In the SHADOW of DETROIT

GREAT LAKES BOOKS

A complete listing of the books in this series can be found online at
http://wsupress.wayne.edu

In the SHADOW of DETROIT

Gordon M. McGregor, Ford of Canada, and Motoropolis

DAVID ROBERTS

W

WAYNE STATE UNIVERSITY PRESS DETROIT

Manufactured in the United States of America.
10 09 08 07 06 5 4 3 2 1

Library of Congress Cataloging-in-Publication Data

Roberts, David, 1949 July 1–
In the shadow of Detroit : Gordon M. McGregor, Ford of Canada, and Motoropolis / David Roberts.
p. cm. — (Great Lakes books)
Includes bibliographical references and index.
ISBN 0-8143-3284-6 (cloth : alk. paper)
1. McGregor, Gordon M. (Gordon Morton), 1873–1922. 2. Automobile engineers—Canada—Biography. 3. Industrialists—Canada—Biography. 4. Ford Motor Company of Canada—History. 5. Windsor (Ont.)—History. 6. Detroit (Mich.)—History. I. Title. II. Series.
TL140.M35R63 2006
629.222092—dc22
2005028656

∞ The paper used in this publication meets the minimum requirements of the American National Standard for Information Sciences—Permanence of Paper for Printed Library Materials, ANSI Z39.48–1984.

Grateful acknowledgment is made to the United Steelworkers of America, Local 1998 (University of Toronto), for its generous support of the publication of this volume.

Design by Elizabeth Pilon
Typeset by Maya Rhodes
Composed in 11/13 Janson

CONTENTS

PREFACE vii

Introduction 1

CHAPTER 1
Riverside 11

CHAPTER 2
The Ford Motor Company of Canada 23

CHAPTER 3
Mr. Ford's Canadian Model T 55

CHAPTER 4
Victory Bonds 115

CHAPTER 5
Lockout 173

CHAPTER 6
Motoropolis 217

CHAPTER 7
McGregor's Legacy 257

NOTES 265
INDEX 303

Gordon M. McGregor, 1908.
Courtesy of Mary McGregor-Clewes.

PREFACE

I began this study in 1997 out of curiosity and for fun, which are not bad reasons to write a book. I worked in fits and starts in my spare time and was finished eight years later, a devilishly long period fraught with many other personal challenges. My intent at the outset was to prepare an article-length biography of Gordon M. McGregor, founder (with Henry Ford and others) of the Ford Motor Company of Canada, describing his relationship to his community and his industry. My project slowly grew in size, scope, and time; new ideas and concepts came together as material was discovered; a book evolved.

Gordon M. McGregor (1873–1922) grew up in Windsor, Ontario. For thirteen years he presided over the Canadian production of the famous Model T, the car that revolutionized automotive transportation in Canada as it did in the United States. With no automotive background, minimal technical expertise, and only a few years of experience in business, he came to Ford in 1904 from a failing wagon-building firm. But, attaching himself to Henry Ford's meteoric rise, he achieved remarkable success, becoming for a time Windsor's preeminent industrialist and civic leader.

I have never been content, however, with the heroic veil placed over McGregor and his achievements by his company and many writers. Corporate leaders can be elusive, their characters contrived and limited. I have attempted, sometimes to my complete satisfaction, to intertwine McGregor's corporate, civic, and personal lives and to trace his rise and pioneering role in the region's automotive industry, which straddled the Windsor-Detroit border and eventually reached out across Canada and into the far-flung British imperial market. In an ill-researched historical field—in Canada—the large themes and important questions came into focus only gradually, stimulated in part by the examinations of the early Michigan auto firms and personnel by Donald F. Davis, Wilkins and Hill, George S. May, and others, whose published works are acknowledged in my endnotes. Company growth, the technical and cultural concept of the automobile, the impact of automotive transportation, technological reliance on Detroit, company parent-branch relations, the effects of border proximity, industrial and political lobbying, labor relations, secondary manufacturing, public involvement, and the Great War: all were issues that engaged Gordon McGregor. Unlike most of the car men of his time and place, he put himself and his company forward with a brashness inspired by Henry Ford's unparalleled success and nearby presence. The legendary Ford needs minimal introduction, despite his almost inscrutable business persona, but his true relations with his Canadian firm—and what he saw in McGregor—merit attention.

Even as I recognized the broader themes stimulated by an investigation of McGregor, I came to realize that in the absence of collections of personal and company papers, it would be impossible to produce a conventional biography of McGregor with strong development of his character and personality as family man or corporate manager. There is no ambition here whatever to present a study on the scale and depth of, to name a well-known few, Michael Bliss's portrait of Sir Joseph W. Flavelle, Heather Robertson's examination of General Motors' R. S. McLaughlin and his distinguished family, or Joy Santink's work on Timothy Eaton and his once-famous department stores. Gordon McGregor left virtually no correspondence; his movement in the ranks of Canada's leading industrialists was quiet; and in the eyes of some, then and now, he was merely an agent of Ford Detroit.

One source that figures prominently in the notes and provides much of the narrative thread (seemingly as a corporate mouthpiece), distinctive automotive flavor, and richness of detail, is the Windsor newspaper of the time, the *Evening Record* (renamed the *Border Cities Star* in 1918). Without this source there would be no base—the amount of information it provides on McGregor and his local presence, on Ford Canada, and on the rest of the industry locally is extraordinary—but its gaps and lack of critical reporting provide as well a succession of pitfalls. Some I have discovered and addressed; some no doubt remain.

Over the several years it has taken to complete this study, I have happily discovered kindred souls, and I have incurred debts. I am obliged to the Honorable William G. Davis for his early support. Ford Canada long ago disposed of most of its early business records and corporate correspondence. For access to what material has survived, including the invaluable company minutes, I am grateful to the Ford Motor Company of Canada, especially Norman J. Stewart, Martha P. Campbell, and Sandra Notarianni. For their assistance at other distant archives, libraries, and universities, I sincerely thank Marilyn Armstrong-Reynolds, Karin Bacon, Fred Bauman, Milka Brown, Deborah C. Brudno, Shaun M. J. Bugyra, Richard H. Carr, Linda Chakmak, Wendy Craven, Jean-François Drapeau, Michael Fish, Cecelia Gallagher, Jenni-ann Littsey, Don MacIsaac, Karen Marrero, Jeremy Morrison, Ronald Onuch, Brock Silversides, Linda Skolarus, Gary R. Tetzlaff, John A. Turley-Ewart, and Paul Voisey. I am beholden as well to the scattered members of the McGregor clan who, without exception, have been enormously supportive. Encouragement, recollections, and the loan of photographs and private records have come from the McGregor, Dodds, Mingay, Brush, Carruthers, Auguston, and Rock families. Mark Coatsworth provided photographic assistance. Other guidance and specialized information have come from Trent Boggess, Patrick T. Brode, Ann Bartlet Brush, Eric DeLony, Eric Edwards, Adrian Ryan, and John Weiler. Kevin Mowle, whose interest has been contagious and whose knowledge of early Ford cars and history is exhaustive, has been particularly helpful in friendly and critical ways. Robin DuBlanc edited the manuscript with extraordinary care and respect. In a timely display of aptitude, Jesse C. Roberts prepared the index. Finally, I acknowledge all my family for their tolerance, Wayne State University Press for its professional willingness and patient guidance, and Local 1998 (University of Toronto) of the United Steelworkers of America for its contribution to the cost of producing this book.

Introduction

For more than two decades after 1900, the flat borderland of the Windsor region of Ontario, including the so-called Border Cities (Windsor, Walkerville, Ojibway, Ford City, and Sandwich), experienced sustained industrial growth in the form of branch plants of American firms. In this context "branch" can have a number of aligned meanings: partial American ownership, wholly owned subsidiaries, closely connected firms, warehousing operations, and other types of cross-border association. Much of this development was defined by the overshadowing proximity of Detroit across the river, hence the title of this work. With the exception of the Niagara area of Ontario and New York, no other border region along the Great Lakes has developed such a transnational identity.

The growth itself was nothing short of phenomenal, advancing over twenty years from a nucleus of distilling and chemical firms through a new core of bicycle makers and mechanical tinkerers to an array of heavy machinery firms and burgeoning automotive and parts factories in the Windsor region, an area identified as Canada's "Motoropolis" after World War I. The automotive plants, which expanded from small, casual assembly operations to heavily mechanized, assembly-line manufacturing complexes, turned out the vehicles, the parts, and the ethos of speedy mobility that gave a lasting identity to the region. Ultimately, it was the trainload after trainload of Ford automobiles that transformed transportation throughout Canada.

Central to the Border Cities' automotive culture was the Ford Motor Company of Canada, established in 1904 by Windsor's Gordon M. McGregor, then a thirty-one-year-old salesman and ineffectual president of a wagon works in nearby Walkerville. His fortuitous alliance with auto maverick Henry Ford and Fordist technology, which would make McGregor rich, shaped his rapid evolution into an auto executive devoted at once to Ford Detroit (and all it came to represent) and his company's Canadian identity, never more than during the Great War. With input from Ford Detroit,

McGregor devised teams and domestic and foreign strategies, many of them innovative, if not unique, in Canada, to make Ford Canada the foremost auto manufacturer in the dominion and the British empire. Until his premature (and not fully explained) death in 1922 at the age of forty-nine, he ran the company with a mixture of authority and subservience to Ford Detroit. In the process he became the border region's industrial star, praised by many and denigrated by others inside and outside the industry. From his positions as head of Ford Canada and chairman of a powerful utilities commission, he exerted extraordinary influence municipally and wielded some power both in the province of Ontario and throughout the Dominion of Canada.

If one equates Gordon McGregor with the number of Ford automobiles his company produced, he, his teams, and the technology they represented had an enormous impact on transportation in Canada, easily as great as its famous and heavily studied railways. But the technology and many of the modes of business were imported, a fact that qualifies McGregor's importance as an innovator in manufacturing and business. (His production manager of many years remembered Ford Canada having a say in the modification of only a single part.)

Until recently the literature on the early automotive industry in Canada—subsidiary or indigenous—has been thin: a few commendable company chronicles, Durnford and Baechler's pioneering survey of 1973, pieces of corporate nostalgia, and broad, important studies of tariffs and economic development, all limited by a dearth of historical sources on the inner workings of the industry itself and studies of the car men who brought the companies to success or failure.[1] Ford Canada's own historical consciousness peaked in the era from 1954 to about 1968, during which the company's "historical consultant," Herman L. Smith, produced cozy but well-informed blurbs, and the company's doors were fully opened to other researchers. McGregor has remained an idolized figure in the company's memory; his carefully preserved oak desk quietly graces the entrance to Ford Canada's present headquarters in Oakville, Ontario.

Borders—the international, political, geographical, and economic boundaries that we all cross knowingly and unknowingly—can be shifting, independent, but sometimes overlapping. Michigan historian David R. Smith recognizes this fluidity in his challenging examination of the boundaries of the Great Lakes region and of spatial patterns there of migration, transportation, labor, and capital. "The Great Lakes connect the disparate resources and peoples of a transnational region," he explains in one summary paper. "The international boundary that divides the Great Lakes, however, does not correspond with the wider boundaries of the basin's economy in which labor and capital migrate."[2] It is in this broad, continental context that Smith and others examine the concept of integrated economies, particularly the phenomenon of factories and businesses that are established as branches of parent companies, which (in this book) are based in the United States. This idea of shifting borders is also another way of conceptualizing corporate territory. In this sense early perceptions of Ford Canada as just one of Ford Detroit's American branches have validity.

To broaden this contextual sweep, the 1890s are seen here historically as the start of important American capital investment abroad. In the Great Lakes basin, the distances between Ontario and Michigan, across the Detroit River, were minimal—short rides by ferry at most points. Drawing upon a study published in a Toronto Board of Trade journal in 1927, Smith advances the finding that about 60 percent of Canadian industry was then controlled by American-owned manufacturers.[3] Certainly, as Tom Naylor demonstrates in *The History of Canadian Business*, businessmen, politicians, and commercial journals and associations throughout the dominion were receptive to foreign capital, regardless of national origin.[4] In regional terms, Smith agrees with others in concluding that the economy of the Great Lakes region "operated with little reference to the international border."[5] This intriguing proposition will be touched on with reference to Ford Canada and Gordon McGregor. While McGregor strived with much success to cast his firm as a Canadian company, Ford Detroit periodically issued parental reminders of Ford Canada's status as just one of its manufacturing and assembly plants in North America—the agent of the American company's "Canadian trade," as Henry's early advertising described the relationship.

International boundaries and vested interests in Canada led to tariffs to protect Canadian business and industry, which in turn provided rationales for the formation of branch plants to avoid the tariffs. This pattern of branch formation, which opened up unending debate and complaint about the relation between prices and tariffs, has received extensive study, ranging back to analyses by the Ontario provincial government after 1900 and Cleona Lewis's revealing *America's Stake in International Investments*, published in 1938.[6] Smith charts their findings: 12 American branch plants established in Canada before 1898, 51 in the period 1898–1908, and 138 in 1909–19. Not surprisingly, within the Great Lakes region, extraprovincial licenses issued by Ontario, Smith notes, "reveal that companies incorporated in the State of Michigan comprised the single largest source of foreign capital in the province, with $14,475,500 invested between 1898 and 1928."[7]

The first wave of American investment favored such border towns as Windsor, Walkerville, Chatham, Sarnia, and other urban centers in Ontario. The American tendency to try to straddle the border easily made the Windsor-Walkerville area attractive to firms in Detroit. By comparison, in Quebec and the Maritimes, the American investment presence tended to joint ventures with local capital, with an infusion of British investment in the former. By the end of the nineteenth century, waves of mergers and large multidivisional firms began entering Canada from the United States in addition to instances of direct investment. One result by the time of the Great War, as Naylor notes, was a closer integration of parent and subsidiary, with branch plants becoming heavily dependent on the parent companies for parts, machinery, and basic technology.[8]

The flood of new branches was significant. Before the turn of the century, Detroit and other U.S. border centers attracted Canadian workers, but sometimes the flow slowed and sometimes it even reversed. On the Detroit River, a steady traffic of ferries daily transported commuting workers in the thousands, to and fro. Ontario's border towns and other urban centers received most of the American plants. By 1914 there were a total of 454 American branch plants, affiliates, and major warehousing operations in Canada, but only 20 British branch plants. Of the 454, most were in Ontario (317), Quebec (78), and Manitoba (33); the leading cities were Toronto (94), Montreal (53), Hamilton (46), Winnipeg (30), and Windsor (26).

In addition to economic and commercial factors, there are other significant elements in a wider consideration of borderlands: the dynamics of cultural contact, similarity and differentiation, social interaction, and identity in adjoining geographical spaces. In

Canadian-American borderlands, these elements have been examined (to select but three regions) for the prairies (with excursions into native and fur-trading history), the Eastern Townships of Quebec, and the Windsor-Detroit area, where Neil Morrison's account of Canada's "liveliest border area" for the Essex County Historical Association in 1954 is appropriately entitled *Garden Gateway*.[9] It is these dynamics that add nuance and subtle complexity to the meaning of "in the shadow of Detroit."

Proximity to Detroit was a prime factor in Windsor's rapid growth after 1910, and central to that growth was the burgeoning automotive industry—the indigenous and branch plants; the makers of tops, fenders, spark plugs, and a wide range of other parts; the dealerships; and the personnel who set up and ran the plants and garages. Morrison tells us too that the region's flat gravel roads and mild, favorable weather fostered the proliferation of automotive use; though similar geography could be found in other regions, harsher winters curtailed the growth of a car culture. Newspaper reports of early vehicles on the roads of Essex County appeared with frequency in 1900, sometimes displaying alarm.[10] One report from Kingsville (on the north shore of Lake Erie) on 24 August 1900—"An Automobile from Detroit Struck Town Tuesday and Created Quite a Sensation on the Streets"—captures a common tone. A sense of disgust and resistance appeared in another news item, this from Amherstburg in 1909: "Reports show that the auto has practically driven farmers' wives and daughters off the road altogether and deprived them of much pleasure."

Such resistance, however, soon faded. "Speed maniacs" and fines by magistrates became ordinary, and so too did jobs in the auto plants of the Border Cities and the related infrastructure in Essex County—ad hoc development that proceeded with minimal planning beyond simple proximity and quickly granted municipal encouragement. Between 1916 and 1920 the number of passenger cars in Essex jumped from 1,450 to 5,134, while in Windsor the number rose from 828 to 2,614; on holidays and horse-racing days many more arrived by ferry from Detroit. During the same period motor vehicles used for commercial purposes went from 100 to 518 in Windsor and from 84 to 449 in the county. And so the motorization of the Border Cities expanded, to the point where the county was saturated with vehicles and automotive work was the predominant form of branch plant activity.

With the growth came social consequences, such as a severe shortage of local housing, and real political tensions between the needs of the region and the separate municipalities. Here, with Gordon McGregor's penchant for public engagement, Ford Canada became a prime player. Residential sprawl resulted in Windsor's expansion into the adjoining townships of Sandwich East and Sandwich West. In 1912 the village of Ford City was carved out of Walkerville in recognition of specifically industrial needs. Central to this new village—it became a town in 1915—and the region's automotive industry was the Ford Motor Company of Canada, the town's prime developer and industry, described in 1917 as Ford City's "wet nurse" and its "great overshadowing industry." Indeed, Ford was at the core of the "Auto Centre of Canada." The Border Cities' local newspaper abounded with such boastful epithets and delighted in paying homage to Ford, Hupp, Maxwell, Studebaker, truck companies, part and accessory makers, other suppliers, and state-of-the-art dealerships. By 1922 Ford Canada reportedly employed 40 percent of the Border Cities' population and was having a major economic and social impact nationally. Personifying this development and impact more than any other local auto man was McGregor, Ford Canada's secretary-treasurer and guiding head. Unlike Detroit, the Border Cities did not have a large resident contingent of car men, a situation that rendered McGregor's presence and many local roles starkly prominent.

Into this industrial branch plant ferment came the social and cultural consequences of a borderlands relationship. Among other aspects, there was the ceaseless flow of labor across the Detroit River, the cross-border taxation of income, wartime cooperation (and friction, before America's engagement in 1917), the brief flirtation of businessmen with an American-style model of city governance, and feelings among Border Cities boosters that the rest of Canada did not properly understand the region's Americanized existence. All of these facets distinguished life there, and all engaged Gordon McGregor, Ford Canada, and such champions as the *Evening Record/Border Cities Star* newspaper.

Before the 1920s Ford Canada's prominence was virtually unparalleled both in the Essex region and in Canadian industry as a whole. No doubt it was dominant during that decade too and later, but this study ends, somewhat arbitrarily, with McGregor's death in 1922, before the clear decline of Ford and the competitive surge of General Motors of Canada, which also had roots in the Border Cities. Ford's authority nonetheless set the tone later for rosy reflections and recollections. "Men looked upon their association with the company as a distinction," Neil Morrison recalled in 1954 (the year of Ford Canada's fiftieth anniversary). "When Ford employees went downtown on Saturday nights, 'they wore their company identification badges proudly on the lapels of their best suits.'"[11] McGregor took pains to recognize and promote such proud affiliation. Many employees did take pride, if not in their work then in their many company sports teams and social activities. But this study is no celebration of Ford Canada, the industry, the workers, or McGregor, who was quite capable of locking out workers in 1918, just as his employees brusquely set aside any company pride to push for higher wages, shun European coworkers in wartime, or leave at the drop of a hat for other jobs in the automotive sector in the Border Cities or Detroit.

It is difficult to see McGregor fully and accurately in relation to the Border Cities' automotive and truck fraternity, the executives and crews who directed not just Ford but Menard, E-M-F, Hupp, Chalmers, Studebaker, Maxwell, Gotfredson-Joyce, Canadian Industries (General Motors of Canada), and a host of other early outfits and parts manufacturers. The *Evening Record/Border Cities Star* favored McGregor, intensely and seemingly to the exclusion not only of other important auto executives but also the heads of the other major industries in the area, including the salt, distilling, heavy chemicals and paint, and pharmaceutical manufactories. (The family of Hiram Walker is one old-money family that comes readily to mind.) A progressive voice for regional development, the *Record/Star* praised McGregor's career and family, provided a biased outlet for distributing corporate news and statements, and backed his civic ventures and positions. To some extent this near-exclusive attention was a measure of McGregor's status locally.

McGregor, unusually among the car men, was the local son who stayed put to give shape to the industry. His crews implemented endless technical specifications from Ford Detroit, found more and more Canadian suppliers, and became extremely adept at defining and serving the Canadian and imperial markets. McGregor recruited his managers with care. Many executives of other companies were brought in from Michigan for short periods, in temporary assignments to the branches; some commuted to or from Detroit; most received little attention in the newspaper. One who received some notice was Michigan-born Howard Blood of Canadian Industries (an early producer of General Motors of Canada), who came with an impressive combination of technical and business skills. But none of these other executives was as publicly involved in the Border Cities as McGregor, at least as reported in the press and other records of local activity.

Recorded instances of the activities of other auto men are few, but these are noted in the chapters that follow for the sake of perspective. Moise Menard (Menard trucks) spoke out on reciprocity in 1911; Norman Allan (Saxon) bravely challenged the powerful Border Chamber of Commerce in 1918; the local heads of Studebaker, Fisher Body, and Kelsey Wheel in 1920 frankly attributed their presence to the tariff; and Frank Joyce (Gotfredson-Joyce trucks) confirmed, in the car-pricing debate of 1921, Ford duplicity of some sort. McGregor's assistant manager, the reserved W. R. Campbell, shunned public involvement for the most part. There was some anonymous participation in corporate actions that had impact on the communities. Rarely, however, do we see McGregor acting beside or against other car men in the Border Cities, though they all knew each other and had a stake in the well-being of what came to be known as Canada's Motoropolis.

This study examines not simply how automobiles changed the Border Cities and gave the region a distinct Canadian-American identity but also how one company and its head integrated themselves into the economic, social, and civic fabric of the community. Consideration of this integration is where this book veers from a straightforward analysis of the company, including its relations with labor, to shed light on the rest of McGregor's short life and career. By 1908–11 he was emerging as one of the auto industry's first true lobbyists as well as, following his father's political example, a dyed-in-the-wool member of the Liberal Party. His and his company's engagement in the tumultuous years of World War I provide a backdrop for examining the impact of this traumatic conflict on the Windsor and Detroit area. McGregor's election in 1916 to an unusual regional body, the provincially created Essex Border Utilities Commission, launched him into years of often frustrating involvement in municipal politics, backroom maneuvering, and the regional governance that is unique to the Windsor region.

As the commission's head for five years, from 1916 to 1920, McGregor tried repeatedly to sell the concepts of common regional needs—water and trunk lines, public health, and parks—to suspicious and resentful town councils and the water and power commissions of the separate but adjoining municipalities, all of which drew from the heavily polluted Detroit River. Repeatedly, over apportionments, engineering reports, and differing urban visions, McGregor was slammed by labor councillors and others who saw his efforts as autocratic—just as they viewed his role at Ford. This was gritty sewage politics at their most complex and fascinating (if sewage can be fascinating)—necessary background for an understanding of the formation in 1935 of the single amalgamated City of Windsor. In the postwar recession, as a physically ailing McGregor grappled with attacks from municipal and provincial politicians, agrarian radicals, and even disgruntled housewives in search of cheap cars, he acquiesced to repeated, sometimes demeaning demands from the office of Henry Ford. In 1922 he died, on the verge of a major corporate expansion that he surely had a hand in shaping.

In strict biographical terms, this study is incomplete, perhaps woefully so. McGregor's character, his family affairs, his relations with his associates in Ford Canada, and his take on other automobile makers in Canada remain sketchy for the reasons given, as do the many company decisions, rationales, and operations not covered or fully explained in the corporate minutes. Still, the efforts and findings are instructive, as the multiple perspectives of a Great Lakes regional economy, borderland identity, American investment in Canada, automotive technology, corporate story, and local and area history are brought together to shed light on one region, one company, and one illustrative individual with some insight, I trust, and with the exposure of some dim corners. *In the Shadow of Detroit* is meant to offer readers and future researchers some direction in an ongoing corporate and regional saga that deserves fresh examinations.

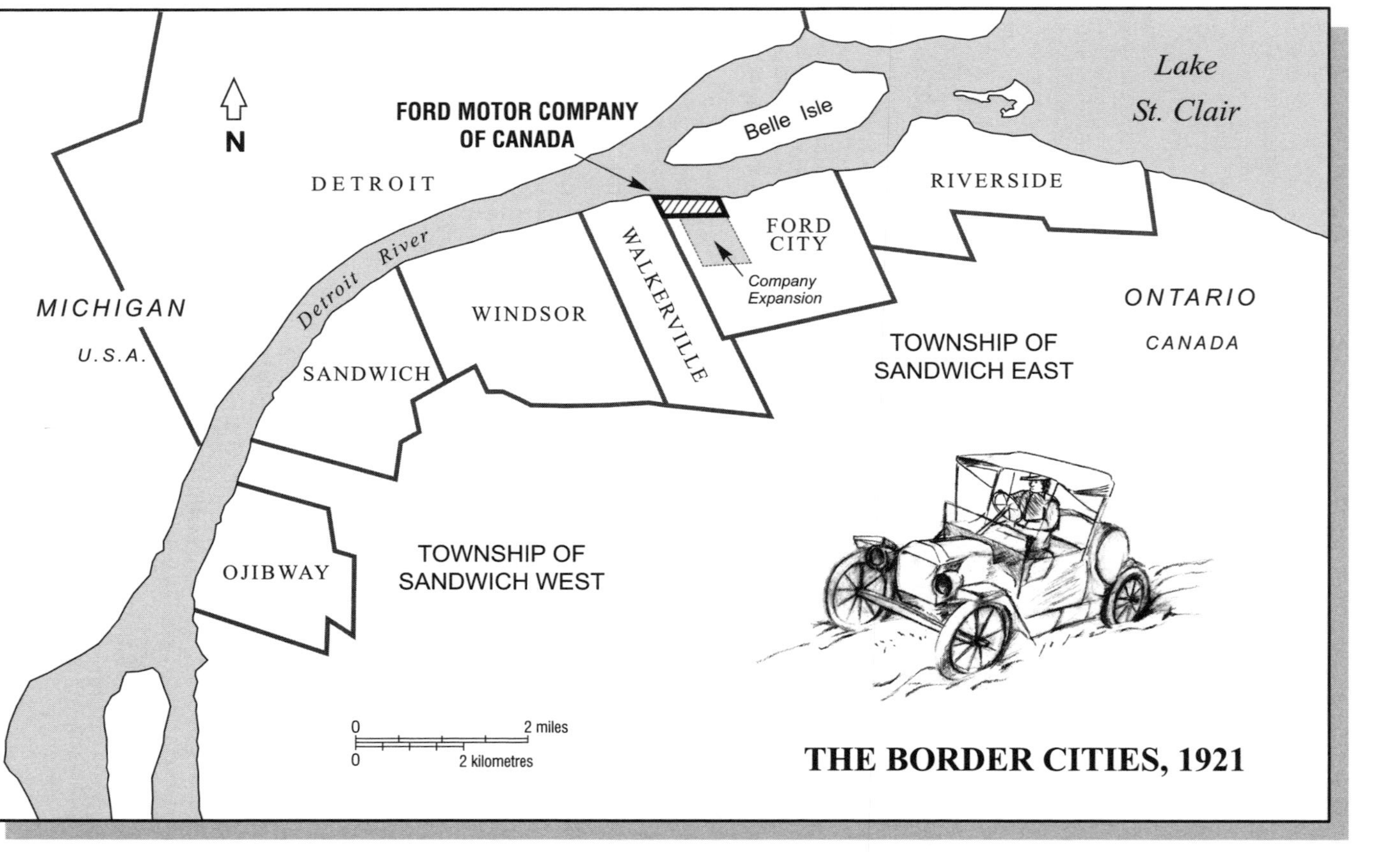

The Border Cities, 1921. Drawn by Jane Davie, Cartography Office, Department of Geography, University of Toronto.

CHAPTER I

Riverside

Locale and the rambunctious advent of the automobile define this story. Gordon Morton McGregor was born on 18 January 1873 on the 1,000-acre family estate on Sandwich Street, just south of Windsor, Ontario, and within hailing distance of the Detroit River. Flowing from Lake St. Clair to the west end of Lake Erie, this river separated—and joined—Windsor and the bustling American city of Detroit, Michigan. Construction of a railway tunnel had been abandoned in 1872 because of engineering problems, though the later perfection of electric engines and the elimination of ventilation problems would make possible the completion of a tunnel in 1910. Still, in the 1870s and subsequent decades, ferries continually plied back and forth, their passage taking mere minutes.

Gordon and his brothers and sisters were the third generation of McGregors to experience this Canadian-American duality of life on the Detroit River. McGregor's Presbyterian grandparents, John McGregor and Margaret Leishman, had immigrated from Paisley, Scotland, in 1830, married, and settled briefly near Montreal. They moved to Toronto and next to Sarnia, Upper Canada, where their third son, William, was born on 24 June 1836.[1] Two years later the family located in Amherstburg, Upper Canada, on the southern stretch of the Detroit River. According to an account written by a cousin of Gordon, John, a brush maker and farmer, died while felling a tree in 1864. Margaret would live until 1896. On 21 May 1866 their son William, then a merchant, private banker, horse dealer, and real estate agent in Amherstburg, wed Jessie Lathrup Peden of Amherstburg, daughter of Robert Peden, a Scottish-born Presbyterian minister, tutor, and author of some controversial theological tracts as well as of "Emigrants Lament" and other little-known poems.

William McGregor's house on Detroit River, Windsor, Ontario, 1873 or 1874. Courtesy of J. McGregor Dodds.

(Linked somewhere to the family were the Mortons, one of them a coachbuilder in Kilmarnock, Scotland.) The McGregors, who settled in Windsor in 1870, had seven children: Margaret Anne (1867), Malcolm Peden (1869), Gordon, Walter Leishman (1875), Edith Ellen (1877), Jean Mabel (1882), and William Donald (1884).[2]

The McGregor children were raised in modest gentility in a tall yellow-brick house (long since demolished) with a white picket fence, newly planted trees, and black servants.[3] A photograph of this house shows William posing in a neat black suit and a young Malcolm perched atop a gatepost. Family life was infused with a distinct sense of Scottishness. A photograph of Malcolm as an even younger boy shows him wearing a tartan sash; as an adult he collected McGregor family and other Scottish memorabilia, including a copy of the British act of 1681 suppressing the clan Gregor. He named his summer residence in Amherstburg Bognie Brae, after the ancestral home in Scotland.[4] Gordon's sense of this Scottishness would surface in song, in the good-natured nostalgia shared by the family, and through corporate banter and advertising. His brother Walter would raise a kilted regiment during the Great War; when he was overseas, with time on his hands, he tried to trace his family roots in Scotland. Writing to his mother on Christmas Eve, 1917, he dredged up homesick thoughts and reminiscences: "You brought us all up as Scotch sons and daughters and we don't say these things much do we."[5] Whatever the family's reticence, the four McGregor boys were close.

In Ontario the children had also witnessed their father's commitment to public service and entrepreneurial endeavor. A go-getter, William McGregor was ever one to take advantage of opportunity. He served as reeve of Windsor from 1868 to 1874, mayor in 1873, warden of Essex County from 1869 to 1873, and the Liberal member of Parliament for Essex from 1874 to 1878. After moving to Windsor in 1870, he operated a gristmill and livery (he had sold horses to the North during the American Civil War), dealt in wheat and grain, ran a shipping business, and continued his banking and brokerage operations with his brothers David and Robert Leishman. In addition, he was a founder in 1872 and then manager of the Sandwich, Windsor, and Amherstburg Railway.[6] Business took him on occasion to Michigan, part of the steady cross-river traffic reflected in advertisements in Windsor and Detroit newspapers of the period.[7]

McGregor's financial interests collapsed in the economic crisis of 1877, though he continued in milling. In 1882, likely following his defeat in the federal election that year, he moved with his family to Winnipeg, where a brother had started a livestock business. There he became a cattle dealer and the manager and treasurer of the North West Trading Company Limited, headed by Amherstburg-born John Christian Schultz.[8] In Winnipeg Gordon continued his public school education and worked part-time as a telegraph messenger boy.[9] Walter would later recall that he excelled at mathematics and being taken around by a school inspector until he was replaced by "a little wizened up Jew kid who beat the spots off me" in arithmetic.[10] Whatever Gordon's boyhood impressions of Winnipeg in the 1880s, they went unrecorded.

For reasons that are not clear, in 1887 the family returned to

Windsor, where William McGregor went back into the livery business and real estate, which included town lots, land for railways, and natural-gas rights. From 1887 to 1892 Gordon, who lived at home, worked as a salesman/clerk for Mabley and Company, a men's clothing store in Detroit. Years later, an obituary writer claimed that after leaving school McGregor "engaged in the clothing business in Windsor and Detroit, being an employee of the Oak Hall clothiers for some years as a boy," but this account seems too compressed to be totally accurate.[11] The experience gave him some mercantile inclination and a flair for fashionable attire. After 1892 he went into business with his father, as William McGregor and Son, real estate and insurance agents, with offices in the British American Block in Windsor. While William McGregor reentered public life as the member of Parliament for Essex North (1891–1900), a member of the board of management for St. Andrew's Presbyterian Church, and president of the humane society, Gordon pursued the social interests of a young bachelor, with few financial worries.[12]

Crossing the river on a regular basis had put both Gordon and his brother Malcolm, an up-and-coming lawyer with offices in Detroit, into the "migrating crowd" that so distinguished Windsor's workforce in the 1880s and 1890s. Workers flowed across the muddy, polluted waterway in daily droves: "back and forward all the time," as one contemporary observed in 1887.[13] More Windsorites worked in Detroit than vice versa. Ferries departed every ten minutes. Windsor labor unions that had affiliations with Detroit were viewed with nationalistic suspicion elsewhere in southwestern Ontario; the annexation of Canada was a topic of street talk in Detroit.[14]

Drawn by Canadian locations that would save them tariff charges on imports, many American manufactories had established branches in Windsor and adjacent Walkerville. By 1887, though the area was not known as a "manufacturing center," its industries, with the notable exceptions of the Hiram Walker distillery and the Stephens box factory, were predominantly American-based or capitalized. Foremost were D. M. Ferry and Company (seeds) and two pharmaceutical firms, Frederick Stearns and Company and Parke Davis and Company, which would remain the area's leading industrial producers (by comparative value) until after 1911.[15] Throughout the 1890s the Windsor Board of Trade fielded inquiries from American businesses eager to establish branches in Canada.[16]

By early 1896 Gordon, at age twenty-two, was known more for his social comings and goings and bass-baritone voice than for his commercial aptitude or leadership. At the fancy dress ball at Crawford House on 14 February, the highlight of Windsor's social season, he appeared as a seventeenth-century lord; his girlfriend, Harriet (Hattie) Dodds, daughter of wholesale druggist John J. Dodds of Detroit, was Lady Gainsborough.[17] The two moved from event to event: Hattie's frumpy looks belied her social verve; the bespectacled Gordon, "a leading vocalist," sang at a succession of birthday parties, musical club evenings, and church socials.[18] Confined by an unspecified but serious illness in June, he went to Winnipeg for a restorative holiday. He was well enough in August to perform there at Westminster Church: "He is possessed of a fine sympathetic voice of good range," the *Winnipeg Tribune* reported, "and it shows careful training."[19] After a tour of the region, including Brandon, he returned home later in August, and that fall he entered another season of guest appearances and easy living. Quite capable of performing classical pieces by Gabriel Fauré and others as well as lighter popular fare, he sang "Abide with Me" to acclaim at St. Andrew's Church and "The Red, White, and Blue" and "The Bonnie Banks o' Loch Lomond" on St. Andrew's Night at the Crawford; at an Oddfellows Hall recital by Miss Franklin Phillips, a gifted youngster from Leamington and a pupil of F. J. Thompson, he was the accompanist.[20]

Gordon initially remained aloof from the partisan politics plied by his father, who was returned to the House of Commons in the general election of June 1896, when the Liberals came to power under Wilfrid Laurier, who had visited Windsor earlier that month.[21] One ongoing dispute that concerned William McGregor, and which carried over into 1897, was the restriction, on both sides of the river, of the movement of workers. McGregor's sharp exchanges with Detroit congressman John Blaisdell Corliss, who preached control as well as annexation, ended when the immigration bill containing the "obnoxious" Corliss amendment aimed at Canadians was vetoed by President Grover Cleveland.[22] The time spent on such disputes (the gritty reality of McGregor's partisan devotion) may have exacted some cost. In applying for appointment as collector of customs at Windsor, a position that would elude him until January 1902, he told Laurier in November 1897 that his staunch support of the party had "dissipated" his earnings.[23] He was certainly not destitute, however. In 1896, with Henry Banwell, he had formed the McGregor Banwell Fence Company Limited, which his son Walter would later manage.[24]

By the fall of 1897 Gordon was becoming politically active in his father's shadow, with something of the elder's grasp of politicking and glad-handing. In November he was an alternate candidate at the provincial nomination meeting in Essex North and he attended the banquet given in Petrolia, Ontario, by businessmen to honor Sir Henri-Gustave Joly, the new minister of internal revenue. The following February and March he was on a ward committee in Windsor for the provincial campaign of William Johnson McKee, a lumber merchant and the Liberal incumbent for Essex North.[25] Gordon would have witnessed too his mother's active involvement in the women's foreign missionary society of St. Andrew's Church in Windsor.

Gordon's relationship with Hattie Dodds also took a step forward. On 2 November 1898 they were married at Westminster Church in Detroit, in what Windsor's *Evening Record* billed "an international union of hearts and hands." After a honeymoon in Chicago and other midwestern cities, they returned to live in Detroit, where Gordon was bookkeeper for the Photokrome Company.[26] Spare-time trips to Windsor for singing engagements and parties were easily handled.

Of the several accounts that later emerged to explain his attraction to Michigan's fledgling automotive industry, the earliest story, set in Detroit about this time, has him talking to Henry Ford about Ford's automobile parked outside the Presbyterian church where Gordon sang and which (implausibly) the irreligious automotive engineer also attended.[27] By 1902 the McGregors had taken up residence in Windsor, with Hattie settling into homemaking and a comfortable pattern of social largesse as a hostess of tea and "pedro" (card game) parties and a patroness of the Agawan Club, which arranged dances for young people.[28] Gordon probably continued to work for William McGregor and Son, which had tried promoting sugar beets for a time, but another new venture by his father set him on a course that led to the brink of failure and then to unimagined success.

The Milner-Walker Wagon Works Company, which had begun production just east of Walkerville in December 1897, was formed by distiller/capitalist Hiram Walker and William Milner, a veteran English-born wagon builder who excelled in efficient operating plants. After Walker's death in Detroit in January 1899, his succession by Frank H. Walker, and Milner's departure for a new venture, the works declined. In December 1900 the property and plant were acquired by William McGregor and John Curry, a Windsor banker. The two also acquired Walker's large farm for subdivision, an area in which they had demonstrated expertise.[29] With an injection of new capital, they reorganized the works as the Walkerville Waggon Works Company Limited, along with Walter McGregor (then a distributing agent for an oil company), W. J. McKee, and William George Curry, a Windsor brick maker. Their intent was "to manufacture and sell waggons, sleighs and wheeled vehicles of every description."[30] Though not an incorporator, Gordon McGregor was installed as manager after his father was appointed collector of customs in January 1902. The extent of his contribution to the works' early success is uncertain; in September he supervised its display at the Toronto Industrial Exhibition, Ontario's premier stage for showing off new industrial products. The works also gave McGregor direct exposure to a mixed Canadian-American workforce: in November the works was one of a number of Walkerville area industries that closed to allow its many American workers to celebrate the American Thanksgiving.[31]

The degree of American involvement in industries in Windsor and Walkerville was exceptionally high, a clear illustration of the transnational economic region delineated by historian David R. Smith.[32] In January 1903 Frederick B. Smith, president of the Chamber of Commerce and Convention League of Detroit, lamented Canada's "tariff wall." In fact, Detroit industrialists had been busy scouting the Windsor area for sites, and many American firms had already built branch plants, among them the W. E. Seagrave Company (fire engines) in 1901, the J. T. Wing Company (metals), Saginaw Salt and Lumber, and Peters Cartridge.[33]

Few represented the fluidity and aggressiveness of this cross-border trade better than Frederick Samuel Evans, who, during the bicycle rage of the mid-1890s, had developed, with machinist brothers John Francis Dodge and Horace Elgin Dodge, the famous Evans and Dodge (E&D) bicycles made by the Canadian Typograph Company Limited of Windsor, of which Evans was manager and secretary-treasurer. A supreme hustler, he also launched the Universal Fastener Company. His drive prompted the *Evening Record* to claim that, if not for Evans, Windsor "wouldn't be on the map" as far as manufacturing was concerned.[34] In November 1899 he headed the formation of the National Cycle and Automobile Company Limited, an American-Canadian holding syndicate that involved Albert Pope and A. G. Spaulding, two American bicycle tycoons who were edging toward the emerging automotive industry. Formed as a direct challenge to Canada Cycle and Motor Company (CCM) of Toronto, National (according to Durnford and Baechler "Canada's first automotive branch plant")[35] produced a steam-driven automobile in Hamilton for a short time in 1900, only to be undercut by the rapid decline of the bicycle market, CCM's successful counter takeover bid of 1900, and Canadian suspicions, which focused on Evans but were not widespread in Windsor, that National had been out to facilitate the American takeover of the Canadian bicycle industry. Undeterred, in 1903 Evans, whose daughter later married Gordon McGregor's brother William Donald (Don), formed the Commercial Motor Vehicle Company in Detroit and contemplated an automobile transit operation between Detroit's city hall and Belle Isle park, a popular playground opposite Walkerville in Lake St. Clair.[36]

For the Windsor area, and for Gordon McGregor, the legacy of the bicycle craze and Evans's automotive misadventures were profound. Speeding, often abusive cyclists, popularly known as scorchers, added a mild element of danger and excitement to the streetscapes; some wondered about the propriety of female riders; cycling shaped sermons and adages ("he that rideth with wise men shall be safe; but a companion of scorchers shall be destroyed"); Evans's worldwide shipment of E&D bicycles provided practical lessons on exporting and freight classification; the saving of the 30 percent duty on the Canadian-made E&D was easily appreciated by local buyers; and bicycle exhibitions drew crowds, as did Harley Davidson, the "crack" E&D racer.[37]

In manufacturing terms, the E&D, like so many other makes, necessitated the fine machining of metal parts such as bearings, which E&D advertising boosted especially, and the production of the necessary cutting and finishing tools. It was an easy shift for the colorfully crude Dodge brothers to apply their mechanical skills to building "special machinery," including the production of auto parts for the Olds Motor Works in Detroit in 1901. In 1910 two Canadian Typograph/E&D workers, Adolph Morrell and Lorne Wilkie, established the Windsor Machine and Tool Works. In marketing, few in Windsor in the late 1890s and early 1900s could push bicycles better than Andrew Douglas Bowlby, a dry goods, sewing machine, and men's clothing dealer on Sandwich Street. Before the rage's subsidence by 1902, he merchandized several makes, among them the E&D, the Brantford Red Bird, the King of Scorchers, and the Detroit. Starting with solid-tired high-wheelers, Bowlby took credit for bringing pneumatic-tired models to the city. Windsor had been struck by the wheeled phenomenon.[38]

The automobile, however, crept slowly into Windsor and the public psyche, encouraged in part by F. S. Evans. The appearance there of a "gasoline bicycle" in 1896 had been a curious crossover. The following year an odd-looking automobile, reportedly built in St. Louis, Missouri, arrived. Readers of the *Evening Record* and Detroit newspapers began learning of European makes; of the debate among the proponents of the steam car, the electric car, and the gasoline car; of "frightful" crashes by unskilled drivers; and of the steady concentration of manufacturing activity and promotional racing in the Detroit area before 1902. Races and hill climbs at Belle Isle and Grosse Pointe, Michigan, and the potential for unheard-of speed, caught the fancy of Windsorites in 1902–3. When a car went out of control at Grosse Pointe in September 1903 and killed a spectator, the *Evening Record* found the event morbidly newsworthy. When Henry Ford's racing machine, the monstrous "999," set a speed record on a sanded track on the ice of Lake St. Clair in January 1904, readers were told of the "wildest ride in the history of automobiling" in a small piece in the sports columns of the *Evening Record*.[39]

Even less conspicuous were the commercial ventures stimulated in fits and starts by Ford's racing successes: the Henry Ford Company in 1901–2, the Ford and Malcolmson Company in 1902, and finally, in June 1903—some distance back in the small pack of rival manufacturers—the Ford Motor Company. When the Walkerville Wagon Works began experiencing difficulty late that year, it was to Detroit's automobile industry that Gordon McGregor desperately turned under a charter that allowed for "wheeled vehicles" of all kinds.

William McGregor had died on 14 May 1903 at age sixty-six, after a short illness. His funeral and burial in Windsor Grove Cemetery were attended by his grieving family, including his brother David from Winnipeg and the seventy-five men of the Walkerville Wagon Works.[40] His estate, which would survive until after 1914, included considerable real estate and stock, notably his holdings as the principal shareholder in the wagon works, which soon became a serious liability for his heirs and administrators. Though the company was favorably faced with a backlog of orders and capable of producing 2,800 wagons and 1,000 sleighs annually (according to the press), Gordon McGregor, the works' new president, and his fellow executors were unwilling, or were unable, to inject the capital needed to meet the production demand. As a result they began negotiating to dispose of the works. Most likely, McGregor was facing stiff competition and could not meet the challenge. In the year after March 1903 his workforce dropped from 102 to 78; by 1904, according to a lawsuit of 1913, the company verged on failure with a debt load of $75,000. In January 1904 the *Evening Record* reported that the works' three-story frame building was to be acquired by a large, unnamed American stove company and that the business and plant were to be taken by the West Lorne Waggon Company Limited, newly established in Elgin County by William Milner, the one-time operator of the works.[41]

Production ceased in July. Although the plant was apparently moved out, possibly to West Lorne, the negotiations for the factory building fell through. Assuming great risk, and a new direction, McGregor found an interested party in Detroit—Henry Ford. How the match came about is not known for sure, but certainly local interest in automotive production had not abated since Evans's efforts. By late January a syndicate had been formed to build automobiles in Windsor under the supervision of a Mr. Kay—the pioneer industry was littered with such fleeting attempts—and in March the enterprising A. D. Bowlby opened a local sales agency for the Ford Motor Company of Detroit.[42]

As early as January the McGregor brothers had been talking

grandly about automobiles. Don McGregor, whose engagement to Fred Evans's daughter Lillian exposed him to much automobile talk, recalled meeting Gordon and Walter one day in January at the wagon works. "There are men in Detroit, like Henry Ford, who say every farmer will soon be using an automobile," Don remembered Gordon musing optimistically. "I don't see why we can't build autos right here. I think I'll have a talk with John Curry."[43] Such recollections would blend easily into Ford Canada's portrayal (as recently as 1997) of Gordon's rosy "vision" that "wagons would soon be a thing of the past" and that he "was determined to be part of a new Motorized era that was now on the horizon." Allowing for some foresight, however dreamy, McGregor's initiative was driven by opportunism born of a willingness to risk potential failure and the street instincts of a traveling salesman.[44]

CHAPTER 2

The Ford Motor Company of Canada

If Gordon McGregor saw his salvation in the reuse of his factory for making automobiles, vying technologies complicated the risk. In the pioneer era of production, electrically propelled, steam-driven, and gasoline-engined vehicles competed for motive domination, as did various styles for preference: the carriagelike high-wheeler, the lightweight cycle car (a cross between a motorcycle and an automobile), and the European-style two- or four-cylinder version modeled on the 1901 Benz, which would emerge triumphant and be embodied in early Ford automobiles. By 1904, in North America, Michigan-based companies had gained the lead on the strength of various makes of cheap runabouts—a two-seater horseless carriage with an internal-combustion gasoline engine mounted underneath. Gasoline itself was considered a by-product, made in the distillation of petroleum to make kerosene. The attrition rate among Michigan's early automobile producers was extremely high, with correspondingly high rates of operational risk, strong aversion by most of Detroit's financial establishment, and slow public acceptance of this new mode of transportation, both in Canada and the United States.[1]

Authorized by John Curry, the secretary-treasurer of the Walkerville Wagon Works, to reduce its indebtedness by any means, McGregor gambled on the fume-belching, gasoline-powered automobile and on a maverick producer with, initially, scant interest in Canada. According to Don McGregor, when Gordon opted in early 1904 to try making automobiles, he initially approached the venerable Henry Martyn Leland of Detroit. At the time, however, Leland's machinery firm was producing motors and transmissions only for Olds and the Cadillac Automobile Company in Detroit, and he would not take over management of Cadillac until late in 1904. Gordon certainly never mentioned Leland in subsequent accounts. "After considerable trouble I got in contact with Mr. Henry Ford, Detroit," he later testified with tantalizing brevity, "and succeeded in getting him interested." Initially Ford was skeptical, but evidently McGregor's assurance that he could raise the needed capital and that Canada was an ideal location for expansion proved persuasive.[2] What else they could have seen in each other and in each other's prospects bears examination, however speculative.

To many, Henry Ford was an unattractive ally. A gaunt, folksy mechanic, racing car driver, and erratic administrator, he was filled with contradictions. An early automobile dealer accurately described the pioneer automobile fraternity as "pretty crude."[3] Even so, the enigmatic Ford hovered on the edge, an outsider cut off from Detroit's social and financial elites, much like his hard-edged secretary and business manager, the squat, ill-humored James Joseph Couzens, a native of Chatham, Ontario, and one of a number of Canadians in Ford's inner group. Of the investors in Ford's 1903 company, few had strong social or financial standing. Canadian diplomat Charles Vincent Massey later took Ford's measure as well as anyone: he had a "profound belief in mechanical organization; boundless energy and eager curiosity, combined with quick judgment and not very profound thinking when out of his own field."[4] Within the industry, Ford had abandoned his efforts to join the Association of Licensed Automobile Manufacturers, formed in February 1903 in a bid to control the licensing of patents and production. An associated lawsuit had been launched in late 1903 against his company (among others) by the holders of the Selden patent, who claimed the rights to the gasoline-powered vehicle and saw Ford as an irritating pretender.

Characteristically, Ford refused to buckle and pay any licensing fee, thus generating a lengthy legal storm and much free publicity. At the same time, his plans for expansion were extraordinarily focused and he possessed acknowledged mechanical ability; some said it bordered on genius, others attributed his technical capability to his associates. Though not a team man, he had attracted a talented group of innovative, young mechanics and engineers, including the colorful Dodge brothers, and some hard-boiled business types.

Jessie McGregor and her four sons (left to right): Donald, Gordon, Walter, and Malcolm, c. 1914. Courtesy of Walter L. McGregor.

Most notable was Couzens, whose sure control of business matters, especially his aggressive approach to uninterrupted production, sales, and wide recruitment of dealers, was a decisive factor in the company's startling success in 1903–4. By April 1904 the company had sold 658 automobiles, had a backlog of orders, and was paying remarkable dividends.[5] Though McGregor came to respect Henry Ford's vision and authority, it was to the Chathamite Couzens that he would regularly turn for practical direction on matters big and small, and he would remain dependent on Couzens's business advice long after Couzens and Ford had parted ways. Couzens was only four months older than McGregor (and Ford nine years), but McGregor routinely addressed them as Mr. Couzens and Mr. Ford.

Ford saw in McGregor, in his links to the likes of banker John Curry and in the beleaguered Walkerville Wagon Works, an ideal opportunity for expansion with minimal financial risk and a tested route for circumventing the high Canadian tariff. Ford probably recognized McGregor's family pedigree, his sales savvy and sense of self-interest, his initiative and willingness to work, his proximity, and, as would become apparent, his pliability and tolerance of

Ford's social crudity and seemingly whimsical approach to business. Socially they differed, but McGregor's somewhat desperate position and lower-tier status in business created an affinity. As well, Ford enjoyed some meanness in his associates—the bullish Couzens was a good example. For all his sociability, McGregor could be a scrapper and had been known to use his fists, brother Don attested. His autocratic gestures in public life and as a company head would hint at an underlying hardness.[6]

McGregor's plans did not constitute Ford's introduction to the Canadian market. In 1903 Canada Cycle and Motor Company in Toronto had offered Ford motorcars for sale. Henry Ford's piloting of 999 on Lake St. Clair in January 1904 generated attention from the *Toronto Daily Star*, which praised CCM's decision to handle Ford cars and other makes, including Packards and Stevens-Duryeas. On 26 April Henry Ford visited Toronto to talk of his racing feats and promote the automotive show sponsored by CCM at "Automobile Corner" at Bay and Temperance streets. Ford, the *Star* reported, enthused (with much exaggeration) "over the enormous strides being made in automobiling in Canada."[7]

McGregor made many trips to Detroit in the late winter and early spring of 1904, some of them occasioned by the death of his father-in-law in mid-March.[8] The business plan laid before Ford by McGregor between March and June was impressively thorough. Though Ford automobiles had been selling in Canada, the 25 percent tariff on assembled American cars entering Canada boosted the price. The duty on components brought in for assembly in Canada was much less. Here was a chance, McGregor proposed, to meet Canadian demand at somewhat reduced prices. Ford was clearly conscious of this demand: in late April his board of directors would decide that, since their contract with CCM in Toronto had been satisfied and there were still "unfilled contracts on our books," no new Canadian orders would be accepted.[9] McGregor had a factory that would be suitable for assembling automobiles, which was all Ford was doing at this point in Detroit, and parts could be easily transported by ferry and stockpiled in bond. In addition, McGregor proposed to find the financing, though both understood that Ford Motor investors would likely hold stakes in any new venture.

Against this plan Henry Ford weighed the uncertainties of the Canadian market, where the public had yet to fully appreciate the automobile as a viable alternative to horse or train. Ford was likely aware that there were only a few hundred automobiles in Canada, and that attempts there to manufacture (among them the Queen City Cycle and Motor Works in Toronto) had floundered, often on account of weak technology. At some point in 1904 Henry Ford drifted through southwestern Ontario; in Berlin (Kitchener) he learned of the financial problems of the short-lived Redpath Motor Vehicle Company.[10] He was nonetheless optimistic, and prior to accepting McGregor's proposal, he visited him to assess firsthand the manufacturing potential. Together they examined, in addition to the wagon works, the local plants of the Canadian Bridge Company (which they believed could make frames for automobiles), Walkerville Malleable Iron (malleable metals), Kerr Engine (brass parts such as lamps and radiator shells), Canadian Typograph (engines), and manufacturers in Chatham (wheels and bodies). McGregor showed Ford how the city of Walkerville was prospering and how the Walkerville and Detroit Ferry Company had added extra service; he boldly assured Ford that Curry, Chandler Merrill Walker (the well-to-do nephew of Hiram Walker, of local distilling fame), and other area residents could be relied on for support.[11]

McGregor undoubtedly emphasized, too, though Ford knew, the sympathetic economic climate being promoted by Canada's federal Liberal government—in short, the golden opportunity to exploit the price differential created by the tariff and to secure the benefits of any trade preference among the colonies of the British empire. McGregor and other local businessmen were eager to help maintain the belief of finance minister William Stevens Fielding, expressed in his budget speech of 7 June 1904, that tariffs were "high enough to bring some American industries across the line."[12] Partially as a result of a campaign by the Canadian Manufacturers' Association for increased protection, a new tariff schedule was introduced that included a provision to raise the duty on American automobiles to 35 percent effective February 1905.[13] In such ways, McGregor later boasted, "We received the unqualified support of the Liberal government."[14]

Ford took his impressions and McGregor's proposal to his directors, who reviewed them through June and July 1904. No news of any consideration surfaced in the *Evening Record*—"there just wasn't very much interest in the automobile," Don McGregor recalled—but Gordon evidently received conditional approval from Henry Ford. By 22 June, McGregor had started to raise funds.[15]

Finding the $125,000 capitalization projected by McGregor—a modest amount compared to some start-up costs among Michigan automobile firms—was likely the most difficult job he would ever undertake for Ford. This was "where the Man came in," huffed the *Evening Record*, McGregor's proud champion, in 1914.[16] Manliness aside—and the early industry was laden with masculine association[17]—the automobile industry was rightly regarded by investors in Detroit as an extremely risky speculation. Competition there for automotive capital had become stiff, and a number of respected, wealthy businessmen had been upset by their encounters with Henry Ford. In Canada, as future automobile giant Robert Samuel McLaughlin of Oshawa was to conclude, success in the industry simply could not be planned or predicted.[18]

Added to these difficulties, the pool of possible support in Windsor and Walkerville was much smaller than in Detroit, the industry had no real foothold on the Canadian side, and McGregor remained burdened with a failing wagon works. To launch the new company, just over 50 percent of its stock was allotted to the Detroit parent; the remainder was to be subscribed, with $5,000 worth going to the owners of the wagon works. Curry and McGregor worked for a week to secure local subscriptions, to no avail. McGregor then asked Curry to let him handle the issue on his own. Curry agreed, so McGregor would relate in court in 1913, and for another week McGregor, assisted by his popular brother Walter, canvassed the area, but again with practically no success. To interest potential investors, even placing one share at a time, Gordon recounted (possibly with some exaggeration for legal emphasis), was a "seemingly impossible" task. He told Curry and the other executors of the McGregor estate of his difficulty and discouragement. The executors then agreed to give him $1,000 worth of stock (to be bought by the estate) to urge him to continue his efforts to find money. Again he met refusals. "Curry tried to encourage me," McGregor later testified, "but I showed him that if we went ahead there was no profit to me. I then suggested that he do the same as the McGregor estate had done. He demurred but finally agreed. With this as an incentive I again went to work in Windsor and vicinity, but met with no success. I then went to Plymouth, Mich., and placed the balance of the stock." Later accounts of McGregor's hardship stress his despair rather than the incentives he squeezed out of his associates and Curry's quiet disregard of his promised bonus. "Gordon went a-begging," his secretary would recall.[19]

By 23 July McGregor had completed his stock list, including the "parties in Michigan," and had begun "negotiating with the Ford Company getting up our Articles of Agreement so as to get the best possible protection," he told Robert Gray of William Gray and Sons Limited, carriage builders in Chatham and by now the anticipated builder of automobile bodies. McGregor had reserved five shares for Gray and wanted to confirm his commitment; Gray wanted to foist off on McGregor a used car as payment. (Gray's persistent campaign to sell it would carry into 1906.) McGregor's prospectus for the proposed Canadian company, his diplomatic attempts to place Gray's car (neither Ford Detroit nor CCM wanted it), and his assurances that no stock would be called until September 1904 won Gray over.[20]

In the end, McGregor received commitments for most of the needed capital, most of it coming from family, businessmen, and some professionals in Windsor, Walkerville, and Chatham (including James Couzens's father, a soap maker), Ford investors and company men in Detroit, and (at the suggestion of Charles H. Bennett, the maker of Daisy Air Rifles and a Ford executive) new investors in Plymouth and DeWitt, Michigan, where Henry Ford's earlier stock had reportedly sold well. By year's end, 67 percent of the shares were held by Americans. The largest investors were, predictably, Henry Ford and his American associates and, in Walkerville and Windsor, John Curry and C. M. Walker; including his incentive from the estate, McGregor himself put in $3,500. The local investors also included a number of small merchants, a hotel keeper, a liquor dealer, a plumber's assistant, and a shipping clerk at the wagon works, which still retained a handful of employees.[21]

For Ford's group, the incitement was the prospect of securing, through a Canadian company, not only a domestic tariff advantage but also preferential tariffs throughout the British empire. Although tariff structures among the imperial members permitted varying degrees of market access, Canada hoped for reciprocity, and not without reason. In 1904 Britain's colonial secretary, Joseph Chamberlain, supported imperial preference, and by late summer in

1904, preferential tariffs had been concluded between Canada and the South African customs union and between Canada and New Zealand.[22]

On 10 August 1904 McGregor, Ford, and the shareholders reached an agreement for a branch plant relationship. In a key exchange that would free the Canadian firm from technological experimentation and cost, the American company would provide the patent rights, plans, and supervision needed to construct Ford automobiles, beginning with the 1905 models. Henry Ford himself would provide "reasonable and sufficient oversight." (Subsumed in this transfer was a parent-branch sharing of manufacturing systems, an exchange that would give the Walkerville firm an important edge among Canadian producers but also create problems, later on, of cost variation created by vastly different scales of production in Detroit and Walkerville.) In exchange, the Walkerville company would receive the sole right, under McGregor's charge, to manufacture and sell its automobiles in Canada and throughout the British empire, excluding Great Britain. The rights there were already held by an English agent until 1 December 1907, at which time, it was hopefully agreed in 1904, the Michigan and Canadian companies would combine their efforts to sell in Britain. From the start, it was estimated by Henry Ford that a Canadian-made automobile would have to cost some 10 percent more than a Detroit vehicle in order to cover the cost of bringing in parts.[23]

The agreement of the 10th immediately set in motion a flurry of legal and official action to secure an Ontario charter for the new company. It was issued by the provincial secretary's office on the 17th, and the next day Henry Ford, as required by Ontario law, authorized the use of his name for the new company. Thus assured, both McGregor and John Curry were eager to move forward; though he did not have the actual charter in hand, Curry called a meeting of shareholders for the 29th. "Our American friends," he explained, "are very anxious to start work in order to have Automobiles on the market on January 1st." Expedited by the political friends of W. J. McKee, the wagon company's vice president, the charter arrived in time for the inaugural meeting of the Ford Motor Company of Canada Limited on the evening of the 29th, as planned, in a private dining room at the Crawford House. After a short statement by Henry Ford, the company's officers were named:

John Simon Gray (president of the American company) became president, Henry Ford vice president, John Curry treasurer, and McGregor managing secretary. The public read of the organization the next day in the *Evening Record*. It was generally understood that McGregor would be the functioning head of the new Canadian firm—Henry Ford abhorred titles and strict corporate organization—but that Ford's wishes, when exerted, would prevail.[24]

It took McGregor about two months to ready the three-story brick wagon works and arrange for the start-up of production. Situated on the river and adjacent to the Grand Trunk Railway siding, the dimly lighted, "barn-like" factory was an 85 x 133 foot shell with a small office attached to the west end. Among the outbuildings were a blacksmith's shop, three warehouses, and a powerhouse with a badly leaning stack. Following the removal of machinery to West Lorne, the stilled works contained piles of discarded and broken wagon parts. It smelled of painted wood, treated leather, and must; the floors and walls, heavily worn and gouged, were covered in places with thick layers of dried multicolored paint. But little more was required: in function the works would be an assembly plant, like Ford's Detroit works, where costs and capital outlay were substantially reduced by buying from outside suppliers. Canadian Typograph dropped out of the picture. The Dodge brothers, of E&D bicycle fame and the makers of Ford's chassis and engines, would also supply Walkerville. Beginning in September, the other American-made components were brought to Walkerville by ferry and placed in bond in a locked warehouse at dockside. When they were needed, a customs officer would release them and charge the duty. As in other early automobile firms, mechanics assembled vehicles one at a time on stationary wooden trestles, fitting the pieces with hand tools to make that particular machine work. Probably no more than six automobiles could be assembled at any one time on the works' main floor.[25]

Progress over the remainder of 1904 was slow. The public stubbornly held concerns over the automobile's staying power as a legitimate form of transportation. Some saw it as a demonic reincarnation of the bicycle, destined to desecrate the Sabbath; one matron dismissed it as the plaything of "childish" men; others questioned the wisdom of sitting above a motor driven by exploding gas. The criticisms were legion. A smaller number, the mechanically curious, itched to take the motors apart. Newspaper editors throughout Canada, indignant over the new speeds, the inexperienced drivers, the recklessness, the noise, the run-over dogs, the terrified horses, called for regulation. Many ridiculed the primitive technology. As one wit put it in August 1904 in the *Monetary Times* (Toronto), "My engine will break when standing motionless on the barn-floor, simply through the power of gravitation."[26] In Windsor, however, skepticism was tempered by prospect: the *Evening Record*, which had castigated the "devil wagons" and the "auto terror," reported on 2 November that Ford Canada was "hurrying ahead its works."[27] Any pride or curiosity was reinforced by the seepage into Canada of automotive advertising and periodicals from the United States, and, for those who attended the Industrial Exhibition in Toronto from 1900 on, by the persuasive automotive promotions of the CCM.

In Walkerville, one of McGregor's first operational steps was the transfer of personnel from the wagon works to the Ford company. The legal acquisition of the riverside site would not occur until 1908, after some profit had accrued. In October and November 1904 a handful of workers was quietly moved from the payroll of the wagon works to that of Ford Canada.[28] Much help came over from Detroit, and a number of employees lived there. Two mechanics, Frank Hagen and Art Hoffmeister, came across the river from the parent company to supervise the initial assemblies, creating a staff of seventeen in all.[29] The Canadian Manufacturers' Association's journal, *Industrial Canada* (Toronto), noticed this start-up, adding optimistically that the new company hoped to employ about sixty hands over the winter.[30] By November the company's officers were recorded as drawing monthly salaries: Henry Ford ($400), James Couzens ($166.66), McGregor ($333.33), and his secretary, Grace E. Falconer ($21), with Ford and Couzens pulling in another $283.33 between them.[31]

At directors' meetings in November, with Henry Ford presiding, more precise corporate shape was given to his new branch.[32] On the 8th, on a motion by Ford, the Detroit parent was authorized to enter contracts for any foreign territory assigned to the Canadian company. Though any agreements were to be submitted to Walkerville as a formality, this decision effectively gave Ford Detroit discretionary access to the imperial market. To develop a greater Canadian presence, and recognizing the considerable promotional value of exhibitions, Henry also moved that McGregor and John Curry make arrangements to exhibit at the CCM's in-house automobile show scheduled for 27 February–4 March 1905 at "Automobile Corner" in Toronto and to launch general publicity through the Detroit advertising agency of O. J. Mulford, the firm used by Ford Detroit. In terms of production, the Canadian company was formally authorized to purchase chassis from either the Dodge Brothers or Ford Detroit. The meeting of 21 November attended to contracts: with CCM for exclusive rights to sell Ford cars in the Toronto area, Manitoba, the Northwest Territories, and British Columbia; with Wilson and Company in the Ottawa area to market up to five automobiles; and with William Gray and Sons Company of Chatham for automobile bodies and Chaplin Wheel Company, also of Chatham, for wheels and bodies.

When McGregor drove the first "Canadian"-assembled Ford down Windsor's Sandwich Street, he was supposedly cheered by all seventeen employees. The *Evening Record* missed the event, but company historian Herman L. Smith states that work started on 10 October 1904 and that the first Ford rolled out later that month.[33] Some of the Ford cars assembled that fall were bought by area customers and personally delivered by McGregor. As directed, others were sent for sale by CCM of Toronto, an existing distribution outlet. It had exhibited Detroit-made Ford cars at the Industrial Exhibition's Transportation Building in 1903 and was the sole agent and exhibitor in 1904 for Ford, its own short-lived electric Ivanhoe, and five American automobiles (Peerless, Packard, Thomas, Autocar, and Stevens-Duryea).[34] The exuberance displayed at the exhibition, however, did not reach far beyond Toronto. Automobiles were still rare in Canada's urban centers, rarer still in the countryside. By 10 November 1904 William H. Avery, the American consul in Quebec City, had seen only four automobiles there, though, like hopeful consuls elsewhere in Canada, he predicted "there must be a market for a great many more."[35]

McGregor's works was a slow, comparatively quiet operation, where hand tools were wielded by former carriage makers in greasy overalls. Aside from a steam-driven elevator, the only machinery was a drill press, reputedly powered by a belt that ran off the rear wheels of an automobile. The top floor of the works, or loft, was reserved for painting and storage; the low basement, with a rough brick floor, was used for occasional storage.[36] The only other occupants of McGregor's office were Grace Falconer and a part-time bookkeeper, H. E. Miller, who could tap-dance. When things were quiet, which was often, he strutted his stuff, teaching Grace a "few steps." "You can see how busy we were," she drily commented later.[37] McGregor himself held a second job until about 1907, as a sales agent for a company that distributed "souvenir postals" (probably postcards) and "art goods," with an office in the Medbury Block on Sandwich Street, close to that of Sutherland, Kenning, and Cleary, the law firm that had handled the Ford incorporation.[38] By the end of 1904 McGregor had turned out about twenty-five Model C Ford automobiles.[39]

Business picked up slowly for McGregor in 1905, but not without a blatant reminder of Henry Ford's isolation among the American producers. In January McGregor attended his first New York automobile show, at Madison Square Garden, the early industry's most important annual promotional event and an essential stop for the aspiring Canadian producer. With its extravagant array of electric lights, muscular salesmanship, displays of disassembled motors, and brilliant paintwork, and with more than 250 exhibitors of automobiles and accessories, it was the largest show ever held under one roof, the *New York Times* boasted. Moreover, the show overlapped the Importers Automobile Salon at the Herald Square Exhibition Hall. McGregor was undoubtedly struck by the scale of these shows compared to Toronto, by the variety of vehicles, and by Detroit's minor place in the busy Garden. Of the thirty-one American manufacturers represented, only four were from Detroit: Cadillac, Northern, Olds, and Packard. Despite its success, the Ford Motor Company was conspicuously absent, not surprisingly since the show was sponsored by the National Automobile Club and the hostile Association of Licensed Automobile Manufacturers. (Ford belonged to the American Motor Car Manufacturers Association, organized by the unlicensed companies.) Substantive advertising confronted McGregor and every prospective buyer: "Do not buy a lawsuit with your automobile! See that a Selden license patent plate is on the car before you purchase." The heaviest sales were in lines of reliable, light runabouts rather than the large, stretched-out touring models. To the majority of visitors, the automobile—any automobile—was a novelty; parents and children alike were thrilled just to climb in and out of the highly polished, brass-fitted vehicles, which most could only dream of owning.[40]

Thus informed, McGregor returned to the sympathetic environs of the Detroit River. Initially, advertising by the American Ford company stressed production, carefully crafted statements of Henry's reputation, and above all the simple concept of the automobile as a mode of transportation. In fine print, the "Canadian Trade" was directed to Walkerville. Advertisements for Canadian Ford cars had begun appearing in a few periodicals in December 1904 and in full, graphically sharp fashion in *Industrial Canada* and technical periodicals in January. Typical of early automobile advertising, the copy highlighted mechanical specifications, for the genuinely uninformed, and the maker's personal prestige. As a branch head, McGregor had not yet acquired any cachet. "Ford Motor cars are now made in Canada under the direct supervision of Mr. Henry Ford, the most successful designer of Automobiles in America," ran one pointed ad in *Industrial Canada.* Through such advertising the Canadian company, which lagged far behind the American company in its development of a sales network, also issued a general call in the spring of 1905 for new dealers: "We want good live agents all over the dominion." No mention was made that Ford cars still cost more in Canada than in the United States.[41]

McGregor's production, and his first advertising flyers and catalogues, centered on Ford's Model C. A dark green automobile with red or cream running gear, it contained a 10 horsepower, horizontally arranged two-cylinder engine under the seat and featured an optional tonneau (detachable rear seat), headlamps, and folding top. This model, which cost $1,000, or $1,100 with the tonneau, was touted as the "Ideal Doctor's Car": "No horse to hitch in the middle of the night. The FORD is always ready." Even at this point, differences, some of them more than cosmetic, were appearing in the Canadian product: in the tonneau, the Walkerville version had side entrances, while the American cars were entered from the rear. Illustrated only with mechanical pieces, the operating manual for the Canadian C was aimed at the novice driver and owner: "It is well to think twice before tampering with any part of the machine, inasmuch as you are liable to tamper with the wrong portion." Also offered was the larger, more elegant and expensive Model B. Its engine, a 24 horsepower, four-cylinder affair, was now situated un-

$3,200

" MODEL K " is a luxurious touring car with a world of *reserve power*, with speed to meet every requirement, with an engine so simple, so smooth in its operation, that the presence of a motor on the car could almost be questioned. A car that is the growth of a lifetime of study and practical development in automobile construction.

There is no feature in this car that has not been *worked out*. There is no danger from experiments. They are radical features but they are *proven features*, backed up not only by the best mechanical views, but by *actual experiences*.

Model C, $1,100.

A practical family car. Carries comfortably four people. The power of the motor is sufficient to drive the car *on the high speed* up all ordinary hills.

Model C has proven itself to be the most economical car to maintain, and in flexibility and ease of control its double opposed engine compares favorably with 4-cylinder motors of double the power.

We also make Model N, the Four-Cylinder Runabout for two people - $650

For Catalog and full particulars write :

The Ford Motor Co. of Canada

Combined advertisement for Ford Canada's Model K (top) and Model C (bottom). *Industrial Canada*, May 1906. Photograph by Mark Coatsworth.

der the front hood. The B, however, proved distinctly unpopular in Canada. The Canadian brochure for the C promised a car "free from vibration, and practically noiseless."[42]

Not all observers found that promise to be true. The 1904 Ford of Oliver Hezzelwood, bookkeeper of the McLaughlin Carriage Company in Oshawa, sounded like a threshing machine to one acquaintance, who also noted that it "stopped about every 5 minutes for repairs."[43] Nor did the Model C have standard headlamps. When Don McGregor borrowed Gordon's personal C one night to take his fiancée for a drive—the use of automobiles for courtship being one of their original functions—he blindly hit a pile of sand and broke the car's drive chain.[44]

By the end of January 1905 McGregor, working with the commissioner of customs in Ottawa, John McDougald, had established the dutiable value of the components being imported by Ford Canada, including hoods, fenders, chassis, and other parts. (The "red" chassis, valued at $266.30, and the "yellow" chassis, at $271.30, both purchased from the Dodge Brothers, were for Model Cs.)[45] The duty on fully assembled automobiles remained at 35 percent; on engines and frames the tariffs were 27.5 percent and 30 percent, respectively.[46] By late August or late September 1905—some sources say at the end of six months of production, and the total count varies—McGregor's small workforce had assembled 114 automobiles (107 Model Cs and 7 Bs), well short of his original projection of 400 but not worrisome.[47]

Henry Ford, whose attendance at corporate meetings would decline after 1905 (though at least one American director was always present), apparently liked what McGregor was doing. He gave him room to maneuver, setting in place the balance of corporate adherence and managerial autonomy that McGregor would experience in the years ahead. Any differences that McGregor had with John Curry—the two did not always see eye-to-eye[48]—were overshadowed by Detroit's support and the flow of new cars. The other solid relationship established by this time was with the *Evening Record*, whose exuberant liking of the automobile and uncritical support and promotion of McGregor solidified as Windsor and Walkerville grew to form Canada's premiere automotive center.

On 28 February 1905, during the CCM automobile show, McGregor made his first shipment of automobiles by rail, most destined for Toronto and probably the CCM; on 13 March a carload went to Montreal. Locally, the *Evening Record* puffed McGregor's operation as "already an established favourite." On the morning of the 27th two members of the newspaper's editorial staff were thrilled to be taken for a "spin" in a Model C tonneau operated by James R. Dixon. A former traveler with the wagon works, Dixon and A. D. Bowlby, the bicycle specialist and clothing merchant, had recently been appointed agents for Ford Canada in Essex and Lambton counties.[49] In May McGregor was authorized by the company to grant discounts to his "more important" agents in Canada and those "on the frontier" in order to compete with the reduced prices recently put into effect for American-made Ford cars,[50] an early harbinger of the price differentials that would later motivate sharp nationalist debate over the tariff and put pressure on Ford Canada. And in 1905 McGregor needed to take notice of American prices, since motorists in regions of Canada that he was not yet reaching in volume, such as Nova Scotia, were willingly paying the duty to bring in fully assembled American vehicles. McGregor certainly understood that his automobiles were selling primarily to urban-based professionals, especially doctors; in September 1905 Ford sales in Canada were concentrated in Toronto, Winnipeg, and Vancouver.[51]

To help cope with this business, on 22 August 1905 McGregor took on as assistant manager Wallace Ronald Campbell, a dour twenty-three-year-old local bookkeeper for a Standard Oil company. He knew the McGregor brothers well.[52] Sales were strong enough, in fact, to allow Ford Canada to declare a 6 percent dividend on 2 October[53] and to give McGregor reason to be optimistic about his Canadian expansion, which included a growing number of accounts with Canadian suppliers, among them Gray in Chatham, who tried to interest McGregor in other local manufacturers. On 18 October McGregor wrote him regarding "Vosburgh" (an unidentified producer) and about possible work for the foundry of McKeough and Trotter:

> I had hoped to be able to furnish plans for the car which we intend to build on this side during this season previous to this date, but one thing and another had held it up but will hope to give you an opportunity to figure very shortly on at least some of the parts and maybe a little later on the motor. We put the Detroit concern in

> rather a nasty position in this matter for you will understand in the automobile business it is their desire, and the desire of every other manufacturer to hold back with their new models until the very last moment so as to prevent other concerns copying the same model. This, of course, also puts our business back in the same way but you can rest assured that just as quick as we can furnish the drawings and plans necessary so as to get a start on the manufacturing on this side, we will be only too glad to give McKeough & Trotter an opportunity to figure on our work.[54]

Whether the firm received any work is uncertain, but McGregor was clearly talking about Ford's forthcoming, much heralded Model N. He was certainly conscious of change in design and technology, a thinking that would carry into the Model T years, a period normally regarded as static in terms of design.

Two major events in 1906 in Detroit had direct effects on Ford Canada and the type of vehicle McGregor was obliged to make. Following John S. Gray's death in July 1906, Henry Ford was elected president of both Ford companies. That same month he concluded an internal power struggle by buying out his principal backer, Detroit coal dealer Alexander Y. Malcolmson. Ford, who had precipitated the ouster by forming a manufacturing division (Ford Manufacturing) without Malcolmson, could now concentrate without resistance on the recently launched Model N, a reliable and low-priced runabout, but not before Malcolmson, who had been behind the unpopular Model B, had also pushed the introduction of his pet: ill-fated six-cylinder Model K.[55] Its production carried over to Walkerville, which, like its parent, had to force the massive, expensive (priced at $3,200 in 1906) vehicle on Canadian dealers. There were problems. The K gained an unwarranted reputation for a weak planetary gear transmission. Mechanically this behemoth was sound, but the transmission was open faced and required regular lubrication, which many owners neglected. Moreover, it was expensive, but not costly enough to put it in the same luxury market as Mercedes, Locomobiles, Pierces, and Wintons. An American-built K was shown at the Granite Rink show in Toronto in March 1906, and many would have noticed its folding hood, a new feature on Ford cars. (On previous models, hoods lifted off.) One reviewer, writing for *Canadian Graphic*, was struck by "the piratical looking

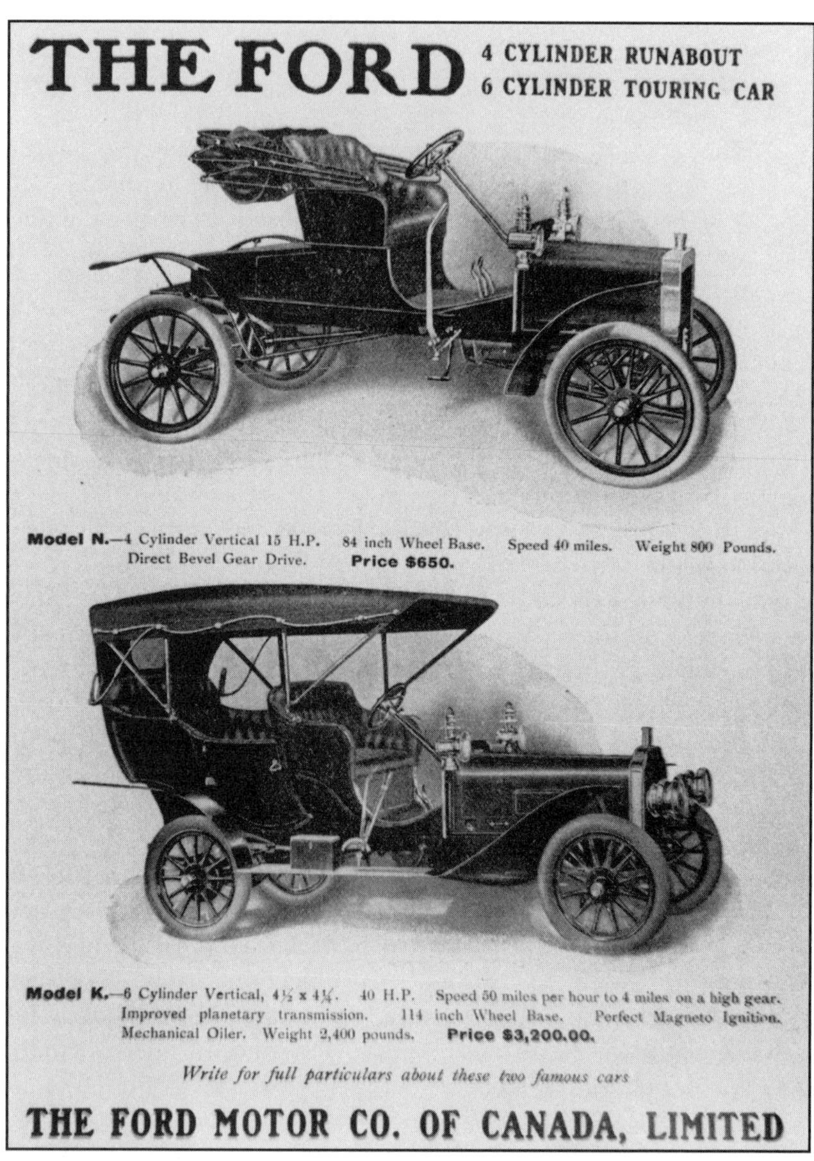

Combined advertisement for Ford Canada's Model N (top), a precursor of the Model T, and Model K (bottom). *Industrial Canada*, March 1906. Photograph by Mark Coatsworth.

six-cylinder Ford, with its long, sleek lines, about the price of which perhaps the less said the soonest mended." On 30 May McGregor personally tested his plant's first K, achieving a speed of 50 mph, and in July he dutifully drove one on promotional trips to Hamilton and Sarnia. The latter excursion was reportedly written up in *Motoring*, an early Canadian automobile magazine.[56]

The Model N (an important precursor of the famous Model T) had embodied Henry Ford's persistent call, fully outlined in *Automobile* in January 1906, for a "light, low-priced car" of ample horsepower that could go anywhere. "The engines must be simplified," he reasoned, "to get them within the comprehension of the ordinary owner."[57] To McGregor's good fortune, the N represented Ford technology at its best: in the estimate of the Ford museum in Dearborn, Michigan, it was the first successful car to include most of the modern mechanical features of the 1903 Benz Parsifal in a lightweight, inexpensive American car. Well adapted to poor roads, the Model N struck a chord in Canada, at the same time that the public started to become familiar too with Ford's new winged script logotype on radiators. Ledgers indicate direct sales and shipments to buyers in Vancouver, Winnipeg, Fort William (Thunder Bay), Goderich, and Fredericton. Local orders were still delivered directly; on 25 September 1906, for example, a Model N was driven to a buyer in Ridgetown, Ontario.[58] Prices ranged from $650 to $750.

In larger centers, multiple-make dealerships continued to be common. Ketchum and Company, at Bank and Sparks streets in Ottawa, for instance, handled Ford, Reo, Hupmobile, and Rolls-Royce. Representing only one make was risky. At least one dealer, Joseph Maw of Winnipeg, who sold Oldsmobiles and Cadillacs, had told McGregor outright that "unless the Ford [Company] turn out a very different machine to what they have at present I would not want to entertain handling it and drop the others." In a number of communities across Canada, where the extra cost of duties had not inhibited sales, Ford cars were already known, along with such other successful early American cars as the Oldsmobile and the Rambler. In Moose Jaw (Saskatchewan), to cite just one instance, Fred Hawkins bought a 1903 Model A Ford, which he sold in 1906 to Fred W. Green, a progressive farmer who promptly took it apart and reassembled it to learn the mechanics of the internal-combustion engine, a response repeated untold times throughout the dominion. He then kept it on his farm at nearby Boharm. For his "city" car he bought a larger, more luxurious automobile, the recently introduced Russell, made by Thomas Alexander Russell of CCM in Toronto, which boldly advertised it (with clear affront to McGregor's and other American-engineered vehicles) as "The Thoroughly Canadian Car: Canadian Material, Canadian Labor, Canadian Capital."[59]

Walkerville's production of the Model N in 1906 and 1907 marked the start of a new phase of accelerated production (still using stationary trestles) and distribution (including a break with CCM). In 1905 Ford and a few of his associates had formed the Ford Manufacturing Company to make the components of the N, specifically its front axles, cylinder blocks, wheel spindles, pistons, crankshafts, and transmission cases. (The Dodge Brothers continued building Ford's planetary transmissions.) This significant move into large-scale manufacturing necessitated Ford's acquisition of specialized machine tools, their sequential placement in the Detroit factory (part of a major reorganization of work there), the implementation of progressive assembly, and a new and imperative emphasis on the interchangeability of parts.[60] Whatever Ford did in Detroit, Walkerville and McGregor were expected to follow suit, as facilities allowed. In October 1906 Ford's new manufacturing bosses, Thomas S. Walborn and Max Wollering, determined that the twenty-three-year-old George Dickert, a talented machinist who had been with the manufacturing company less than six months but who had experience making automobile frames and small gasoline engines, should go to Ford Canada to supervise production. "I cannot tell you how I was chosen to go to Canada," Dickert recalled. "All I know is that they came and told me they wanted me to go over to Walkerville to work. I think Tom Walborn had spoken to Max, and Tom went over with me to see Mr. McGregor."[61] Some of the company's other early mechanical stars were likely hired directly by McGregor. Daniel Mitchell Sorenson, for example, an eighteen-year-old native of Windsor, joined his shop as an apprentice mechanic in 1906 and rose quickly, becoming head of the mechanical division of Ford's Toronto branch in July 1908.

When Dickert started work, he was struck by the smallness of the Walkerville operation. "At times they did not have more than a half a dozen on their staff, all told, including the office and shop."

There were still the trestles; the only thing driven by the steam engine was the elevator. Dickert began with the assembly of the Model N and the K, which they turned out at the rate of one a week "or something like that. There were not many of them." The K chassis and motor were tested for more than a week before they were deemed finished. Dickert supervised assembly operations: motors from Ford, bodies and wheels from Chatham, frames and housings from A. O. Smith in Milwaukee (for whom he had once worked), and differentials from the Dodges. According to Dickert, McGregor and Campbell, who handled sales, "had to do a lot of peddling to sell" the K. The easygoing Dickert got to know McGregor well: he "was a very pleasant man," "a nice man to get along with." The relations of McGregor and Campbell with Henry Ford, he observed, were harmonious: "[T]hey would come over and discuss policy with Mr. Ford. It was a case with them mostly of coming over to Detroit."[62] McGregor's corporate correspondence, most of which has been destroyed, was augmented by frequent visits and telephone calls to Ford's offices in Detroit.

Under Dickert production continued as a stationary assembly of parts. "When we received an order for a car, the first step was to place a frame on two horses. Then you would put your front axle on, then your motor and dashboards and body. We assembled everything right on these horses. We would take these horses out, put the car on the floor, and push it away. We would lift it by hand."[63] Recalling his early years, Dickert believed in 1952 that equipment was installed to machine front axles and spindles about 1907, though the *Evening Record* had noted the installation of undescribed "new machinery" in November 1906, the same year that McGregor hired George Dixon, possibly his first toolmaker. Later accounts confirm the installation in 1906 of two lathes and, to drive both the drill press and the lathes, an electric generator that Henry Ford had obtained from the Edison Company in Detroit.[64] Dickert cited this stage as the start of the plant's technological growth.

Whatever the function of the new machinery, and whatever new patterns of work flowed from Detroit, production edged forward in fits and starts that year, to the point that McGregor found it necessary to hire a purchasing agent, Sergeant Joseph D. Isaacs, whose initial job was trucking parts from Ford's new Piquette Avenue plant in Detroit in a Model C poetically named Sappho.[65] At some point in 1907, because of a downturn related to a short business recession that year, or because of an overaccumulation of axles, Dickert was laid off for a few months. He simply remembered the period as "hard times."[66] Even as production increased, the pace of activity could seem casual. In 1907 when Robert Conklin, an implements dealer from Kingsville, Ontario, dropped in unexpectedly to buy a car from Gordon McGregor, everyone in the office was at lunch. To kill time, he wandered through an adjacent shed, "where a few Ford cars of the B, C, K, and N class were in the process of manufacture," but there was no one there either. When McGregor finally did return, Conklin ordered a Model N, which, in stripped condition, cost him $710 (windshield, top, horn, and lamps were extra).[67]

McGregor's small plant turned out 101 vehicles in 1906: 54 Model Cs, 35 Ns, and a mere 12 Ks, generating a profit to 30 September 1906 of $4,095.76.[68] In 1907, Dickert's first full year, the total shot up to 327, comprised of a few Ks but mostly Ns and two new modified versions: the somewhat heavier and more expensive models R and S, which featured running boards.[69] The company's balance sheets to the end of September 1907, in addition to revealing a healthy profit of $19,168.61, show too an investment in equipment: the firm's machinery was valued at $7,341.93, its tools at $4,550.32, and miscellaneous equipment at $2,986.20. Significantly, expenditure on advertising and catalogues increased from $1,583.92 in 1906 to $4,601.47 in 1907.[70]

Moreover, production was being matched by a proliferation of testimonials and a growing Ford mystique. In the summer of 1907, undoubtedly with McGregor's blessing, W. J. Gourley drove a Ford from Windsor to his hometown of Calgary, clocking 3,000 miles without a tire puncture and 3,700 without a breakage (except for a spring). He generated publicity the whole way and, following the pattern of transcontinental automobile trips in the United States, confirmed the motorcar's utility. The publicity carried into the Toronto exhibition of 26 August–7 September, which McGregor attended, the first time that Ford Canada exhibited on its own there apart from CCM.[71]

With McGregor's progress and needs being monitored by his associates in Detroit, the same two-year period of 1906–7 also witnessed his turn to overseas marketing through Ford's existing system of exportation. McGregor seems to have been involved in the plans charted by Henry Ford and Couzens. In the spring of 1906 Ford was visited by Percival Lea Dewhurst Perry, an English car enthusiast who had already sold three Model Bs for use as taxis in London and wanted the exclusive rights to market Ford automobiles in Britain. Perry found Couzens a "spiteful man" but McGregor, whom he met in Walkerville, struck him as "one of the finest men who ever lived." When McGregor began shipping abroad in 1906, he was hardly charting unknown waters. Some Canadian Ford cars had apparently gone to Calcutta and New Zealand in the fall of 1905. For years American consuls, who understood that American automobiles did not compete well in Europe, had been calling attention to the potential for the sale of small, practical American runabouts in British imperial colonies. In October 1904, while McGregor was still getting organized, Ford Detroit engaged the New York export agent Robert M. Lockwood to handle Ford business outside Canada; the first Model A Ford cars had appeared in Australia in the spring of 1904. In March 1906 "large shipments" went to New Zealand and to Denmark, the first instance perhaps of McGregor filling in for Detroit in the supply of nonimperial destinations. Between September and December, working through Lockwood and various shipping firms, Ford Canada sent vehicles (mostly Model Ns) to Australia, New Zealand, India, Egypt, and Natal (South Africa). The high-riding, light, and relatively powerful Ford cars quickly gained reputations for their adaptability to widely varying rural road conditions not unlike Canada's. Model Ns landed in Durban were quickly sold throughout Natal's inland farming districts; in India and Australia dry conditions and flat landscapes drew vehicles "away from the roads altogether."[72]

Australia, where franchises were established in 1907, would quickly become Ford Canada's largest foreign market—and its most problematic, as official trade and tariff talks lurched backward and forward, leaving Ford Canada exposed to heavy duties on assembled cars and car bodies, a factor that would later influence the style of both Canadian and Australian Ford cars. Ben A. Morgan, a trade commissioner for the Manufacturers' Association of Great Britain, "was nonetheless impressed with the scope that existed throughout Australia and New Zealand for the sale of motor vehicles of all kinds. . . . If one eliminated the exports of two or three British firms, the market would be found to be practically in the hands of German, French, and American houses."[73] Still, the number of Canadian Ford cars exported to Australia and New Zealand was appreciable in relation to overall output. The Canadian Department of Trade and Commerce recorded the total numbers of all automobiles (most of them undoubtedly Ford cars) exported to New Zealand—15 (1906), 7 (over nine months of 1907), 13 (1908), 18 (1909)—and to Australia: 2 (1906), 24 (over nine months of 1907), 34 (1908), and 48 (1909). Overall, exports sustained Ford Canada in 1906: though production dropped to 101 units for the year ended August 1906, 76 of them were exported (a number that would rise to 114 in 1908).[74] Prior to the fiscal year 1908–9, Ford Canada sent 224 cars abroad.

On 1 January 1907, by which time Henry Ford was becoming quite rich, McGregor's modest success in Canada and abroad was recognized by the increase of his annual salary to $3,000. Of course he drove Ford cars—in February 1907 he took possession of a new Model N sent over from Detroit. Later that year he bought in much of his company's stock at 75 percent of its value from shareholders "who had become timorous as to the safety of their investment." He would often cite these purchases as a benchmark of stability and his own personal relief. Commensurate with the growth of the firm, he started to become active in public life, much as Detroit's automotive kingpins (except for Ford and Couzens) would enter the city's associational life, notably its board of commerce. Certainly, too, McGregor had his father's example to follow. In May 1906 he and others had tried unsuccessfully to revive Windsor's defunct board of trade. In January 1908 he was named chairman of the board of management formed to direct the construction of First Presbyterian Church in Walkerville, the cornerstone for which was laid on 1 June.[75]

Having achieved some success, McGregor could view with satisfaction the quick maturing of the automobile industry in Canada. The process included the establishment of branch plants to provide infrastructure. For example, the Trussed Concrete Steel Company of Canada Limited, patented on 23 January 1907 and based in Walkerville, was formed by Gustave Kahn and three civil engineers to provide a range of new reinforcing and window systems for reinforced-concrete factories. Kahn's brother Albert had built Detroit's first reinforced-concrete plant, for Packard Car in 1905, and would soon be favored by Henry Ford and Gordon McGregor. Exhibitions, too, were essential to the industry. There the way was pioneered by Robert Miller Jaffray, a journalist born in Galt, Ontario, and onetime manager of a cycling journal. In November 1906, with his wife and others, he incorporated Automobile and Sportsmen Exhibition Limited in Montreal, though he soon gravitated to the Detroit-Walkerville hub. Since 1903 the Canadian National Exhibition had been showing automobiles, including Ford cars, first by CCM and then by the Dominion Automobile Company Limited. In 1906 a second show was added, in March at the Granite Rink in Toronto. New trade journals such as *Canadian Motor* and *Motoring* provided print support and advertising.[76]

On the tariff front, at the end of January 1907, in committee debate on tariff revisions in the House of Commons, maverick Tory MP (member of Parliament) William Findlay Maclean of Toronto, anticipating an important argument of later years, tried to get the government to push American carmakers in Canada toward total domestic production. "At present the tariff does not encourage the industry, but only increases the price of an article that many want to buy. . . . We want to see big machine shops." Anxious to move ahead in debate on a long list of tariff changes, finance minister W. S. Fielding was quite content with the busy branch plants—Ford in Walkerville and Olds, then being made in St. Catharines by Packard Electric Company Limited—and 35 per cent, "one of the highest duties on the tariff."[77] Certainly the number of cars registered in the various provinces confirmed that the mode of transport, regardless of origin, had a tentative hold on the traveling public in Canada.

Different regions in Canada were taking to the automobile in different ways, a fact McGregor and his sales associates recognized and would act on. Sales in Saskatchewan would soon take off, for instance. Comparatively, Quebec lagged in terms of per capita ownership. In New Glasgow, Nova Scotia, the *Eastern Chronicle* of 28 July 1908 cheered the temporary absence of the "stink wagon" from the town's streets as a result of accidents and disposals. Farmers generally remained resistant. But few could deny that the motorcar was on the rise. In March 1908 *Industrial Canada* described motoring as "in the springtime of its popularity in Canada." *Saturday Night* had held a more definite opinion in March 1906: "The automobile has

Table 1

Number of car registrations in Canada, 1907 and 1908		
Province	*1907*	*1908*
New Brunswick	79	104
Quebec	254	396
Ontario	1,530	1,754
Manitoba	0	418
Saskatchewan	0	74
Alberta	55	45
British Columbia	175	263

Source: Historical Statistics of Canada, ed. M. C. Urquhart and K. A. H. Buckley (Cambridge, 1965), S227–35.

come to stay. It is the modern Aladdin's lamp that annihilates time and distance."[78]

Welcoming such assessment, McGregor vigorously pushed business, though the production of 324 automobiles in 1908 was three fewer than the previous year. (By comparison, in 1907–8 Ford Detroit turned out more than 10,000 vehicles, of which 6,398 were sold that season.)[79] Ford Canada's first branch was set up in July 1907 at 53–59 Adelaide Street in Toronto under the brassy management of go-getter Frederick Isenbard Fox, a native of London, Ontario, who would compete head-to-head with T. A. Russell and CCM.[80] At year's end on 30 September 1907, the company posted profits of $19,168.61, and in 1908 the Walkerville plant's collection of machinery was enlarged. The period January–March 1908 witnessed a relative surge of exports to Australia, New Zealand, Pretoria, Trinidad, Jamaica, and India.[81] At home, in January McGregor lured Harold S. McMullen away from the Chatham Motor Car Company in Chatham, Ontario, first to fill in for Fox while he took an "extended trip in the interests of the company" and then in March to join the Walkerville office to give "special attention" to sales in Ontario.[82]

At the Toronto automotive show of 21–28 March in the St. Lawrence Arena, visitors were likely impressed by the low prices of Ford

Ford Model R (a more elaborate version of the N) with unidentified family group, 1907. The Esplanade: Archives, Medicine Hat, Alberta, image no. 0411.0001.

cars (in the $750 to $800 range) compared to Oldsmobiles ($3,000–$4,750), McLaughlin-Buicks from Oshawa ($1,050–$2,750), and "Canadian by birth not by adoption" Russells ($1,600–$3,750).[83] By 1908 the parent company's new winged pyramid trademark was becoming prominent in Canada, as was Henry Ford's idea of a car for the masses, a concept that would easily sideline the Russell's nationalist thrust in marketing and surpass the market for luxury vehicles. Canadian advertisements for Ford's Model S deftly promoted it on the one hand as the "Edition De Luxe" of the now famous Model N (the S had fully enclosed fenders and splash aprons) and on the other hand as "everyman's" car. "The idea behind the Ford Cars," one ad ran, "is a determination to give the public a car of the widest range of usefulness, built in sufficiently large quantities to make the cost as low as possible."[84] Despite the limited size of his Walkerville plant, with its stationary assembly, McGregor completely bought into Henry Ford's ethos of greater production to lower cost—he had little choice—and would soon make plans to expand.

During his time at the Toronto automobile show of March

1908, McGregor witnessed a vigorous demonstration of industrial pride and of how automotive interests were beginning to mesh and flex some muscle. Staged with great flair and color, "ablaze" with electric lighting, and opened by the lieutenant governor, it was held in the St. Lawrence Arena, to the rear of the St. Lawrence Market on King Street. Billed as a sportsman's show, it was in effect a major, full-scale showing of all makes of automobiles, the largest outside New York, Chicago, and Boston. For a full week, a record number of visitors gazed upon polished automobiles (including Ford cars), chassis and motors laid bare for scrutiny, displays of tires (some "puncture proof"), secondhand automobiles, and motorboats. At the same time, the newly formed Ontario Motor League met in convention at the nearby King Edward Hotel. At its closing banquet at the National Club, speaker after speaker enthusiastically condemned government regulation of automobiles and motoring. Preferring corporate weight to personal flamboyance when away from Walkerville, McGregor stayed in the background while T. A. Russell held center stage, escorting the lieutenant governor and, as the president of the Ontario Motor League, championing both his car's "Canadian" quality and the splendid growth of the industry. McGregor knew that the success of the show owed much to its organizing manager, his friend R. M. Jaffray of Windsor, who would soon, in Detroit's glow, gain recognition as Canada's number one automotive showman.[85]

During the summer of 1908 McGregor traveled to the west coast to strengthen his sales network there. After his return, Canada's governor-general, Lord Grey, visited Windsor on 24 August. McGregor provided the viceregal party with automobiles and personally and swiftly chauffeured the Greys. "McGregor gave His Excellency a speedy trip in some places," the *Evening Record* reported. "On Belle Isle Earl Grey's fedora was blown off. Mayor Thompson assured the party that speed ordinances would not be enforced."[86] Two weeks later McGregor appeared at the Toronto Industrial Exhibition, where automobiles formed half the transportation exhibit (then situated under the grandstand because of fire damage elsewhere, but strategically close to the racetrack, where automobiles roared) and were "a decided success," in the estimate of the exhibition's annual report.[87]

The success of Ford Canada drew other manufacturers to

Windsor-Walkerville, a trend that would give the area a distinct identity and eventually produce a local automotive fraternity dominated by Ford personnel. The appearance of the Menard in early 1908 was a matter of little consequence to McGregor, whose control of Ford technology and sales would keep him in the forefront in Canada until the 1920s. In any case, the reliable Menard highwheeler, a vestige of carriage days, was soon destined to fall from favor and former carriage maker Moise-L. Menard of Windsor would wisely move into the production of trucks in 1910.[88]

What did trouble the speedy, citified McGregor was the regulation of automotive use, a direct result of the growth in numbers and the incidence of thoroughly upset horses, run-over dogs, infuriated farmers, and cautious pedestrians. To many the automobile was the rich man's toy. In Windsor and Walkerville the levels of sound, smell, speed, and threat were set by Ford employees test-driving motorized chassis up and down Sandwich Street, by "auto scorchers" racing on the streets, and by the likes of Dr Henri-Raymond Casgrain and other repeat crashers. In March 1906 Walkerville's municipal councillors, however, solicitous "to protect one of their pet and growing industries," opposed provincial regulation intended to place stringent penalties on speeding automobiles.[89] Public concern in Ontario had generated regulatory by-laws—Toronto's passing early, in 1902. Provincial statutes followed in 1903, 1904, and 1905. Swayed by strong rural resistance and attachment to horse-drawn vehicles, other provinces and a host of municipalities followed similar courses: British Columbia in 1904, Saskatchewan in 1906, Alberta and Quebec in 1906 and 1907, Nova Scotia in 1907 and 1908, and Manitoba, New Brunswick, and Prince Edward Island in 1908. In Ontario, additional legislation of 1906 was brought up for amendment two years later. By this time McGregor had had enough.[90]

Two opposing delegations waited upon a committee of the legislature in Toronto on 31 March 1908 near the end of the St. Lawrence automobile show. One group, headed by representatives of the Dominion Grange and other agricultural bodies, along with rural politicians, wanted among other proposals to limit use to certain hours or days and force automobiles to stop within 100 yards of a horse. "The automobile keeps a thousand women off the roads in my constituency," reasoned one delegate. "Not only is the auto a danger, it is a nuisance. We can't keep our doors or windows open for dust and the nuisance is greatest on Sunday. Why should we pay for good roads when we are driven from them by the automobile? The people are up in arms against it."[91]

The automotive proponents—possibly the earliest such lobby in Ontario—were represented by officials of the Ontario Motor League (OML) and "allied interests" headed by T. A. Russell, the outspoken political science graduate turned automaker. Concerned about overregulation and buoyed by the OML convention and the success of the show, they described the automobile's importance in terms of both business and pleasure. For his part, Gordon McGregor directed the committee's attention to the value of the industry. Tying its prosperity to unfettered use, he cited orders his company had taken conditional "upon no further drastic legislation being promulgated." A week later the committee proposed a modest set of amendments, which received assent in April: professional drivers had to be provincially licensed, no one under seventeen could drive a car on public streets and highways, motorists were to give way to funeral processions and assist vehicles drawn by frightened horses, and they were to give their names and addresses to injured parties.[92]

Ontario's acts—another would follow in 1909—blended into the call by the Ontario Municipal Association and others for the application of license revenues to road improvement. In Quebec, the Good Roads Association lobbied the provincial government there. McGregor supported the good roads movement, but he still remained critical of regulation. Speaking through the *Evening Record* in September 1908, he ventured the conclusion that Ford sales in the Maritimes had been hurt by regulatory legislation and bylaws there that barred cars from streets on certain days. In reality, in Halifax County, as elsewhere, regulatory laws were largely unenforceable and were routinely violated. People still bought cars. "The by-law is a dead letter," one Dartmouth editorial snorted. "In time, the auto will be as common as carriages are today, so it is better to prepare for them."[93]

Ford Canada was indeed beginning a modest surge of success. At the end of September 1908, a few weeks after his now-routine appearance at the Toronto Industrial Exhibition, McGregor basked in company profits of $18,549.08. The following month his firm was able to pay the Walkerville Wagon Works (the legal entity) $16,000 plus interest, the balance due on its property. On 24 December, following similar action at Ford Detroit, McGregor gave his employees their first bonus, possibly based on seniority. The gesture, whatever its role in shaping labor sentiment in an open-shop environment, was gladly reported by the *Evening Record*, which by then had settled into a pattern of unapologetic promotion of Walkerville's rising star. McGregor valued this free promotion and carefully nurtured the journal as his favored mouthpiece. On 28 September it had claimed in an article that the works, with seventy-five men, was selling more than ever before, and that Ford cars were outselling all other makes in Canada. Tucked into the piece was the understated announcement that the company would launch a new touring model for 1909.[94] In the last few days of 1908 a handful of the new Model Ts were shipped to Walkerville.

In 1933, when Henry Ford was asked by the *Toronto Star Weekly* to reflect upon his Canadian plant, his first factory outside Detroit, the skepticism that McGregor had encountered in early 1904 had given way to an eminently promotable corporate bond. "It was the approval, and the confidence, of the Canadian public that more than anything else made me confident I was on the right track," Ford concluded. "I had just that much confidence in the Canadian estimate of everything—such as the material used, the scale of values, and all that sort of thing—that I was encouraged and reassured from the start."[95]

CHAPTER 3

Mr. Ford's Canadian Model T

From 1909 until his untimely death in 1922, McGregor made no other car but the Model T Ford—and it made his fortune. Simultaneously, no other car had such an impact upon Canada's early automobile culture. Though it was designed and engineered in Detroit by the parent company, with virtually no technical input from Walkerville personnel, who included few automotive engineers and no designers, McGregor labored mightily to cast his assemblies as "Canadian" automobiles. But the underlying concept was American and purely Fordist. According to James Couzens, with the Model T, Ford Detroit reversed the traditional process of meeting customers' demands: "We worked out a car and at a price which would meet the largest average need. In effect, we standardized the customer. We set the price of the car as a goal to reach and depended for profit upon the economies that we might effect in volume manufacturing."[1]

Designed around the engineering principles of solidity and simple operation needed for a "universal" car that ultimately could be mass produced, the T was accordingly made dependable, light, sturdy, and increasingly inexpensive. It was easily repaired, fitted with interchangeable parts throughout, and adaptable to the roughest road surfaces. Rigidly rectilinear in shape and seemingly disjointed, with a distinctively bold, squarish brass radiator, it was mechanically undistinguished and, to present-day eyes, lacked aesthetic unity. With other cars rivaling it in this respect, historian D. F. Davis nonetheless singles out the Model T as "almost perversely utilitarian—by all accounts the plainest and perhaps the ugliest car of its era." Terry Smith, in his perceptive analysis of the "technology of modernity," sees the T's evolution as the "revolutionizing of the ordinary."[2] But discernment of beauty was subjec-

Advertisement for two versions of Ford Canada's famous (but here unnamed) Model T. *Industrial Canada*, March 1909. Photograph by Mark Coatsworth.

tive: some progressive architects of the time viewed the Model T as modernism on wheels. The T would emerge as a powerful symbol of industrial transformation from the remnants of carriage design (the tonneau and wooden spoke wheels, for instance) to minimalist simplicity.[3] Whatever the faults or merits of its design, the T caught the American public's imagination like no other new vehicle in 1908–9. In the United States descriptive circulars went out to dealers in March 1908; introduced in October, the car was an instant success, "the greatest creation in automobiles ever placed before a people," one agent crowed.[4]

In Walkerville, with a much smaller operation and publicity machine, McGregor did not follow the same pattern of introduction and promotion. After a prodigious reorganization of its plant (engineered by Peter Edmund Martin from Wallaceburg, Ontario), Ford Detroit turned out 309 Model Ts in late 1908. Walkerville assembled none that year. In the early months of 1909 it turned out only a few, as it continued to use up parts for more models K, N, R, and S.

George Dickert confirmed that at the time "we were getting ready for the T." The *Evening Record* mentioned it only in passing in a feature article on the Canadian company in September 1908. In October, McGregor occupied himself with setting Ford Canada's prices for the T and, following a pattern set by Ford Detroit, taking steps to establish new agencies and dealerships, a vital process that involved the granting of territorial rights in exchange for signed commitments to meet specified volumes of business. Established dealers such as Fred Fox in Toronto, who was already receiving a generous combination of salary, commission, and bonuses, were eager to push the new model. So-called factory letters—technical specifications and modifications—began flowing into the Walkerville plant in mid-February; the shipping records of Ford Detroit indicate that T chassis were starting to arrive in Walkerville in March 1909; by August, 458 had been produced.[5] A red Model T with black fenders, on display at the Canadian Automotive Museum in Oshawa, Ontario, is believed by the museum to be the earliest surviving Canadian-built Model T in the country, though much-prized examples with earlier serial numbers survive in collections in Woodstock and Gorrie, Ontario. Other early examples undoubtedly exist.

The response to the T in Canada was initially subdued. It struck many as only a modest progression from preceding models. The T, which came in red, green, or gray, made its exhibitory début at the St. Lawrence automobile and sportsmen's show in Toronto on 18–25 February 1909. However hard McGregor and his staff worked on expansion and sales, the impact of the new model could hardly be predicted with assurance. No mention had greeted it in the press at the famous Olympia show in London, England, in November 1908. Though at the outset the T cost more than the S or the N, McGregor could market the touring version at $1,000 and the roadster at $975 (compared to $825 in the United States) and still call it the "lowest priced 4-cylinder touring car in the world." At the St. Lawrence show, every other make cost more (among them the Cadillac at $1,850, the Oldsmobile from $3,000, the McLaughlin-Buick at $3,100, the Russell from $1,950, and the Overland at $1,775), with the exception of the $550 Tudhope-McIntyre, the almost obsolescent two-cylinder high-wheeler out of Orillia, Ontario.[6]

For reasons of price, and with the reputation of the S and the N behind it, the Model T slowly started to receive notice. In advertising McGregor tried hard to give it a native identity. Although Canadian-made bodies and other components were placed on American chassis, advertisements in February had claimed that the T was being "manufactured entirely at the Ford plant" in Walkerville.[7] (Other makers, such as Russell, did not equate assembly with manufacture.) From the beginning the Canadian T, in addition to a Walkerville Ford nameplate, did possess some technical features that distinguished it from its American counterpart—the result in part of Canadian production and subcontracting of components—but these were minor and were never singled out for advertising purposes. The T's Canadian-supplied tires, for instance, were 30 inches x 3 1/2 inches all round, whereas the American version had 30 x 3 inch tires in front and 30 x 3 1/2 in the rear. The Canadian uniformity made replacement much easier. Other differences in the Canadian version included the two-piece front seat cushion (to facilitate access to the gas tank), the vertical seams down the back of both front and back seats, and a slightly greater overall width. The Ts made in Walkerville for export often had right-hand drive steering, other controls were also placed differently, and many received custom-made bodies in the countries of destination. Widely separated imperial markets and customs regulations dictated a range of regional variations,[8] but overall a Ford car was a Ford car. Of greater consequence for McGregor was the recognition he was getting, slowly and sometimes grudgingly, as a manufacturer who had the good fortune to be sustained by an automotive corporation that had developed a winning formula.

Despite breaking a bone in his leg earlier in February, McGregor attended the St. Lawrence show and, with three colleagues, the Ontario Motor League banquet at the nearby King Edward Hotel on the 24th. McGregor, Fred Fox, and associates H. Angove and C. H. Nash "were present in the flesh," the *Toronto Daily Star* noticed, with maybe a hint of admiration.[9] Though Tommy Russell and his Toronto-made car continued to receive the greatest adulation—it was the local product, after all—the Ford gang now had presence. So too, as 1909 wore on, did the indomitable Model T: news and sales spread, drivers became converts, and initial mechanical and supply problems were worked out in Detroit. Even then Canadian newspapers still reflected some resistance to the concept of the automobile. In July the *Toronto Globe*, for example, professed to speak for the anonymous farmer: "He regards it as a kind of modern juggernaut, which scatters death and destruction wherever it goes." But such grumbling was fading out. By May the Walkerville works was faced with "orders beyond their capacity."[10]

Demand was generated in part by an increasing number of dealerships in Canada. The exact numbers are unknown, but in the United States dealerships skyrocketed from 215 in September 1908 to 859 in September 1909. Ford Canada may have operated at a tenth of that range or less, and would not pass the 700 level until late in the Great War, some years after the immense boost generated by the wartime economy, western prosperity, and Ford Canada's remarkable program of dealership development in 1912–13.[11]

During the summer of 1909, in concert with Ford Detroit's aggressive promotion of the Model T and development of its nonimperial foreign market, Gordon McGregor planned a big adventure: a round-the-world trip to promote and consolidate the foreign business of Ford Canada.[12] On 25 August he bid farewell to his family and headed out by rail, stopping periodically in Canada's western provinces en route to Vancouver, where he embarked. This trip was a grand undertaking for the former clothing and postcard salesman. In Fiji he tried to interest the local chiefs in automobiles—his automobiles, even if he had none in hand. The pitch was not a complete gimmick: the queen of Fiji had reportedly learned to drive in 1907. McGregor, for all his heartiness, was ever the consummate salesman, always ready to cajole, argue need and utility, and persuade. From Fiji he went to Australia (his main destination), New Zealand, Calcutta and Bombay in India, and Ceylon (now Sri Lanka).

To formally set up an Australian branch, McGregor evidently secured the "voluntary" withdrawal of his existing agents, Davis and Fehon of Sydney, and in September or October he gave the responsibility to a Canadian, Robert J. Durance, and his Australian-born wife, who established a branch office in Adelaide. Prior to this appointment Durance had been a carriage builder and the innovative sales manager for Dunlop Tire in Melbourne. McGregor had known him since he was a young, Toronto-based commercial traveler for Dunlop in Ontario and he admired his salesmanship. Following his appointment, Durance promptly hit the road to begin building up a network; he understood Australia and how Model Ts and dealerships could best be placed. Though he initially "found the selling rather hard," he cleverly developed a successful technique. He drove a Model T into a town, asked the local bank manager to direct him to the wealthiest businessman in the area, and then entreated this businessman to take on the Ford dealership. "In every case," Durance wrote, "the man would be greatly flattered, and in not a single case did I fail to sign these people up."[13]

In Melbourne, Durance secured Tarrant Motors Proprietary Limited, a long-established firm that already handled Ford cars. At the end of his first tour, which took some months and did win converts, Durance cabled Walkerville with an impressive order for 200 Model Ts. By November 1909 advertising for the T was appearing in the *Australian Motorist.* Over the next three years the T found a ready market; it was more than capable of withstanding "the pounding from the dirt tracks that passed for roads in the Outback." Australians took to it with enthusiasm, and the commonwealth's embryonic car manufacturing industry died young.

In New Zealand, McGregor reaffirmed his business arrangement with the Rouse and Hurrell Carriage Company of Wellington, which had secured an agency from Ford Canada in 1908. It placed its first order for twelve Model Ts in October 1909. McGregor's visits to the empire's Asian colonies laid the groundwork for the large export house of Markt and Hammacher to set up agencies in India, Ceylon, Burma, and Malaya. Although he did not visit South Africa, steps were taken by R. M. Lockwood through Ford's New York exporter, Arkell and Douglas, to have its manager in Port Elizabeth begin to find dealers to sell Model Ts. It was a Swedish firm, Gadelius and Company, that placed the first local advertisement for Ford cars in Singapore's leading newspaper, the *Straits Times,* on 20 December 1909, though organized selling did not begin until 1911.[14]

Continuing around the world, with stops for sightseeing and some business in Italy, Paris, and London, a mightily enthused McGregor worked in smooth concert with Ford Detroit and Jim Couzens; Couzens, encouraged by strong sales in the United States, had also left the Detroit River behind, in August 1909, to formalize the opening of a branch in England. It had been the focus of negotiations since 1906 between Ford and British distributor Percival Perry. In Canada on 5 October 1909, during the absence of both McGregor and Couzens but with their compliance, the directors of the Canadian company waived whatever manufacturing and marketing rights it had in the United Kingdom under its agreement of 1904 with the Detroit parent. In a letter of 24 November to Wallace Campbell, who was in charge in Walkerville during McGregor's tour, Henry Ford noted paternally that the waiver was "duly appreciated."[15] To make sense of the Canadian firm's action, historians Wilkins and Hill offer this explanation: "When in 1904 the agreement was made, there was a chance of an English protective tariff with imperial preference. In 1909 this had not yet come into effect. The English Ford business had developed separately from the Canadian, and to inject the Canadian company into it at this point would be not only superfluous but also maybe destructive. It made far more sense, McGregor recognized, to have the English operation an offshoot of the American Ford Company."[16]

Indeed, in 1904 the implications for the British market of forming a Canadian firm were barely considered and in 1909 McGregor's focus was on other imperial markets overseas. Underlying the waiver too was the developing reciprocal relationship between Walkerville and Detroit and, to a degree, McGregor's subservience to Henry Ford as president of Ford Canada and Ford's own organization for foreign business. In 1910 Ford's contract with Lockwood in New York was allowed to lapse, and Couzens created a "foreign department" with salaried employees to serve both the Canadian and American companies. Though crating cars for export continued to be done in Walkerville as well as in Detroit, the New York office, which would act for Ford Canada for a few more years, reported primarily to Detroit.[17]

McGregor returned to Walkerville from his global trip in late January 1910. The *Evening Record* accorded him a hero's welcome and presented the saga of his trip more as a travelogue than as a strategic business venture. Here was the emergence of Ford Canada, through accounts of its foreign business, as the border communities' outreach to the world. During McGregor's absence much had changed. By the time of his return, Windsor and Walkerville were taking shape as centers of automotive manufacture, a bustling mixture of branch plants and parts makers in a dizzying succession of publicized starts and silent collapses. The competitive environment here had no parallel elsewhere in the Canadian industry. McLaughlin Motor in Oshawa, Russell in Toronto, Reo in St. Catharines, and Chatham/Anhut in Chatham, among others, attracted far less ancillary business and had no adjacent parents. In October 1909 the *Evening Record* announced the intention of two Detroit firms to cross the river to build the Regal Motor Car and (with the backing of the Walker family) the E-M-F, both of which were in production in early 1910. At this point E-M-F Canada reportedly had the largest automotive plant in the dominion; a few years later it folded into Studebaker. In the fall of 1909 the local branch of Seagrave Fire Engines had moved into motorized vehicles. To make the American Gray car, Canadian Gray Motors Limited was incorporated in January 1910, the same month that two American auto men formed Dominion Motors Limited and that Victor Manufacturing Company of Detroit combined with Walkerville Carriage Goods Company to build auto bodies. Within months Paterson Automobile Company of Flint moved to set up a branch in Windsor, and Walker Motor Car Company was formed to take over a Chatham operation. Later in 1910 Canadian Commercial Motor Car Company Limited and Gramm Motor Truck Company of Canada Limited began to compete with Menard in the truck-making sector. At year's end Canadian Auto Top Company was established in nearby Tilbury by a Jackson, Michigan, parent, and American Auto Trimming Company of Detroit set up in Walkerville.[18]

This entrepreneurial rash, most of it concentrated with municipal blessings and bonuses on the fringes of Walkerville and Windsor, intensified the automotive character of the community, creating there, as in Detroit, what Clarence Hooker calls a symbiotic relationship between the different automobile and parts works and the community. Service garages sprang up, one in October 1910 by Eli Parent, who had reportedly turned out the first auto in the Border Cities. Accidents caused by "auto scorchers" and the "reckless manner" in which test-drivers and vile Yankee upstarts tore around became a source of renewed complaints to public officials, who, though hesitant to disturb the golden goose, levied fines for speeding against E-M-F and Hupp. The sole local agent for Ford automobiles was former bicycle dealer A. D. Bowlby, long a fan of fast vehicles, on two wheels or four. Ford workers themselves began achieving a less contentious identity through such means as the factory's baseball team, which toured from Kingsville in the south of Essex to Detroit in the summer of 1910.[19]

Between 1910 and the end of the Great War, McGregor, the Model T, and Ford Canada had an incalculable effect upon the industry and the proliferation of the automobile in Canada. To be sure, McGregor could bask in the breakthrough represented by the resilient Model T ("the car for everybody," Canadian advertisements called it) and in the slipstream of Ford Detroit, where the opening of a revolutionary plant in the Detroit suburb of Highland Park in January 1910 increased the American company's volume of operation tenfold.[20] From this point on, McGregor's challenge was similar: to meet steadily increasing production targets, a goal that would ultimately produce many thousand Model Ts before its sameness led to decline.

Buoyant after his overseas trip and convinced of the automobile's permanence, McGregor no longer worried much about the domestic regulation of auto use. "They're off on automobile legislation once again at the legislature," the *Toronto Daily Star* moaned in February 1910 while he was at the St. Lawrence show, but there was no lobby in response.[21] In the "Canadian-made" debate and in its coverage of the record-breaking auto show and the desired "trend" to Canadian cars, the Toronto press, which never completely understood the dynamics of the Border Cities, continued to portray the Russell as "the leading Canadian make" and ignore McGregor's version of Canadian manufacture. In 1912 the Tudhope Motor Company of Orillia advertised its product as the no-tariff motorcar (thus anticipating a future debate) and its new six-cylinder model as "Canada's Car de Luxe." Still, auto show coverage benefited all and, as McGregor knew, the market for the Russell, as for the McLaughlin-Buick, remained constricted by their prices. R. M. Jaffray, the show and journal promoter (*Motor Times*, *Gas Power Age*, and *Motor Trade in Canada*), got it right in September when, dismissing the relevance of nationality, he labeled Walkerville and Windsor the "hub of the industry in Canada."[22] Of the nine automakers that had formed a new branch of the Canadian Manufacturers' Association by June 1910 to promote the industry in Canada, four were based in Walkerville: Ford, E-M-F, Dominion, and Regal.[23]

After making small changes to the factory's office and showroom—in 1910 he still had only four office employees—McGregor launched the works' first major expansion in the summer of 1910: a

Ford Motor Company of Canada factory, machine for milling cylinder-block castings. *Canadian Machinery*, 25 December 1913. Photograph by Mark Coatsworth.

three-story addition on the riverfront to the rear of the old wagon works. He had "consulted" first with the Detroit office, which, consistent with its goal in the United States, "wanted to expand and produce more in Canada to reduce the cost" of the Model T.[24] In addition, the consultation directed McGregor to the architectural firm Henry Ford had chosen to give structure to his revolutionary concepts of manufacture. Started in August and completed in January by the contracting firm of Wells and Gray, which would become Ford Canada's favored builder, the square, heavily fenestrated block was the work of the Detroit architectural firm of Albert Kahn, Ernest Wilby, and John R. Boyde, which had designed Highland Park, the Hudson auto plant, and the Dodge works. Kahn was no

Ford Motor Company of Canada factory, multiple-spindle machine for drilling cylinders. *Canadian Machinery*, 25 December 1913. Photograph by Mark Coatsworth.

stranger to Windsor-Walkerville, having designed offices for Hiram Walker and Sons in 1894 and the residence of Detroit-born Edward Chandler Walker in 1905. For the Walkerville project the firm worked out of an office at 240 Ouellette Street in Windsor. The structural engineering that went into the addition had just preceded it into Ontario. Integral to Kahn buildings was a novel system of window framing and steel-bar reinforcement, which was configured to produce thinner walls and floors that gave more room with less superstructure. The system was being promoted in Canada by the Trussed Concrete Steel Company of Walkerville and Toronto, with Albert's brother Gustave as general manager and C. S. L. Hertzberg as engineer. Gustave Kahn and Hertzberg would be joined by Wilby in promoting their system and writing about concrete construction for the Canadian Cement and Concrete Association in 1910 and

Ford Motor Company of Canada factory, heat-treatment department. The parts in the foreground are engine crankshafts. *Canadian Machinery*, 25 December 1913. Photograph by Mark Coatsworth.

1911.[25] In the later year Trussed Concrete was federally incorporated, and subsequently it secured work across Canada, with a profound impact on industrial construction.

The new Walkerville plant, though relatively small, was a much-hyped and radically functional piece of work. Like Highland Park, it embraced the stark new machine aesthetic of automobile production but on a much smaller scale. As a multistory building, it did not facilitate straight assembly-line flow. In contrast to the old wagon works, however, the addition boasted tall expanses of windows made possible by the use of reinforced concrete, and it signaled the beginning of a changing workplace. The most dynamic change in the move of 1910–12 to greater production was the purchase and installation of more and increasingly sophisticated machine tooling, which Ford Canada, as it moved from assembly to manufacture, had begun inventorying in 1909, as had Detroit. Consistently accurate machine work was, without doubt, the basis of mass producing the Model T, in Walkerville and Detroit, where Ford had adopted major innovations in the automatic grinding of steel parts. For his supply of such specialized machinery, McGregor gradually shifted from American to Canadian suppliers.[26]

If McGregor was less concerned about the legislative regulation of automotive use, the machine trade for one did not want the automotive industry upset by anything. As the *Canadian Machinery and Manufacturing News* (Toronto) explained in April 1909, "The fine work required in the manufacture of the automobile parts and accessories made a better class of machine tools necessary and manufacturing industries, generally, have reaped the benefit. Let us not knock away the rungs of the ladder by which we have climbed."[27] Demands in hollow-core casting, for engine blocks and cylinder heads, exerted similar demands on the founding industry.[28] McGregor's production manager, George Dickert, recalled that the 1910 building allowed, as part of the expanded operation, for the assembly of radiators and the machining of differentials, axles, and other parts.[29] Though not large by Detroit standards, it facilitated the designed goal: production jumped from 486 in 1909 to 1,280 in 1910, an increase absorbed by the export business, Toronto, the Winnipeg branch (established in 1909), and the branches opened in the fall of 1910 in Hamilton and Montreal.[30]

McGregor could not build fast enough to meet the surging demand for the Model T, abroad and at home, or on the scale that would reduce the cost of production to the level desired by Detroit. His marketing trip of 1909–10 was undoubtedly a factor in the strong overseas sales in 1911–12, including 1,157 in Australia, 586 in New Zealand, 456 in South Africa, 106 in India, and 179 in Malaysia. Equally vital were the regional marketing arrangements. For instance, beginning in 1911, an American trading company based in New York, Dodge and Seymour, handled the sale of Canadian Ford cars in India, Ceylon, Thailand, Burma, the Dutch East Indies, Borneo, Malaya, and Aden. In mid-1911, V. A. and Henry T. Dodge—not the Detroit Dodges—had arrived in Malaya with a Model T. They contracted with C. F. F. Wearne and Company, an

Table 2

Ford Canada export sales, 1911–23

Area[a]	1911–12[b]	1912–13	1913–14	1914–15	1915–16	1916–17	1917–18	1918–19	1919–20	1920[c]	1921	1922	1923
Australia													
Passenger cars	0	0	2,266	2,137	5,234	432	0	0	551	18	0	0	13
Chassis	1,157	1,862	360	471	1,268	532	4,412	2,337	3,014	1,744	2,857	7,212	13,708
Trucks	0	0	0	0	0	0	14	503	803	345	388	773	7,350
New Zealand													
Passenger cars	586	830	802	1,085	1,936	958	1,048	1,302	2,776	1,154	50	1,748	4,946
Chassis	0	0	0	35	60	44	84	144	186	41	108	234	384
Trucks	0	0	0	0	0	0	7	652	870	439	0	234	1,266
New Caledonia													
Passenger cars												3	0
Chassis												2	0
Trucks												0	6
New Britain													
Passenger cars													3
Chassis													1
Trucks													12
Papua													
Passenger cars													3
Chassis													0
Trucks													3

Area[a]	1911–12[b]	1912–13	1913–14	1914–15	1915–16	1916–17	1917–18	1918–19	1919–20	1920[c]	1921	1922	1923
West Samoa													
Passenger cars										4	0		3
Chassis										0	2		0
Trucks										2	5		0
Fiji													
Passenger cars	1	5	10	27		15	8	20	22	10	19	21	30
Chassis	0	0	0	0		0	1	0	0	0	0	0	0
Trucks	0	0	0	0		0	3	0	10	4	18	15	17
Java													
Passenger cars				101	335	402	194	474	969	706	728	456	697
Chassis				0	1	4	0	0	18	0	12	0	0
Trucks				0	0	0	0	112	174	264	233	0	0
Sumatra													
Passenger cars			3					165	202	226	169	103	377
Chassis			0					0	0	0	2	0	6
Trucks			0					7	34	55	130	60	31
Celebes													
Passenger cars												7	25
Chassis												0	0
Trucks												2	6

Area[a]	1911–12[b]	1912–13	1913–14	1914–15	1915–16	1916–17	1917–18	1918–19	1919–20	1920[c]	1921	1922	1923
Malaysia													
Passenger cars	179	255	111	131	517	1,063	403	677	928	871	7	176	885
Chassis	0	0	4	0	3	10	16	0	0	0	0	24	0
Trucks	0	0	0	0	0	0	52	48	68	226	78	36	153
Borneo													
Passenger cars													114
Chassis													0
Trucks													0
India													
Passenger cars	106	316	494	584	764	335	60	998	3,498	1,206	549	1,242	1,608
Chassis	0	0	23	56	24	22	175	174	106	30	42	0	56
Trucks	0	0	0	0	0	0	0	16	646	497	261	199	609
Burma													
Passenger cars		85	36	52	198	60		115	254	124	7	0	237
Chassis		0	2	2	4	0		1	0	0	1	0	0
Trucks		0	0	0	0	0		6	51	40	12	18	63
Thailand													
Passenger cars				19	35	41	42	18	30	49	85	15	77
Chassis				0	9	4	4	0	6	0	16	0	10
Trucks				0	0	0	2	6	9	19	40	35	124

Area[a]	1911–12[b]	1912–13	1913–14	1914–15	1915–16	1916–17	1917–18	1918–19	1919–20	1920[c]	1921	1922	1923
Ceylon													
Passenger cars		55	46	38	90	60		71	248	134	0	164	204
Chassis		0	0	6	12	0		22	10	0	0	4	6
Trucks		0	0	0	0	0		9	35	47	21	77	194
Aden													
Passenger cars			7	25	34			27	35	31	37	15	30
Chassis			0	1	0			1	3	0	0	0	0
Trucks			0	0	0			2	2	0	1	12	25
Madagascar and Réunion													
Passenger cars	30					5		6	5				
Chassis	0					0		0	0				
Trucks	0					0		0	0				
British South Africa[d]													
Passenger cars	456	1,448	1,107	742	1,504	2,737	852	1,084	2,535	535	738	2,341	3,520
Chassis	0	0	14	14	57	210	266	150	0	0	108	37	30
Trucks	0	0	0	0	0	0	43	121	225	168	0	248	373
British East Africa[e]													
Passenger cars	31	51	50	152	182	25	56	92	246	80	101	102	606
Chassis	0	0	3	2	5	0	10	18	52	6	8	0	80
Trucks	0	0	0	0	0	0	0	10	45	10	22	45	140

Area[a]	1911–12[b]	1912–13	1913–14	1914–15	1915–16	1916–17	1917–18	1918–19	1919–20	1920[c]	1921	1922	1923
British West Africa[f]													
Passenger cars	14	9	29	37	164	33	93	94	421	74	32	35	159
Chassis	0	0	35	77	316	21	0	0	357	84	40	19	118
Trucks	0	0	0	0	0	0	6	11	341	67	0	4	60
H.O. special order[g]													
Passenger cars	74	119	146	16	22	4	50	1,355	46	4			13
Chassis	0	0	0	0	0	0	0	6,581	1,500	2			2
Trucks	0	0	0	0	0	0	0	12	1	13			1

Source: FMCC, "Export Sales: Shipments to Dealers and Sales by Overseas Branches" (copies courtesy of Kevin Mowle).

Note: Export shipments before 1911 were not tabulated but were totaled: 224 (prior to 1908), 119 (1908–9), 483 (1909–10), 1,089 (1910–11). Some "first" shipments were also noted: Calcutta, 10 Oct. 1905; New Zealand, 8 Nov. 1905; Australia, 2 Aug. 1906. The company's tabulations continue past 1923, the year after Gordon McGregor's death.

[a] In the original tables, the geographical areas were broken down by specific colony or town and by model types (touring, runabout, coupe, two-door, four-door, delivery, chassis, and truck).

[b] The year given is Ford Canada's fiscal year, to the end of July. In 1920 recording shifted to the calendar year.

[c] This covers the period August–December 1920.

[d] British South Africa included Cape of Good Hope, Natal, Transvaal, and Orange River Colony.

[e] British East Africa included Uganda, Kenya, Tanganyika, and Zanzibar.

[f] British West Africa covered Ghana, Nigeria, Sierra Leone, Gambia, and Cameroons.

[g] "H.O. special order" likely means special orders for the Ford head office in Michigan. For details on Ford Canada's fulfillment of such special orders in 1918, see chapter 5.

Table 3

Annual exports of automobiles from Canada, 1916–22, selected destinations

Country	1916[a]	1917	1918	1919	1920	1921	1922
United Kingdom	2,536	166	5	1,472	807	1,358	2,804
United States	50	60	82	52	83	796	100
Australia	6,606	3,352	3,222	4,080	3,937	3,289	4,897
New Zealand	2,346	1,065	1,157	1,588	2,820	2,326	426
India	0	0	0	900	4,949	1,557	979
Ceylon	0	0	0	13	317	168	28
Straits Settlements[b]	0	0	0	641	978	999	68
British South Africa[c]	1,660	1,953	1,506	990	3,163	1,431	1,240
British East Africa[c]	0	0	0	0	0	263	129
British West Africa[c]	0	0	0	98	546	480	80

Source: Monthly Reports of the Department of Trade and Commerce of Canada (Ottawa).

Note: The *Monthly Reports* do not specify makes, but a comparison (even with different reporting periods) to Ford Canada's export sales point to the company as Canada's major exporter. Before 1916 the *Monthly Reports* tabulated exports only by value.

[a]The figures given are for the year ending in March.

[b]The Straits Settlements included Singapore, Penang, Malacca, and Labuan.

[c]See notes to table 2.

Australian outfit, to sell twelve cars in the Malaysian state of Perak, while Gadelius and Company and Paterson, Simons Company of Penang handled the rest of the colony. Later, the Dodges granted Wearne the sole agency for Singapore and Malaya, with a contract for sixty cars a year. Wearne placed an advertisement in the *Straits Times* in November stating its appointment effective 1 October. Though the numbers of cars sold were not large (and they came with regionally made bodies), Ford Canada's alliances with Dodge and Seymour and then with local firms and Chinese entrepreneurs allowed McGregor's company to break into the Malayan market, where the Chinese and British formed a large proportion of car buyers. Dodge and Seymour may also have handled the Caribbean, though on a smaller scale; in 1911 right-hand-drive Model Ts were being sold in Jamaica through the garage of the Kingston Industrial Works.[31]

At home, the Toronto auto show of February–March 1911, now in larger quarters (the city's armories), was a good barometer of the domestic market. Amid military bands, lectures, vibrant decorations, strings of lights, theme events, cheap gimmicks, and tearooms, more than 100 models competed for attention. The *Toronto Daily Star* read the attraction astutely: "Each ticket to the automobile show entitles the purchaser to step inside and look like a millionaire." Ford cars were heavily advertised, their falling prices accompanied by a wildly exaggerated claim to "several thousand" dealers in Canada. Piqued E-M-F executives in Walkerville billed their car as "[m]ade up to a standard—not down to a price." But Ford too provided a standard—and at a lower price that appealed to institutions and businesses as well as private customers. Struck by "auto fever" in 1909, the City of Toronto bought five Model Ts from Fred Fox for its works department in March 1911.[32]

In May, within months of the completion of his three-story addition in January, McGregor (on behalf of the company) purchased Detroit River frontage from Windsor hotelier Barney Maisonville for another major addition, the start of a long, four-story expansion jammed along the waterfront. Designed by the Kahn firm and begun that August, it was completed by March 1912. The death of a worker under a "massive weight" in August 1911 did little to distract attention from the sounds and sights of construction and negotiations for more land along the riverfront. Without missing a beat, additional frontage was acquired to the west in July 1911 (at a record price of $100 per foot) and 250 more feet were added in June 1912 to complete the space needed for an extension, which was pushed to completion by January. Space was created near the extension for a testing court for new cars. The purchase in June had caused a stir: the owner, Walkerville butcher Fred Johnson, received a "fortune" ($40,000), the cost of moving his house, and a new Ford car. (The property title was actually held by his wife, Sarah.) Once again, McGregor claimed the purpose was to have a building and equipment "for the complete manufacture of every part of the Ford car" (a goal that would be largely realized in 1913).

In October 1912, with no more frontage available, McGregor, working through the Bartlet law firm, bought land for a new power plant south of Sandwich Street, opposite the old works. According to Bartlet lore, Walter Bartlet, who had recently joined the family firm, was given the daunting task of assembling the land package. Going door-to-door, the young man secured enough options on properties

Likely taken in the late winter of 1912–13, this picture nicely shows the evolution and tight riverside siting of the early Ford Canada factories: the original wagon works along the street, the 1910 addition (middle), the office building (forefront), and the two-part riverfront extension. *Industrial Canada*, June 1913. Photograph by Mark Coatsworth.

for a major site for Ford. For the rest of McGregor's time at the helm of Ford Canada, the company was in an almost steady state of property acquisition, negotiations of one sort or another, planning, construction, and internal reorganization. Photographs of the tall, long riverfront expansion starkly highlight the modernistic plant's encroachment on the sewage-laden river, the side streets and lots to the west and south, and the now miniaturized wagon works.[33]

Within the new structures, major mechanical reorganization allowed the company to move toward its goal of greater production. The riverfront building, following Ford Detroit's experience, allowed for the installation, apparently in 1911, of Ford Canada's "first power conveyor," described by Dickert as "a standard T rail with a chain driven by a motor and saddles" for the chassis' axles to sit on.[34] Overhead conveyors for parts, for which the building was not initially well suited, would come later.[35] The impact was dramatic in all areas: from 1,280 automobiles in 1910, production surged to 2,805 in 1911 and 6,388 in 1912. As a result, McGregor traveled steadily on business, and a succession of new branches was opened: Vancouver in 1911, followed by Saskatoon, Calgary, and London in 1912. Detroit expected McGregor to cooperatively follow its pattern of production-driven expansion. In January 1911 the Canadian board agreed that if it could not meet overseas demands, then Detroit would come to its aid in the form of shipments of cars.

That June a dividend of 100 percent was declared by McGregor, who claimed that his company was making one-fifth of the cars produced in Canada.[36] The excitement generated by these strides was matched in terms of publicity only by Henry Ford's prideful victory in January 1911 in the Selden patent suit, though by this time the decision was irrelevant to a company that was making about 20 percent of the automobiles produced in the United States.[37]

By year's end the provincial charter of Ford Canada was found inadequate. On 18 December 1911 it was reincorporated under a federal charter, and the capital stock of the firm was upped from $125,000 to $1,000,000 "to provide for its increased business." As part of the reincorporation, in February 1912 McGregor carried out the replacement of shares in the "old" corporation with stock in the "new Company." In asking James Couzens, John Stodgell of Walkerville, and probably all other shareholders to submit their stock certificates for a lucrative six-for-one exchange, he requested, to avoid the embarrassing scrutiny given the unusually high dividend payments in the past, that they do so in strict confidence, "as we do not care to have any publicity in connection with the re-issue of stock."[38]

The workforce overseen by McGregor in Walkerville remained small in comparison to that at Ford Detroit, but in 1911, in the census district of Essex North, automobiles had overtaken patent medicines as the most productive industrial sector by value: 195 employees in four automobile plants generated $1,827,385 in value compared to 347 employees in medicinals generating only $787,408.[39] At Ford Detroit, employment levels surpassed 1,000 in 1909 and reached 5,000 in 1912. Ford Canada employed a fraction of these levels. The number of Canadians who lived in Detroit and worked at auto plants there was 5,280, or 16 percent of the workforce; a good many more commuted from the Windsor area. The high-wage reputation of the industry attracted masses of workmen to Detroit, and Henry Ford was not reluctant to declare incentives.[40] In pace, McGregor issued employee bonuses in January 1911. The steady cross-border ebb and flow of workers had been identified as early as November and December 1910, when Walkerville factories were being "besieged" by workers from Detroit (with many "foreigners" among them) looking for work, most in the automotive and shipbuilding industries.[41] It was not just the factories and the

Walter McGregor in Canadian-style Model T Ford coupe, 1912. Courtesy of Walter L. McGregor.

movement of workers that were defining the automotive identity of the Border Cities. American customs officers were beginning to worry about the number of Canadian motorists who were crossing over to buy cars, secure cheap repairs, and delve into the blooming parts and accessories market, not to mention incessant attempts to smuggle American automobiles into Ontario.[42]

In the three years after the introduction of the Model T, McGregor happily took a more prominent place within the social and political elites of Windsor and Walkerville. No longer the inconsequential singing salesman, he enjoyed the good fortune and celebrity status of an extraordinarily successful automaker, albeit a spin-off from Ford Detroit. With scant recognition of the contributions of other local producers, among them A. J. Kinnucan of Dominion, Moise-L. Menard, Louis Logie of Lozier (and later Maxwell Canada), and Edmond-Georges Odette of Canadian Top and Body, the *Evening Record* credited McGregor with the Border Cities' ascent, somehow seeing him as responsible for the Model T phenomenon.[43] No other manager in Windsor or Walkerville received such extensive, free coverage, not even the old money that tried to enter the fluid ranks of auto and machinery makers. In November 1910, Chandler Merrill Walker joined Detroit automaker Michael Augustine Delany and others to form the short-lived Walker Motor Car Company Limited, and in 1912 Hiram H. Walker, then of Detroit, helped form the stable, longer-lasting Wilt Twist Drill Company of Canada Limited.[44]

Generally, the car men were a young, slightly brash lot in search of winning formulae. McGregor's case was somewhat different; there was some distance between him and the other makers, whose presence in the border towns was usually fleeting. The auto landscape was littered with look-alike prospectuses, failed negotiations, weak technologies, and poorly planned factory starts. Through it all McGregor could not have been better positioned. Ford made him nouveau riche; his family name and connections gave him status. In 1909, on the founding of First Presbyterian Church in Walkerville, he was made chair of its board of management and he would remain a "staunch supporter and loyal friend." A photograph taken a year earlier, in the C. M. Mayes and Company studio in Detroit's Fine Arts Building, captures a formally dressed McGregor, still of medium build, suggestive of some affluence, and with a high, tipped-end collar, a stickpin neatly in place, and the ever-present wire-rimmed glasses (see frontispiece).

Socially his favored haunts were the summer cottage, the fine resort, the golf club, and the ballroom, where Hattie's own fashionable attire was the stuff of social columns. In August 1910 McGregor bought a cottage lot on Lake Erie, just on the fringe of Kingsville, which was fast developing as a fashionable summer retreat for the well-to-do of Windsor and Detroit. The Walker family had already constructed a railway to Kingsville and, in 1889, the glorious Mettawas Hotel. With his brother Walter, Gordon belonged to the Oak Ridge Golf Club in Sandwich, which in October 1910 was incorporated as the Essex County Golf and Country Club Limited.[45]

Marriages strengthened the ties within the "Ford family." In September 1910 Wallace Campbell married Gordon's second cousin Gladyes Emily Leishman of Toronto. In December, four months after attending branch managers' meetings in Detroit and Walkerville, George Alexander Malcolmson, the lanky manager of Ford's Winnipeg branch (established in the fall of 1909) whose parents lived in Chatham, returned to Windsor to marry Gordon's younger sister Edith Ellen.[46]

Amid the many associated teas, luncheons, and dinners, in venues resplendent with orchestras, bouquets, maids, and Union Jacks, McGregor found time, in October, to show his plant to the members of the federal royal commission on industrial training, headed by educational expert Dr. James Wilson Robertson. Bolstered by production and streams of prospective workers, and aware of Henry Ford's keen interest in this field, McGregor testified in support of such training. (Other industrialists favored learning along the "road of toil.") He provided some "splendid" but undescribed information to the commission; whether he talked about the minimal training needed for his factory is unknown.[47]

The reciprocity debate, tariffs, and the federal election of 1911, matters of real concern to the Liberal McGregor, gave both the public and the political party some indication of where the thirty-seven-year-old head of Ford Canada stood. By December 1910 negotiations between the Liberal government of Sir Wilfrid Laurier and the United States for a new trade agreement were well under way. With tariffs at the heart of the automotive industry in Walkerville and Windsor, debate there and in Detroit was intense but often ill informed. At the end of January the proposed new common rate on automobiles and parts was publicized: 30 percent, which represented a 5 percent reduction by Canada and 15 percent by the United States.[48] Detroit automaker Hugh Chalmers, who would set up a branch in Walkerville in 1916, favored a reduced tariff on automobiles. The president of the Detroit Board of Trade, Milton A. McRae, maintained that the Canadian reduction was insignificant and unlikely to alter the pattern of branch plants. Conscious of the protective nature of the tariff and its role in fostering the local industry, the Walkerville Board of Trade, at its first annual banquet in February, opposed reciprocity outright, to the disgust of the Liberal, Ford-leaning *Evening Record.* The Walkers too voiced their opposition. Essex County's two MPs, Oliver James Wilcox (the Conservative returned in Essex North in 1909) and Alfred Henry Clarke (Liberal, Essex South) had nothing to say on the matter in the House of Commons throughout 1911. Interviewed by the *Toronto Daily Mail and Empire* at the Canadian National Exhibition (CNE) in early September, Windsor truck maker Moise Menard mistakenly understood reciprocity to mean the virtual elimination of tariffs. If adopted, he heatedly exclaimed, with veiled reference to McGregor and others, the "Canadian automobile industry will breathe its last. . . . The only auto manufacturers in Canada who will benefit by the agreement, if passed, will be those who are running branch offices of the United States manufacturers." Other Canadian auto men agreed. In September, Robert McLaughlin of Oshawa, like many industrialists, angrily left the Liberal Party. Articulate opposition came too from Toronto's T. A. Russell, who viewed the issue both as an automaker fearful of competition and as chairman of the tariff committee of the Canadian Manufacturers' Association.[49]

In a style that would characterize his future responses on many public issues, Gordon McGregor had no objection to reciprocity, a partisan position he could afford to adopt. The proposed reduction in the tariff was minimal, his firm was solidly established, and any impact of a reduced barrier, which smaller producers such as Menard feared, was more than offset by McGregor's access to the imperial market and Ford Detroit's need for and confidence in its Canadian branch. In June 1911 Couzens told McGregor that "being close to the Management, and to the progress of the business, . . . I could not say that I was surprised" to receive a Canadian dividend of $6,800. In corporate terms McGregor, in supporting the reciprocal trade agreement, was safely echoing Couzens's bold opposition (since at least 1908 and well before the stimulus of the Model T) to any increase in tariff protection in the United States.[50] Faced with no genuine threat and backed by John A. McKay, the owner of the *Evening Record*, McGregor could easily afford to throw his full weight behind reciprocity. On 12 August, at the North Essex Liberal convention—the federal election had been called for 21 September—he took the limelight by standing up on the floor and declaring reciprocity to be the "best proposition" Canada had ever received or made.[51]

On 8 September, Laurier arrived in town to wave the Liberal banner. He was picked up at the train station by McGregor in a new Model T touring (top down) and, accompanied by party organizer William Costello Kennedy and railways minister George Perry Graham, they set out at the center of a "monster parade." At the ensuing speaking engagement, McGregor sat on the platform, quiet but every bit as conspicuous as Liberal candidate Dr. Peter A. Dewar, Michigan senator W. A. Smith, and M. A. McRae of the Detroit Board of Trade.[52]

Gordon McGregor chauffeuring Liberal dignitaries W. C. Kennedy (front), Prime Minister Sir Wilfrid Laurier (rear left), and G. P. Graham (rear right), Windsor train station, 8 September 1911. Courtesy of Essex County Historical Society, Windsor.

The election, which was a complete disaster for the Liberals, including Dewar, had little consequence for McGregor and Ford Canada. A special industrial issue of the *Evening Record* on 15 December, three days before Ford Canada's federal incorporation, portrayed Walkerville as a "beehive of industry"; of the automakers (Ford, E-M-F, Dominion, Seagrave, and Gramm), Ford was highlighted. With a population of only 7,059 in 1911 (Windsor had 17,829), Walkerville was reminded of its great industrial and imperial reach. Model Ts made there took part in December in the "magnificent" durbar at Delhi in India, attended by King George, Queen Mary, and thirty Indian princes, few of whom, other sources reported, understood much about the Ford cars they rode in. The T sold briskly among the tea planters of Ceylon, and it won races in

Gordon McGregor (right) relaxing at his lakefront cottage in Kingsville, Ontario, c. 1919. Courtesy of Estate of Mary Mingay.

South Africa. Behind the image of a buzzing industry, a publicist's dream, was McGregor, whom the *Evening Record* fashioned as the model executive: "[T]o his splendid business ability, genial manner and strictly honorable business methods much of the success of the company is due." Last season, the newspaper went on with less exaggeration, 3,000 cars had been sold before they were made; to meet orders expected for 1912, 6,500 were to be made. (The actual production figures for the two seasons were 2,805 and 6,388.) As advertising, the portrait was a throwback to the old-fashioned, founder-centered promotion attached to Henry Ford.[53]

The tangible rewards for McGregor were significant. In June 1911 he began preparing his cottage for summer use and, with other cottagers, pushed the town of Kingsville to annex their lakeside area in order to give it municipal water and fire protection. McGregor came to love this cottage; he and Hattie were generous hosts and frequently held large family gatherings there. The convivial Gordon, a nephew would recall, sang "at the drop of a hat." In 1912

Gordon earned $25,000, of which $18,000 represented bonus payments. Early in the year he bought a grand new house at the corner of Victoria and Wyandotte in Windsor, a well-to-do area of large trees and stately homes. Bursting radiators delayed its occupation. In September he bought an adjoining lot to secure "suitable grounds to make his new residence one of the most beautiful in the city."[54]

With Windsor leading all other Canadian cities in building starts as a result of the automotive industry, civic officials, Ford officers, and the *Evening Record* competed for superlatives and grand imagery in their almost smug consideration of the industry. Vehicle regulation was no longer an issue. Ontario's Motor Vehicles Act of 1912, the most intrusive piece of user regulation to date in Canada, passed virtually unnoticed. Now, rampant growth was the focus. "One firm attracts another," claimed the newspaper correctly in April; the "auto industry here is looming up like a bright star on the industrial horizon." Out-of-town journalists visited to cover the phenomenon. Never one to lose an advertising opportunity, McGregor brought over Ford men from Detroit to witness the scene. He was particularly eager for James Couzens to see his expanded factory and new office wing, which he and his delighted staff occupied on 6 April. "Personally," he told his Detroit mentor, "I feel a great d[eal of] pride in what we have accomplished and I think you would have some considerable pride in looking at the growth of this institution in this territory." Later in April, eighty-five Canadian agents were treated to breakfast in Detroit and a tour of the Walkerville plant under the direction of McGregor's staff and the brilliant manager (since 1907) of Ford's sales department in Detroit, Norval A. Hawkins. It was his demanding standards of performance for company-owned branches and the dealers they supervised and his system of breaking down Model Ts for shipment in crates that did much to elevate the Ford market in both the United States and Canada.[55]

McGregor's image in Detroit, and elsewhere in Canada, differed markedly from the way he was seen and publicized in Windsor and Walkerville. In contrast to well-placed figures such as T. A. Russell in Toronto, he received little coverage in the daily press elsewhere in Canada, which seemed to have trouble grasping the import of the Border Cities' Americanized nature. He was hardly a household name, like Toronto's John Craig Eaton or Joseph W. Flavelle.

Closer attention came from such trade journals as the *Canadian Foundryman* and the *Canadian Machinery and Manufacturing News* (Toronto), which understood the mechanical systems at the heart of Fordism and had a serious interest in the automotive industry. The American edition of *Ford Times* gave considerable illustrated coverage to the Canadian and imperial markets—they held an almost exotic appeal—but at the same time it grouped McGregor, his factory, and his branches together with the American branches and personnel. Poems, cartoons, and corporate banter appear throughout *Ford Times* and other company literature, but never in the subdued Canadian edition, launched in August 1913.[56] As directed by Walkerville, the Canadian *Ford Times* was respectfully content with photos of Henry Ford and his quaint sayings and less inclined to feature McGregor directly. In the American edition McGregor was amusingly cast in verse as one of the "Fordcrafters" and "our Canadian high priest," best known to other Ford executives for his singing voice, his Scottish persona, and his widely recognized "sales talk and wit."[57] The handful of family letters that survive reflect this exuberance.

McGregor had attended the Detroit convention of Ford managers during the first week of July 1911, a "strictly Ford family affair," where he fit in remarkably well. Few purely Canadian automotive companies could muster the large turnout (McGregor included) photographed at the Log Cabin Inn on 3 July. In its description of the closing banquet on the 7th, *Ford Times* presented distant American Ford owners with a snapshot already familiar to many in Detroit and the Border Cities. "Did everybody hear that sweet Scotch voice of McGregor's when he sang 'The Union' at the banquet? Mack's voice sounded like an order for more cars, although 7,500 for 1912 will be going some for Walkerville."[58] Ever reluctant to infringe on the primary image of Henry Ford, McGregor would rarely sanction such American-Canadian camaraderie in the Canadian edition of *Ford Times*, which, in issue after issue, stressed instead the Canadian identity of his Ford cars. Northerly photographs and such literary injections as Emily Pauline Johnson's poem "Canadian Born" invariably served to reinforce this identity.

The momentum generated by the completion of the new factory in Walkerville in 1912 and the resulting escalation in output produced real benefits not just for McGregor and his executives but also for the workers and the shareholders. A healthy 20 percent dividend was declared in July. On 8 April the *Evening Record* had reported, prematurely, that Ford Canada employees were being given an unexpected wage increase of 15 percent and a reduced working day, from ten to nine hours. (A number of them may have remembered that in 1907 the Machinery Moulders Union in Detroit had struck unsuccessfully for the nine-hour day and a minimum wage.) Whatever the need in 1912 to forestall labor unrest or curb turnover (wage increases had a pattern of generating temporary docility), the paper reported that the announcement—by whom is unknown—"soon put the entire plant in an uproar."[59] The problem, however, was that the concessions had not been authorized, and McGregor was evidently forced to make an unreported and probably embarrassing retraction.

The plant extension begun in June 1912 would create work for 2,000, McGregor estimated optimistically in a press statement meant to impress labor as well as the public.[60] With expansion and production cresting, and some backroom skills up his sleeve, he was in a confident position to weather political scrutiny, though, unlike the unperturbable Henry Ford, he did not see a silver lining in every kind of publicity. He could be oddly skittish and fretful over inconsequential incidents, but he was confident on most political matters. One early skirmish started as a nasty "little family quarrel" in the House of Commons in March 1912, when O. J. Wilcox, Essex North's Conservative MP, unwisely challenged his own minister of militia and defense, the irrepressible Samuel Hughes, for ordering twelve Ford cars in February for regional inspection officers, without tender and without consulting him as Walkerville's representative. Convinced that Ford cars were the cheapest, strongest automobiles on the market, Hughes hit back, claiming that he was doing Essex North a favor and that Wilcox was reacting on the grounds that his candidacy in September had been vigorously opposed by McGregor, who, the minister claimed, had "placarded his shop all over with appeals to his men to vote against" Wilcox. The still-green MP retorted, implausibly, that he had evidence that "McGregor never took any part in politics."[61]

Hardly a political know-nothing, McGregor especially valued sales to businesses and to any level of government—they guaranteed free, effective advertising—and he was not about to bow to pressure from a Conservative backbencher. In his response to the affair, he went beyond the simple provision of automotive and price details. Before the purchase had surfaced in the Commons, Wilcox's complaints had been leaked to McGregor, who not only had an unnamed Conservative shareholder privately confront the rash MP but who also, playing on Ford's favor in the public eye, had spread the story that Wilcox had tried to have his government's order shifted from Ford to another local maker (Reo, Hupmobile, or E-M-F), a charge that meshed with Hughes's championship of Model Ts. When the dust settled, the Ford order stood, the vehicles were distributed through the Toronto branch, and Wilcox had been made to look disloyal to both his minister and his riding. Though downplayed by the *Evening Record*, McGregor's political savvy was coming into focus.[62]

The summer and fall of 1912 were buoyant, vibrant months for McGregor, particularly as the factory extension neared completion. The automobile industry in Windsor-Walkerville was booming, with Detroit auto men continuing to vie for factory sites and concessions. Windsor had a reputation for its ready granting of bonuses to the industry. If anyone personified the much-editorialized "cult" of the automobile, it was Gordon M. McGregor, who, in contrast to the Walkers and other old money, took no pains to hide his Ford-funded affluence and social celebrity, which were closely reported. In October 1912, at a board meeting chaired by Henry Ford, he reported an annual profit of $838,862.25 on a net earning of $1,065,977.78. In September, with brother Walter, he had attended the auto show at the CNE in Toronto. The following month he was elected president of the newly formed Essex County automobile club, which the organizers meant to affiliate with the Ontario Motor League. Such a club was a fitting adornment for Canada's "automobile center." The *Evening Record* boasted, "[T]here is no other single city to challenge our supremacy."[63]

Later that month, in a syndicate with Walter and Wallace Campbell, McGregor bought the Victoria and Curry buildings in Windsor and the old Bartlet skating rink at Ferry and Chatham, where he intended to erect a major car dealership for Don McGregor and their brother-in-law John Morton Duck. The Universal Car Agency, a showcase dealership mainly for Ford cars, opened in February.[64] (In addition to George Malcolmson's position with Ford in Winnipeg, Hattie McGregor's brother Bruce Dodds was also a

Ford dealer, in Detroit.) By all accounts, the McGregor brothers were extremely close. When Don married in 1912, Gordon gave him a share in Ford Canada. In October the family had rejoiced at Walter's engagement to Esther Margaret, the eldest daughter of Lieutenant Colonel Ernest Solomon Wigle, the head of another established Essex family, a Windsor lawyer, and a very strong personality. He once threatened to throw Walter out of his office for trying to sell him shares in Ford. The clan was beginning to fear that Walter "could not be pleased" and was likely to remain a bachelor. One of the pieces of family correspondence to have survived, Gordon's congratulatory note to Esther on 30 October, written from Toronto en route to a hunting trip in northern Ontario, is warmly welcoming and gently humorous. The marriage took place on 30 December at All Saints Anglican Church in Windsor.[65]

Other good news came that month when, under an Essex County bylaw, the area around the Ford plant was carved out of the Township of Sandwich East and erected as a separate village, to provide municipal services to the Ford-based community. It was appropriately named Ford City. With industry booming, its population doubled within the next eight months. To avoid a confusion of name and location, the company's designation as Ford Walkerville continued for many more years. Cognizant of the electrical needs of its main industry, though at times desperately unable to cope with rampant residential and industrial sprawl (many factories had located there to supply Ford), a sympathetic council soon entered into negotiations to switch over from the Walkerville Electric Light and Power to the larger, much-heralded grid of Ontario Hydro, which aggressively courted new municipal customers. It was these negotiations that first engaged McGregor in the knotty politics behind the utility services of the adjoining municipalities in the Border Cities.[66]

The plant expansion of 1912 and the resultant surge in production required managerial responses from McGregor and his crew that were purely localized or routinely dependent on Ford Detroit. As the expansion neared completion and the company continued to find more and more Canadian suppliers, 800 new manufacturing machines were ordered from A. R. Williams Machinery Company of Toronto. McGregor predicted that if business kept growing, he would have to significantly reassess the allocation of functions and building plans for his growing complex of adjoining properties. The aim, as always, was to manufacture all of the company's components in Canada, and the company wanted buyers to know this: by 1912 it was stamping parts, including the radiator, with a "Made in Canada" logo. In methods of production and design, however, McGregor's plant continued to follow closely the technology and operations of Detroit, though the pace of implementation and machine replacement lagged. If there was any sense or talk in Ford Canada of "scientific" or systematic management, which included studies of time and effort—and such talk did permeate other Canadian industries—it emanated from Henry Ford's production engineers. As a smaller, separate corporation with different resources, independent finances, and a different market, McGregor's company could not be a mirror operation. However, moving assembly operations, as introduced at Ford Detroit over the course of 1913, were carefully installed at Ford Canada, as layout allowed. Though Ford Detroit was vastly more productive in terms of volume, George Dickert vigorously pushed Canadian line production at least to match Detroit's time-cost ratio: "We tried to meet their minute cost if we had the same equipment," he explained. He also supervised the integration of more and more manufacturing functions. In May 1913, for instance, the plant began machining and assembling its own engines (the castings themselves came from Michigan until 1919). In September the Canadian company terminated its supply arrangements with the Dodge brothers in order to begin making its own transmissions and other engine parts.[67]

McGregor was adept at attracting talent in areas that required initiative and flair, at both the head plant and the branches. The slim, youthful-looking Augustin Neil Lawrence, who had taken charge of sales in September 1912, was responsible for establishing a company network that could effectively absorb and service the 11,584 Ford cars made in 1912–13 (up 6,388 from the previous season). Where McGregor, who was not averse to raiding other automakers and businesses, had recruited him is uncertain, but Gus Lawrence—he later preferred Neil—was a dynamic salesman with impressive credentials. His wife was a daughter of the American army's judge advocate general, who lived in Washington and had a vacation home in North Hatley, Quebec. Lawrence understood intimately Ford's complex system of dealerships, dealer contracts and deposits (a major source of company finance), quotas, enforcement, territories, wholesaling to branches, and advertising. He also knew the regional markets within Canada and the potential in each for sales, which he did much to cultivate. Like McGregor, he had a firm grasp on the production-centered ethos and methods shaped in Detroit by Couzens and Hawkins.[68]

By 1909 American farmers were fast taking to the Model T in an extraordinary wave that built as prices fell. It spread into rural Canada between 1909 and 1912. In one community after another, the automobile, usually a Ford, broadened horizons by breaking down the limits of time and distance associated with the horse-drawn wagon. Propelled by income from wheat crops and liberal credit sources (though not from Ford), an almost crazed flood of automobile buying ensued, with Alberta, Saskatchewan, and Manitoba representing the hottest markets. In their grasp of the automobile's transformative magnitude, prairie farmers became pioneers of modernity. Edmonton had had a Ford agency since 1904, a Ford traversed the Edmonton-Calgary trail in 1906, and on 26 July 1906 the *Weekly Herald* proclaimed that "the automobile is in Calgary to stay." The first good-roads convention in Alberta took place in Leduc on 19 August 1909, and the number of registered drivers jumped from 275 in 1909 to 3,733 in 1913. In Saskatchewan, the 22 cars recorded in 1906 shot up to 2,268 in 1912; in North Battleford, to pick one locale among many with stories of Ford's sweep, the first automobile appeared in May 1909. That fall a local dealer sent a representative across the border to the auto exhibition at the Minnesota state fair to purchase a Ford. Six more appeared the following spring. In Manitoba, where McGregor's future brother-in-law ran the Ford branch and would soon help to set up the Winnipeg Motor Trades Association, American consul general John E. Jones reported in early 1910 that dealers were finding it impossible to meet the demand, mostly for Canadian-built American cars. (This view, of American cars that happened to be built in Canada, was not uncommon.) *Gas Power Age* (Winnipeg) acknowledged that Ford Canada had produced a light car fit for the west. Plans were afoot to hold western Canada's first auto show in February 1911 in Winnipeg, during bonspiel week, when people would be in town. Even with the success of such venues, in 1913 some western buyers also began appearing at the Toronto shows (then in the hands of the

In preparation for a contest against an iceboat, Ford's Toronto manager Fred Fox puts his record-setting "Ford racer" through test runs (and spins) on Toronto Harbour on a snowy 22 January 1912. City of Toronto Archives, fonds 1244, item 452C.

Automotive show, Transportation Building, Canadian National Exhibition, Toronto, possibly September 1913. Canadian National Exhibition Archives, General Photo Collection, file 266, box 17.

Automotive show, Transportation Building, Canadian National Exhibition, Toronto, February 1914. City of Toronto Archives, fonds 1244, item 51.

newly formed Toronto Automobile Trade Association, headed by a group that included Michael A. Kennedy of the Ontario Motor Car dealership and Fred Fox of Ford's Toronto branch). "The automobile has become a prime necessity with the rancher on the prairie," Arthur C. Wyndham of Calgary told the *Toronto Star* in February 1913.[69]

Gordon McGregor's early exposure to auto shows in New York was not wasted effort. Ford Canada placed much emphasis on the shows in Toronto, at both the CNE's new transportation building and the city armories. The show at the CNE in February 1913, a grandly festooned event organized by E. M. Wilcox, was typical; the press puffed that half the space was devoted to cars made in Ontario, though virtually all of them were of American parentage. Pitched to farmers, women, and "men of moderate means," this automotive "Mecca of thousands" appealed to all. Maybe the claim of the press that, for the price of a ticket, one could feel like a millionaire for a while held true in some cases; people could certainly get close to such hitherto unknown luxury cars as the Pierce-Arrow, the Stoddard-Dayton, the McLaughlin electric from Oshawa, and, from Saint John, New Brunswick, the Maritime Six, which had its transmission and gears in the rear axle (to position its weight best for "Canadian road conditions"). The mechanically curious pored over stripped-down chassis. Gimmicks ranged from the mock funeral of the canary brought in from New York (to cheer the crowds) to the latest nonfactory accessories, including the electric starter installed in a Model T Ford. Long a mainstay of the Ford group, the successes of souped-up Fords in races (particularly Fred Fox's famous stripped-down T) and polo matches (with tumbling Ts instead of horses) at the CNE grandstand were not lost on the local show crowds, nor was the sales psychology behind product change. Of the many attractions, reported the *Star* in 1913, suggestive of shows before and since, "the designs of the bodies of all the new cars show distinct advances." In 1914 the most "radical" featured development was the "automatic" (sliding) gearshift, an advance shunned by Henry Ford. Politicians glad-handed, buffs buzzed, unionized musicians groused about the use of unorganized players, Russell cars from Toronto got their usual due, and Ford cars usually claimed the most sales. Banners promoted such related organizations as the Ontario Safety League, founded in 1913 by the Ontario Motor League and other interested parties to address the shocking number of accidents involving automobiles. But the influence of these auto shows still had limits.[70]

The rural areas of some provinces, especially those without enriching wheat crops, proved less responsive to the automobile, Ford or otherwise. In Quebec the diffusion of Ford automobiles and other motorcars was inhibited by such factors as the close proximity of farms, the poor road system, the prevalence of horse-drawn vehicles, and the absence (perhaps until 1914) of any Ford Canada sales brochures and manuals in French. The Montreal branch of Ford Canada nevertheless made a particularly strong push in 1911 to gain market share and get Ford cars on the province's roads. It would not be until after World War I, with a surge in road building under a new department of roads, that the number of automobiles increased substantially—from about 7,400 vehicles in 1914 to seven times that in 1921—and clear patterns of regional use began to emerge. In Quebec's Eastern Townships, for instance, French Canadians preferred new cars, while anglophones were less averse to driving older vehicles. In Prince Edward Island as well poor roads checked the spread of cars; as late as 1917 there were only 133 automobiles registered, 53 of them Fords. An analysis of these registrations that year, according to historian Sasha Mullally, "suggests that many rural Islanders still perceived automobiles to be only marginally useful to their particular working context, even with the 'good times' provided by the wartime economy or the extra income generated by fox farming endeavours." Newfoundland, though not yet a province, was still a British colony, but it drew no attention from Ford Canada—there were few roads and fewer automobiles. And so the regional patterns went, from sea to sea, with contrasts and variations known well by the Ford branches and local dealers.[71]

McGregor's response to the market was to initiate concrete steps to strengthen demand nationwide. In 1912–13 Neil Lawrence, in consultation with McGregor and Campbell, moved to systematize Ford Canada's sales and create a "formula for organized selling," as assistant sales manager Harry S. Pritchard (a former Toronto lawyer) would later term this major corporate thrust. It may have reflected what Hawkins and Couzens were doing in the United States. The first step in Walkerville was the construction of a large map of Canada, a war room–like task that took several months. Sales department representatives then drove through virtually every rural section of Canada, noting its physical condition, crops, and population; in urban areas, the residents, industries, and wage scales were studied. Based on these surveys, the numbers of Ford cars that "should be sold" were methodically calculated, an industry-leading approach taken by no other automobile company in Canada before the 1920s, as far as is known. The projections were then imposed on the Ford dealers; where no dealers existed, they were aggressively recruited; where this was not possible, the company had grounds for projecting future growth and distribution. Dealers were linked to their branch offices and each other by traveling "road men." Their job was to "instruct and assist" the dealers, coordinate data on business, roads, and crops in an area, and gather statistics "showing population, assessment values, and all interesting information which may be of value in furthering" the dealers' sales.[72]

Finding dealers or servicemen was not always an easy task, in Canada or abroad. Mel S. Brooks, an experienced Canadian Ford executive assigned to finding dealers in New South Wales before 1924, made a comparison. Unlike R. J. Durance, Brooks did not necessarily pick businessmen, but at the same time he was wary of professed mechanics. "Australia seems now to be in the stage that Canada was a few years ago, where a man knowing anything about a motor car is considered a genius."[73]

As part of this systematization, advertising began shifting from its roots in rational explanation and technical data. With no advertising department to speak of at Ford, in either the United States or Canada, there had been no coherence in early Ford advertising in the markets for the range of Ford automobiles. Newspapers would remain the favored medium. In 1912 McGregor's office came out with an unusual but delightful forty-one-page booklet, *Six Talks by the Jolly Fat Chauffeur with the Double Chin*, a light, comical promotion of Model Ts in conversational format and cartoons. In its humor, it reflected McGregor's style, though it would not set a pattern; as distributable publicity, it served as a prelude to *Ford Times*. In July 1913 the weekly *Ford Sales Bulletin* was launched for dealers and salesmen, followed in August by the monthly Canadian edition of *Ford Times*, which strategically took the company (and Henry Ford's photograph) to the customers and into their homes and farms far more effectively than the staid newspaper advertising of the company and its dealers at this time. Lawrence's medium, the extraordinarily assertive *Bulletin*, was festooned with sales figures, challenges to try harder, cartoons, and snapshots of Ford Canada's young corps of branch managers, optimistic dealers, and cocky salesmen, many of whose resourcefulness pushed the limits of ethics. Occasionally dealers were warned, in chummy fashion, to stay within their territories and stock parts made only by Ford. Lawrence also let them know that his department was tracking their advertising. A masterpiece of promotion, the *Bulletin* did not mince its message. "Every Ford representative is expected to hustle," Lawrence exhorted. One challenging but happy result for McGregor, who was alone among Canadian auto producers in this respect, was a market in which demand steadily outpaced supply, thus allowing for the consumption of more Ford cars and the desired reduction of prices through volume production. Another apparent consequence of the strong market, and of the degree of company control among dealers, was the rarity of legal action by dealers, who, if weak, dissatisfied, or outmuscled by neighboring dealers, just dropped out of sight or switched to other automobiles.[74]

McGregor was proud of both the *Bulletin* and the *Ford Times*, which few other Canadian producers could afford to match. He kept gilded, leather-bound sets of both the Canadian and American editions of the *Times*, as well as the *Bulletin*, and he clearly understood their purpose.[75] At the center of each publication was the Model T, called from the start the Universal Car, which was publicized in homey chat of the Henry Ford variety, sketches, incessant statements of simplicity, technical data (there were still legions of customers to educate), testimonials, and stories and pictures from the Yukon to the Australian outback. The writers of *Ford Times* worked steadily to encourage the use of Ford cars in wintertime, especially in Quebec and the west, knowing well the tendency of Canadians to store their cars away from snowdrifts, debilitating cold, and mud. In the winter of 1909–10 car owners in Winnipeg began using their machines throughout the season for the first time, thus spreading the sales season. The winter of 1911–12 saw a similar trend in Montreal. But, recognizing the general patterns of low off-season use and sales, McGregor, Campbell, and Lawrence counted on the off-setting compensation provided by sales in the imperial market: "The peak demand from our foreign territory," Campbell explained,

"Opposition 'Knocks' Help Ford Dealers." *Ford Sales Bulletin*, 1 November 1913. Photograph by Mark Coatsworth.

" . . . comes when our domestic demand is at its lowest ebb."[76] In either market Ford Canada targeted the new buyer, at first the wealthy professional and the enthusiast—doctors and others who tended to upgrade—and then the middle-income earner and the rural buyer. (The used-car market and the market for parts and service were just taking shape.) "The Ford is farm machinery," the *Ford Times* reasoned. Give the farm boy a Ford and nothing could lure him to the city, though in reality the Model T, soon the most popular vehicle on the prairies, gave distant farm families new accessibility to towns and agricultural service centers. At the same time sales were often clinched as much by social factors as by the economic advantages of motorization. Urban markets, as Fred Fox knew in Toronto, now posed intensifying competition, which in turn led to the traffic problems that were taking shape daily in Toronto in the 1910s. *Ford Times* had the effect, too, of helping to promote publications by the auxiliary industries. *Goodyear No-Rim-Cut News*, for example, was launched in Toronto in 1913 by the Goodyear Tire

Ford Canada's sales manager, A. N. Lawrence, as depicted in *Ford Sales Bulletin* on its first anniversary. *Ford Sales Bulletin*, 4 July 1914. Photograph by Mark Coatsworth.

and Rubber Company, which was happy to promote any car that used its product.[77]

Throughout the Canadian *Ford Times*, McGregor's place within the Ford family was downplayed, though like most makers, Ford Canada pressed such familial identity among its customers. Instead, both the *Bulletin* and the *Times* pushed the Canadian national bandwagon that McGregor had launched in 1904 and that he would drive at full speed into the Great War. As dealers were told in early August 1913, "Canadians take a just pride in industries within their own borders, financed by Canadian capital, employing Canadian labor, boosting Canadian interests. . . . Even Canadians will be astonished at the magnitude of the Ford industry, of which the first description at all comprehensive will appear in the August *Ford Times*."[78]

The few buyers who left any unsolicited record of their choice

A 1913 Model T in New Zealand. The cars then being sent from Canada were complete, but the description on this photograph suggests some local bodywork: "A Ford Model T (Pauling Roadster), made by Chavannes, Wanganui." Alexander Turnbull Library (Wellington, New Zealand), Teslas Studios Collection, PAColl-3046, ref. no. G-17348–1/1.

of automobiles, however, never mentioned national labels, though by 1910 American consuls as far afield as Yarmouth, Nova Scotia, Winnipeg, and Victoria had noticed, with bias, a new but decided preference for American automobiles, Walkerville Fords included. Of concern to buyers were availability, price, reliability, service, and parts. Lawrence's formula worked marvelously well. By the end of 1913, according to registrations, there were 11,217 "Canadian-made" automobiles in Ontario versus 4,947 "American-made" cars. Coincident with the upswing in production in 1912–13 was the strong demand from Australia and New Zealand. The 303 Canadian Model Ts taken from two vessels in New Zealand in May 1913 reputedly constituted the largest shipment of vehicles ever landed in the Southern Hemisphere. After a period of drought, Australian buyers turned from high-priced English cars to the lower-priced Canadian Ford, and made it the most popular auto there by 1914. By early 1914 Ford Canada was incorporating larger radiator tanks in its export versions to control hotter running temperatures. To facilitate the supply of Ts, which were Canada's leading export to Australia, Ford Canada pressured the federal Department of Trade and Commerce to push for a preferential trading arrangement with Australia, to which it was shipping from 150 to 175 cars a month but still wanted help to compete with American imports. In Ceylon, in 1913–14, the Canadian Ford became the most popular vehicle in the low-price range ($1,000–$1,850), though the American consul in Colombo drew attention to strong regional dissatisfaction with the finish of Ford cars, which suffered in sea transit and rusted quickly in hot humidity, and bland colors (dark blue or black). Almost invariably, the consuls viewed Walkerville Fords as American vehicles. Of little concern to McGregor was the domination of the higher price ranges by the British Wolseley and the German Adler.[79]

Supported by the talents of Dickert, Lawrence, and Campbell, the quiet assistant manager who often held the fort, McGregor, in the laudatory estimate of Wilkins and Hill, remained the "creative pilot and complete boss of the corporation he had brought to life."[80] In the absence of sustained corporate correspondence, however, it is difficult to see this slightly exaggerated assessment in active play. McGregor could not ignore his subordination to company vice president Couzens and president Henry Ford, despite the latter's tendency to beg off company meetings. Analysts of the period understood that the Canadian company, despite its separate corporate existence, followed the same operating methods in terms of production, branch assembly, and sales approach as the parent company. In contrast to the continuing flow of factory letters, Wilkins and Hill claim that no managerial directives or letters went from Detroit to Ford City, one result of a relationship that was always informal, cordial, and heavily dependent on the telephone and personal interaction.

At the same time, the public record, primarily the *Evening Record* (despite its uncritical coverage), reveals the Canadian nuances of a border-side industry. By 1913 the managerial challenges facing McGregor were inextricably linked to the Border Cities' unrelenting attraction of auto-related industries and workers, a campaign pursued with great earnestness by Windsor's industrial commissioner, Charles L. Barker, and taken up by the board of trade and then the Border Cities Chamber of Commerce. Between March 1912 and mid-1913, Hupp, Overland, Baker Electric, Tate Electric, Tudhope, Fisher Body, National Auto Body, Dominion Stamping, American Lamp and Stamping, and Kelsey Wheel had all set up branch works, with, as one trade journal put it, the "usual" and expected municipal exemptions and a high degree of participation by Trussed Concrete Steel. Intermingled were such local suppliers as Canadian Bridge (frames), Auto Specialities Manufacturing and Walkerville Malleable Iron (castings), Kerr Engine (brass parts), and Canadian Typograph (engine parts). All jostled for business alongside the predominant Ford and other primary makers.[81] Throughout Canada, the flood of Model Ts led to a growing secondary market, with used Ts becoming a regular filler of the classified pages of rural and urban newspapers.

At the core of the exuberance displayed by McGregor and others at Ford Canada in 1912–13 was productive capacity and the preponderant drive to meet targets and backlogs of orders by speeding up the assembly process. As *Iron Age* (New York) put it in June 1912, the "spirit of catching up is omnipresent."[82] In this regard Ford Detroit, where every step and the rates of output had been precisely clocked and calculated, was a model. In Ford City, McGregor could still mark the results with a facade of cheer and fun. In 1912, when production reached twenty-five cars a day, shipping superintendent Arthur R. Graham recalled, McGregor declared a half holiday on a Saturday, took a group of employees to a Detroit Tigers baseball game, and then rented a streetcar to take the party to dinner at a roadhouse "up the river from the plant." In a significant shift from the casual days of assembly stands, speed was paramount too at Ford Canada: in the winter of 1913–14 the assembly line there was run at "full tilt" to gain ground on the anticipated rush of meeting spring orders.[83]

At the same time, side by side with employee banquets and the formation of workers' clubs and competitive sports teams, the turnover of workers, discharges, fights among workers, factory accidents, and legal actions against Ford Canada by employees betrayed tension. Only the workers knew the full impact of repetitive line work; many simply registered their disgruntlement by leaving. One worker, Albert C. Ward, who started at Ford Canada in 1913, clearly remembered the mounting pressures from the line foremen.[84] This tension in turn was exacerbated by the recession in Detroit in 1913–14 and reaction there to the force of speedup.

A frequent visitor to Highland Park, McGregor could not have been unaware of a series of significant events: extraordinary turnovers at Ford Detroit; the unemployment demonstrations; the strike in Ford's core room in 1912; the bitter, failed attempts at labor organization at Ford in March–April 1913; the strikes in June in Detroit at Studebaker, Cadillac, Krit Motor Car, and Timken Axle; and the machinists' strike at the Ford assembly plant in Buffalo, New York. The Detroit strike reportedly involved 4,000 autoworkers.

Labeled the "Detroit of Canada," Ford City and Ford Canada did not go unaffected during a period of even wider industrial boom. Though the International Association of Machinists' campaign in Ontario for fair wages may not have touched the Border Cities, Ford City had other problems. With its population doubling between 1912 and 1913, the influx of unemployed autoworkers created an acute shortage of work and housing, forcing McGregor, partly out of some sense of civic responsibility and with few options open to him, to apply to the council for allowance to house workers in tents. By July 1913 his company was employing "several hundred" American autoworkers, whom he paid a premium because of the housing shortage. Unable to find work or affordable housing, American and foreign-born laborers turned around and left in droves, creating the specter of desperate workers drifting back and forth across the river. Over the course of the year, and into 1914, houses and subdivisions sprang up, built by private companies with little or no organized municipal planning. Such spontaneous development was oblivious to the reports done for the International Waterways Commission on the highly polluted water being taken in by the Walkerville and Windsor utilities, a field that would engage McGregor in a few years.[85]

For McGregor the flashpoint came in April 1913, in the most unexpected form of a liquor application to the North Essex Licence Commission. The applicant was Arsas Drouillard, whose unwitting mistake was the location of his intended tavern: almost opposite the main gates of a company whose American president, Henry Ford, was a known teetotaler. The application elicited an immediate response from a deputation of Ford City manufacturers headed by McGregor and including his brother Walter and John H. French of Dominion Stamping. In a statement released before the commission's decision, Gordon McGregor declared no need for another licensed hotel in Ford City, certainly not one in such close proximity to his susceptible workforce of 1,400. Both Toronto and St. Thomas, Ontario, he argued, had refused to sanction hotel bars next to factories. (He did not mention this, but Detroit City Council had taken similar action in 1907.) At a hearing on the application on 24 April 1913 in the suburb of Tecumseh, tempers flared, with McGregor and French accusing commissioner John Lickman of pandering to a "mere saloon." The operation of the 700 machines in his auto plant required "sobriety," McGregor claimed, as if Drouillard's pub would intoxicate his entire workforce; to drive home his point he cited the instance of a drunk employee who fell three stories. With minimal thought to how his workers would respond, he then turned to nativist stereotype for his main threat: "We have probably 300 or 400 foreigners at work. I tell you, gentlemen, if those men can get liquor openly it will be a serious problem." Walter McGregor, whose other business associates included virulent racists, followed his brother by drawing the commissioners' attention to Hungry Hollow, a slum area behind the Ford plant where fights and trouble, fueled by the Dew Drop Inn, were said to be common. In concluding his attack, Gordon, in a hollow gesture of virtuous conciliation worthy of Henry Ford, offered to open "a public restaurant and charge the public the same as our men" if the application was turned down.[86]

Unswayed, the commissioners approved Drouillard's application, as well as another for a liquor shop, on the grounds of a public petition showing strong support. From an assessment base of 256, 138 had favored Drouillard's application, while only 63 opposed it. Unwilling to bend to public sentiment, McGregor refused to let the matter rest. In a blatant attempt to outmaneuver the commission, his group appealed to William John Hanna, a director of the Imperial Oil Company (a major supplier of Ford Canada), the Conservative MLA (member of the Legislative Assembly) for the adjacent riding of Lambton West, and Ontario's provincial secretary, whose department had jurisdiction over liquor licenses. In the meantime,

McGregor's characterization of his foreign workers legitimized a broader, sustained assault by the *Evening Record* (already known for its hostility to the area's French Canadians) against the eastern and southern European communities of the Border Cities. No good could be expected of Ford City's southern European contingent, who, the diatribe ran, "were unaccustomed to the strong drink of North America" and had "little knowledge of the laws and custom of the Canadian people."[87]

In the months that followed, the newspaper gave selective coverage to the efforts of municipal health authorities and law officers in Ford City "to clean up the Polish district" around Marion Avenue, where overcrowding, boardinghouses (a particular target of Ford moralists), fights, illegal stills, and disease elicited particular disgust, despite the willingness of foreign workers to take some of the most grueling positions at Ford, including foundry and heat-treating jobs, that required only a day or two of training. By 9 May, Hanna had vetoed the Ford City licenses, overriding the taxpayers of Ford City as requested by its premier industrial spokesmen. Liquor production and consumption continued behind closed doors, and no restaurant was built by McGregor.[88]

From this victory, which revealed more of his political connections and autocratic tendencies, McGregor proceeded in confident fashion later in May into litigation over the Ford stock promised by John Curry back in 1904. The transfer, McGregor claimed on 29 May at the sitting in Sandwich of the High Court division of the Ontario Supreme Court, had been repeatedly put off by Curry on the basis that the original debts of the Walkerville Wagon Works had not been cleared, evidently a condition of the original agreement. In 1911, however, McGregor had disposed of some land from his father's estate, settled the debts, and gone after Curry, but on 11 May 1912 Curry had died, followed by his wife on 31 October. Represented by Toronto lawyer James B. McLeod and pressed for taxes, the estate refused McGregor's claim, stating that it could not be substantiated. McGregor consequently sued for ownership of the stock and the bonus shares and dividends issued on it, all now worth more than $300,000. He had taken physical possession of the actual certificates at the corporate turnover at the end of 1911 and held onto them. The legal grounds of his claim were not reported; the *Evening Record* found no need to question it, and there were no doubt several who could testify to Curry's original promise. At the end of the trial, Justice Lennox reserved judgment after first encouraging an out-of-court settlement, though none was reached.[89]

McGregor's testimony in May did more than present his case legally. As reported by the *Evening Record*, so soon after the patent license victory, his recollection of his dealings with Curry had the additional benefit of sanctifying Ford Canada: its early struggle against ruin, its "meteoric rise," and McGregor's "perseverance"—the stuff of automotive romance in the "auto centre of the Dominion," the newspaper editorialized in July.[90] And so it was. Windsor was ever ready, the *Canadian Foundryman* had recorded in June, to offer "the usual exemptions" to Kelsey Wheel and others willing to erect plants. On 12 July, the reciprocity debates safely behind it, the *Evening Record* took delight in quoting from the Canadian Manufacturers' Association's *Industrial Canada:* "Do not advocate free trade in Windsor, Walkerville or Sandwich, or you will be laughed at. These three border communities are enjoying the spectacle of great United States industries crossing the Detroit River and locating branches within their boundaries." After falling out with E-M-F, in August 1913 Walter E. Flanders of Detroit moved to set up a branch plant for making Maxwell automobiles, the bankrupt Tudhope company of Orillia was bought and moved by a Walkerville consortium, and more parts companies sprang forth from Detroit parents. In November, George K. Parsons of Detroit set up the Parsons Motor Car Company of Canada Limited. There was still "plenty of room" for American producers in Canada, boasted Louis Logie, the Windsor representative (though he lived in Detroit) of the Lozier Motor Company of Detroit. American firms would win out over purely domestic manufacturers, he calculated frankly, because of "superior resources and advantages," particularly in technology transfer and the vital production and distribution of parts. Reliable technology was crucial. In Toronto, in its top line of cars, Russell had been using a British-designed sleeve valve that promised to overcome the engine knocking caused by early fuels and value defects in the conventional poppet-valve engines. But when Russell, to preserve his patent rights, began making his own sleeve-valve motor for 1913, he got into technical trouble and fell seriously behind in production. For McGregor, by contrast, it was a simple matter of having Ford's main patents, for such components as the planetary transmission, legally transferred without change and registered to his company.[91]

In September 1913 McGregor left off discussions with the reeve of Ford City, Charles Montreuil, over the sharing of power from Ontario Hydro to travel to Halifax with his brother Walter, their wives, and Ernest George Henderson of Canadian Salt for the annual meeting of the Canadian Manufacturers' Association, where Gordon's status as a major auto producer was known. After his return he received good news, in October, in the form of a favorable decision on the Curry shares, but the stubborn estate appealed, sending the case to the appellate division for consideration the following spring. In November and December 1913, to push and coordinate development, and with early thoughts of municipal cohesion, Gordon and Walter McGregor backed the fledgling Ontario Border Development Bureau and together they headed its financial solicitation committee. By the end of October, McGregor had resumed contact with Ontario Hydro. These talks over power supply drew Ontario's hydro czar, Adam Beck, to Walkerville to speak at a municipal meeting on 5 December. There was no question which industry was the leading consumer and was expected to take the lead. "When the Ford Motor company install hydro we can save that firm $10,000," Beck argued. "That should convince them that they cannot afford to do without hydro." To the likely chagrin of Walkerville Light and Power, the bylaw accepting provincial power passed by a large majority. Even with a steady supply of hydroelectric power, Ford Canada still relied on internal combustion as a major source of power for its plant. In August it had installed a 5,000-horsepower gasoline engine, which reputedly attracted "considerable attention" as "the most powerful gas engine in the world."[92]

The Ford shareholders' meeting of 27 October, held in Walkerville, was carefully orchestrated by McGregor, both in its agenda and how it was covered by the *Evening Record.* Despite the upswing in business—McGregor had told dealers on 4 October to stock up for an exceptional 1914—he declared no dividend at the meeting, a step not seen since 1904–6. The reason, he explained with false gravity and no detail, was the company's "present financial situation." To reinforce the supposed seriousness, the *Evening Record* revived the ever-useful image, recently used in the Curry case, of McGregor scrambling for capital in 1904. But in 1913 he was hardly cash-strapped: he was authorized to distribute bonuses at the executive, branch, and dealership levels, and on a motion by Wallace Campbell and McGregor, $5,000 was subscribed to the Walkerville and Ford City hospital, of which McGregor was vice president, thus establishing his and his company's philanthropic presence. The withholding of dividends, however, had more to do with the need to finance another sector: to catch up with Ford Detroit.[93]

At the directors' meeting also held on the 27th, but in private, McGregor was finally authorized to institute the shorter nine-hour day and pay raises and bonuses for the workers at his earliest opportunity. In terms of hours, pay, and working conditions, he obligingly recognized that the general policy of Ford Canada was "to be as consistent with that of the Detroit company as is possible." To strengthen this harmonization, the now disfavored John Dodge, who had resigned as a director of Ford Canada and had had his engine contract terminated, was replaced as a director by Frank L. Klingensmith, the secretary of Ford Detroit.[94]

The harmonization was carefully timed. To relieve the pressures created in Detroit in 1913 by labor's mounting distaste for the new assembly-line system and the speedup policy, the high rate of labor turnover, and growing signs of union activity, particularly among the most militant group (the machinists), management in Detroit had instituted several labor reforms, including the announcement of an across-the-board pay increase averaging 13 percent on 10 October 1913 and 10 percent bonuses on 31 December. A second increase in wages, called "shared profits," was being considered by Henry Ford and Couzens. On the other side of the river, McGregor and Ford Canada were already paying laborers, machine operators, and assemblers rates that were 32.5 to 45 percent above the prevailing rate for labor in the Border Cities. On 28 November 1913 McGregor publicly announced the nine-hour day and the pay raises—an "entirely altruistic" gesture, he maintained without hesitation, that he predicted would cost the company more than $30,000 a year.[95]

During the week of 29 December 1913, McGregor hosted at his factory the first annual convention of Canadian branch managers. They came from eleven cities and included Don McGregor and John Duck of Universal Car, which was frequently granted favored status in company functions. Ostensibly called to discuss company policy, the convention featured a tour of the Detroit plant, a motion picture made by Ford (a medium soon to be exploited effectively by McGregor), and a banquet at which he was presented with a silver loving cup. The convention coincided nicely with a feature article on the Ford in *Canadian Machinery*. (Dealers would be invited to Ford City in April.) Within days of the managers' convention, Neil Lawrence, well recovered from a serious auto accident, had returned from a seven-week business trip through British Columbia, Alberta, Saskatchewan, and Manitoba. His aim had been to assess the impact of the systematized sales strategy and his report surprised no one: "Fords predominate. . . . They are thick." More Model T Fords had been shipped west in 1913 than all other makes combined. There they would be used, tested, fixed, raced, and studied endlessly. *Gas Power Age* would note the response to Ford's showing of models from 1909 to 1914 at the Winnipeg auto show in February 1914: "Each successive machine had a little added in the way of improvement and a little taken off, making the newer models appear less and less cumbersome."[96] Here again was the concept of model change.

In the Border Cities, Lawrence's predictable news was not the focus of the rush of publicity facing McGregor in January 1914. On 5 January Henry Ford shocked the industry by adopting the $5 day, a pay scheme with a reputed profit-sharing component (likely devised by Couzens) that would guarantee a steady stream of new employees and provide an incentive to stay on the line. (The turnover rate that year, to maintain a workforce of 14,000, was an astounding 379 percent.) Ford Detroit, and eventually Ford Canada, insisted on labeling the scheme a profit-sharing plan, then a popular form of welfare capitalism. Actual profit-sharing plans had enormous variety. The National Civic Federation in New York tracked the many forms, which could include production bonuses, stock distributions, actual percentages of annual profit, and such "special distributions" as outright bonus payments. In the federation's view, the Ford scheme was a "radical deviation" from any plan in operation in the United States or Canada; it was, in truth, nothing more than a wage increase. But to Ford, a "sharing of profits" sounded wonderfully altruistic. For those wishing to qualify—and not all qualified for the new wage; certainly no women did—the scheme meant an investigation of their private lives to ensure conformity to Ford's standards of sobriety, rectitude, family life, residential status, and work ethic. For some, qualification would also lead to genuine aid, such as English-language classes, which some critics viewed as forced Americanization.

Such possible scrutiny discouraged few. The immediate reaction in Detroit was riots caused by workers seeking jobs at Ford. Couzens vigorously defended the scheme, claiming that employees deserved to share in the company's good fortune. Despite the clear, though unstated, intent of using wages to reinforce managerial control, Henry Ford steadfastly denied any intent to forestall labor troubles. Though big business had been debating profit sharing for years, Ford's announcement still created a shockwave. Unconvinced socialists in Detroit attacked the scheme, while pastors there praised its generosity. Organized labor uniformly dismissed profit sharing as an evasion of paying union wages. Unable to offer wages anywhere close to Ford's, other American automakers were reluctant to follow suit. Some Ontario newspapers found the scheme newsworthy—the *Toronto Globe* criticized it—but few analyzed it carefully. Some manufacturers outside the Border Cities raised serious questions about the pay program, which one Toronto businessman dismissed as "a nice little advertising scheme." The *Canadian Foundryman* predicted the scheme would have an unsettling effect on other trades. Few Canadian companies could match the scheme because the "Ford Company is largely in a class by itself." British businessmen immediately saw the link to labor relations and dismissed the scheme as "unsound business."[97]

On 15 January the *Evening Record*, in a rare moment of semi-independence, asked outright if the scheme would be adopted by Ford Canada. This inevitable question would be repeated over the coming year, especially since profit sharing was adopted by Ford in Britain and by some Windsor companies, among them Canadian Salt, but McGregor remained silent.[98] The financial requirements of implementation were beyond his resources so soon after the pay raises of late November, and he may well have been caught off guard by Henry Ford's action. It is more likely that labor conditions in McGregor's works did not yet warrant the scheme, which remained an extremely valuable tool to hold in reserve. Even without the $5 day, the Ford City plant had all the workers it needed, whatever its turnover. In February, Neil Lawrence, while announcing a new record in production—on a single day (the 24th) 105 cars were built and 129 were shipped—noted that up to 2,000 applications for work were being received daily. Even allowing for exaggeration, the number is impressive. James Dark, who joined Ford in 1914 as a concrete tester in its building department, remembered the long lines of men seeking employment stretching back that year "as far as the Peabody Bridge." Late in February, McGregor, during one of his frequent visits to the Detroit plant, told Frank Klingensmith, in a discussion of business in Canada, that "conditions were the best there that they have ever been."[99]

Throughout the dominion, Ford trade continued to be pushed aggressively. In October 1913 McGregor had been authorized to open a branch, the company's tenth, in Saint John, New Brunswick, through a lease of a portion of the property of Jack A. Pugsley's Maritime Motor Car Company Limited, a manufacturing venture well on its way to failure. That same year Ford took over the bankrupt Tudhope premises in Vancouver. In Toronto, Ford manager Fred Fox announced in February 1914 the construction of a five-story assembly factory at Dupont and Christie; months later a plant was announced for London, Ontario, following the "American policy" of shifting assembly and the related costs and accounting to the regional centers and thus relieving pressure on the main factory.[100]

McGregor's summation of these developments is neatly contained in a long revealing letter on 26 February 1914 to James Couzens, then on vacation in Santa Barbara, California. The letter was both a courtesy and a responsibility; McGregor dutifully felt Couzens needed to be informed. Keeping up with orders, McGregor reported, was the main task. With 5,500 cars shipped on the year's output, Walkerville was producing 100 a day, its maximum, though he was pushing for 125. "The Detroit factory seems to be setting an awful pace and we are trying to do our share to keep up with them." Severe weather conditions in the west had discouraged agents from sending in orders and taking early deliveries, but "we have been forcing them to the limit." (This was particularly aggressive given the emerging debt crisis among western farmers.) Exports were up by about 35 percent. Finances, too, were in "good shape," he reported, and the company's bank overdraft of $200,000 (a winter necessity to prepare for the "spring rush") was less than he had anticipated, knowing full well that Couzens understood the Canadian company's need for financing (something normally shunned by Henry Ford). In a gentle aside, and a rare glimpse of his humorous side, McGregor noted that he had not been over to Detroit much lately, but he had seen Henry Ford "a day or two before he went south. Mr. Ford seemed to be in particularly good spirits, although he is very thin. I think you and I could each let him have fifteen or twenty pounds in weight."[101]

Moving the factory's unrelenting output also meant giving vigorous attention to imperial markets, including the smallest untapped colonies. Ever since his trip of 1909–10 McGregor had underlined this challenge. Every photograph in the *Ford Times* of a Model T in a colonial setting, often the local garage or hazardous terrain, bears witness to his success. He assigned the responsibility to Neil Lawrence, who refused to be slowed down by bureaucratic inadequacy or the approach of war in Europe. Mindful of the American consuls' utility as sources of trade news, his own systematic approach in Canada, and the enormous reach of Ford's foreign department, he methodically canvassed British colonial representatives in territories where Canada had no direct representation. Minimal response led him to redouble his efforts. The case of British Honduras in Central America, if not typical, is illustrative of his brazen methods.

In April 1914, with McGregor coordinating several fronts, Lawrence asked Robert Walter, the colonial secretary in Belize, if there was any market for automobiles (read Fords) in British Honduras, even if it was largely inaccessible and undeveloped. Walter's abrupt response—"[T]here are no roads suitable for motor traffic and [I] would not advise you to attempt to do business here"—spurred Lawrence to complain in disbelief on 22 July to Canada's Department of Trade and Commerce on the ground that he had the right at least to "correct information." As evidence, Lawrence explained that Ford's foreign office in New York City had already lined up a dealer in Belize, who had immediately placed an order for one tourer from Walkerville ("right drive, regular equipment"). Despite the "unsettled condition of affairs abroad," meaning the buildup to war, he felt that the matter was of sufficient importance that Francis Charles Trench O'Hara, the deputy minister, should convey his concern to the Colonial Office in London through Canada's high commissioner there. On 14 August a cowed O'Hara asked William Linny Griffith, the secretary of the high commissioner and a former exporter himself, to review the correspondence on the matter and then, at his discretion, pass it on to the Colonial Office. With some gratuitous promotion added, O'Hara clearly saw Ford Canada as part of a whole: "I may say that the Ford Motor Company of Canada is one of the largest concerns not only in Canada, but on this continent, and they are shipping motor cars to all parts of the world, ship-loads in fact to Australia and New Zealand alone. While they manufacture a good class of car, yet they make a very durable runabout which they sell at a very moderate price, and their sales are enormous." In early September, singularly unimpressed by the sale of a single car and convinced that the colonial secretary was right, that no trade was possible, Griffith quashed Lawrence's complaint. Ford's response is unknown.[102]

Against the backdrop of such negotiation, social and recreational outings—dances, dinners, golf matches, and horse races—kept pace with McGregor's success in business. Personal disappointments were quietly endured, including the loss on 14 January 1914 of their three-year-old son, Gordon Jr.[103] (Gordon and Hattie had four more children: William, Harriet, Elizabeth, and Nancy.) Early in February, Gordon and Walter sold Curry Hall in Windsor for more than $65,000. Later that month Gordon, Hattie, and brother Malcolm, the Detroit lawyer, left for a fortnight's vacation in Hot Springs, Arkansas, the first of Gordon's annual vacations at large American resorts. In April the appeal on the Curry estate was dismissed, but he still could not claim his prize: the executors, refusing to concede, wanted the case pushed on to the Judicial Committee of the Privy Council in Britain, then Canada's court of final appeal. The following month, when the governor-general, the Duke of Connaught, and his daughter came to the Border Cities, McGregor chauffeured them on a tour in a Ford, only to collide with the accident-prone Dr. Casgrain.[104]

McGregor's life was permeated with the sight, the smell, the use, and the promotion and sales of automobiles. The Border Cities understood his influential presence—public criticism was guarded—and the community knew that he would have a dominant position on the automotive concerns that defined so much public debate. On the reorganization of the Essex auto club on 6 April 1914, he stepped down as president, though his brother Don remained as secretary, but he did take the opportunity to push reciprocity in auto licensing. Attention to this form of reciprocity, which would allow out-of-province automobiles to enter Ontario and vice versa, especially to Detroit, helped force a bill on the matter in the Ontario legislature in May. How much weight was attached to the Border Cities' concern is uncertain, but the link to W. J. Hanna suggests that McGregor could claim an audience at Queen's Park (the seat of the provincial legislature) even if the government was Conservative. Now Windsor's key Liberal organizer, in June he backed the Liberal candidacy of James Craig Tolmie in the new riding of Windsor in the provincial election. Tolmie, whom McGregor had known for many years as a residential neighbor and as the pastor of St. Andrew's Presbyterian Church, won the election, as did the Liberal candidates in Essex North and Essex South. These results were the start of a most enjoyable summer. In June McGregor also participated in the golf tournament between the Essex Country Club of Sandwich and the Ann Arbor Country Club from Michigan, followed in July by a large family outing to the Windsor horse races and a ball given by Hattie and others in the casino of the Mettawas Inn in Kingsville. In between came his announcement, later in June, of Ford's first dividend in two years.[105]

Perceived in Detroit as an integral member of the broader Ford family, McGregor promoted that sense of family on his own and through Neil Lawrence in sales. They did not need Henry Ford in person for that purpose. When Ford did visit, in the spring of 1914, he was most interested in talking about natural conservation with tile and brick maker Jack Miner near Kingsville. Henry Ford often arrived at business matters by such tangential paths. In May, in a staged visit to London, McGregor had rubbed shoulders with Ford owners, extolling their shared "fraternity." This Henry Fordism was evident too in his many pep talks at conventions and head office indoctrinations. McGregor's address in April to the gathering of Ford dealers in Ford City is worthy of quotation, in part because of its reflection of Henry Ford's own rhetoric about his company. "Frankness pays," McGregor reasoned. Businessmen and the public alike appreciated openness rather than a "secretive and snobbish policy." "So it is in the automotive industry. No one any longer keeps his activities a secret. One reason for this is that the automobile is no longer in the experimental stage and there is little difference in the fundamentals between one car and another."[106] No matter that Ford was the only major producer still using the legendary but outmoded planetary transmission instead of a manual shift and that sales bulletins in February 1914 needed to remind dealers that Ford gears were always smoothly in mesh while sliding-gear transmissions led to grinding and damage.[107]

McGregor's efforts at transparent policy were not always sustained in practice, his distorted reporting of company finances being an example. At other times he took pains to explain that the policies and practices of his company could not completely duplicate those of the Detroit company. When workers were laid off at Ford Detroit in May 1914, he announced that he had no need to do so at his plant. Due largely to the western wheat economy, in Lawrence's estimate, business was brisk: some 1,500 workers were employed and about 85 cars a day were going out (on a target of 20,000). The Canadian market was based on climate, seasonal demands, and other peculiar variables that produced a uniquely Canadian pattern of requirements. In any case the car-buying public cared for policy only when it delivered a cheaper product and service. On 1 August, Ford Canada dropped its prices by $60 and instituted, for the next twelve months, another much-publicized and opportunistic form of "profit sharing," a rebate to buyers of $40 to $60 from Ford "profits," provided that 30,000 Fords were sold during that year. Later that month, on the eve of the Great War, it was an easy matter for the *Evening Record*, in a series of articles on board of trade members, to once again extol McGregor's role in raising formative capital in 1904: "This was where the Man came in."[108]

CHAPTER 4

Victory Bonds

At the outbreak of war in August 1914, McGregor had some indication of how his company would have to respond to the conflict. Mindful of the scrutiny of Ford Detroit, he was confidently poised to boost production significantly. A rising industrialist and local benefactor, he likely knew that he personally would want to play a part in the local war effort. The people of the Border Cities met the war with quiet resolve; the grim consequences would not begin to register for several more months. Walkerville's municipal council formulated a well-meaning plan to place the wives of soldiers on its payroll. The first group of local volunteers left on short notice for the training camp at Valcartier, Quebec, in late August. Canadian and British-born autoworkers in Detroit crossed the river to enlist. In September, Ford Canada, among other local industries, announced it would give preference to the hiring of veterans when the war was over. By October the first group of reservists and volunteers from Ford, twenty-five in all, had left; later that month the company and other manufacturers, in advertising dominated by Union Jacks and plucky bulldogs, proclaimed their commitment to "keep the wheels going" and "the dollar at home." As an extension of Ford Detroit, the Walkerville plant had no intention of turning to war production. The United States had not entered the war and would not until 1917. By early 1915 Henry Ford's antiwar sentiments were becoming a matter of record, though many in the Border Cities would turn a blind eye.[1]

Among Canadian automakers, a small amount of army business, including armored trucks, staff cars, and shell contracts, went mostly to the politically connected T. A. Russell in Toronto, whom the federal government in Ottawa appointed purchasing agent for motorized equipment for the Canadian Expeditionary Force (CEF).

In the fall of 1914, seven Ford cars and twenty-four Walkerville-built Gramm trucks were sent overseas with the 1st Contingent, but they performed poorly. Later, several thousand unmodified Model Ts would go into service with the CEF, the British army, and the New Zealand and Australian forces. A good number of these were made in Walkerville, though not under any special contract or with Henry Ford's endorsement. (Wilkins and Hills estimate up to 41,288 from Ford Canada, Flink credits 50,000 to Ford England, Adeney gives 30,000 to Ford England.) Along with the Ford employees who went to war, these vehicles were highlighted in a special war issue of the Canadian *Ford Times* in mid-1915; one Canadian military officer attested to their reliability. McGregor made sure, in a careful way, that readers understood that the Ts were standard, assembly-line automobiles and his plant was not converting to production for war. Industrial activity in the Border Cities altered only slightly during the last months of 1914—the real stimulus of the war upon the economy had yet to be felt. By November the automotive sector was experiencing cutbacks through shorter hours, the *Evening Record* reported.[2]

The overall mood was nonetheless buoyant, sustained by the undiminished and aggressive campaign of Windsor's industrial commissioner, C. L. Barker, to attract industry. (More than thirty new plants had opened between the beginning of 1913 and August 1914.) In September a major industrial exhibition opened, organized by veteran impresario R. M. Jaffray. As part of the show, on 12 September Ontario Hydro commissioner Adam Beck inaugurated Windsor's entry into the Niagara power grid, and on the 16th the Windsor Board of Trade hosted a "Detroit Night," with many Detroit manufacturers in attendance, but not including Henry Ford, who was selective about when he came across the river and where he would appear in public. Displays were mounted by Kelsey Wheel, Tate Electric (in its last year of making electric automobiles), and Windsor Auto Sales (Studebakers). Don McGregor and his Universal Car agency proudly showed two 1915 Ford cars, possibly the new models: the hardtop, center-door sedan and the coupelet.[3]

Gordon McGregor adapted to the war with extraordinary zeal and efficiency. His company was in excellent financial health: at the annual meeting of October 1914 shareholders were told that sales had increased by $1,637,531.67. McGregor was positioned to become, in the later estimate of the *Evening Record*, the most important cog in the cities' civilian war effort, a role that would show him at his best and at his worst. By December, to expedite the internal movement of parts, production, and increased sales, plans were in place to replace the old wagon works part of his factory with a major, Kahn-designed six-story addition, with an advanced system of ventilation and a massive traveling overhead crane that could link assembly lines and parts storage through all six floors from railway sidings directly below. Combined with brilliant marketing and unhindered by the production of war materials, the enhanced plant would facilitate a staggering increase, from 15,657 automobiles in 1914 to 46,914 in 1918, and a corresponding drop in price, from $650 to $495. In 1914, of the cars registered in Canada, 38 percent were Ford cars.[4] McGregor only shared the responsibility for this phenomenal growth—the biggest factor remained the transfer of technology and policy from Ford Detroit's Highland Park plant. Less obvious were the careful reexamination of sales projections and the fine-tuning of the branch and dealer systems.

In the early months of the war, McGregor shifted effortlessly between flag-waving and corporate promotion. Typically, in December he chaired a patriotic concert given by the schoolchildren of Ford City in the Oddfellows' Hall. At the end of the month he hosted a three-day convention of optimistic branch managers. Two results of this gathering were the shift of the *Ford Sales Bulletin* from a weekly to a biweekly publication, and the cancellation of the Ford catalogue for 1915. Coverage would be inserted in *Ford Times*, which would be sent in bulk to the branches. The managers believed buyers made decisions based not on demonstrations and catalogues but on the recommendations of Ford owners, though it was likely too that Ford no longer needed a catalogue. The convention's concluding banquet at the Essex Golf and Country Club, McGregor's favorite venue, was attended by Henry Ford, an entourage of other Ford Detroit headmen, and McGregor and his usual crew: the dour Wallace Campbell (a club regular and an excellent golfer), Neil Lawrence, and representatives of two of Canada's largest dealerships, Don McGregor and John Duck of Universal Car in Windsor and G. S. Bullis of the Saskatchewan Motor Company in Regina.[5]

The key marketing platform for Ford Canada was the "Made in Canada" movement. Adopted throughout Canadian industry, it was promoted in earnest by the Canadian Manufacturers' Association from at least 1909 and was modestly employed by McLaughlin, Russell, and other domestic automakers.[6] After 1914 the movement provided strong impetus in industry's rapid commercialization of the war. Even the Canadian Shredded Wheat Company of Niagara Falls, in its illustrative advertising, geared its product, made from "the choicest Canadian wheat," to housewives who "bear the brunt of those burdens that make the home a perfect place in which to develop sturdy men fit for war or the pursuits of peace." The movement found some of its most fervent champions in the late summer and early fall of 1914 in the Border Cities and in particular in Ford Canada, where McGregor needed a marketing umbrella for increasing the Canadian content of his cars and sidelining criticism of his rejection of war production. Ford figured largely in the Made in Canada week celebrated in the Border Cities in November.

For the duration of the war, this theme would define the company's marketing approach, link it acceptably to the war effort, and pervade the pages of *Ford Times*, the *Ford Sales Bulletin*, the *Evening Record*, and Ford advertising across the dominion. On 15 August the company had calmly advised dealers to remember that Canada was in no danger of invasion; prospective customers who used the war as a reason to back out of deals were just not exercising "good judgment." "The firing line in Europe is depending on the work line in Canada," reasoned a cartoon in the *Evening Record* in December.[7] A month later the *Ford Times* argued that "the thousands of Canadians at home are not fulfilling their duty unless they are doing as much to keep Canada's business booming as Canada's troops are doing to keep Canadian honor unsullied." Even a Henry Ford homily was quoted, or created: "Keep the wheels moving, the crops growing, and your dollars in Canada—buy Canadian made goods."[8] *Canadian Machinery* called this approach "industrial patriotism." Sales manager Neil Lawrence was quick to connect greater Ford production, sales, national industrial prosperity, and the war effort, a strategy that effectively bridged the demands of Ford Detroit for more cars and Canadian patriotic imperatives. "A strong 'Made-in-Canada' campaign will make Canada commercially great," quipped the ever-quotable Lawrence during the celebratory week in November.[9]

Few would argue otherwise. The endorsement of the movement by respected economists such as Adam Shortt, who wanted to see closer cooperation between farmers and manufacturers, added extra momentum.[10] Ford for one was ready. Company advertisements pitched the Made in Canada Ford as "a necessity—not a luxury," as well as the farmer's car, the woman's car, the merchant's car, the municipal vehicle of choice, the car most people could afford. Coating his company with patriotic guise, and charged with a bogus militaristic vocabulary, "Field Marshall" Lawrence called Ford sales "practical patriotism," and he took great pains in his sales bulletins to confirm Ford's old refrain on the Model T as a Canadian-made motorcar sold by Canadian dealers and serviced by Canadian technicians with Canadian-made parts.[11] Whatever message was received by farmers and other buyers, for whom practical factors such as cost were likely more important, the appropriation of the Made in Canada movement by McGregor, Lawrence, and their colleagues stood out as smart marketing, even in an environment of industrial advertising saturated with patriotic motivation. Ford Canada's boastful claim to be "the vital factor in Canada's industrial awakening" generated skepticism among London and Toronto businessmen and municipal politicians, but if Ford's output was any indication, the claim was not without foundation.[12]

Although the Ford plant was "practically at a shut down" between October 1914 and March 1915 while the crane building was being completed, sales records were still being set at the Saint John, London, and Winnipeg branches. Nor was McGregor idle. In a "pep" meeting on 19 January, he and Lawrence hosted dealers from Essex, Kent, and Lambton counties to discuss Ford policies, tour the Walkerville plant, and attend the Detroit auto show. Rumors and public scrutiny of the firm—a corollary of its high profile—could lead to misunderstandings that would frustrate and annoy McGregor. In January 1915 the firm's cancellation of its Ontario charter, which Ford Canada no longer needed because of its broader federal charter, panicked some journalists and Ford watchers into believing that Henry Ford was pulling out of Canada. Strong denials by McGregor's office appeared in the *Evening Record* on 19 January and in the *Ford Sales Bulletin* in February.[13]

Even Henry Ford himself could be a cause for worry. Ford's erratic path was a matter of proven concern to McGregor, although he exercised great discretion in any commentary. The *Evening Record* was especially cooperative. It published a summary of Henry Ford's testimony in New York City on 22 January before the American government's industrial relations committee. His year-old profit-sharing plan, the paper reported, had increased efficiency, given some money back to his workers, and reduced daily absenteeism from 10 percent of his workforce to 0.3 percent. What the sympathetic report did not convey was Ford's fumbling performance after reading a prepared statement. When pressed, according to the transcript, he could not clearly explain the "machinery" and viability of the scheme, particularly how future profits and employee productivity could be accurately forecast. Underlying the interrogation was the fact that the scheme had little to do with profits at all. Questioned about his attitude to organized labor, Ford (without reference to the company's repression of worker resistance, including the unproductive efforts in 1913 of the Industrial Workers of the World) responded coyly that he ran an open shop. "I don't know anything about organized labor. We have never had any of it, to my knowledge, around our place."[14]

McGregor had experience trying to manage the impact in Canada of Ford's public pronouncements. Just as challenging was implementing Detroit-made policy and dealing with cross-border trade conditions in wartime. Adept at calculating currency differences, McGregor's accountants set to work to figure out how manufacturing costs could be adjusted to absorb (or so the company advertised) the new war tax of an additional 7.5 percent on imports from the United States, effective 12 February. Ford Canada still used some "special" steel and other materials from the United States.[15]

Such concerns, however, never tied McGregor to his office. One gets the impression that he was never addicted to work. On 20 February he and his wife left for a vacation in one of James Couzens's haunts, Asheville, North Carolina, where, among other resorts, the newly opened Grove Park Inn and golf course were attracting the likes of Henry Ford, his friend Thomas Alva Edison, and American president Woodrow Wilson. A nephew recalled McGregor coming back from one of his southern trips in Henry Ford's private railway car.[16]

By mid-February 1915, McGregor's plant, with the expansion nearly completed, had reopened, and immediately the factory set to work to reach new levels of production. "Faster" production was the goal, reported the *Evening Record*, which recorded a rapid escalation of daily output: 85 automobiles on 23 February, 100 on 4 March, 144 on 23 March, and 171 on 23 April. In March a night shift was instituted. The introduction of more and more automated machinery increased the number of "unskilled" laborers, a trend noted by the federal *Labour Gazette* in May. Even the thirty punch-in clocks obtained from the International Time Recording Company of Toronto and installed the previous December were billed as "30 units in Ford efficiency" by *Maclean's Magazine*.[17]

Elsewhere, the company's new Toronto branch, a five-story building on Dupont Street, opened on 22–27 February with a profusion of flowers, palms, and bay trees. At a luncheon one day, area dealers were addressed by Neil Lawrence and entertained by pianist Jules Brazil. With the cancellation because of the war of the regular CNE show sponsored by the Toronto Automobile Trade Association, the branch hosted its own event, including "a motion picture show of the latest Ford films" and another address by the effervescent Lawrence. In March, the branch entertained a group of top municipal officials from Peterborough, Ontario, led by Ford dealer and alderman Joseph James Duffus. Earlier, in January, McGregor and Lawrence had attended Montreal's annual auto show, the only spring show still running within the empire. Opened by federal secretary of state Louis Coderre and set with displays of Canadian-made warplanes and armored cars, it was hosted at Ford's new Montreal branch building. Staff there had been taking solid strides in selling Ford cars. A "general educational campaign" had been launched to demonstrate the Model T's stated capability of running under severe winter conditions. (Until Montreal started clearing its streets in the winter, beginning around 1914, most car owners put their vehicles away for the season.)[18]

Such progress was good news. McGregor spent an inordinate amount of time, with Campbell and Lawrence, tracking branch finances and capabilities. As the Ontario Motor League's *Canadian Motorist* would explain in July, Ford Canada's "home factory is up against a problem. It is already the largest automobile manufacturing plant in the British Empire, with an output of a car every three minutes—still this does not supply the demand. The only logical way to increase production is to erect assembly plants where the demand is the heaviest," ship the partly disassembled Ford cars in crates, and charge the costs to the branches. The company did exactly that.[19]

After his return from North Carolina in the spring of 1915, McGregor and his executives, acting under pressure from Henry Ford and James Couzens, met with them to plan an important, not totally surprising initiative by Ford Canada. On 20 April its board of directors formally approved an increased wage scale for employees. The following day, at noon on the shop floor, surrounded by a prearranged, tightly packed group of workers, McGregor announced his company's adoption of a minimum wage of $4, an eight-hour day, and a forty-eight-hour week, effective 16 April. As anticipated, pandemonium ensued: elated workers cheered the increase and McGregor and his staff flashed "beams of joy," the *Evening Record* reported. A photographer captured the moment. The account in the Ford-loving *Canadian Motorist* was even more effusive: in a "monster demonstration," the workers cheered Henry Ford, McGregor, and the other officers present, "whose popularity with the working force is unbounded."[20] This assessment was clearly an exaggeration—within months McGregor would be secretly hiring Pinkerton detectives to sniff out mysterious problems in his plant, as we will see below.

The April announcement put Walkerville in line with the policy at Highland Park. That was critical, but the move also calmed any simmering concerns within the labor force, reducing turnover so that aggressive production was not impeded. The size of the increase and its delayed timing undoubtedly had much to do too with the finances of Ford Canada, which McGregor monitored, including the salary rolls. The increase came laden with the populist rubric of profit sharing. The $4 day was less than Ford Detroit was offering, but it was still well above the industry standard in the Border Cities. How many actually benefited from the plan is as uncertain as the degree of benefit at Ford Detroit. One historian suggests that no more than 5 to 10 percent of the workers there were barred from the scheme. Another asserts that in 1916 Ford Detroit had thousands of workers on probation, paying them cut rates, and dispensing with them as necessary as a controllable workforce. A machinist of the time recalled that the wage was paid only after a worker had been with the firm for six months and had proven his ability to maintain a high quota. In his stinging critique of Ford's experiment in welfare capitalism, Stephen Meyer concludes that no more than 50 percent of Ford workers were eligible.[21]

McGregor's announcement, which extended to the branches, caught the attention of the press in Toronto and London, Ontario. After the initial rush of publicity, however, Canadian workers, like their Detroit counterparts, came to realize that not everyone would receive the increase in what the *American Machinist* had dismissed as "Henry Ford's bonus game."[22] To qualify, McGregor himself explained, following the precedent of Ford Detroit's sociological department, employees had to undergo in-home examinations by a small staff of "investigators" to ensure that acceptable standards of living, cleanliness, and thrift were followed. At the same time, employees would be given access to doctors, lawyers, "educational clubs," and, for foreign workers, interpreters and classes in reading and writing English taught by volunteers from within the company.[23] *Ford Times* told the public the classes were for "making new Canadians" and "good citizens." This "Department of Education," or "Sociological Department," was to be headed by Ford Canada's assistant superintendent, Lawrence W. Lee, brother of John R. Lee, the former engineer who ran Ford Detroit's sociological department. "The Ford idea is to make a life, not a mere existence," L. W. Lee later explained, before enlisting and going overseas.[24] In content and intent, the program at Ford Canada merely substituted Canadianization for Americanization, with a deep-rooted, middle-class paternalism.

In Lee's seemingly honest estimate, between April 1915 and June 1917 the plan contributed to a stunning 1,000 percent decrease in the turnover in hiring. Ford Canada's intensification of automated machinery had created a new level of technology and a large unskilled labor force. The situation had drawn workers from throughout southwest Ontario, a flow that went back and forth across the Detroit River. As a result, the housing shortage in Ford City became acute. The population of 563 at the village's incorporation shot up to more than 3,000 in the fall of 1916—a sure sign to the board of trade types of the industrial vibrancy of the Border Cities. Ironically, a company cartoon on the wage raise in the *Ford Sales Bulletin* in May 1915 depicts a worker dreaming, with new hope, of owning a lovely house and being able to concentrate without worry on his

Ford Canada's interpretation of its workers' response to the pay raise of April 1915. *Ford Sales Bulletin*, 1 May 1915. Photograph by Mark Coatsworth.

"REAL job" at the Ford plant. This cartoon gave graphic illustration to the sociological department's view of the single-family home as the anchor of moral and social values.[25] (Henry Ford disliked boardinghouses.) It was not by coincidence that at Ford Detroit the highest percentages of "good" family homes (in the estimate of the sociological department) were held by Canadian (97 percent) and English (96 percent) workers. Even with increased pay packets for many, the situation was rife for union activity.

By late 1916 jurisdictional disputes had surfaced within the auto industry in Detroit among the American Federation of Labor, the International Association of Machinists (IAM), and the Carriage, Wagon, and Automobile Workers. It was the IAM that carried the gauntlet across the border. Ford workers may have known of (if they were not involved in) the dispute in Canada between the machinists' union and an incipient autoworkers' union in 1915. The IAM led organizing activity in Toronto in 1916, and in June–July 1918 it conducted a strike over female membership at Russell Motor Car.[26] There is no clear evidence of organized activity at Ford Canada in 1915–17, although there were instances of suspected industrial sabotage, but the IAM, whose auto plant members witnessed a dramatic change in skill levels, would gain a foothold there before the war was over.

The decrease in turnover cited by Lee was one of the company's main objectives. McGregor sternly denied any paternalistic intent: "undesirable" employees would be warned and then disqualified for any pay increase or have it withheld. In a profession of concern for "community conditions," he risked insulting some of his employees by taking particular aim at the eastern European element in Ford City and on Marion Avenue in Windsor.[27] Throughout the war, the *Evening Record*'s reports of fighting, sickness, boarders, bootlegging, and liquor raids among the "Poles" and the riot-prone Russians—Ford City remained a dry town—illustrated McGregor's concern, though criminal and unsavory activity among other sectors of his workforce was not unknown. To offer justification of McGregor's concern, on 23 June the *Evening Record* printed a letter from one Isadore Cherniak under the headline "Since Ford Wage Increase, Polish Colony on Marion Avenue Has Undergone Transformation." The residents there, many of whom worked at Ford, had experienced improvement: "they have been instructed in better home-building and encouraged to improve the standard of citizenship."[28] To put the impact in beneficial perspective, the company reported the numbers in Lee's English reading and writing classes, ranging from 247 in 1916 to 120 in 1917.[29]

Production head George Dickert later recalled the sociological department's investigations, which he believed did not go as far as those at Ford Detroit, nor did they provoke any resentment "as being paternalistic." Some of the employee files maintained by the department survive in Ford Canada's archives; they are too few to allow of any comprehensive analysis, though some confirm input by McGregor. An assessment of the Walkerville department, however, might reflect some of the findings of historical analyses of the department in Detroit: its infringement of privacy, its genuine aid to some, its role in labor management, and its promotion of work and domestic ethics. Labor management in particular springs from Lee's comments on turnover. Concurrent with the sociological department and the new pay scales were new, centralized employment practices that also reduced, dramatically, arbitrary discharges by foremen and allowed the company to counter casual attitudes to attendance and curb absenteeism. Ford was not the only automaker to create employment departments to take control of erratic discipline as a way of curbing worker resistance and departures. Paige-Detroit, Packard, Haynes, and Saxon Motor Car all created formal employment departments in order to reduce labor turnover, and it would be surprising if McGregor had not known of such results.[30] Any discontent bred of escalating production in Walkerville in 1915, plant expansion, unrelenting pressures for workers to speed up, quotas, and discipline may well have been tempered by McGregor's pay and work announcements of 21 April 1915. At Ford Detroit there had been a rush to secure jobs there, an attraction that did not fade until the 1920s.

The drive for industrial efficiency (including the control of labor) in this era carried moral and patriotic meanings that would not be lost within Ford or the Border Cities in wartime.[31] The ethos of efficiency and its measurement pervaded the Ford system; among the machinists, efficiency meant pressure to meet high quotas on finished parts. The efficiency clubs found among Ford employees in Detroit in 1915 may have existed in Walkerville. In September 1916 one Ford Canada official boasted, "[E]fficiency has been reduced to an exact science." That same year company advertising even promoted the "efficient" service and customer relations to be found at local Ford garages and dealerships, though photographs found across Canada reveal some truly dingy outposts. Reports of efficiency as the percentage ratio of orders against estimates of sales fill the Canadian *Ford Sales Bulletin* from 1913. The company vigorously promoted "efficiency clubs" at the branch and dealer levels and measures to increase speed on the assembly line. The Toronto branch, for one, held frequent internal "efficiency meetings." In public, McGregor viewed the speedup in simple terms as a positive: the production of a record number of cars by the same-sized workforce in fewer hours was proof, he told *Canadian Motorist* (echoing Henry Ford) that "it is just good business to pay men well."[32]

After his April announcement, McGregor had every reason to look forward to months of solid production and the personal leisure that was now an enjoyable adjunct of his executive success. On 25 April he left for Winnipeg and Vancouver on business. In Winnipeg he had to complete the legal work for the new assembly building that was being opened there. The following month the *Financial Post* found him bullish on Canadian business in general and looking for a "coastal" site somewhere for another new assembly plant.[33] At the end of July the company cancelled its buyers' rebate program because sales for the year (18,774 automobiles) had failed to reach the target needed (an overly optimistic 30,000) to allow the company to honor the "profit sharing certificates" issued to buyers. The company's claim that the increased American tax on steel was a factor contradicted its intent to absorb the tariff, as boasted in advertisements. Once again profit sharing was more of a lure than a reality: in the end, the program had provided superb advertising and incentive. To the press McGregor reported a 50 percent increase in Ford's export trade due largely to Britain and France being "out of business"—he was not above exaggeration—but in reality his own overseas business was being affected by the war. In Australia, sales fell off dramatically in early 1915, leaving dealers there with thousands of unsold Model Ts. Negotiations with a representative sent by McGregor reportedly led to a hold on new shipments and heavy price slashing, which advertisements attributed to the Canadian company's increased production and reduction in manufacturing costs.[34] Reports of a hold on shipments are seriously undermined, however, by Ford Canada's aggressiveness, as demonstrated by its own record of exports to Australia in 1915–16: 5,234 cars and 1,268 chassis.

None of these circumstances appears to have worried McGregor excessively—there were always ebbs and flows in the automobile industry—and the war provided no reason to alter his lifestyle and pattern of social advancement. He was first elected on 7 May to the board of directors of the Essex Golf and Country Club, his daughters Elizabeth and Harriet drew smiles as flower girls at a garden party put on in June by the Mary Gooderham Chapter of the Imperial Order Daughters of the Empire (IODE), in which their mother was active, and the family headed into a summer at their cottage near Kingsville. Wallace Campbell and Walter and Don McGregor also had summer homes there, and Detroit novelist William Levington Comfort was a neighbor. The Ford factory closed as usual for inventory for two weeks in July–August. (Shutdowns at other times would be caused by, among other factors, shortages of natural gas from the fields in Tilbury Township.) In September the three McGregor brothers, Gordon, Don, and Walter (then president of McGregor Banwell Fence, which made wire fencing and springs and seats for Ford cars), joined others at the flag-festooned golf club to fête Captain George Wilkinson, who had been wounded in Europe.[35] Brother Malcolm would not come over much from Detroit until after 1926, when he bought a summer home in Amherstburg.

In July Gordon had returned from his cottage to address the board of trade, which was as keen as ever to bring new industries to the Border Cities. As always, McGregor advocated better roads—the good-roads movement was now in full swing throughout Canada—and he proudly invited members to visit his expanded machine plant when it was finished. It was being built out into the Detroit River parallel to his factory, a sure sign that Ford was being constricted on its narrow lot between the river and Sandwich Street. He also urged members, prophetically, to begin thinking of the adjoining border towns as "practically one urban community."[36] (Within a year he would be giving solid substance to this message.) The following August the industrial promotions of McGregor and others resulted in the formation of the Windsor Bureau of Industry. At the end of September, after a second successful industrial exhibition—"the usual large number of Ford worshippers" flocked to the exhibits of Universal Car—the *Evening Record* ran a special article on Ford City ("the town that an industry built") and drew commentary from McGregor. It could always count on him for a quotation, however flat, on his company and its prospects. In this instance, western Canadian prosperity meant good fortune for Ford and other eastern industries: "If the crop indicated in the west is successfully harvested and marketed, the manufacturers of the east will profit largely, just as will the merchants of the west," claimed McGregor, who understood what historian G. T. Bloomfield has described as "the complex linkages between wheat prices, farm incomes and the cycles of automobile buying" in this period.[37]

If plentiful western crops were good for business, so too was the economic stimulus of the war and the Made in Canada opportunity. On 21 June a shocking disruption struck the center of the Border Cities. A massive detonation rocked Walkerville's Peabody garment factory, which was then manufacturing military uniforms. The Windsor Armouries were also targeted but the explosives there did not go off. Furthermore, dynamite was found planted at the Gramm Motor Truck works in Walkerville and in a boardinghouse in Ford City, occupied, the *Evening Record* claimed, by "Ford labourers of many nationalities." Investigations by the local police and Pinkerton detectives called in by Arthur Percy Sherwood, head of the Dominion Police, focused on Albert Kaltschmidt, a German national married to an American and resident in Detroit. He had legitimate business interests there and in the Tate Electric car plant in Windsor, where the Peabody and armories explosives had been assembled. Inquiries, arrests, and trials carried on through the summer, reports filled the *Evening Record*, and the Home Guard was omnipresent.[38]

The public did not know about the security threats faced by McGregor between July 1915 and January 1916, even as he was delivering optimistic messages to the board of trade and elsewhere. Unwilling to risk any public investigation, further scares, or possible loss of confidence and business, he secretly opened a "special" private account at the Merchants' Bank of Canada in Windsor. On 8 September he deposited $2,000. Over the next five months checks from the account were written to, and only to, the Detroit office of the Pinkerton National Detective Agency for the following services, rendered as stark bank statements:

2–21 July 1915, "Susp. Depr. [Suspected Depredations], Ford City Plant"

12–13 August, account "in re 'Stephen Cozak'"

1–31 October, "Suspected Depredations—Ford City"

1–31 December, "Susp.—Depredations—Ford City"

The nature of any depredations, the puzzling identity of Cozak, and Pinkerton's findings are unknown, but this financial evidence points to some form of industrial sabotage that a greatly concerned McGregor was determined to cover up but not ignore. In a community traumatized by the Peabody blast, this cover-up was no small achievement, though it was not unusual to see Pinkerton's men around town checking into the blast and assorted petty crime at the Windsor racetrack.[39]

Far more problematic for McGregor was Henry Ford's unwitting insensitivity to Canada and his Canadian managers in wartime. One major concern stemmed from farmers' demands for cheap gasoline-powered tractors. Many simply adapted their Model Ts—conversion kits were available in Canada as well as the United States. In the spring of 1915, with maximum press coverage, Henry Ford announced his intention to build a tractor. A prototype was demonstrated at the Michigan State Fair in September, and within a month a plant was being erected in Dearborn, but delays set in and the first production model of the Fordson tractor would not appear until 1917. In the initial flurry of promotion, Ford stated in September 1915 that a tractor plant would also be built near McGregor's factory in Ford City, then in the midst of a chaotic industrial and real estate boom. Any plans for a tractor factory there, however, were soon abandoned as production schemes in Dearborn fell apart. Undoubtedly dismayed, McGregor began wondering if his original agreement with Ford entitled him to build tractors on his own.[40]

But it was over the war, not tractors, that Henry Ford truly became a publicist's nightmare and, at times, an unshakeable burden to McGregor. At some levels, accommodating Ford's legendary spitefulness was easy, though the results could look strained, even if cloaked in wartime associations. For instance, Ford's dislike of the Dodge brothers for using their Ford dividends to finance a revival company surfaced in May 1915 in the Canadian *Ford Sales Bulletin*, where a comparison of their "mediocre" mechanical ability to Ford's technical originality was likened to a cockney corporal next to British military leader Lord Kitchener, whom Canadians would know well. Dealing with Ford's own position on the war was another matter. Fed on a rich diet of publicity and adulation, and drawn by the pacifist notions of populist William Jennings Bryan, Ford cast himself as an antiwar spokesman, but with none of the religious or intellectual underpinnings of a true pacifist. Speaking through the *New York Times* and other channels, in early 1915 he began developing his own populist interpretation of the European war as a murderous fracas driven by munitions makers and New York financiers. At a press conference in June on tractors, he set out his vision of creating a machine that would allow the small farmer to work his land and forestall the absentee owner; in pure, twisted Ford logic, by keeping its rural folk working, America would never be drawn into the war. That summer Ford took part in an unofficial peace conference along with Thomas A. Edison and Philadelphia merchant John Wanamaker, whose sage advice on persistent advertising was given cachet in Ford Canada literature.[41]

Ford's sentiments inevitably found their way across the Detroit River. Initially, McGregor and the *Evening Record* received them without comment. Ford had some sympathizers in Ontario, among them James Alexander Macdonald, editor of the *Toronto Globe*. Ford's naturalist friend Jack Miner would recall Ford's folksy resolve during a visit to his Kingsville home. Ford looked him "straight in the face and, with pale-faced earnestness, said 'Jack, if I could stop the war I would willingly give every cent I have on earth, and I'd start in, anew, with my naked hands.'" The antiwar position of Macdonald, his participation in peace rallies in the United States, and his links with American leaders who resisted involvement in the war all stirred controversy in the Toronto press. His address on disarmament in Detroit on 11 April drew from Ford the "spontaneous gift of a motor-car as a tribute."[42]

Ford's reaction to the Allied war loan pulled the hitherto quiet, and genuinely patriotic, McGregor into the controversy. On 10 September a joint Anglo-French high commission had landed in New York for the purpose of securing a loan. J. P. Morgan and Company obliged by signing a contract on the 25th and spreading the loan over a syndicate of sixty-one financial houses in New York. Ford responded with hostility and some sensationalism in the New York press: "If any of the Banks which have money belonging to the Ford Motor Co., or to me personally, participate in the Anglo-French Loan, I will withdraw every penny from them. If I had my way, I would tie a tin-can to the Anglo-French Commissioners and send them back where they came from."[43] The remarks sparked immediate reaction in wartime Canada, nowhere more than in the Border Cities, where McGregor and his staff hastened to control the damage.

On 30 September the normally adulatory *Evening Record* branded Henry Ford a "lamentable failure" for his statements on the war loan. Stinging critiques came from the Toronto press and Border Cities clergy, newspapers scrambled to cancel Ford advertising, the federal minister of militia and defense, Samuel Hughes, fired off statements of dismay, and even the British press had a say. In Toronto the *Monetary Times* wondered, if Henry Ford wanted to end the war, why he did not fund the loan. "That act would help in the most practical way to accomplish the end, the theoretical aspects of which Mr. Ford seems to cherish devoutly." The City of Toronto implemented a boycott of purchases of Ford cars for municipal departments. Accounts circulated of decisions by the Dodge brothers and Windsor businessmen Edgar Nelson Bartlet (McGregor's brother-in-law) and A. D. Bowlby (an early associate) to sell their shares in Ford Canada. Bartlet and Bowlby later explained that they had sold only some of their shares, and those before Henry Ford's incendiary remarks; the Dodge sale put $800,000 worth of stock on the market.[44]

On 6 October the *Evening Record* repeated the inevitable question, first posed by the *Globe:* was Ford Canada "in any way committed to the policy announced by Mr. Ford of withdrawing Ford company funds from any bank which participates in a loan to the allies?" In a difficult and highly embarrassing position, McGregor defended his company as best he could, with no initial support from Detroit. A sympathetic *Evening Record* gave him an opening: it doubted if Ford Canada was committed to the "Ford boycott." McGregor quickly responded that, of course, his mostly (78 percent)

Canadian-owned company and his staff were "absolutely with the allies." He was committed with others to organizing a Ford City branch of the Canadian Patriotic Fund and to raising funds for the Red Cross Society. Moreover, over 300 Ford employees had left for the European front. Diplomatically, but lamely, he tried to distance himself from Henry Ford without being offensive: he doubted if his boss had been correctly understood and if his remarks were ever intended for publication. Behind the scenes, he asked for some show of support from his Detroit associates and from Ford himself. On 14 October Ford obliged, in the form of a $10,000 check to the Canadian Red Cross Fund, an unusual gesture in light of Ford's reputed preference for closely directing the philanthropies he supported. (His tax returns, however, suggest a wide generosity.) In addition, according to McGregor, Ford instructed him to tell Canadians that he was "with them heart and soul." Other contrived releases would follow in November. In reiterating his plans for a tractor factory in Ford City, Ford maintained "it will be a Canadian industry, built up by Canadians for the advantage of Canada. That is the kind of thing I want most of all to do." On 8 November the *Evening Record* reprinted the soft interview with Ford by his friend J. A. Macdonald of the *Globe*, who had caught up with the auto tycoon in Colorado—Henry Ford was not one to stay in Detroit to soothe Canadian sensitivities. In typical vacillation, he flatly denied the statements attributed to him about the war loan. Although he denounced militarism, he professed support: "I feel with all Canadians in this awful time, and if I thought that Canada was in peril every wheel in the Ford factories would be set to turning out munitions." Blunter, more aggressive words by Ford, in the *Globe* of 14 October, did not surface in the *Evening Record:* "As for the threats in Canada to boycott me or my product, they are the machinations of politicians. All the boycotts that Canadian politicians are threatening will have nothing to do with the public demand for the Ford cars."[45]

Ford was right, but for McGregor the "Tin Can Episode" (as the *Monetary Times* dubbed it) needed more than Ford's words for resolution. Unlike the flinty Ford, he worried greatly about boycotts and negative publicity. As a Canadian and a major industrialist, he saw the need for concrete, newsworthy gestures of local support by Ford Canada for the war effort. Organized on 11 October, the Ford City branch of the Canadian Patriotic Fund was very much a Ford Canada–McGregor operation: Walter McGregor was president, Neil Lawrence headed publicity, and Gordon McGregor and others directed the all-important industrial committee. Here was the start of Ford Canada's dominant role in the war effort in the Border Cities. By 28 October the leading contributors to the Ford City fund were Henry Ford (his $10,000 donation to the Red Cross), Ford Canada's officers and shareholders ($22,725.75), Ford's employees ($36,578.64), Gordon McGregor ($5,000), and Wallace Campbell ($1,500). Within the Ford ranks, the motivation may well have been a blend of some coercive sense with patriotism. Money also poured into Windsor's patriotic fund, and McGregor prematurely announced (with Canadawide publicity) that his company would raise $1 million for the Canadian war loan (separate from the Allied loan), with subscription lists to run from 22 to 30 November. Within days, however, Henry Ford was back in the news with his naïve "peace ship" initiative, dreams of a European peace conference, and still hazy notions of how "money" was the cause of the war. This time, fortunately for McGregor, editorials in the *Evening Record* and publicity elsewhere were personally derisive and aimed straight at the "Skipper," meaning Henry Ford. From another quarter, Dominion Police commissioner A. P. Sherwood had begun taking serious interest in Ford's antics.[46]

Throughout the Ford fiasco, business had been carried on steadily, with one notable break, the startling resignation of Ford's strategist and McGregor's mentor, James Couzens, as vice president, treasurer, and general manager of Ford Detroit on 12 October and as vice president of Ford Canada a day later. Whatever the professed causes—Couzens's statements in the press over a fundamental disagreement with Ford's stand on the war are contradictory—an irreparable rift had been developing between these two headstrong figures for some time. According to John Dodge, Ford believed that Couzens's methodical approach to growth was too cautious. Couzens, who was now in public service as chair of the Detroit Street Railway Commission, claimed he had become "nauseated" with just "making money," though he would retain both his seat on Ford's board and his substantial stake in the company. At the Canadian directors' meeting of 13 October, McGregor was formally appointed vice president, treasurer, and general manager for Ford Canada, with Wallace Campbell succeeding him as secretary. Still a director, Couzens moved to increase McGregor's salary. (His salary for 1915 at year-end was $25,000, plus dividends, bonuses, and other income.) In a warm letter of thanks on the 18th, McGregor asked him to remain on the Canadian board "so that I may have the benefit of your experience and counsel same as in the years gone by. There are many reasons why you should retain your association which I want to discuss with you." (Couzens would stay, as second vice president.) Two days later, with a chuckle, McGregor declined to comment on rumors from a newspaper in Chatham (Couzens's hometown) that Couzens would join the Canadian company as a working executive, that it would break away from Ford Detroit, and that Henry Ford had agreed to sell his shares in his Canadian firm.[47]

McGregor was forever being pelted with such rumors, some from the Detroit side, others from small-town Canada. Despite the formal break with Couzens as a kingpin in Ford Detroit, McGregor continued to correspond with him, in friendly exchanges on Canadian business and for advice, for the next three years at least, until Couzens, as police commissioner and then mayor of Detroit, no longer had time or sufficient knowledge of Ford's inside workings. Though no one could match his long experience and skills, he was replaced in Detroit by Frank L. Klingensmith, who had started as a clerk under Couzens and had risen to become his assistant. McGregor could work with him—he had replaced John Dodge on the Canadian board in 1913—but McGregor would never be as dependent on him as he had been on James Couzens.

McGregor rode out the year in fairly buoyant fashion. A well-timed gesture, Henry Ford's $10,000 check for the Red Cross arrived on 14 October, though it was slow to reach Red Cross officials. The Canadian Ford company was flourishing. In commentary and in photographs—of the bustle at quitting time or of 1,750 Ford employees blocking a street for an impressive group shot—the *Evening Record* gave the company attention that was bestowed on no other local enterprise. On 25 October shareholders voted a massive 600 percent dividend on an annual profit (to 30 September) of $3,202,458.15. By contrast, Russell Motor Car, in the two years ending 31 July, had suffered losses of more than $700,000, and would soon have its motorcar business taken over by Willys-Overland of Ohio. In November, McGregor had Toronto city alderman Robert

H. Cameron lobby the municipal board of control over its ban on Ford cars—the company's public image was more at stake here than numbers of automobiles. In opposition, city controller Francis Stephen Spence had no sympathy: since Henry Ford was president of Ford Canada, "anything he did reacted on those under him."[48]

Nonetheless, business went on. In Ford City, more property was acquired for expansion south of Sandwich Street; one lot was purchased from John Stodgell (an original shareholder) and his wife, Emma, for $11,000 on 17 November. On 14 December a special meeting of shareholders authorized a needed increase in the company's capital stock from $1 to $10 million, and, in another stunning display of profitability, a 100 percent dividend. That same day, the Judicial Committee of the Privy Council in England confirmed McGregor's personal claim to the ten original shares from the Curry estate, now worth some $200,000, not counting bonuses and dividends.[49]

This good news coincided with the completion in December of the machine shop expansion, a key sector for greater speed in production through the use of ever-bigger, largely automated machines (1,300 in all on a single, two-acre floor)—gear cutters, multiple drilling presses, mammoth milling and cylinder-boring machines, lifting and loading devices, and overhead rails. One new machine could mill forty-eight engine cylinders "at once with perfect accuracy." "Manufacturing Magic," *Ford Times* proudly called this expansion, which almost doubled the capacity of the former shop and reduced the plant's dependence on Detroit to just a few manufactured parts. Here, skills were defined by the maintenance and operation of complicated machinery. In January 1916 the firm would give notice that it planned to extend the plant farther out into the Detroit River. None of the internal assessments calculated the increase, or loss, of workers and skills caused by these expansions and upgraded equipment.[50]

In December, the same month that R. M. Jaffray did a feature piece on the local auto industry for *Motoring* (Toronto), McGregor's sense of well-being was high. His plant was approaching peak efficiency, the Pinkerton's investigation was winding down, Henry Ford was in neutral gear, and Ford Canada was doing its best to steer clear of a sordid little scandal in Ford City. Its police chief, Edward Marand, was under investigation for running an extortion racket

The McGregor clan at one of Gordon's favorite haunts, the Prince Farm clubhouse of the Essex County Golf and Country Club. Taken around 1917, during the Great War, this photograph includes Gordon and Hattie McGregor (upper left) and their children Bill and Harriet (front row, third and fourth from left). Courtesy of J. McGregor Dodds.

in which newly arrived foreigners were allegedly being swindled of their meager savings on promises of jobs at Ford Canada. Enriched, with increasing leisure time, and impressed with the progress of the patriotic fund, McGregor still felt he could or should do more. On 23 December, after the financially pressed Essex Golf and Country Club had acquired additional acreage, he assumed its cost and took steps for the course's remodeling and expansion, for which he lined up Ernest Way, a professional groundskeeper from the Detroit Golf Club, where his brother Malcolm was a member.[51]

The clearest exposition of his energized philanthropic drive came in an exchange with James Couzens, who, post-Ford, was devising his own concepts of corporate and personal responsibility. In politics and social policy, Couzens mixed Republicanism with views that some found "socialistic." On 16 December, McGregor brought him over to speak to the board of trade on his notions of "social science." Without reference to his work at Ford on wage increases, Couzens urged employers to take a genuine interest in their workers and pay them a worthwhile wage. He was critical of a public system in which social workers "were trying to do things without money." The following day, thinking he saw opportunity, McGregor wrote to Couzens, inviting him to join in meeting the request of the Essex Health Association (EHA) for financial aid to expand the two-year-old tuberculosis hospital at Union-on-the-Lake, between Kingsville and Leamington. A member of the advisory board of the EHA, McGregor laid out its case, including a statement from its treasurer, Annia R. Baird. In the frank, almost lecturing tone that McGregor had come to accept, Couzens said no. His allegiances were now to Detroit and to Michigan, which had their own tuberculars. He did not mention that he had already given $10,000 to a home for crippled children in Detroit. Not satisfied, McGregor wrote back on the 18th to point out that the Border Cities had few truly rich men "outside of the Walkers and probably a dozen others," that "practically half of this community" was dependent on the automobile industry, and that (with a reference to Couzens's birth in Kent County) an appreciable part of his wealth had come from Ford Canada. Some of its employees had been treated at Union, and because of a lack of space there, McGregor had recently had to make arrangements to send a man to a tubercular hospital in Muskoka, many hours north of Toronto. He then came to the crux of his appeal, and the restraints he had faced because of his link to Ford Detroit, which reflected its founder's aversion to public largesse:

> For years I have tried to carry out the regular policy of the Company and have made practically no contributions to any work of this kind, although I really have felt as a company that we should make some contributions to objects of this kind and then this money would be distributed equitably over the shareholders according to their holdings. However, I have tried to carry out the policy of the American Company in this respect and have refrained from making contributions which I really felt we should take care of and which were worthy, to say nothing of private subscriptions. The result of a condition

> of this kind is such, that being the head of this institution, wherever these things come up, I have had to refuse so far as the Company is concerned but it has left me the opportunity of heading personally practically every list which is brought out of this community for anything of this kind.

Shareholders in Detroit, who had received between $600,000 and $700,000 from Ford Canada, should join him. McGregor was ready to contribute—he would write his first check for the hospital project in October—and he thought that Couzens should be prepared to give, too. "I thoroughly believe that you and I have more money than we know what to do with and more money than any one man is entitled to and if we do not take up works of this kind, I do not know who else should. There isn't only the money, but there is a certain moral affect in interests of this kind which is of great benefit."[52] There is no record of McGregor ever expressing such motivation in public.

Unswayed by McGregor's beneficence and candor, Couzens, who openly acknowledged that he did have more money than he was entitled to, saw no connection "between citizenship and the source of our money." Government should do more, he added, "and in that connection I am a very strong advocate of the policies of Lloyd George," Britain's prime minister, who had introduced national health and unemployment insurance. There the matter rested, though McGregor would follow through in his support for the sanatorium building at Union, which would eventually open in October 1917, thanks in part to his donation of $9,000 and $5,000 from his father's estate. An obituary of G. M. McGregor would claim that his donation was made in memory of his infant son, Gordon, who had died in 1914.[53]

McGregor and Couzens resumed correspondence after Christmas, first regarding a sales flyer put out by the hitherto unknown George H. Smith, the Chevrolet dealer in Lucknow, Ontario. This cheaply made flyer featured the new Chevrolet 490, the model targeted to compete with the Model T and now being made by McLaughlin Motor Car in Oshawa. But that was not what had caught McGregor's eye. Into his pitch Smith brought Couzens, who, he claimed, had left Ford because of "Henry Ford's pro-German attitude regarding the war" and who was soon to throw his weight behind Chevrolet. The "pro-German" statement was actionable, McGregor thought, though he quickly added, "I do not know that we are particularly anxious to stir up any more publicity in this matter if we can avoid it." At the least an apology or a retraction should be demanded for the misrepresentation of Couzens's association, but McGregor first wanted his authorization. Not as sensitive as McGregor, Couzens advised him by telephone on the 28th definitely to steer clear of any statement on Henry Ford's attitude and to consider doing nothing about the Chevrolet flyer, which he felt would soon be forgotten—"the keeping up of the controversy always is more advertising for the other fellow"—and at any rate Smith hardly had a large audience.[54]

Gordon and Hattie McGregor and their children celebrated New Year's Day 1916 at a dinner given by Gordon's mother in honor of his sister and brother-in-law, George Malcolmson, who were visiting from Winnipeg. At work, he was relieved that Henry Ford's recent return from his dismally unsuccessful peace mission had generated no backlash against Ford Canada, though there was some indication that his ties to Detroit and the discredited Henry Ford were not ideal credentials within some financial circles in Canada. In appointing an agent to handle a transfer of stock to Couzens in early January, McGregor rejected the use of a trust company in Toronto because of the potential for delay and one in Detroit, which would cause "some objections in view of the present attitude in this country." In the end he delegated a young man in his office to handle the matter. Within weeks he had to contend with a more direct, clearer consequence of the war.[55]

As McGregor and Ford Canada moved into 1916, it became increasingly evident that the continued growth of the company, even with wartime stimulus, would still have to be reconciled with the fiscal and economic actions of the national government. In early February, after a short vacation in New York City with Hattie, Walter, and Walter's wife and mother-in-law, McGregor went to Ottawa, both to visit Essex South MP Mahlon K. Cowan, then in the hospital, and to talk to government officials about the forthcoming federal budget. Proposed on 15 February, it introduced (retroactive to the beginning of the war and effective until 4 August 1917) a direct tax on the excess business profits of companies, defined as a quarter of net profits above 7 percent. Some industrial journals grumbled, but there was no widespread objection to this politically necessary levy. The minister of finance, William Thomas White, was certain the tax was "comparatively small" and would force no company to discontinue operations. Only modest adjustments were made to the tax scheme—by March the starting date had been moved up to 1 January 1915. Nationally the assessment and collection processes were slow and complicated. As late as October 1916 a compliant Ford Canada was still holding $716,136 in reserve pending a final federal assessment. In the meantime, the tax had stirred debate in the Border Cities. The *Evening Record* felt that the tax would discourage new industry, and it cited the plans of two Detroit automakers (possibly Chalmers and Maxwell and perhaps a third, Saxon) to set up plants. "We need these American branch factories. They have been our life-blood in this district," the paper editorialized on 23 February. The Windsor Board of Trade agreed, and in a near unanimous vote moved that all local branch plants established since the war began should be exempt. (The Hiram Walker distillery would later claim exemption, unsuccessfully, on the grounds of reduced business because of Prohibition.) Only Gordon McGregor opposed the board's resolution. On big, national matters, compliance looked good; he likely knew, too, that the cross-border mindset was not fully understood elsewhere in Canada. There should be no discrimination, McGregor argued, though he did object to the retroactive nature of the tax. The matter was comfortably referred by the board to a special committee, of which McGregor was made a member. Though he would grow to resent the tax, he shifted his arguments as expedient to cover corporate decisions. What the Ford City Board of Trade, of which Walter McGregor was president, thought is unknown.[56]

So much news in the *Evening Record* was auto based, and not just on dry issues such as taxation. Over a period of days the newspaper reported that a test-driver for Hupp hit a group of students and was charged with manslaughter and a ring of auto thieves was making car owners nervous. R. M. Jaffray remained a tireless promoter (he still frequented all the major auto shows), and social and industrial news and views from Ford Canada were constants. The newspaper gave the impression that the automotive industry set the standard for response on most issues. Though a number of producers had fallen by the wayside, the list in February 1916 was still impressive: three auto manufacturers (Ford, Hupp, and Studebaker, with Maxwell, Saxon, and Chalmers reportedly on the way), four truck makers (Gramm, Canadian Commercial, Menard, and New Dominion), and, in the fastest-growing sector, twenty-one parts and accessories manufacturers. Of all the heads of these outfits, none had a greater public profile in the Border Cities than McGregor, and none had the strength of his association with Detroit, although (in 1917) the managers of Maxwell (Louis Logie) and Studebaker (J. E. Grady) lived there. The manager of Chalmers, E. S. Jackson, lived on McGregor's street, but he never entered public discourse or participated much in society. Collectively, these auto men did not dominate associational life in the Border Cities to the extent that their counterparts and superiors in Detroit headed activity there.[57]

At Ford Canada the business profits tax was a minor diversion from meeting the monumental tasks of promoting and distributing the increased output made possible by the expansion of 1915. Ford and the *Evening Record* giddily reported one record after another as annual production jumped from 18,771 in August 1915 to 32,646 in August 1916, economies of manufacture forced prices down, and demand continued to outstrip supply. In February the company was boasting the emergence of a new car every three and a half minutes, but that was not enough. Some dealers, not content to wait for shipments, came to the plant to drive cars away. Although the output paled beside that at Ford Detroit (508,000 Model Ts by August 1916), it left Ford's Canadian competitors gasping: McLaughlin, for one, turned out only 7,796 Chevrolets in 1916. Making record numbers of Model Ts was one thing, avoiding congestion at the plant, getting the Ts to the dealers, and selling them were other matters. Though the market was developing—profits from servicing cars and selling parts were quickly catching up to retail sales—the flood of new Ts dictated that dealers handle only new automobiles. Dealers were pushed to sell the new coupelet and the closed sedan as distinctive models and to promote the concept of style change, though basically the cars remained Model Ts and underwent no substantial technical modification. At the time, "our company never took in used cars," explained H. R. (Pat) Cottingham, a road man and go-getter working out of the Montreal branch, though by September 1916 Don McGregor's trend-setting Universal Car Agency in

Windsor was advertising used Ford cars. (Company policy on handling used cars would not change until early 1918.)[58]

Buyers existed at every level for Ford cars. The rural press throughout Canada continued to identify the automobile in general as an essential tool, and companies were appearing to finance purchases and insure automobiles. The first transaction of Guaranty Securities Corporation in 1916 was the financing of a Ford chassis for a truck.[59] Though economies of manufacture allowed Ford Canada to reduce its prices, it could never take its eye off the ever-lower prices set by Ford Detroit. In 1916 Ford Canada dropped its prices, just as it had in 1914 and 1915, in part to remain competitive with the American T; foreign sales had to be made at American prices, which reduced the margin of profit. The most important structural change at Ford Canada in 1916, however, was devolution through the branches, which were made exclusively wholesale and assembly centers, with added responsibility for handling contract deposits and rebates from the dealers. "The idea of the Branch," shareholders were told by management on 23 October 1916, in strict accounting terms, "is to give us an output from the factory and make the Branch carry itself. In that case every possible expense which can be charged to the Branch is charged." As a result, automobiles were shipped out to the branches "broken down" in compact crates, but at the same freight charges as fully assembled automobiles.[60]

At the same meeting, company officials confessed without explanation that they were beginning to face "some very annoying and serious conditions in this country." The *Financial Post* had blithely claimed in July that "Canada has probably not been very seriously injured by the war so far," but conditions were changing fast, as McGregor and Ford Canada recognized. The decision to forgo any dividends was explained in this context, which shareholders could understand, though Henry Ford's decision in 1916 to cut American dividends severely, in favor of more funds for production and new factories, cannot be dismissed as unrelated. The main problem, however, was transportation. At some point in 1916 McGregor hired as traffic manager Frank A. Nancekevill, the former eastern representative of the American lines of the Canadian Pacific Railway. He had considerable experience analyzing and resolving transportation problems. The procurement of shipping to Australia and New

Zealand was also becoming problematic. No Ford cars were sent to Australia between September 1916 and August 1917, partly because dealers were still selling off the backlog from 1915–16. Moreover, one dealer there recalled, "trains were held up everywhere" because of the war.[61]

Within Canada, by June 1916, at which point the company was used to sending out a full trainload of motorcars daily, securing sufficient railway cars for automobiles was proving difficult. In a system where moving food and fuel had priorities, the problem, which was continentwide, flared as winter approached. On 23 November the *Detroit Free Press* sounded the auto industry's alarm over the railway car "famine," a concern soon heard in the Canadian press. Ford Detroit was forced to close between 22 December and 3 January. Recognizing the problems in sending sufficient numbers of automobiles to the branches, whose targets had already been set, Ford Canada had urged dealers to overstock "before the lack of means of transportation makes this impossible." In terms of contractual obligations to his branches, McGregor took steps to forestall problems. On 5 December, "on account of a condition which has arisen today," he wrote to the company's nine Canadian branch managers and one Australian head, asking each of them to confirm in writing that he had no contract or bonus clauses that the company would be obligated to honor. All complied—they had no choice. Though evidently clear to all at the time, no explanation of the "condition" was offered. The transportation, commercial, and daily presses, as well as Ford's corporate minutes, are mute, except to confirm railway car shortages and delays and low supplies of natural gas in the Border Cities. Anticipated backlash from Henry Ford's departure on 4 December on his peace expedition would be an understandable but remote possibility. The key probably lay in the convolution of the railway network, but still production and shipments climbed.[62]

As production geared up in 1915–16, so too did publicity. Filled with tips, photographs, and Ford stories from all across Canada and the empire, the ever-readable house journal, the *Ford Times*, was renamed (following the American edition) the *Ford News* in August 1916. Early that year McGregor had no difficulty luring the talented George E. Ranson away from Frederick Stearns, a Windsor pharmaceutical and confectionary firm, to establish a new publicity department at Ford. New, energetic advertising appeared that cleverly pushed the oneness of Ford production and efficiency, Made in Canada, and patriotic devotion. On 25 February 1916 the *Evening Record* ran a Ford advertisement that, on the one hand, seemed to distance the company from war production and Canada's sacrifices in Europe and, on the other, took victory for granted:

> The executives of the Canadian Ford Company make no consideration of the war. They are so thoroughly Canadian in their ideals that they take the prosperity of Canada and the triumph of Britain and her allies as accomplished facts.
>
> No stops have been made in their plans for progress—not the slightest hesitation has been evidenced in developing this great Canadian Plant to its highest degree of efficiency on account of the war.

As proof, other advertisements boasted that Ford had spent more than $1 million on new equipment since the beginning of the war and $1,724,000 on new buildings across Canada. The cost of non-Canadian parts was brought down to $16.88 per car in 1916, and hence the prices of the Model T could be cut.[63]

In February and March, in a rare, never-to-be-repeated venture into personalization, the company tried selling McGregor himself to non–Essex County readers through a full-page advertisement in the *Toronto Daily Star*, the *Canadian Motorist*, *Industrial Canada*, and probably elsewhere. (A feature on the unpopular Henry Ford would have been a difficult sell at this time.) Entitled "McGregor of Ford," the piece constituted a tightly linked chain: marching kilties, McGregor's Scottishness, his corporate heroics, Henry Ford's success, and Canada's foreordained victory in war. Even the wage increase of April 1915 had a place: "What an immense expression of confidence in the ultimate and unquestionable success of British Arms and the allied cause was this great wage increase." So too did film—silent film with subtitles—where Ford would shine: "the Company is spending thousands of dollars in moving pictures which are offered free to assist in recruiting work all over the Dominion."[64]

Ford excelled at the production of promotional film among industrial practitioners of the art. It was not new in 1916. By 1910 the Canadian Pacific Railway had pioneered the use of film to promote immigration to Canada. Much work originated in the border region. In 1914 a Windsor firm headed by American cinematographer Frederic Colburn Clarke, the All-Red Feature Company (meaning the red of the British empire), produced *The War Pigeon*, a drama about the War of 1812. It was released across the border, with little impact, by the British American Film Company of Detroit. For a few weeks after the start of World War I All-Red released weekly newsreels. By early 1916 films were being used in Canada for "industrial education"—the edification and enjoyment of employees.[65] Ford Canada tapped the new sense of Canadian self-awareness stimulated by the war, which in turn reinforced the company's campaign to create a Canadian image. In April 1914 Ford Detroit had established a motion picture department and begun the free release of factual one-reelers, the *Ford Educational Weekly*. It was this department's work that was shown at the Toronto branch opening in February 1915. The production of Model Ts was a popular early topic.[66]

Ford Canada had entered the cinematic field as early as February 1914, when highly popular lantern slides, stills of Ford automobiles, were being sent to moving-picture houses across the country to be shown between the regular reels—these directed viewers to their local Ford dealers. By April 1915 feature films made by Ford Detroit and special "Ford Nights" were drawing record crowds at cinemas throughout Canada. Supplied through the branches and pushed heavily by Neil Lawrence, the films cost the cinema proprietors nothing; the advertising value for Ford was immense. Though it is hard to imagine now, audiences were reportedly thrilled by films depicting "the final assembly of a thousand Ford cars in a single day in the Detroit plant and also the making of a Ford piston." Dealers were expected to take full advantage of this opportunity. Staples and Brebner of Ingersoll, Ontario, for instance, lined the street in front of the local cinema with Model Ts, placing on each a sign, "Ford Night," coordinating the event with newspaper advertising, circulars, and complimentary film tickets for prospective buyers. In Moose Jaw, Saskatchewan, dealers Manley and Slater distributed flyers that combined the film program with Ford advertising, and they ran a Model T through town "decked in Ford pennants."[67]

Ford film thus presented a winning opportunity that helped consolidate Ford's Canadian and imperial identity. Motion pictures were being produced at Ford Canada's plant before December 1915, when the venture was featured in *Ford Times.* There was an adventuresome, almost exotic quality about Model Ts in deep mud, deep snow, and deep dust. An alluring film by Ford Canada of a grueling motor trip across the Australian interior (*The Edge of Beyond*) and a corresponding travelogue in *Ford Times* were made before the announcement in March 1916 of George Ranson's plans to begin filming Canadian events as silent newsreels and travelogues.[68] Fascinating, if fragmented, footage survives (from Australian archival sources) of Windsor's boat race week in 1916 and of a *Ford Monthly* newsreel made that year featuring a variety of topics: Niagara Falls in winter, snowshoe racing in Montreal, the aftermath of the Parliament Buildings fire in Ottawa, a harrier race by the Vancouver Young Men's Christian Association, views of Cheakamus Canyon and Brandywine Falls in British Columbia, winter activities in Toronto's High Park, and the "amphibious" Model T made for military use and launched in Windsor by that "ingenious inventor" Oliver A. Light.[69] Although such films were not direct advertising, audiences likely made conscious connections between Ford, Canada, and popular entertainment. Ranson left Ford in November to return to Stearns, but his motion picture department remained a vital part of McGregor's publicity machine. It allowed a strong mix of advertising, nationalism related to the war effort, and the Made in Canada attachment. The fast imagery of motion pictures blended well with McGregor's effusive style of promotion and the sometimes-forced bonhomie engendered by Ford's heady success.

The emerging automotive clique in the Border Cities relished recognition, none more than McGregor. In May 1916 the board of trade was addressed by R. J. McLean of Detroit, former president of the board of trade in Wilmington, Delaware, and one-time secretary of the chamber of commerce in Spokane, Washington. "As Detroit is the leading automobile centre of the United States, it follows that Windsor will be the leading automobile centre of Canada," he told a receptive audience, McGregor among them. "This will be due to the fact that the automobile companies operating in Detroit are in a position to exercise close personal supervision over their plants in Windsor, on account of your proximity to Detroit." Here was Detroit's shadow looming large. After McLean's remarks, McGregor, who personified the connection, duly invited board members to visit his showpiece plant.[70] The invitation also went to the other boards of trade and the municipal councillors of the Border Cities. On Thursday, 11 May, they paraded—500 strong, according to one, surely exaggerated, report. Members proceeded in a "fleet of Fords" to the factory, where they were greeted on the top floor of the new crane-way building by McGregor, Wallace Campbell, George Ranson, and other officials. After lunch, at which Henry Ford was the special guest, the group inspected the plant, where the focus on production was omnipresent. They were impressed by the massive overhead traveling crane and "the evidence of efficiency," particularly the "scoreboard," which tallied 205 cars on Monday, 197 on Tuesday, 190 on Wednesday. When asked a few days later by the *Evening Record*, in an abrupt change of tone, about Henry Ford's change of plan on the tractor plant, to build not in Ford City but across town in Sandwich (but still with no hint of construction), McGregor uncharacteristically refused comment.[71]

The *Evening Record* rarely put its favorite industrialist in such an awkward position. Hardly ever did it look at Ford with an independent eye. When it came to the public activities of Ford employees, the same accommodating spirit guided the paper's choice of harmless events to report: the dances, the annual boat excursions and picnics, the Ford orchestra and glee club, the educational club, and the other groups and the sports teams. Such activities reflected the fact that, despite staff turnovers, not all workers were being demoralized by the infamous speedup in production or the numbing drills of "efficiency." Many workers thrived at Ford, and said so. The clubs and other internal organizations were not faceless groups: glee club president and Glasgow native George Macdonald was renowned for his "clever impersonations" of the famous Scottish comedian Harry Lauder—humor that McGregor enjoyed and commended.[72]

Few within the auto industry would have had much sympathy at year's end with the attempt by the hapless Mrs. Charlotte Heck, who lived near the Ford plant and whose health and sleep were reputedly being disrupted by its incessant noise and vibrations, to seek an injunction to stop the company from operating. The court hearing was adjourned to allow company officials to do "everything possible" to remedy the alleged conditions.[73] The outcome is unknown, though a settlement could be suspected—a small cost of doing business—and the machines kept on banging and grinding. Of all the atmospheric conditions that permeated the Ford plant, it was sound—the drone of production—that had changed most intensely since the static assembly days of 1904, a change that no newspaper recognized.

Despite the small nuisances and large problems that confronted McGregor and Ford as 1916 and early 1917 unfolded, McGregor seems to have delegated more and more authority. He found time for vacations, as usual, and eminently respectable public engagement, much in the manner that automakers in Detroit had come to dominate the board of commerce and the Employers' Association there. On 20 March he and his wife left for two weeks in White Sulphur Springs, a prestigious resort in West Virginia; on 28 June they moved for the summer to Kingsville, where brothers Don and Walter, sister Jean, and their families also had cottages, as well as a migratory host of other Windsor-area residents. Gordon urged Kingsville's council to repair Lakeview Avenue, which ran behind his cottage, and he later petitioned it about his water supply. Son Bill, who had once helped save three boys from a sinking duck boat, continued to enjoy the waterfront. In late July and early August the Ford plant closed for about two weeks for customary stocktaking. Between 26 October and 18 November, Gordon and Hattie were in Hot Springs, Virginia, another famed resort locale. In January 1917 they went to Winnipeg for a few days, arrayed in full evening attire, for what Walter called "their quarterly honeymoon." They left without taking any lunch, Walter added light-heartedly, "as Gord hates to carry packages and baskets. . . . They actually gave the impression that they were prosperous when they left." Later that winter, on 24 February, they set out for California to join brother Malcolm, his wife, and the travel-loving Mrs. McGregor Sr. for a month, a trip that included a visit to the Universal Pictures film studios in Hollywood.[74] The family reveled in the prosperity brought by the Model T, for which Ford Canada dropped its prices on 1 August.

McGregor's associational involvement reached new levels in 1916–17. So, too, did automotive traffic from Detroit following reciprocal car licensing. The discovery of dynamite in the Chalmers auto plant in Ford City in June caused some alarm among industrialists. But there were no signs of any sabotage at the Ford plant, and the smooth-running lines of production did not require McGregor's constant presence. Steadily he emerged as his company's chief contributor to the war effort and local philanthropies. The Essex Health

The McGregor family visits the "Cairo" set at Universal Pictures film studio, Hollywood, California, 1916. Courtesy of J. McGregor Dodds.

Association, the local chapters of the IODE and the Victorian Order of Nurses, the patriotic funds, and the YMCA all claimed his time and resources. Joining him were his wife (at teas, dances, and benefits) and Ford associate Wallace Campbell; the public came to know the McGregors' daughters, too, whose public performances of Highland dancing delighted no one more than their grandmother. Gordon McGregor's company and factory provided the staging for much of his public involvement. At a fund-raising affair put on by the IODE in October 1916 for the British Red Cross, Ford films were shown, featuring "Essex's Pride" (the 99th Battalion, formed the previous year with financial support from McGregor), the Rocky Mountains, and the lumber industry of Quebec. "That the audience greatly appreciated the efforts of the Ford Motor Co. of Canada to show the advantages and natural beauties of Canada was shown by continued applause," the *Evening Record* reported.[75]

Equal effort was expended by McGregor's mild-mannered brother Walter, who in June had been made lieutenant colonel and commanding officer of another Essex battalion, the 241st (the Canadian Scottish Borderers). Walter was quite prepared to recruit in the United States as well as Essex—at departure, a quarter of the battalion would be American—and in a typical display of Scottishness he was determined, with the help of $25,000 from Gordon, to dress the battalion in kilts of McGregor tartan. In the end he had to settle for khaki kilts and glengarries, but morale remained high, sustained by lawn parties, concerts, other fund-raising events, and picnics with the Clan Campbell organization of Detroit. Camp McGregor, a temporary base for the new battalion, was established in the area of Windsor south of Shepherd Street between Pelissier and Dougall. In November Gordon opened his plant and diverted staff time (valued at $2,500 by the *Evening Record*) for a huge parade and recruiting meeting in his crane-way building, all duly filmed by company crews. By December, however, the requisite number of recruits had not been reached. In desperation, recruiting committees were formed in every church in Ford City, Walkerville, Windsor, and Sandwich. As elsewhere, the war was taking a brutal toll in the Border Cities: columns of local patriotic news were counterpoised in the *Evening Record* by grim lists of casualties, Ford employees included.[76]

The state of enlistment and the need and value of Gordon's promotional machine are poignantly revealed in a January 1917 letter from Walter to their mother, then still in Hollywood. He did not care that the enlistment of Americans was illegal since the United States had still not entered the war. He thought that his battalion had too many Americans, but that was the way it had to be. At an IODE meeting in Walkerville, he was slated "to make a heart rending appeal to mothers and sisters to send their sons or brothers & who have already resisted any appeals made to them heretofore. . . . I do not expect one recruit as a direct result. Not a man from Windsor has joined in January. What we get are from Detroit. Some are British or Canuck born but mostly U.S." With mention of the bounteous auto industry, he credited this situation on enlistment first to the "prosperity here and second because all know now what war is no more romance. No flag waving patriotism not knowing what is at the other end." The strong, patriotic types, he knew, had gone "long ago."[77]

Despite Gordon McGregor's prominence and wartime involvement, he had always avoided elective office and direct military participation, preferring instead to exert his influence through his company, the board of trade, and the backrooms of the Liberal Party. In the provincial election of 1914, Essex North, Essex South, and Windsor had all elected Liberals, including J. C. Tolmie, McGregor's pastor and neighbor on Victoria Avenue. In June 1916 Sir Wilfrid Laurier canvassed McGregor to help fund the party's cash-strapped Information Bureau in Ottawa. "I understand from our friend John Bain," Laurier told McGregor, with reference to a local businessman and party organizer and then to McGregor's father, "that you are a true chip of the old block; that your heart is with the old cause, and that you are willing to help."[78]

Whatever attention McGregor could command in Ottawa, where Sir Robert Laird Borden's Conservatives were in power, his political interests still focused on the Border Cities, which he and others continued to view progressively as a metropolitan region with common needs. In 1916 the federal Commission of Conservation sponsored a local conference at which Ford City, Windsor, Sandwich, Walkerville, and Ojibway—all conscious of the turmoil caused by the housing shortage, industrial sprawl, and competing utilities—agreed to cooperate in a town-planning scheme. Little materialized beyond plans for the transformation of Ojibway into a steel town. In January 1917 the Windsor Board of Trade was reorganized as the more broad-reaching Border Chamber of Commerce. A provisional director, in March McGregor was elected a director at large and named to the organization's labor committee.[79]

Of equal or greater significance, in the spirit of the Progressive Era, were the local discussions in the fall of 1915 over creating a commission to control transportation, water, sewage, and light systems throughout the adjoining municipalities. The matter was reviewed the following February (without transportation), and the next month the councils petitioned the province for an act to constitute a joint utilities commission. Authorized by statute in April 1916 and organized in June, the Essex Border Utilities Commission (EBUC) was directed to create a common water system and build a trunk sewer and disposal plant. To the extent that it rationalized civic service, the EBUC reflected something of the draft plan of reformer Samuel Morley Wickett in 1913 for a metropolitan government for Toronto. The Essex commission was to consist of twelve members: the mayors of Windsor, Walkerville, Sandwich, Ford City, Ojibway, and Sandwich East Township, and an elected member for each municipality. Nominated for the balance of 1916, they were to be selected at the municipal elections for the coming year. For Ford City, McGregor joined mayor Charles J. Montreuil, who ran a sand and gravel dealership near the Ford plant, and in late December McGregor was elected unopposed.[80]

Almost immediately, common cause dissipated, and the EBUC fell victim to opposing interests among the members and the utilities commissions of the respective municipalities, which still existed to resolve local needs. Inaction in January 1917 over sewage problems in Ford City upset Montreuil and McGregor, who became the commission's chairman for 1917. By the spring, when McGregor was in California, these problems still had not been solved, though proposals for a disposal plant for Ford City had been placed on the agenda and attention had returned to discussing a joint system and the vexing problem of apportioning costs. After McGregor's return in May, the commission's engineer worked out a plan for both a joint sewage system and an overall metropolitan district plan. The united municipalities, it was proposed, were to be called Vimy Ridge, after the glorious Canadian victory in France in April. (Dr. Thaddeus Walker, the president of the Border Chamber of Commerce, would later, in November, seriously suggest "South Detroit" as a more appropriate name.) The *Evening Record* called in vain for a joint industrial policy, a goal McGregor recognized but did not strenuously pursue. By July, under his guidance, the EBUC had returned to its mandate and had worked out acceptable apportionments on a sewage and water system, though Ojibway still viewed the commission as just one route for the delivery of water. The issue was shelved as the war effort, the corporate preoccupations of members, and the departures of McGregor and others for their cottages intervened.[81]

At Ford Canada, the rise in production to 50,043 automobiles in 1917 (the highest level achieved during the war) came with some fine-tuning of the product and adjustments in marketing. The

Model T comprised more Canadian-made components than ever before, some of them (such as the folding tops) differing noticeably from the American-made equivalents. Modeling changes—in Ford's perspective—included the efficient use of a single color (black), painted-steel radiator shells (instead of brass), fenders with a crowning ridge and curved edge, and an overall "stream line effect." As a result of the elimination of retailing at the branch level, the company was able on 31 July to close its branch in Hamilton, Ontario, while in Vancouver business was restricted to parts. In Saskatchewan, where the number of automobile registrations (including new Ford cars) trailed only Ontario, "local conditions" compelled the continuation of retail in Saskatoon for another year.[82]

Farmers in droves bought Ford cars, and demands for better roads escalated. It was on the prairies, too, that the sale of used Model Ts by non-Ford garages was strong. As one fortunate result, the region has yielded wonderful anecdotal evidence of social impact, not least the rich variety of family and group photographs taken in all manner of settings using Model Ts. In the summer of 1917 Ernest Davidge, a young Methodist minister, bought a used Ford tourer for $370 from a garage in Gleichen, Alberta, and took it home to Buffalo Hills. Fiercely pleased with their first car, for over a week he and his wife parked it heading downhill (to help start it). It was "the object of our admiration and pride. We practiced opening the doors and climbing into its seats and out again." They soon summoned up the nerve to drive it, and the thrill "opened up a whole new world of adventure, expense, and novel situations." In addition to the stream of testimonials that appeared in *Ford Times* and *Ford News*, from coast to coast recollections, photographs, statistics of registration, and local histories record the overwhelming presence of Ford cars—the earliest motorcar to appear in a legion of communities.[83]

McGregor and his crew understood this impact—they had been instrumental in shaping it—and they did everything in their power to see the association repeated and advertised again and again throughout Canada. Such promotion could emerge only from a company headquarters that kept pace with developments in office and records management, advertising, and divisional need. The reach for efficiency and rationalization on the line extended into McGregor's own office, where his original secretary, Miss Grace Fal-

Model T Ford on the huge 76 Ranch in southwest Saskatchewan, c. 1913. The Esplanade: Archives, Medicine Hat, Alberta, image no. 0206.0003.

coner, continued to preside; from four employees in 1904 the office had grown to almost 200 in 1916. (The only other place for female employment at Ford was, apparently, in the assembly of magnetos, for some reason.) In 1917 the office purchased from the Tabulating Machine Company (the predecessor to International Business Machines) up-to-date equipment for the recording and analysis of an array of information on punched cards. Advertising had emerged strongly from the marketing campaign of 1912–13; in 1914 the department was headed by R. W. Mickam. On 1 August 1917 the head office took over from the dealers responsibility for all newspaper advertising and, to standardize it, engaged the well-known London, Ontario, agency of McConnell and Fergusson Limited, which had been doing work for Ford since 1904. Although McGregor's office had been supplying distinctive Ford advertising materials for several years, including standardized copy, stationery, storefront signs, photographs, lantern slides, and pennants, problems had emerged before the war with dealers who refused to use Ford copy and materials, who preferred the letterheads of accessory manufacturers, or who sinfully neglected advertising altogether.[84]

The slight dealer resistance provoked by the shift in 1917 was easily overridden by Ford's tougher control, through head office and its branches, of franchises, contracts, and sales territories, which could be constricted or left open for raiding and takeover by other dealers. Ad constancy was a tenet. An advertisement for Model Ts in the *Toronto Daily Star* in June 1917 urged husbands, "Give your wife one . . . the Ford is as easy to operate as a kitchen range." The point was not necessarily the appeal to women—Ford dealers were being encouraged well before the war to sell to women—but the appearance of the same ad across the entire country.[85]

The Canadian thrust of 1917 in advertising, which would blossom in the 1920s in splendid graphics and pitches, constituted a marked departure from the approach taken by Ford Detroit. There the lack of attention to consistent advertising and a discernible house style led in 1917 to the abandonment of national advertising because Henry Ford deemed it unnecessary for the low-end market. American dealers were left to fashion their own advertising, using a limited range of standardized logos and slogans and building on the company's ideas for sales, its motion pictures, and the *Ford Times*.[86] McGregor's semi-independence allowed a different approach.

In marketing, domestic sales in Canada overtook foreign sales. In addition to restrictions on foreign steel and coal supplies, shipping problems and legal actions intensified, principally in the Asian Pacific regions, where embargoes were imposed on shipments to India and the Straits Settlements. Locally made bodies had been appearing on Ford cars sold by Wearne Brothers Limited in the Straits and the Malay States in 1916. Strong prices for rubber and tin from 1911 to 1917 sustained record sales in Malaya; imports of automobiles were apparently prohibited there in 1917–18, though a few hundred Fords were still brought in. After August 1917 only chassis could be sent to Australia, when, because of the shortage of shipping space, the country imposed an embargo on car bodies. Though relaxed after 1918, this limitation spurred an already vigorous body-building business Down Under, creating some very unfamiliar-looking Canadian Ford cars. Given the problems with the Australian market, which included lawsuits with two shipping companies, Ford Canada was compelled to make special shipping arrangements and to allow a "substantial reserve" to cover any liability.[87] The company still, however, was able to take advantage of the chassis-only restriction: after sending 532 chassis to Australia in 1916–17, it shipped 4,412 in 1917–18 and 2,337 in 1918–19.

In Canada, McGregor was forced to postpone the introduction of Ford's new one-ton truck chassis, a delay that helped encourage the appearance of such independent firms as the Forduplex Truck and Auto Company of Canada in Walkerville to provide truck bodies for Ford chassis. More troublesome was the long-delayed introduction of Ford's gasoline tractor. The steel-wheeled Fordson that finally appeared on the market in early 1917 was made in Dearborn, Michigan. Henry Ford's bombastic promises of a Canadian plant had led to nothing—he had dropped the Sandwich site because its estimated cost ($250,000) was considered too high. This situation left McGregor a slightly embarrassed observer, even though he became the manager of sales for the tractors through his Canadian dealers. Canadian production head George Dickert recalled that in any case the tractors were brought in duty-free on account of the war, thus removing any need for a Canadian plant, and "there was never enough market to pay for the tooling necessary." In responding to Britain's wartime need for tractors, McGregor may have played only a small part. Reacting to strong diplomatic pressure from the British government, which sorely needed tractors to sustain agricultural production, Henry Ford dealt directly, as he always had, with Percival Perry, the head of Ford operations in Britain. Perry's request in April for the loan of drawings and personnel to build the tractor was met by Ford's promise of cooperation. The entry of the United States into the war that month also softened his attitude somewhat. On 25 April his assistant chief of production, Charles Emil Sorensen, left Detroit by rail for Halifax with a boxcar filled with tractor parts, patterns, and farming implements. McGregor and Henry Ford accompanied him to Halifax to see him off on 3 May. McGregor went along presumably since they were crossing his territory, and he may have arranged the transit. He would undoubtedly have recognized the hostility shown Ford by the British public on account of his unforgettable peace ship escapade.[88]

McGregor had almost been bypassed one other time in the scramble over tractor production. In February 1917 a group headed by Toronto lawyer John Francis Boland, seeing an opening, had incorporated the Ford Tractor Company of Canada Limited in a brash legal bid to corner the rights to manufacture a "Ford" tractor in Canada. The bid failed, but after his initial surprise McGregor moved quickly to determine what entitlement his company did have. Both his Windsor lawyer at the time (Alexander Robert Bartlet) and Henry Ford's lawyer (Alfred Lucking) advised him that he had no rights at all in Ford's tractor business under the original agreement of 1904. Not convinced, on Bartlet's recommendation McGregor went to "the best man to advise us on the technicalities of that agreement," Arthur White Anglin of the noted Toronto law firm of Blake, Lash, Anglin, and Cassels. In May Anglin confirmed that Ford Canada had no rights under the agreement, which covered only automobiles and established no claim to Henry Ford's subsequent mechanical developments or the separate tractor company he had formed. A still-doubtful McGregor ran the decision by James Couzens, whose interest in such matters was waning, and then by the company's shareholders. Unlikely to take any kind of negative position on the manufacture of tractors for Britain, McGregor nonetheless remained a teammate. Not only had he gone to Halifax with Ford and Sorensen, but in late July, at his Kingsville cottage, he hosted Henry and Clara Ford and Percival Perry and his wife, who had all come to visit Jack Miner and his bird sanctuary near Kingsville. In February 1918 he would quietly facilitate the Ontario government's purchase of 100 Fordson tractors to be sold to farmers at cost.[89]

If the tractor could not be part of McGregor's manufacturing operation, the motive of agrarian aid was not lost on him or on those throughout Ontario for whom food production was a most worthwhile patriotic activity. The provincial Organization of Resources Committee, authorized in April 1917, asked farmers to produce larger crops, but the shortage of farm labor posed a serious obstacle. More attuned to metal than soil, Ford Canada was nonetheless quick to pick up on the gardening plan proposed by local bakery head Henry (Harry) James Neal. Ford's response had all the hallmarks of corporate patriotism tinged with gimmickry. In May the company purchased a large shipment of potatoes and secured a fifty-acre plot of open land in Ford City. The company would plough the land with a Fordson tractor (a feat captured in a Ford film—perhaps of a later date—with several grinning dignitaries standing by), and seed potatoes would be sold to company employees at cost, with preference given to married men. The project was endorsed by Windsor's War Production Committee, of which McGregor's brother-in-law E. N. Bartlet was secretary. The potato patch fit well with the program of Canada's new food controller, former Lambton West MLA and McGregor's friend W. J. Hanna, whose board included McGregor's cousin James Duncan McGregor of Manitoba. McGregor prevailed on Hanna in early August to announce that Ford management had voluntarily offered to close its entire plant for four to eight weeks if his men could be used to help farmers take in their crops.[90] There was no closure—that probably was never the intent—but the announcement again brought public attention to McGregor as a master of the patriotic gesture.

McGregor's network was comprehensive. In April Couzens's secretary, H. S. Morgan, who had promised to get information on the retraining of crippled veterans for a Red Cross official in Detroit, asked for his help. Through branch manager Fred Fox in Toronto, McGregor obtained a full summary from William Kerr George, chairman of the federal Military Hospitals Commission and a Liberal businessman.[91] McGregor was also unstinting on behalf of both the patriotic fund and the related work of the IODE; so were his wife and daughters. By May 1917, $50,000 had been committed to the patriotic fund by the workers at the Ford plant. On 27 October the "girls" there proudly held a patriotic bazaar, concert, and dance, which together raised more than $1,000 for "comfort" boxes for the "Ford boys" at the front. Another Ford-McGregor project also came to completion at the end of October: the opening on the 27th of the sanatorium at Union by the IODE's head (and Amherstburg native) Mrs. Albert Edward Gooderham (Mary Reford Duncanson) of Toronto, who pointedly thanked Henry Ford and Gordon and Hattie McGregor for their contributions.[92]

Less sustained interest was paid by the community and the *Evening Record* to events that did not conform to the largely Anglo-imperial character of the local war effort. One instance was the laying of the cornerstone in late October for Holy Trinity Church in Ford City, the first "foreign" Roman Catholic church in the Border Cities, with a congregation made up mostly of Hungarians, Poles, and the infamous "Marion Avenue colony." A month earlier little debate or reaction seems to have been generated by the public proposal of Walkerville councillor Harry Crouchman to segregate the Poles, just as blacks were "restricted" in the United States, he said, in order to prevent the "foreigners" from buying property in the "exclusive and aristocratic" sections of town. The telling aspect was not what action was taken (none) but that the proposal came forth at all. The opening on Windermere Street of a Polish or Austrian boardinghouse—true ethnic identifications were usually blurred in such debates—had provoked righteous indignation.[93] Henry Ford opposed boardinghouses because they offended his perception of single-family homes and values. As an employer of many workers of European origin, McGregor carefully weighed his public participation in such debates.

Recognition of the military effort was another matter. On 23 April, as the United States prepared for war, Walter McGregor and the kilted 241st Battalion left Windsor for Halifax and overseas. Throngs of emotional, cheering well-wishers saw them off. Whistles screamed, mothers' tears flowed, the Union Jack, the Canadian Ensign, and the Stars and Stripes waved everywhere, and "Auld Lang Syne," "Dixie," and "O Canada" were sung repeatedly. "Fully one-fourth of the battalion were Americans," reported the *Detroit News* in the fullest coverage of the "spectacle," which combined "carnival and funeral." After accepting a $1,000 check for the battalion from A. W. Joyce of the Fisher Body Company, Walter McGregor gave a short speech. As the train pulled out of the station at 9:50 A.M., "he waved a miniature Union Jack from the officers' coach." Claiming in family correspondence to be bound by duty, he felt he had to go to war. "Walter could do nothing else, and live up to his standards," his wife told Mother McGregor. "Your sons are wonderful, nothing on earth could be nicer than to feel that you had given to the world men like these." Equally proud was the poet T. D. Niven:

> It's ower tae France at duty's ca',
> The kiltie lads will mairch awa,
> In freedom's cause tae strike a blow
> They'll on and face a savage foe.
> An' wha are they wi' dirk and gun
> Wad gang abroad tae fecht the Hun?

They're the Twa Hunner and Forty-first,
An' they'll a' win tae the front or bust.

In July, some of the battalion was ordered from England to bolster the British army in France, but Walter would not continue as their commander. By December he was working in the Claims Office of the British 1st Army, feeling keenly Scottish, homesick, and ambivalent about his diminished command. He confided to his mother that he did not have the ability to discipline and "rant."[94]

At home the family devoted itself to wartime activity. Older sister Margaret assisted with mail and war packages. Her husband, E. N. Bartlet, was secretary of the War Production Committee, which maintained a register for willing harvesters. Gordon supported this cause by offering to compensate any of his workers who took up lower-paying farm jobs, though few did. He kept in close touch with his brother Walter by letter and cable, and he took pains to share Walter's news with the rest of the family. There was never any suggestion that the forty-four-year-old Gordon would go into the forces. Ford was his regiment, the assembly line his front line, and domestic support his patriotic best. In a now-familiar pattern, he spent the summer of 1917 at his Kingsville cottage, commuting back and forth to the Border Cities to check on one cause or another. On one trip he and other drivers from the chamber of commerce brought back a group of Boy Scouts who had been camping on a lake near Kingsville. The construction of a large addition to McGregor's house on Victoria Avenue by the Windsor branch of Wells and Gray Limited of Toronto, the contractor for most of Ford Canada's construction in the Border Cities, delayed the family's return, and when they did move back in mid-September they were forced to take up temporary quarters at the golf club.[95] McGregor was more than well off: after forgoing dividends in 1916, his company paid a 5 percent dividend in October 1917 on profits to 31 July of $2,322,646.88.

The initiation in the fall of 1917 of a new phase of national fund-raising, the Victory Loans, followed by only a few months the launch of an intense campaign for greater industrialization under a dynamic new industrial commissioner hired by the Border Chamber of Commerce, whose perspective was clearly shaped by such directors as McGregor. Industrialization knew no bounds and was guided by no official plan; industrialists worked hand in hand with major realtors and developers. At the chamber of commerce, in July 1917 F. Maclure Sclanders, enticed by the challenge and the offer of a $5,000 salary, was drawn to the Border Cities from his position with the board of trade in Saskatoon, where he had gained a reputation for his level-headedness, his shrewd understanding of land development, and his recognition of the automobile as "the new thermometer of prosperity." Without waiting in his new position of industrial commission for any form of joint industrial policy, as advocated by the *Evening Record*, or for any productive debate on such chronic problems as the shortages of natural gas, this civic hustler moved quickly to attract still more industry. In October he beat the drum in eastern Ontario; in November he went to Chicago to lure an unnamed automobile manufacturer; in December, after issuing the chamber's new promotional brochure, he hurried off to Grand Rapids, Michigan, to meet with prospective branch plant prospects there. *Border Brieflets*, the punchy, twenty-one-page brochure, played up branches, tariff advantages, Made in Canada, the absence of labor troubles, and the Border Cities' bold claim to be the Canadian center for automobiles, heavy chemicals and drugs, pharmaceuticals, paint and varnish, and salt. The boast—"We are logically ripe for a great industrial awakening"—neatly captured the fervor of such unabashed boosters as Sclanders and his industrial cohorts, McGregor included.[96] Sclanders's campaign had a decided bias toward branch plants (many of which came in on shaky business plans and folded) and automobiles, which permeated life in the Border Cities.

"The great overshadowing industry," as the *Evening Record* properly billed the automotive sector, had reached a new level of maturity. At the center was Ford, "the wet nurse" of Ford City, which kept nine out of twenty local parts makers in business. In terms of employment, there were at least 1,730 workers in the Ford plant and 190 staff in the office. The paper saw nothing unusual in its claim that Ford "exercises such a systematic supervision of the social concerns of its employees as cannot fail to produce beneficial results."[97]

And so the effect went, down through the ranks. At the hub of the local retail trade in automobiles was the "auto centre," a congregation of outlets at Pitt West and Chatham streets that R. M.

Jaffray had had a hand in developing and promoting in early 1916. It included Windsor Auto Sales (Chevrolet and Menard), Woollatt Brothers (Overland), Copeland Motor Sales, the Studebaker showroom and garage, and the dominant Universal Car Agency. Run by McGregor's brother and brother-in-law and viewed by Ford as the model agency, Universal Car promoted itself as Canada's largest retail organization, and it certainly was after the Ford branches had gone wholesale. In the *Evening Record*'s special issue of 23 May celebrating Windsor's twenty-five years as a city, automobiles were named as its primary industry. On 28 May a group of auto dealers from throughout Essex met in the chamber of commerce building to hear F. W. Gottlieb, a "special representative of the Chicago trade." Over the previous eight months he had been working to establish "clearing houses" for used cars (now a major part of the market generally), organize dealers' associations, and create a national association to address such problem-prone areas as shipping and dealers' contracts with manufacturers. As a result, steps were taken to organize an Essex auto dealers' association, in keeping with similar bodies in other centers and with the object of "correcting abuses in the handling of used cars and otherwise putting the trade on a sound business footing."[98]

Firms quickly sprang up in the Border Cities to fill other gaps in the automobile business. For example, the Champion Spark Plug Company of Canada, a branch plant, was incorporated in April 1917. With Ford having postponed its production of trucks, Universal took up the agency for the Detroit Truck Company's Tonford, a one-ton, chain-driven truck built on a Ford chassis. Forduplex Truck and Auto Company and Tonsmore Truck, another local firm perhaps, made their own versions. Student courses in "auto engine management" were added to the industrial program in the fall of 1917 at Windsor Collegiate Institute, while at the Windsor fair a racing card exclusively of Ford cars modified for speed was presented on 27 September.[99]

The industrial buzz and patriotic intensity of the Border Cities were sustained even as gloomy news sifted through from the war. Daily reports of deaths were made worse by coverage of defeats on the Italian front and the descent of Russia into a revolutionary maelstrom, which rooted the fear of Bolshevism firmly in the local consciousness. The matter of wartime finance entered this discourse that summer and fall. Ford remained exposed to the excess business profits tax: it had paid $150,262 for 1916 and $785,181 for 1917. Under the federal Income War Tax Bill introduced in July 1917, Ford was further subjected to a 4 percent charge on corporate profits, and for the first time private individuals were required to pay an income tax. At the same time, the war's stimulation of the economy was leading to enormous profits in many sectors, including munitions, and public hostility toward profiteering was generating headlines in Windsor as elsewhere. The income tax act, which passed a third reading in Parliament in September, added to the load carried by Ford and produced some confusion locally. Both the *Evening Record* and Thaddeus Walker of the chamber of commerce believed wrongly that the income tax would supplant the more costly excess profits tax. Ford would contribute less, and thereby come out ahead, Walker reasoned publicly, though McGregor, who clearly understood the double taxation, shunned any public discussion of the sensitive matters of Ford's profits and taxes. The $350,000 paid on 15 October 1917 was downplayed. McGregor was far more at ease in his undemanding, uncontroversial support for the patriotic fund, the YMCA, the health association, and the Serbian Relief Fund.[100]

The war loans floated by Canada before the fall of 1917 had not commanded much public notice or easy participation by the person on the street. Launched in October, Canada's first Victory Bond campaign changed this situation. The issue, which brought a new sense of public input in a grinding, sometimes demoralizing war, constituted $150 million in tax-free, interest-bearing bonds with three maturity dates (1922, 1927, and 1937). An elaborate, nationwide marketing organization was quickly set up, headed by some of the country's leading professional financiers and publicists. Significantly, sales of the bonds rested not just with the banks, brokers, and bond dealers, but also with companies, schools, fraternal societies, church groups, and other local bodies, to be directed by a central committee. The entire process was to be infused with a patriotic purpose that would supposedly curb any self-interested urges, in competition or fees, among the sales forces. The purchase of a Victory Bond would be the first foray into such investments by the ordinary citizen, so there was also a novelty factor. With a compelling combination of marketing savvy, intense publicity, professional financial direction, and patriotic motivation, the campaign was expected to be an overwhelming success. As later explained by finance minister Sir W. T. White, "the impetus of a Victory Loan movement, once it got under way, was irresistible."[101]

Gordon McGregor was a natural choice in October to head the Victory Bond campaign in Essex. Evidently White asked him personally. As the head of the county's most dynamic manufactory, then in the midst of a major Made in Canada campaign, and a key figure in much of the Border Cities' war effort, McGregor could bring to the task the needed combination of salesmanship, showmanship, verve, and organizational skill, not to mention the proven resources of his company. The first planning meeting took place on the evening of 16 October at the chamber of commerce building at 14 Sandwich Street West in Windsor. Following the annual Ford meetings the next week (including the announcement of an $8.5 million increase in business) and the opening of the sanatorium at Union at the end of the month, McGregor turned his full attention to Victory Bonds.[102]

The campaign would run from the 12th to the 30th of November.[103] Its intended aim was to sell more than $2 million worth of bonds, with all commissions on sales being turned back to the Red Cross, McGregor assured the public. He was to directly supervise north Essex, which would be blitzed by twenty-one teams of canvassers. South Essex was entrusted to William T. Gregory, the manager of a tobacco firm in Leamington. Born in Stovall, North Carolina, and disappointed that the States had not entered the war sooner, Gregory had already thrown himself into the Canadian war effort as a recruiter. Ford accountant Philip W. Grandjean handled the financial end, Ford film crews covered the campaign from beginning to end and provided cinematic entertainments, and the company and its employees were expected to make substantial purchases of bonds. The entire campaign bore McGregor's imprint, though there were distinct parallels with the conformity that characterized Americanization campaigns in wartime Detroit and subscription drives there for Liberty Loans.

In the Border Cities, the campaign opened early on a Monday morning with a blast: harmless bombs were fired from mortars atop the chamber of commerce building. More bombs would be exploded in the afternoons for every $100,000 subscribed. A mass meeting followed on Monday evening. After the official prospectus of the loan had been explained, the crowd heard from Abner E. Larned, a Detroit businessman and banker and chairman there of the Liberty Bonds campaign. He carefully found the community's pulse: "It was with a feeling of deep humility that I crossed the river this evening to participate in this meeting. I now feel very humble, facing a Canadian audience—an audience of men and women who have laid their sacrifices of the world's finest manhood on the altar of humanity. It is not for me to tell you what to do in this war—you have already done all that can be asked of you."[104]

The address met with thunderous ovation. After the antics of Henry Ford, the audience was emotionally struck by this recognition. It was five minutes before Chairman McGregor could speak. When he did, he was delighted to announce that on Thursday the American "March King," Lieutenant John Philip Sousa, would be coming to town with his 300-piece Marine band to boost the campaign and wind up at another mass meeting at the armories, along with vaudevillian Harry Lauder and his bagpipers. On McGregor's request, Prime Minister Borden—so the *Evening Record* claimed—secured American permission for Sousa to cross the border. In the intervening days, McGregor met with Henry Ford on Tuesday to discuss the important question of how much Ford Canada would subscribe to the Victory Loan. Ford departed for New York once a figure had been determined for McGregor's announcement at the optimal moment. No time was lost, however, assigning a team headed by J. R. Hewer to canvass Ford Canada's employees. Some were no doubt eager to share in the new investment; others (judging by defaults) may have felt obligated. At one point the two candidates for the upcoming federal election, Colonel E. S. Wigle and William Costello Kennedy, joined by the veteran francophone journalist and ex-politician Gaspard Pacaud, formed a delegation that visited the Ford factory to speak on the "advantages" of buying Victory Bonds. From within the company's office, Wallace Campbell, though he had been shot by a burglar and badly wounded at the beginning of the month, coordinated corporate solicitations. A Mr. Williams of the K. W. Magneto Company of Cleveland, for instance, subscribed $10,000. Locally, American Auto Trimming went in for $25,000. With production well in hand, McGregor could cheerfully claim: "I have been so busy looking after the organization of the canvassing forces elsewhere that I almost neglected the Ford factory."[105]

The Sousa-Lauder parade on Thursday afternoon was a noisy, glorious affair. It was escorted across the river by Detroit's mayor, the Great War Veterans' Association, and a group of dignitaries who included proud marshal McGregor. At the armories he had trouble calling the crowd to order. The featured speaker was a father, clad in the dress of the Highlands, whose son lay buried in Flanders. All the emotional and patriotic stops were pulled; of all the advertisements, none could top the one bearing the face of Christ, "the Prince of Peace." Credit for the orchestration was freely given to the head of Ford Canada. "It takes Gordon M. McGregor to put on an all-star cast," the *Evening Record* concluded without hesitation.[106]

By Friday, subscriptions had shot past the $1 million mark, with Ford employees pledging more than $100,000. On Saturday, McGregor and his canvassing committee gave the "boys" a day off. That night the public was treated to showings of four Ford films that had been doing the rounds during the campaign: an interview between W. T. White and Miss Canada,[107] an explanation of the Victory Bonds, the departure of the 241st, and the Sousa-Lauder parade. Unfortunately, none of these films has survived. That same evening the audience was addressed by a speaker brought over by Campbell, Detroit water commissioner John B. Sosnowski. He spoke in both Polish and English, and for a short time the Border Cities' Polish received some respect.

Campaigning continued solidly into the week of 19 November. McGregor announced Henry Ford's much anticipated subscription as president of Ford Canada ($500,000), with Ford Detroit committing to the same amount. On the 21st McGregor gave a typically folksy speech at the Amherstburg town hall. Claiming almost to be an "Amherstburg Old Boy," he said he had heard that the stone building where his mother was born was getting a new roof, though, he hastened to add to a round of laughter, if it was "in as good condition as my mother, it wouldn't require a new roof."[108] Overall, the Essex campaign would raise $4,915,000, a figure exceeded only in Toronto, Hamilton, Ottawa, and London. Not surprisingly, within the Border Cities, the highest amount was generated not in Windsor ($1,195,400) but on Ford's home ground in Ford City ($1,467,450), where Ford employees alone subscribed for more than $200,000. Whether Ford Detroit honored its pledge is uncertain.

Throughout the campaign, McGregor led the charge: speaking, cheering, exhorting, and inspiring the teams with a wonderful mix of enthusiasm, tact, patience, and years of acquired smoothness—all to turn patriotic emotion into fiscal commitment. He brought in Sir Robert Borden to speak to "the premier county of the dominion," read messages of congratulations from securities expert George Herbert Wood (head of the Ontario committee of the campaign), broadcast the true goodness of Henry Ford, put a positive spin on the morale-crushing battle of Cambrai in France, and, ever the salesman, put up a prize of 100 cigars for the campaign team with the most subscriptions. It was won by campaign receiver P. W. Grandjean. He doubled as captain of the "Ford City hustlers," who had secured 847 applications worth $161,300. A wind-up dinner was held on the 30th, and McGregor went to Toronto for a celebratory dinner hosted by Wood.

McGregor's Victory Bonds campaign was conducted alongside other complementary activities. The industrial campaign of Maclure Sclanders and the chamber of commerce had equal intensity, with the overarching Made in Canada theme that embraced the patriotic challenge to drive the wheels of industry. Despite his professed preoccupation with Victory Bonds, McGregor could not ignore the shipping problems that afflicted his company or the plunge of Ford Canada shares on the Detroit exchange, a fall likely precipitated by the uncertainties of Ford Canada's foreign business and by Henry Ford's ongoing battle with the diminishing number of minority stockholders in Ford Detroit, among them John and Horace Dodge and James Couzens. Ford Canada helped discredit the Dodges, who in March 1917 had taken out a dominion charter for a branch plant in the Border Cities, but it discreetly left Couzens alone. At the annual Ford Canada meetings in October 1917, despite a sharp rise in business, McGregor had again announced, the *Evening Record* reported, that there would be no dividend. The company's financial records, however, confirm one of 5 percent on 15 October. If no oversight, the public silence is difficult to explain, though timing and public perception may have been factors. Henry Ford had renewed his bias against stockholders (he called them "parasites"), a position that may have contributed to the fall of Ford Canada's stock on the Detroit exchange from $400 a share to around $160.[109] Throughout the Victory Bonds campaign, McGregor had expressly directed that politics were to be avoided, though candidates for the federal election set for December often appeared at various promotions. With Borden now at the head of a new Union coalition government, the election campaign placed McGregor in an awkward situation. A Liberal, he faithfully persisted in supporting the aging Laurier, who opposed conscription and remained outside the Union coalition. Far removed in England, McGregor's brother Walter would abandon the family's long-running Liberal ties to become a "union man" and support his father-in-law, Colonel E. S. Wigle, in the overseas military vote for Essex North. As the head of the Victory Bonds campaign, however, Gordon had no intention of letting any partisan sentiments undermine the campaign, though as expected he took part in the return of Essex North's incumbent, the anticonscriptionist Liberal W. C. Kennedy. Only once did partisanship intrude, and from an unexpected source, McGregor's cochair, W. T. Gregory. At the Victory Bonds meeting at the armories on 24 November, chaired by McGregor, Kennedy and Gregory (filling in for Wigle) were present onstage. Out of the blue Gregory took a potshot at Laurier: what had this ancient Liberal done to help win the war? Gregory wondered aloud. A shouting match with the audience immediately ensued. Struggling to close the meeting, a barely restrained McGregor tried to check this display of bare-knuckle politics.[110]

McGregor's handling of the campaign had produced stunning results. The *Evening Record* made no excuse for its effusive praise for his generous involvement, but it was a praise that not everyone on the street or the assembly line shared. Ill will toward McGregor would surface, although not until after 1917. It is impossible to document the range of bad feeling Ford management drew by the injuries and deaths incurred during the factory expansion, by the housing and fuel shortages (Ford was a major consumer of gas), by the employees who had to default on their subscriptions, or by rumblings of an autoworkers' union in Detroit. Some, whose lifestyles and values did not conform to the company's ideals—men like John H. Hill, the war veteran and Ford employee arrested in early December for bigamy—may not have cared much at all for the likes of McGregor.[111]

Ensconced for the winter in his newly enlarged house, McGregor mixed with chamber of commerce confrères, proud of the Victory Bonds campaign. He enjoyed his work (which never seemed strenuous), patriotic card parties, and patriotic fund functions. He was gratified too by the frequent supportive performances of the Ford glee club, band, and literary club, by the appearance of Ford moving pictures at a variety of functions, and by the successes of the many sports teams at the Ford plant. (The bowling teams had such wonderful names as the Torpedoes, Sedans, Trucks, Coupes, Touring, Chassis, Toolmakers, and Millwrights, among others.) In mid-December he presided confidently at a dinner given at the chamber of commerce building by Windsor mayor Charles Robert Tuson. In his speech, McGregor expressed his usual optimism flavored with old-boy levity. The public had had enough of voting, he remarked, and since the council had been doing such a creditable job, he saw no need for municipal elections in January 1918.[112]

The natural gas problem, caused in large part by unusually harsh winters and heavy industrial consumption—the Consumers Glass plant in Wallaceburg was the biggest user—did not openly concern McGregor as head of the Essex Border Utilities Commission. Gas supply was not part of its mandate. The problem was so severe that winter, however, that the Ontario Railway and Municipal Board (ORMB) was engaged in January to sort out the jurisdictional and regulatory confusion that concerned numerous municipalities and local gas companies in the southwest. For a few days in February, Ford, among other industries, was shut down by federal fuel controller C. A. Magrath, but the company had more than enough coal to keep going, according to Wallace Campbell. In testimony to the ORMB on 18 January, Ford City mayor Charles J. Montreuil credited Ford with supplying enough coal to keep thirty families from freezing, but all knew that charity was not the solution.[113]

In January and February, McGregor was in a forward-looking frame of mind as chairman of the EBUC. Backed by the chamber of commerce, provincial health officers, and pollution reports from the international waterways commission, and with municipal consent on the apportionment of costs, he called several meetings to explain the bylaws needed to implement the plans and set up the infrastructure for a Border Cities–wide sewage system. To illustrate the need, at one meeting he graphically emphasized the complete lack of any control or treatment in Ford City, where raw sewage from his plant and from his employees' houses flowed directly into the Detroit River.[114]

When other public matters came up for debate, McGregor could usually be found as a participant or relied on for an opinion or quotation in the *Evening Record*, often ahead of any local politician. One innocuous issue was the door-to-door delivery of mail, on which a conference was held at the chamber of commerce building on 2 February 1918. McGregor was there as the representative of Ford City.[115] The chamber of commerce did facilitate a broad viewpoint, and it was within that organization that McGregor, who was reelected a director at large in January and again named second vice president, helped shape priorities in discussions with other business heavyweights such as Maclure Sclanders, E. G. Henderson (the veteran head of Canadian Salt), R. M. Jaffray (the exhibition promoter and now manager of the Rapid Electrotype Company), and a number of officers from Ford Canada. The chamber's many lobbies betrayed a distinct branch-plant mentality, consistent with Sclanders's aggressive promotion. In mid-February, for instance, it sent a deputation to Ottawa to brazenly lobby once again (and unsuccessfully) for an exemption for new American branch plants from the income and excess profits taxes.[116]

It took a different mindset to openly question the chamber's approach. With the dispatch of the deputation, Windsor resident Norman McL. Allan, for one, had had enough. As the manager of the Saxon Motor Car Company in Detroit, he had a different perspective: the chamber was self-absorbed and unrepresentative, he believed, and the deputation's goal was discriminatory and unfair to the branches already in the Border Cities. With some nerve, he said so in an open letter of 12 February to the minister of finance, published in the *Evening Record*. Industrial commissioner Sclanders immediately shot back, not at Allan but at the *Evening Record* for printing the opinion of someone who, in Sclanders's view, dared to dismiss the chamber as a piece of out-and-out "propaganda."[117] No one mentioned McGregor's similar opposition in this issue the previous winter. But if Allan, or Sclanders for that matter, thought the Border Cities' automakers and other key manufacturers always needed the chamber as a front, which it sometimes was, he was wrong.

Of definite concern was the American interest in restricting the flow of alloy steel to Canadian carmakers, who, in the Border Cities at least, had not turned to war production and used all their steel for automobiles. In 1917 the American government had imposed a luxury tax on automobiles and moved to limit the supply of steel to the industry on the grounds that it was not essential to the war effort. Lobbying on behalf of the formidable National Automobile Chamber of Commerce (NACC), Hugh Chalmers (whom McGregor knew through Chalmers Canada) vigorously fought the attempts of the War Industries Board to cut off the industry's supply. In his fight he asked how Henry Ford, a nonmember of the NACC who had begun to shift to war work, seemed able to secure some supplies when other Detroit producers faced serious shortages. When in February 1918 the American board, as feared, placed an embargo on exports of steel to foreign countries, Ford Canada, Chalmers Canada, and Studebaker Canada, as well as "other large importers" in the Border Cities and such bodies as the Canadian Manufacturers' Association, sent a joint appeal to the board in Washington. After "a day of anxiety" and some intervention by the Borden government, the embargo was lifted.[118] Mindful of this close call, in June the Border Chamber of Commerce would move formally to oppose any restriction on the importation of coal and other raw materials.

A more concrete instance of Ford and McGregor throwing their weight around occurred in April 1918, over the controversial issue of adopting the federally initiated daylight saving time, aimed at the more efficient use of daylight hours. From the start Ford had been taking blame for shaping sentiment against the change. Most schools and some businessmen accepted it, but a number of factories, the local trades council and labor federation, and the councils of Ford City, Windsor, and Sandwich followed Ford's lead, partly on the grounds that workers coming over from Detroit would be inconvenienced by the time difference. This opposition attracted attention beyond Essex. Even though daylight saving was drawing strong resistance in the provincial capital, on 27 April *Saturday Night* (Toronto) ridiculed Windsor's singular resistance. Whether McGregor knew of such attention is uncertain, but he did not like negative publicity, even if he had no strong profile personally outside southwest Ontario. His announcement on the morning of the 27th, the day of *Saturday Night*'s barb, was as unexpected at it was unexplained. Ford was reversing its position on daylight saving. To adjust, factory workers would start at 8 a.m. and office staff at 8:45, a half hour earlier than before. The municipalities, schools, and other industries immediately fell into line.[119]

CHAPTER 5

Lockout

The "annoying and serious conditions" recognized by Ford Canada in 1916 only intensified as the war dragged on. Many problems had cross-border origins. The impact of the war on the American automotive industry was closely followed by McGregor. By early 1918, worried that the Canadian government would also try to curtail the production of motorcars as a nonessential use of steel, he had moved to develop a base for responding to any regulation.[1] In January in Montreal, before the lifting of the American embargo, McGregor was instrumental in bringing together thirty-four automotive, parts, tire, and accessory producers to form the Automotive Industries of Canada (AIC), of which he became first president. Organized to foster the industry, spread information, and demonstrate the value of "co-operative action," particularly on restricted production and steel imports, the AIC weakly emulated the NACC. It would eventually decline. McGregor's direction (and Ford Canada's primacy) can be seen in the resolution at the organizational meeting in Montreal "that there be no more motor shows—the Exhibition at Toronto excepted—until the war is over." (The midwinter show in Toronto had already been discontinued in 1915 by the Toronto Automobile Trade Association.) Such voluntary restraint was evidently meant to help create a favorable wartime image for the industry, though most could see that curtailed promotion did not necessarily mean curtailed production. Still, the AIC had seen that the campaign for voluntary conservation launched by the National Automobile Dealers' Association in the United States the previous fall had had some success. Attempts by the AIC to close shows would meet with resistance, however, and force McGregor to push closure again at a board meeting in July, when the war's end appeared safely imminent.[2]

McGregor brought the same, seemingly cooperative approach to the Canadian War Trade Board. Within days of its formation on 8 February, he was lobbying it in Ottawa. He agreed with board member J. H. Gundy that a heavy tax on imported or manufactured motorcars would reduce purchases of nonessential cars. In May the war revenue act of 1915 was amended to bring in, among other charges, an excise tax of 10 percent on cars (excluding exports). Perhaps in response to pressure, this position was modified to the benefit of the industry when, in June, on the board's recommendation, only imports were taxed and luxury imports were stopped altogether.[3] Ford's Toronto manager, Fred Fox, felt that the embargo was unlikely to affect Ford much. Customers who wanted high-priced automobiles might turn, he suggested wistfully, to the well-appointed Model T coupelet, though any trend was some months away. Buyers, he pointed out, usually bought in the winter for spring delivery.[4] More problematic were the disruptions in the flow of steel from the United States.

Production at the Ford Canada plant for fiscal year 1917–18 dropped to 46,914 automobiles from 50,827 the previous year, a decline that would continue into 1919. Shortage of steel for bodies and chassis was the primary factor, though what portion of Ford's need came from the United States is uncertain.[5] The decline worried McGregor, who even toyed with retrenchment, including the idea of closing the Australian branch. This notion, a prelude actually to starting full assembly operations there under a separate company, was likely considered in part out of frustration (and then reconsidered by the Canadian directors) and partly to appease Henry Ford's overseas contractions. The drop in revenue that came with the reduced production of cars was more than offset by the start of manufacture of Ford trucks (the TT, a strong seller), a sharp rise in the sale of parts, the much publicized and duty-free import in February and sale of Fordson tractors through the Canadian government (a preferential deal that upset Canadian tractor makers), and, most effective of all, a $100 (Canadian) price increase on Model Ts beginning on 22 February, in lockstep with the $90 (American) increase at Ford Detroit.[6]

Though Ford Canada had increased prices before, marginally, this time the move sparked a new consumer concern, one that the

Evening Record and McGregor's office could not comfortably address. How, one farmer asked in a letter to the *Toronto Daily Star* on 18 March, could the mass-producing Ford Motor Company of Canada justify a reversal of its publicized trend of falling prices, and, posing the question that would plague Ford in 1920–21, why did Canadians have to pay more than Americans for the same automobile? The *Star* had wondered that too in an interview with Ford's Toronto manager Fred Fox in February. Moreover, was Ford simply taking advantage of the tariff to boost prices and profits? This was the conclusion that many reached when they saw the price differential range suspiciously around the amount of the tariff. Fox, presaging Ford's standard rationale in the low-tariff debate that would begin to heat up in 1919–20, attributed the price difference to the differing scales of production in Detroit and Walkerville.[7]

In Detroit, amid the confusion caused by steel shortages and regulatory interference, wartime enlistment and strong industrial activity had helped foster an acute labor shortage, unprecedented pressures on autoworkers to speed up, anti-German fever, and an upsurge in labor action and membership, particularly within the muscular International Association of Machinists (IAM), which had locals on both sides of the river. The American War Labor Board had stipulated that employers could not prevent workers from joining unions. In Windsor, labor unrest was evident, though the conservative, proindustry *Evening Record* reported it only in generalities and rarely located it by industry. In May, IAM officials reported the "splendid success" of the membership drive and organizational efforts (the "labour forward campaign") of its local Lodge 718, which would be chartered by the American Federation of Labor in July.[8]

In March the Border Cities Trades and Labor Council opened its own ambitious, long-range campaign to organize Windsor as "an out-and-out union city, with an eight-hour working day." On 21 March the council was addressed by Judge Edward J. Jeffries (later a labor candidate for the office of mayor, which McGregor's old associate James Couzens won) and Thomas Fox, the IAM's organizer in Detroit. Two weeks later Fox, James McClennan (the IAM's Canadian vice president), the organizer of Detroit's streetcar operators' union, and the Reverend Arthur Carlisle of All Saints' Church in Windsor addressed the unions.[9] Autoworkers were probably mindful that in June, the same month street railway workers went out in Windsor, the IAM successfully struck the Willys-Overland plant in Toronto.[10]

Then in the midst of a reorganization caused by Thaddeus Walker's resignation as president, which would see McGregor become first vice president, the Border Chamber of Commerce had a different perspective on labor concerns. On a resolution by Philip Grandjean, Ford Canada's assistant secretary and head of publicity, the chamber supported exempting from Canadian taxation those Americans who commuted to work in Canada. Cross-border taxation was a recurring headache.[11] Some categories of workers were left unprotected altogether. In June, under the guise of patriotic righteousness, southern and eastern European workers were subjected to intense harassment (especially over registration for military conscription, which many foreigners did not understand and resisted). They were also exposed to negative publicity in the press, by the Protestant clergy, and behind closed doors by the automotive heads, who nonetheless needed these workers. According to the *Evening Record*, incipient Bolshevism and sedition lay behind any resistance to registration, any bust or arrest for bootlegging, any news of the Industrial Workers of the World (IWW), and every rumor of German spies prowling the border region.[12]

Such antagonisms exacerbated an already unbalanced labor scene. The *Labour Gazette*, in May–July, reported (not altogether accurately) that the auto plants were working at "full capacity," though behind the scenes at Ford there was simmering unease.[13] As reported in the *Evening Record* and elsewhere, McGregor's public and personal activities gave no indication of industrial strife or troubled labor relations. The cheery social functions of Ford clubs and sports teams, patriotic fund-raising and gestures (including the donation of a Fordson tractor to the Border Manufacturers' Farmers Association), the omnipresence of Ford films and film crews (Ford's Canadian travelogues had become extremely popular wartime entertainment locally and across the country), Ford's heavy influence in the daylight saving debate, and the incessant promotions of the chamber of commerce and its industrial commissioner all conveyed a sense of well-being.[14]

Within the Essex Border Utilities Commission, McGregor inched forward the debate over the sewage and tendering scheme.

New offices were secured for the commission in May; in March, McGregor and Dr. Charles Westlake Hoare (an original Ford subscriber) drew upon the report of the International Waterways Commission to highlight the ugly state of pollution in boundary waters. In April, Ford Canada was compelled to lay new water pipes of its own and at its own expense.[15] Insightful critiques and exposures of Ford profit-sharing plans in Detroit and Walkerville by economist Humfrey Michell of Queen's University in Kingston, the National Civic Federation of New York, and others generated no response from McGregor's office.[16]

After McGregor's vacation in West Virginia in April–June, he, Ford company lawyer A. R. Bartlet (on behalf of Walter McGregor, who had wound up behind a desk in France processing civilian claims for damages), and others privately completed the purchase of the National Spring and Wire Company and its reorganization in July as the Ideal Fence and Spring Company, which made wire fencing and seat springs and seats for Ford cars. The deal also led to the transfer of a factory building to Ford.[17]

That same month, the governor-general, the Duke of Devonshire, visited the Border Cities and, with Henry Ford hovering, was given a tour of the Ford plant by McGregor and Wallace Campbell—the tour offered to just about every visiting dignitary. As the duke and duchess were leaving town, the unpredictable Henry Ford "shocked" members of the viceregal party by walking arm-in-arm with the duchess, allegedly to prevent her from falling. At the formal level, the duke claimed to be "profoundly impressed with the industrial possibilities of the district."[18]

Committed to the promotion of such possibilities, the *Evening Record* offered no inkling of the labor disruption that broke out at Ford Walkerville at noon on Friday, 28 June. No one close to conditions there, however, was surprised. "It had been an open secret that labor troubles, together with the increasing difficulty in procuring materials promptly, have made the matter of keeping a full force at work a difficult one," *Iron Age* (a metals trade journal published in New York City) would claim in mid-July. As noted by *Iron Age* and some plant workers, dissatisfaction had been brewing for months. Links can be made to McGregor's earlier decision not to adopt the full $5 day in effect at Ford Detroit. The sequence of events in 1918 is clearer than the undercurrents and floor talk in the Canadian plant. Sometime in early June a group of workers reportedly secured the signatures of two-thirds of the plant's workers, demanding a wage increase from 45¢ to 62 1/2¢ an hour, or $5 for an eight-hour day. At noon on Friday, 28 June, a delegation led by George Currie, assistant foreman in the machine room, marched into McGregor's office, laid the petition on the table, and demanded that the company pay its employees a "living wage." McGregor and Campbell's stern refusal led to a mass meeting of workers that evening in the Trades and Labor Council (TLC) Hall in the Victoria Block, which was owned by Walter and Gordon McGregor and others. Advised by the IAM to unionize fully in order to enforce their demands, the workers present decided to give the company a week before they would ask federal labor minister Thomas Wilson Crothers to authorize a board of conciliation under the Industrial Disputes Investigation Act (IDIA).[19]

The next morning Philip Grandjean declined to give the *Evening Record* a full statement. He did say that the company understood it had three days in which to decide and that McGregor had made it known that the plant would close on 15 July for two weeks or more for its customary annual stocktaking of ten to fourteen days. (In fact, this was an unusually long break, meant to exert pressure on the workers.) McGregor took his family to their cottage at Kingsville on the 29th and then came back to Windsor. After a week of extreme tension, including the revelation of a "revolutionary society of Russian workmen" supposedly operating as a local of the radical Industrial Workers of the World and related accusations of sedition, on Saturday, 6 July, the company unexpectedly shut down the plant. McGregor's office posted notices for the factory's early closure and indefinitely locked out most of the workers. The company affronted them further by directing that they could now help with farm work, as a patriotic gesture. Emotions were highly taut. Watchmen were stationed in the machine room, where sabotage or other trouble was expected. McGregor was not at the scene or at his cottage; he had dashed off to Ottawa to intervene with Crothers. Emboldened perhaps by the machinists' victory at Russell Motor in Toronto and by workers' success in a brief strike at Fisher Body in Detroit (resolved by Automobile Workers Local No. 27), the TLC telegraphed Crothers on 19 July, demanding the reinstatement of workers laid off for joining the IAM, calling for a board to investigate the dispute under the terms of the Industrial Disputes Investigation Act, and threatening to call a general strike in a city already convulsed with a street railway strike, a short-lived postal strike, blistering summer weather, and heated misunderstandings and violent outbreaks over registration for military service.[20]

Three days later, the provincial convention of the IAM added its weight to action against the company for staging an illegal lockout. If Crothers was prepared to prosecute over a general strike, as he threatened to do, why would he not overturn the lockout, workers asked. Certain that Crothers would act, especially in light of the government's labor-favoring declarations of 11 July, which forbade strikes and lockouts and permitted union membership, the workers waited patiently for weeks without any further action. The plant remained unusually idle, but not for inventory. On 12 August, as announced suddenly by McGregor on the 8th, production resumed with a reduced (by about half) workforce on the old pay scale. Because of the lockout such local suppliers of Ford as Fisher Body (Walkerville) and Kelsey Wheel were hit hard. Predictably, Ford attributed its layoffs to wartime shortages of materials. By the 16th the irrepressible Ford Glee Club was active again in patriotic concerts, putting forth cheerful music. The conclusive step was taken on Saturday, 7 September, a day after authorization by Ford Canada directors, when McGregor happily announced that the workers' $5 wage demand would be met and that full production would resume on Monday, though with fewer workers, again, reputedly on account of the wartime drain but no doubt because Ford had not had time to hire new workers or had fired many.[21]

The wage demand had been at the heart of the disruption. Conscious of the level of pay at Ford Detroit, the workers were reportedly disgruntled too over the larger than necessary portion of company revenue being reserved for war taxes, the very argument McGregor had used as grounds for initially refusing labor's demand. To a lesser extent, dissatisfaction was also fueled by the presence, as the *Evening Record* put it, of "Bolsheviki Russians and Austrians" in the Ford plant, particularly in the heat-treating works and other departments where, because of the extreme temperatures and gaseous environment, Ford had trouble retaining Canadian- or American-born workers.[22] The European workers, whom the company never defended publicly and whose numbers were invariably exaggerated in the press, were willing to defy these physically unbearable conditions. In its extensive, pro-Ford coverage of the disruption, the *Evening Record* was quick to amplify and sensationalize the foreign factor. One reported incident dragged the debate down to a stereotypical level. In the midst of the factory disruption, a Scottish-Canadian worker voiced his intent to enlist and go to war. A "foreigner" replied that he would "look after the wife" of the worker, offense was taken, and a fight broke out.[23] There is no evidence that such tensions ever caused Ford to refuse to hire the eastern and southern European workers, who generally were unfamiliar with trade unionism before emigration and were loath to take part in labor actions.[24]

The degree of instability within the Ford workforce prior to the disruption, as a result of reduced production and shortages, is unclear. So too are the numbers of workers involved. The number of signatories to the original petition presented to McGregor varies from roughly 500 to more than 1,000, or something in the range of one-third of the workforce. Equally uncertain is the number signed up by the IAM, which had been making gains in Detroit on account of the official wartime authorization of membership by the American government and in Toronto because of the success of the action in July against Russell Motor.[25] The IAM pushed for more members in the Border Cities and throughout Ontario, though it was reluctant to see the wheels of industry stopped by a full general strike in wartime. The targeted group at Ford was the machinists. The sympathetic *Industrial Banner* (Toronto) claimed that the "greater number" of the employees was enrolled. It further reported, from interviews with IAM representatives, McGregor's distinctly antilabor responses. These were corroborated by no other journals. Asked if he thought a 40¢ an hour wage was enough to support a family, the *Industrial Banner* reported, McGregor claimed that was not his concern—workers knew the conditions of their employment when they began. "If not satisfied, they could go elsewhere," he retorted. On the matter of union membership, in true Henry Ford fashion, "he replied it did not make any difference to him what the men did after hours, but he would not stand for them telling him how to run his business."[26]

Outside the Border Cities rumors swirled about the causes and outcome of the labor disruption at Ford. In adjoining Kent County, the *Chatham Daily Planet* reported claims that the plant would close for the summer to allow the autoworkers to toil usefully on farms and that the government would take over the factory to produce munitions.[27] Opinion over the nature of the disruption and whether it warranted federal investigation was equally confused. McGregor saw it as a customary summertime closure brought on early, he tried to argue, by reduced production and shortages of materials, an argument picked up as far away as England, by the London *Times*.[28]

Even in Ottawa, the government's *Labour Gazette* recorded "an impending strike" at Ford, but no lockout and no investigation. Rather, it identified the disruption as a layoff of over 2,000 men because of "the difficulty of securing materials promptly," with most of those let go being "absorbed by other companies." The IAM and the local TLC, however, saw the disruption as an outright lockout, with McGregor in collusion with Ottawa. Moreover, the TLC claimed in late July, on the basis of workers' affidavits, that the Ford plant had turned to making boilerplates and smokestacks for the Eagle submarine chasers being constructed across the river by Ford Detroit in an ill-fated venture into marine engineering. This Canadian work would be acknowledged by McGregor's head of production, George Dickert, and at Ford Canada's shareholders' meeting in October, when the company openly accepted work on military tanks for the United States.[29] The Industrial Disputes Investigation Act, which originally covered a spectrum of "public utilities," including the communication, mining, and shipping and rail sectors, had been expanded in March 1916 to include industries producing a broad range of wartime materials, including ships.[30] It was on the basis of this extension that the TLC had pressed Crothers. McGregor, however, resolutely denied that his company had taken on any war work, and he likely told Crothers so at the earliest opportunity. Under no circumstances, not even the conversion of Ford Detroit, would McGregor publicly renege on his decision to forgo wartime production and remain with automotive production and a Made in Canada program as his company's best contribution to the conflict. At no point did anyone publicly ask how Ford Canada could produce war materials for the United States but not for Canada. By contrast, in Toronto T. A. Russell had become a purchasing agent for the Canadian Expeditionary Force, secured contracts for Russell Motor Car, and retooled it for the production of munitions.[31]

Antagonized by the TLC's threat of a general strike in the Border Cities, the overburdened Crothers ignored or was unconvinced of Ford Canada's production of war materials. There is no record in his department's files of any disruption in Walkerville in 1918, though some investigation may have been initiated. In the coverage by the *Evening Record*, the TLC was informed on 24 July that Crothers had indeed instructed the local crown attorney to begin investigating the lockout and to institute action against the company in the event of any violation of the IDIA. The *Industrial Banner* completed this account by stating that Crothers took no action on the crown's report. If any finding had come from this report, perhaps it was a factor in McGregor's concession in September.[32]

There was minimal or no involvement in the disruption from the Detroit side of the river. McGregor and Campbell evidently made the decisions; their American associates were already enjoying the labor peace and publicity attending the $5 day and the profits on war contracts, which McGregor was in no position to emulate. In the Border Cities, Local 718 of the IAM, emboldened by wartime sign-ups in the union, was largely on its own in charting a course alongside the TLC. In July in Detroit, the Automobile Workers (likely the Socialist-led United Automobile, Aircraft, and Vehicle Workers of America) had helped achieve success at Fisher Body, but in the embryonic state of auto unionization, the Automobile Workers would not become active in the Border Cities plants until 1920.[33] The drive initiated by the strike-weary IAM at Ford Canada ended with McGregor's timely recall in August and his premeditated concession on wages early the next month. Despite the TLC's opposition to the layoff of IAM members, McGregor, behind the shield of limited production, ensured that many were not reinstated in August, with organizer George Currie being one of the first to go.[34]

On 27 September the *Industrial Banner* put a brave face on the conclusion of the disruption: "[I]t can clearly be seen that there was a reason why the Fords came up with the dough. It was simply a case of having to if they wanted to keep things moving at all." In addition, the journal claimed that Ford Canada's boast of having the "best paid men" was bunkum—the IAM had placed a number of former Ford employees in new jobs "under better conditions and for higher wages."[35]

Despite the IAM's failure at Ford to gain a lasting beachhead (if wage demands are not considered), the disruption did spotlight a new cast of labor activists in the Border Cities, most notably the feisty Archibald E. Hooper, an IAM member, chair of the TLC's board of trustees, and a future labor alderman in Windsor. He would become Gordon McGregor's municipal nemesis. A machinist with the Great Eastern Railway in his native England, he had come to Canada in 1896 and in 1918 was working as a machinist in the Grand Trunk Railway's shops in Walkerville. Workers at Ford, he had stated bluntly in June, had just as much right to organize as did the businessmen and manufacturers in the Border Retail Merchants' Association and the chamber of commerce, which he despised and of which McGregor was the first vice president.[36]

After the disruption, which McGregor would rarely discuss afterward, he moved quickly to promote some semblance of normalcy. He was favorably profiled in a "Get Acquainted" series on 12 September in the *Border Cities Star:* the new name of the *Evening Record* when John A. McKay sold the newspaper that summer to William F. Herman of Saskatoon.[37] That same day McGregor announced his intent to continue making passenger cars, something Ford Detroit had abandoned in order to concentrate on war work. When Ford Detroit received contracts for military tanks and openly passed some of the work on to its Canadian plant, McGregor told his shareholders so in October but steadfastly maintained his public deceit on the flimsy grounds that the government would not want the information given out.[38] Such spurious reserve was not demonstrated by other local branch plants with contracts, among them the Canadian Sirocco Company, a maker of heating and ventilation systems that had a large suborder for munitions from the American government.[39]

In October, Ford shareholders were told too of some internal adjustments within the company: the closing of the assembly plant in Saint John, the elimination of sales and service at the branches (thus reducing branch expenses), and, most dramatically, plans to deal with the troublesome Australian branch. Unchallenged on the matter of war work—his company had built up a huge reserve of patriotic currency—McGregor had many other interests to follow in September and October: the opening of the golf club's social season (he had served as president in 1917–18), the never-ending water and sewers debate (including the opposition of Windsor mayor C. R. Tuson to the joint system, part of which was contracted out in August), chairmanship of the organizational meeting of a manufacturers' section within the Border Chamber of Commerce on 16 September, cheering on good war news ("Byng Bangs Bill's Boches," sang the *Star* on the 28th), making and showing Ford films, a major gas explosion at the Ford plant and up into nearby houses, and the implications of a purchase of thirty-eight acres in Ford City by General Motors of Canada Limited, which had been quietly incorporated on 8 November 1918 by a small Walkerville-based group acting for the American parent.[40] At the time it was in the process of negotiating to take over the McLaughlin interests in Oshawa.

On 4 September, shortly before his wage announcement, a buoyant McGregor was in Toronto to preside over a general meeting of Automotive Industries. A review of the work of the NACC in the United States left members convinced of the value of "co-operative action" within the industry in Canada. This was lofty intent. In an effort to emulate NACC policy, however, McGregor's awkward exercise of authority as president of the AIC and its vapid policies led some to question its value. At its board meeting on 14 July, McGregor, then in the midst of his lockout, again announced that the upcoming National Motor Show at the CNE in Toronto would be the last show allowed until after the war. Without Ford's participation, any Canadian show took a serious risk.

Whether meant as a gesture of industrial restraint or as a practical response to falling production by member manufacturers, the announcement offended the industry-friendly *Canadian Motorist*. It believed that the AIC could hardly duplicate the powerful NACC. McGregor's restriction would only "be a death blow to the professional motor show promoters."[41] Such a severe consequence, however, grossly underestimated the enterprise of the likes of the intrepid R. M. Jaffray and the proximity of armistice. As usual, the CNE was a success, with emphasis on the wartime role of trucks, but it was the industrywide increase in prices that had first caught the attention of the *Toronto Daily Star* in August: "Since last February, when Ford reversed its traditional policies of lowering prices to increase output, it has been patent that the era of low prices in the automobile industry has passed for a time—at least, until peace returns."[42]

With labor seemingly mollified by the wage settlement, Mc-

Gregor's publicists quickly returned to the war and Ford's place in its victorious conclusion. With McGregor and Wallace back from their cottages and Toronto, another grand Victory Bond campaign was in the offing and Ford employees were stepping up their activity. Particularly evident, after the summer's labor troubles and price increase, was the diversionary quality of the Ford activities. Traffic manager Frank Nancekevill entertained his office staff at his home near McGregor's large, servant-filled residence on Victoria Avenue. On 25 September the Windsor and North Essex fall fair began, with the opening parade being filmed by Ford crews for distribution across Canada. Other Ford films were a major feature during the fair, and the auto displays, including Ford cars, trucks, and tractors, were bigger than ever.[43] The impact of the Ford films, and the corporate association that came with them, cannot be overestimated. As the *Toronto Daily Star* had observed in the dreary days of the past winter, travelogues provided nationalistic inspiration: "We need recreation and relief," especially if they promote "clear thinking and resolute action."[44]

In 1918 McGregor's crews were doing their share, with a wide range of films made by a department now headed by advertising manager E. Gifford Hogarth. For over a year the public had been coming to terms with fears that the province could not produce enough food. One Ford film, dedicated to the federal Canada Food Board (of which McGregor's cousin was a member), focused on the Greater Food Production movement. Subtitled to depict the story of the Border Manufacturers' Farmers Association, this film spliced together footage of the mustachioed industrial commissioner Maclure Sclanders, association founder, baker, and former baseball and golf notable Harry Neal, the blast furnaces in Ojibway, the use of factory workers (to allow farmers to toil without interruption), the good-roads movement, and, inevitably, Ford tractors at work in the fields. "Good roads will greatly assist food production," viewers were told. Used for grading as well as tilling, "Fordson tractors are a means to this end as well as to farm production." The annual report of Ontario's Department of Highways confirmed this link: "[T]he road and the vehicle are complementary parts of the one machine." The Ford film would certainly have made sense to audiences inundated with messages of conservation from Canada's fuel controller and food board and a host of provincial emissaries.[45]

Another typical Ford release in 1918, *Interesting Glimpses of Eastern Canada*, which featured the tides of Fundy, the famous Reversing Falls on the Saint John River, scenes after the Halifax explosion of 6 December 1917, a marine diver at work, and the railway bridge at Quebec City, took the viewer to the east coast for under $1. So useful were such films that the new exhibits and publicity bureau of the federal Department of Trade and Commerce undertook in 1918 to circulate reels by Ford Canada, railway companies, and other private cinematographers.[46]

The Victory Loan campaign of 1918, which ran officially in Essex from 28 October to 16 November, was propelled by the success of the 1917 drive, the expertise of Ford personnel led by McGregor, the full cooperation of the *Star*, and the emotional run-up to the armistice. Nationally, the full resources of the federal government, the country's most imaginative advertising firms, and the smartest financial wizards were all marshaled in an elaborate, dominionwide organization to aid local campaigners and create a sense of urgent need, and to fund the end of war and the beginning of demobilization. In several areas, local committees agreed to pay salesmen or allow other incentives to encourage competition. In Essex, assisted once again by Colonel W. T. Gregory in the southern part of the county, McGregor was a natural choice to head the campaign. A proven marketer, he would preside over a carefully orchestrated campaign laced with vaudevillian farce, irresistible salesmanship, and patriotic obligation. By the end of the campaign, he told James Couzens, he was spending "very little" time at his Ford office. For several key positions he again turned to his own staff: sales manager Neil Lawrence took change of publicity, traffic manager Frank Nancekevill handled "special features," and film boss Gifford Hogarth assisted his predecessor George Ranson on the motion picture committee, which planned to film the campaign at every turn, show Ford films of Canada and of "German atrocities," and, working through government channels, secure a special film made with screen stars Mary Pickford, Douglas Fairbanks, and Charlie Chaplin to popularize Canada's Victory Bonds and the United States' Liberty Bonds. (Pickford and Fairbanks were enthusiastic participants in the Liberty Loan campaign.) The campaigning in Ford City, including McGregor's plant, was assigned to Ford Canada's assistant secretary Philip Grandjean and local realtor W. G. Reaume. Campaign headquarters was split between the offices of the Essex Border Utilities Commission and a drugstore in McGregor's Victoria Block. Introductory arrangements were undertaken by McGregor and Lawrence, starting with a launch at a chamber of commerce dinner on 3 October, when McGregor and national committee member W. G. Brett of Toronto both spoke.[47]

From the outset, as a condition of his chairmanship, McGregor insisted to resounding approval that any commissions received by his bond salesmen and other professionals be turned over to the Red Cross or other charities and that, with an eye on speculators, exceptionally large subscriptions be subject to taxation. There was to be no appearance of self-interest. On the 7th, McGregor and Lawrence went to Toronto for a district organization meeting. At the opening of the campaign on the 28th, Ford's board of directors authorized McGregor to purchase $750,000 worth of bonds.[48]

The tone was set early by Lawrence, in an obsessive style typical of his encouragement of Ford dealers: "We want to make every man, woman and child in Essex County think Victory bonds, eat Victory bonds, dream Victory bonds, and then stimulate enough enthusiasm to make them want to buy Victory bonds. If we can do that we can make six million [dollars] look like a beginning."[49]

The mechanics of the campaign resembled those of 1917: door-to-door and institutional approaches by teams of salespeople; "pretty girls" pushing bonds in theaters; a monstrous, two-mile-long parade on 2 November; visits and lectures by the national executive; heavy advertising in the *Star* and a series of bright posters; frequent rallies (many at the Ford plant) replete with dignitaries, celebrities, and Ford personnel from Detroit; and strong commitments from Ford Canada and Henry Ford, whose wielding of the common touch was well understood by McGregor. McGregor and his crew played on the patriotic emotionalism of wartime—the science of sales was their forte—and they skillfully built momentum by steadily moving their quotas and targets upward. In addition, they coordinated their campaign with the Liberty Bond drive in Detroit, an effort that facilitated a sharing of publicity, floats, and speakers as well as a generous response from such cross-border interests as the Association of Border Americans (who lived in Canada). From the patriotic thrust emerged the campaign's burlesque, mock-military theme: the "Battle of the Bonds." McGregor was styled a brigadier general, and campaigners became officers and soldiers in "McGregor's army." Aircraft dropped "bombs" of campaign literature, and Henry Ford's Eagle boats chased imaginary submarines up and down the Detroit River. This military mimicry carried through to the end of the campaign. At a "Victory Dinner" at the Windsor Armouries on 15 November, more than 800 campaign salesmen and workers celebrated. Entertainment consisted of the Ford-made film of the recent victory parade and a farcical skit on the "court martial" of Colonel W. T. Gregory for not engaging all his "troops" and allowing Ontario County and the United Counties of Leeds and Grenville to meet their goals before Essex. The court was conducted by McGregor and his brother Walter, recently returned from overseas service because of their mother's illness, both decked out in clan attire in true Scottish fashion. In response, Gregory turned over $240,000 worth of bonds. The audience, the *Star* reported, roared with laughter. The mood was jubilant, of course, because of the armistice.

On the 7th, news of peace had reached McGregor at noon in his campaign office at the chamber of commerce. Immediately he jumped up on a chair and announced the great news to those present. In a spontaneous expression of relief, the assembly broke into a favorite hymn, "Praise God from Whom All Blessings Flow." Not all of McGregor's staff were on hand to celebrate, however. Neil Lawrence for one had gone to Washington, possibly to deal with some of the business problems facing Ford. The *Star* would try to credit the war's end for the 5 percent dividend quietly announced by McGregor later in November, though increased prices were certainly a contributing factor. At the Ford plant work ground to a temporary halt when the peace became known and happy tumult ensued; subscriptions surged for the Victory campaign. The next day, the 8th, a massive, quickly organized parade headed by Windsor mayor Tuson, McGregor, and insurance agent Thomas J. McConnell wound its way to the armories. The *Star* naturally chose to quote McGregor's address there. After allowing the crowd to thank the Almighty through another round of "Praise God," he immediately reminded them of the Victory Bond campaign and Essex's claim to be the only county where subscriptions had been raised "totally voluntarily," without fees or commissions. "I want to know," he asked an audience eager to make final contributions, "if you are willing to show the rest of Canada they cannot pay us—that we will do this work without hire." Celebrations and subscriptions continued unabated; McGregor was fêted royally. An international victory parade in Detroit, where James Couzens had just been elected mayor, was scheduled for the 28th—to "show the boys in Detroit that our hearts are in the right place," as McGregor put it—but the parade was rained out. In the end, the campaign in Essex raised $9,781,000. In a disappointing coda, it was discovered after McGregor's death that one of his accounting staff, in collusion with a banker, embezzled a sizable portion of the funds held in the Ford Motor Company Victory Bond account, an incident that raises questions about the accounting practices of both the campaign and the company.[50]

There had been other problems during the campaign, though McGregor managed to keep the Victory drive to the front, with the full cooperation of the *Star.* An outbreak of Spanish influenza in mid-October, which struck more than 500 families with grim results, had delayed but could not derail McGregor's orchestration. To make matters worse, firemen threatened to strike, and veterans complained about inadequate medical facilities, despite campaign professions of concern for Essex's servicemen. In addition, an untold number of Border residents were suffering directly from the ongoing housing crisis in an urban area becoming known nationally, as well as among local real estate developers, for its disinterest in effective town planning. And once again, Windsor's council and mayor, C. R. Tuson, McGregor's campaign ally, were having second thoughts on the question of a central water and sewer system and about losing their municipal autonomy to a "metropolitan united service."[51] The *Border Cities Star,* which boosted the "vision of a metropolitan area," continued to back the EBUC. McGregor shared this vision. On occasion he could resort to sniping at Tuson, wondering where Windsor, if it did not purchase clean water from the commission, would get it.

The changes brought to the Border Cities by the end of the war were predictable, with many of the successes and problems having origins in developments of the past few years. McGregor continued to maintain a high public and corporate profile, albeit with emerging levels of postwar and political tensions and ill health. The Victory Loan drive had drained the Border Cities' well of charitable donation, but even after their remarkable achievement, which no other local auto producers could match, McGregor and his crew at

Ford remained convinced that there were other good causes that deserved their support. In November the Salvation Army began planning a drive for a maternity hospital and rescue home, a cause taken up by the Rotary Club. Within days, McGregor (who could draw on his experience with the sanatorium), Frank Nancekevill, the recently returned Neil Lawrence, and Philip Grandjean had put themselves forward as the drive's organizing committee, under the chairmanship of Harry Neal. Begun in early December, this campaign received some financial support from Ford Canada, but by mid-January it had collapsed. With minimal publicity, McGregor half-heartedly tried to restart it. A committed member of his office staff, Lillian St. Louis, ran a "tag day" at the factory, but the effort seems not to have had the appeal of the all-consuming Victory drive.[52] Circumstances simply did not support the hard sell, as auto men saw it.

By this point, McGregor's time outside his Ford office was being consumed by the increasingly intertwined politics of utilities, the uncharted ways of regional governance, and boosting the Border Chamber of Commerce. Like so many other local businessmen, McGregor was glad to contribute to the unceasing promotions of the chamber of commerce. In the "reconstruction period" after the war, it was eager to back fresh initiatives to sustain its call for industrial expansion, which trumped effective zoning and planning. A given was the Border Cities' fortunate proximity to Detroit. Why should American producers go any further into Canada, the *Star* would later ask one more time in an editorial on the dominion's "Motor City," when they can "build plants in the Border Cities, where they can personally supervise them with a minimum of inconvenience?"[53] Led by Maclure Sclanders and supported by the Border Retail Merchants' Association, through the winter of 1918–19 the chamber did its usual job of boosting the local auto industry, brought in various American speakers to promote the link, and feebly attempted a "Buy at Home" campaign to dissuade shopping in Detroit. The chamber did find a new, popular vehicle in the nationwide safety movement, which, generated by committee work at Ford, Dominion Forge, and Hiram Walker and by safety films in the Ford plant, culminated in a motion by McGregor in May to form the Border Cities Safety Council under the direction of F. M. Tobin.[54] As the head of the Canadian Safety Council, Tobin had had wide experience with safety bodies elsewhere in Ontario and had instituted the movement locally in January and February. Ford Detroit had formed a health and safety department even earlier, in 1914. By that time the Ontario Safety League had widened its focus of concern to include all types of accidents, especially those in workplaces.

As a regional body, the chamber of commerce received mixed support from each of the Border municipalities, with Windsor least well disposed of all. In December the chamber faced charges of cliquishness as Windsor's nominees for its directorate on the chamber pulled out. Within a week McGregor, colleague Frank Nancekevill, and other directors had hurriedly formed a reorganized body and new bylaws. Windsor's council, which in January's election lost Tuson and took on four labor representatives, including the obstreperous Archibald Hooper, continued to find the regional chamber and its assumption of municipal authority offensive, whatever it did to promote industrial growth. In February, Sclanders moved to apply to the province to allow Windsor to exceed the $20,000 it could spend on acquiring industrial sites. In April an unimpressed council withheld its annual grant to the chamber.[55] The same type of divisions confounded any regional efforts to deal with the housing crisis. In 1918 the high costs of labor and material had caused building permits to fall by half, though between 1912 and 1918 the population had almost doubled.[56]

The Windsor and Ford City housing commission did what it could with provincial funds intended to alleviate the housing shortage. Sclanders and others recognized the problem and though the Border real estate board, Ford City, and a number of building and loan and realty companies advanced remedial schemes, as well as cheap, rapidly built housing for workers, no larger regional response could be coordinated before the summer of 1919. No industry interested in expansion, especially Ford, was interested in restraining the free-wheeling negotiations and absence of zoning restrictions that facilitated property swaps and purchases.[57] McGregor and Ford Motor did not see the problem of housing as one they needed to address as seriously as sewers and water.

As chair of the Essex Border Utilities Commission, McGregor progressively embraced the call for amalgamating the Border towns, a position encouraged by the advocacy of planning pioneer Thomas Adams for the coordination of utilities, highways, and park projects in the Border region. Such coordination did not rest easily with the councils of Windsor and Sandwich. They tended to self-interest and grave suspicions of the EBUC's unprecedented move to impose new levels of governance without clear electoral mandates. Public debate did not yet focus on the formation of one municipality, despite recurring suggestions of unifying names for the region, such as Ferry City in 1918. Rather, wide-ranging plans for the unified water and sewer system advocated by the EBUC, a regional health board, and better links to Detroit claimed attention. In June 1919, to no one's surprise, McGregor moved the chamber of commerce's support for an international subway under the Detroit River, a massive, overly ambitious undertaking keenly supported by Detroit mayor James Couzens and backed by many on the Canadian side as a suitable war memorial. At the same time, the chamber was unhappy with Windsor's handling of ferry service. A month later, EBUC engineer Morris Knowles (originally from Pittsburgh), in outlining the commission's ambitious regional plan, prophetically proposed a bridge over the river. It was water and sewers, however, that most challenged Chairman McGregor, whose imperious corporate style did not always translate into smooth municipal politicking.[58]

From September 1918 McGregor and the EBUC had clashed repeatedly with Tuson and the Windsor council over a joint system. Over the year's final months, costs, engineering reports, and questions of popular representation were fruitlessly debated, with mounting frustration, barely controlled hostility, and threats to resort to public referenda and bylaws. McGregor was reelected to the EBUC for Ford City in January, defeating Theodore Drouillard by a vote of 387 to 285, and was then returned as chairman. Patiently he weathered Windsor's challenges and complaints. He countered where he could, often using the damning reports of heavy pollution issued by consultants, health officers, and the International Waterways Commission. Significantly, he had the backing of industries and the chamber of commerce's industrial committee for a joint system. The encouragement of Windsor's new mayor, Edward Blake Winter, was short-lived: support in March for an amalgamated system dissipated.

The deadlock was partially broken in April, when McGregor unilaterally proposed plans for a regional health board, to consist of three taxpayers, a medical official appointed by the EBUC, and a chairman. Municipal unanimity was not required to move ahead; in July the province, which had formed the EBUC, retroactively vested it with the authority of a local board of health. This new board, planned by the commission from the beginning of 1919, took shape that summer. In June its members were selected by McGregor and chamber president A. F. Healy of Sandwich. Dr. Fred A. Adams of Toronto, just out of the Canadian Army Medical Corps, was named joint officer of health; he made his first visit to the Border Cities in July. Confirmed as the board's chairman, McGregor eventually intended to resolve the water and sewer problems through this board, and he had support from Windsor's health officer, Dr. George Robert Cruickshank, though not from the council, which was insulted by McGregor's end run and reliance on provincial means. Support for the board came too from the chamber of commerce, which would later back the idea of the EBUC's attempts to coordinate town planning. This alignment helps explain Windsor's coolness toward the chamber.[59] The health board first met on 22 August with McGregor in the chair, and it quickly launched a crusade against dirty cafés and substandard jail cells.

McGregor's ongoing concerns over taxation at different levels—federal, local, and cross-border—stemmed from a mindset formed within a chamber of commerce committed to unfettered growth and as the head of the Border Cities' largest branch plant. The move by American revenue authorities to tax the Canadian branches of American firms generated a flurry of reaction in late January 1919 from the Canadian Reconstruction Association and boards of trade throughout Ontario, including the Border Chamber of Commerce. The problem was aggravated locally in February by the decision of tax officials in Detroit once again to require Canadians working there to pay American income tax. (Related action would later be taken against Americans living in the Border Cities.) On 28 February 1919, 250 Canadian workers employed at Detroit Shipbuilding waited on industrial commissioner Maclure Sclanders, A. F. Healy, and McGregor to have the decision delayed. A terse telegram was immediately sent by the chamber of commerce to McGregor's good friend and member of Parliament, W. C. Kennedy: "Get Ottawa to instruct Washington to call off Detroit collector." Within days Washington, recognizing Canadian tax exemptions for Americans, ruled to allow Canadians similar exemptions.[60]

Of more direct concern to McGregor were Ford City's municipal attempts to assess Henry Ford for personal taxation, attempts that McGregor vigorously stonewalled year after year, and the federal business profits tax. He supported the chamber's call on 23 January for the abolition of this noisome tax, which, he argued, hurt not just Ford but also "the industrial life of this country." Sclanders backed him on this complaint by producing letters from western associates who voiced similar concern, among them the Winnipeg-based Canadian Credit Men's Trust Association. When the tax was not dropped from the federal budget that spring, McGregor's exasperation reached new heights. There was little reaction from business in general to this politically necessary tax, but McGregor was selfishly resentful: "[N]o development of the local [Ford] plant will take place," he threatened on 7 June 1919, adding with much exaggeration that his company had already paid more than $3 million. (For the year ending in July 1918 the company had paid tax of only $167,951 on net profits—from fewer cars than the year before—of $2,445,139.53.) Similar sentiments came from brother Walter and his company, Ideal Fence. A meeting of the manufacturers' section of the chamber of commerce was called for the 9th to draft yet another complaint for the full body to endorse and promulgate.[61]

McGregor's assessment of Ford's postwar position depended on his audience. Within the chamber of commerce, his commentary on the depressive business profits tax found a sympathetic audience. Publicly he claimed the war, which spawned the tax, had been good for Ford. Personally, even with the institution of income taxation in 1917, the gregarious McGregor was in a most comfortable position, ready to enjoy the trappings claimed by Essex's most publicized industrial leader: a box at the Empire playhouse in December 1918, prominence at IODE dances and a host of other social functions, the donation of trophies to sports teams at Ford, another month's vacation at White Sulphur Springs in Virginia in March–April, founding membership in the short-lived St. Clair Auto and Boat Club in April, and renewed directorship in the Essex golf club in February.[62] A casual sportsman and fairly good golfer, he loved the game, its camaraderie and smoothing of corporate discussion, though he did not play as well or as seriously as his next in charge, the intense Wallace Campbell. It was no coincidence that Ford advertisements in 1919 featured Model Ts parked next to the clubhouse and greens in play.[63] On 1 June 1919 McGregor's salary was raised substantially, to $65,000, and probably included the traditional bonus allowances. By this time, too, for his own transportation McGregor had moved up to a luxurious, chauffeur-driven Packard automobile, a marque made in Detroit.[64]

When the Reverend Henry John Cody, Ontario's minister of education, visited the Border Cities in May 1919, the *Star* covered his visits to the Ford and Canadian Steel plants and GM's rising factory and his chummy public debates with McGregor. In part, this agenda was to allow Cody to emphasize the need for technical education. At a banquet sponsored by the public and separate school boards, McGregor, in his guise of civic leader, criticized in a "friendly" way the lack of spaces in Ford City's new school, the resulting division of students into morning and afternoon shifts, the proliferation of subjects, the limitation of physical education, and the foolishness of making children stay in school through "sultry" weather until 15 July to make up for the suspension caused by the outbreak of flu.[65]

As 1918 ended, McGregor was in an optimistic mood. Though there was no clear indication about the actual constrictions of steel supplies—reports varied—the drop in production was more than offset by increased prices. Henry Ford's resignation as president of Ford Detroit (and talk of a new company) on 30 December 1918—a major shift caused by a court decision that forced him to distribute millions to stockholders—shook America, though he retained ownership. With Ford still president of Ford Canada, McGregor headed off rumors with bland public reassurance in March: "Mr. Ford still has his interests here and will continue to hold them."[66] Indeed, McGregor made sure that Henry Ford's interests and financial stake were carefully monitored. By July 1919, after falling to a low of $155 in 1918, Ford Canada stock on the Detroit exchange had climbed to $540, though there were suggestions of manipulation by brokers.[67]

Ford Canada's fall in production to 39,112 in 1919 (of which 17,880 would be exported) did not surprise McGregor, who had anticipated the drop. In January 1919 the Canadian Manufacturers' Association's *Industrial Canada* published a two-and-a-half-page statement by McGregor called "Conditions in the Canadian Auto Industry." Even though he was a member of the association's export trade and industrial relations committees, he rarely wrote such pieces, unlike the more outgoing T. A. Russell. McGregor's article was largely an unabashed encomium on Ford Canada, just as the article in the *Canadian Annual Review* for 1919 on "Canada as a Producer of Motor Cars" was a barefaced promotion of Russell's Willys-Overland of Toronto and its direct contribution to wartime production. The effect of the war, McGregor wrote in his piece, had been "almost . . . beneficial" because of increased purchasing, despite railway congestion, that Ford had partially overcome by shipping its cars "knocked-down," or mostly disassembled, in compact crates. He honestly acknowledged Ford's increase in prices, a situation that would be sustained by the high costs of materials and labor and current inventories, and he stated his intention to maintain reduced production, in part because of reduced postwar demand. Inevitably he challenged government taxation of automobiles as unfair. Scant attention was paid to developments outside of Ford.[68]

A fuller account of the industry would have recognized other developments, among them the fast growth of the used-car market across Canada, the new local branch works of Maxwell-Chalmers and Fisher Body, the appointment in June of George W. Parkes as president and general manager of Maxwell-Chalmers in Canada, and the branch plant begun that spring for Champion Spark Plug (a major supplier of Ford). Typical of the steady movement of personnel and close familiarity within the industry was the selection of Arthur J. Hayes, former assistant manager of Ford and before that manager of the McLaughlin automobile agency in London, as sales manager of Champion Spark Plug. Characteristic of the industry's transitory nature was the flurry of brash proclamations by peripheral upstarts and the rumors of new competition for Ford. In the spring reports circulated that Overland would set up in the Border Cities.[69] The real competition, however, came from General Motors Canada. Its affiliated Canadian Products plant, which started construction in Walkerville in April and went into production within months building axles and transmissions for the Oshawa-made Chevrolet and McLaughlin-Buick, was the first heavy manufacturing arm of GM Canada. At the same time, in April, GM Canada had ambitiously announced a "profits plan" for its future employees. In all, in 1919, forty-four new manufacturing concerns, most of them American, had established themselves in the Border Cities. "Ours is not mere development," industrial commissioner Sclanders had marveled. "It is transformation."[70] In February Pathé Film of Montreal came to the Border Cities to film this transfiguration, notably in Ford City and the Ford plant, assisted by Ford film crews. The Sparks film company made a similar film some months later.

The brevity of McGregor's mention of labor costs in his *Industrial Canada* statement belied some shifts in the local labor movement and local politics, interwoven with countrywide turbulence that would climax later in the year in Winnipeg. In Windsor there was a handful of members of the left-wing, Detroit-based Automobile, Aircraft, and Vehicle Workers, which published the *Auto Workers' News*. On its editorial staff was Windsor's Gordon Cascaden. He belonged to a labor family that was active in both the Socialist Party of Canada and the radical Industrial Workers of the World, though it is not known if any of the family worked at Ford Canada.

Some war veterans who came back to work in the Border Cities saw industrial relations from new points of view. Some were too young to see any change. In February former soldier Frank Rawlings returned to work at Ford, the first veteran to be put back on its payroll. Not yet twenty-one years, he did not qualify for the company's increased wage, but he still complained directly to McGregor. "Take it easy, son," Rawlings remembered him saying in a piece of homey advice used by Ford as a promotion years later, "you've only a few weeks to go until you're 21, and you've got a lot of years ahead with the company." Assuaged, he later recalled McGregor as "a real diplomat. He could explain company policy, even though you thought you were against it, and make you like it."[71]

Not all veterans were as impressed with Ford Canada's refusal to enter war production for Canada, especially as they watched the company draft presumptuous postwar advertising championing the Model T as the "Joan of Arc Machine" that drew praise from British Tommies and did soldierly service in France (where "700 cars out of 1,000 were Fords"), Italy, Egypt, and Mesopotamia in western Asia.[72] In December 1918, in a vote that speaks of family rejection, both Walter McGregor and his father-in-law were defeated for the presidency of the Border Cities branch of the highly assertive Great War Veterans' Association. On 6 February 1919, in an expression of strong nativist sentiment that ran far beyond the numbers involved, the association voted that "aliens" (suspect European workers) be replaced in the automobile industry by veterans. (Ford City mayor Montreuil, in an attempt to straddle the debate, distinguished between friendly and enemy aliens.) Pearson Wells of Ford's labor department countered that Ford *would* replace the twenty-five or so aliens employed at the company, mainly in the heat-treatment rooms where temperatures and gas fumes were excessive, but that no veteran would accept a position in those areas because "it was not a white man's job." By contrast, Henry Ford supposedly made openings for 1,000 "crippled soldiers" at the American plant. The larger issue of placing veterans was debated without clear results by the chamber of commerce on 12 February, with McGregor presiding. "Comrade" Carrick took exception to the employment of German workers at Ford and Canadian Bridge, but the chamber's president, customs officer Robert H. Harrison, resisted committing the chamber to any resolutions along such lines, and there the matter dropped from the columns of the *Star*.[73] At the chamber's elections at the end of the month, McGregor was reelected as a councillor at large.

Far stronger in labor circles than the Automobile, Aircraft, and Vehicle Workers or the Great War Veterans' Association, Local 718 of the International Association of Machinists launched a new membership drive in the spring of 1919, possibly to recoup the losses of 1918 and fight potential wage cuts. In the tide of workers who shifted back and forth across the river, there were many who had undoubtedly been let go when American employers cleaned house as government contracts and union membership had evaporated at war's end. More militant in rhetoric than in action on the floor, the Windsor local of the IAM was reputedly the largest union in the Border Cities, with close to 1,500 members. Of that number, 800 were actual machinists, most in the shops of the Grand Trunk, the Michigan Central, and the Canadian Pacific railways. But there was also an unspecified number, according to local president-machinist-alderman Archibald Hooper, "in the automobile industries, and other metal trades in the Border Cities." When the IAM launched its drive, it had momentum. "Currents of discontent" churned through labor's ranks, but, in contrast to the action of 1918, Ford was not a clearly defined target.[74]

The IAM's agitation took place against a backdrop of local strikes between May and July of cigar makers, garbagemen, and especially the streetcar operators of the Sandwich, Windsor, and Amherstburg Railway. In May one of Windsor's other labor councillors, George Wood, addressed Local 718, condemning the open shop and calling for new members amid rumblings of a general strike. Hooper was even more vociferous. "He is one of the boys," the *Machinists' Monthly Journal* (Washington) proudly claimed. "He stands by his gun until all his ammunition is spent, and then fights with the gun."[75] The labor councillors kept pressure on mayor E. B. Winter, whose support of a joint water system and of May 26 as a national holiday (against the wishes of the banks and post office) was strategically backed by McGregor and Pearson Wells (now with Dominion Forge). Incensed by the treatment of strikers in May and June in Winnipeg, where social and political confrontation peaked in the famous Winnipeg General Strike, the IAM nonetheless balked when the Border railway men called on labor in July to join in a sympathy strike. The "time was not ripe," the machinists felt. Still, their membership drive had been productive. By early August, a new lodge had been formed in Walkerville, and a women's lodge was taking shape within Local 718.[76]

At the Ford plant workers were quiet. Even if Ford Canada was not a clearly defined target of IAM efforts, Archibald Hooper's sentiments became well known. He disliked McGregor's brand of corporate welfare and his autocratic control of the EBUC, and he had no use for the cliquish chamber of commerce. He argued at every opportunity that through its promotions the chamber had lured laborers to the Border Cities but betrayed them by its failure to ensure sufficient jobs and housing. It was in this setting that McGregor had moved to forestall any labor action and to keep ahead of other automotive companies, including GM's Canadian Products and the profits plan it adopted in April.

On 8 May McGregor announced, with no prior notice, a $6 a day wage scale, effective 12 May. Ostensibly, in a now familiar pattern, he was following the plan adopted at Ford Detroit on 1 January. Observers had wondered if this increase would happen, and labor leaders in Toronto had debated the possible impact. What internal demands were at work, apart from a climbing cost of living, is unknown. McGregor's announcement, the *Star* reported, was received "with joy" by his 2,500 workers, who included 400 veterans. "We have tried to do the best possible by our employees and it now remains with them to provide out of this increase, for their future," he explained with a hint of dismissiveness (and no mention of his own upcoming salary increase). In addition to the workers' increase, in September the company would move $100,000 from a surplus account to form the Employees' Welfare and Housing Fund. This initiative, and that of GM, provided some incentive for Studebaker's launch of a new benefit plan for its own workers in July and Fisher Body's adoption in August of a bonus plan. All generated disdainful reaction from Windsor's labor alderman.[77] That summer, McGregor's support for a memorial tunnel under the Detroit River and consideration of a bridge in the EBUC's regional plans helped divert public attention to metropolitan and cross-border needs.

After the pay raise at Ford in May, McGregor had found himself in a comfortable position in his relations with labor, despite the scrutiny of Hooper and the IAM. During the spring a royal commission on industrial relations held hearings in twenty-eight centers across Canada to allow, as historians Heron and Siemiatycki put it, "for an airing of grievances and a show of official concern, just at the height of militancy."[78] No Border automotive representatives were heard from, but senior industrialist E. G. Henderson of Canadian Salt in Windsor and a Canadian Manufacturers' Association (CMA) stalwart, did speak to the commission at its sitting in London. He was queried about the auto industry. His remarks were oblique. He mentioned Ford in his acknowledgment of the cross-border competition between Canadian and American laborers in terms of wages and rates. When asked directly about Ford's presence, and possibly its influence, at chamber of commerce meetings, he tactfully stated that he could not speak for the company.[79]

McGregor certainly needed no champion. He had been reelected president of Automotives Industries earlier in the year, with the irrepressible Robert Samuel McLaughlin of McLaughlin-Buick/General Motors in Oshawa as vice president.[80] (Whatever their corporate rivalry, McLaughlin liked McGregor and would later remember him with respect and a smile, according to one of McGregor's nephews.) Their combined weight did much to define Automotives Industries, whatever its real function, and McGregor and McLaughlin often traveled together to promote its virtues. By midyear they also worked together on the executive committee of the CMA's newly formed Ontario division and as new members of the association's industrial relations committee. Both were eager to share enthusiasm for the revival of the National Motor Show at the Canadian National Exhibition from 23 August to 6 September. Though McLaughlin did not yet make trucks, it was these heavy haulers, including Ford trucks, that were given pride of place at the CNE.[81]

The Ford truck was quickly gaining ground statistically as the favored service vehicle of merchants and businessmen. From coast to coast they delighted in photographs of their fleets in front of their stores and factories. Advertising aimed at farmers urged them to buy a Ford truck and thus save time on travel "and spend more time on the land." Anecdotal support kept pace, not all of it of the sort publicized or desired by Ford Canada. In the Nova Scotian countryside, for instance, Frank H. Sobey's use of his Ford truck's reverse pedal as a brake—a common practice with Ford cars—failed him one day on a tight downhill turn with a load of twenty-eight lambs destined for his father's butchery. Despite Sobey's stand on the running board for counterbalance while grasping the steering wheel, the truck flipped and the future supermarket magnate spent the rest of the day gathering lambs. In the west, the adventuresome use of Model Ts in wintertime led to the innovative fitting of front-end skis and rear-wheel tracks.[82] No other car in Canada produced such a volume of adaptations and stories.

Heading into the fall of 1919, McGregor was in a confident position. The royal commission, which had bypassed Ford, gave way in September to the National Industrial Conference in Canada, a remarkable gathering of capital, labor, and the state. McGregor attended as an employers' delegate for "vehicles for land transportation." Despite the strong representations of the labor delegates, the overall results of the conference were inconclusive. The response from the employers on the key issues of hours of labor and collective bargaining was limited. Ford received little attention, and McGregor was disinclined to say much of consequence to a gathering he did not deem important. Unexpected praise for Henry Ford came from labor leader John A. Flett of Hamilton, whose testimony on 16 September was also marked by ignorance of the concessions made by Ford workers in securing an eight-hour day. McGregor's single intervention followed Flett. After some weak humor and, in typical fashion, factual corrections to misinformation then in circulation about Ford, he offered the company line of forward movement on profit sharing: "[I]f you go into the United States you will find wagons running up and down the streets carrying newspapers that call Mr. Ford everything they can afford to call him because he is not splitting his profits further with his employees." Positioning his own company as an aspirant for a "satisfactory solution—on the question of the working day and the working wage," he blamed labor for any delays, through reference not to Canada but to Australia. "I was there in 1909, and it seems to me that every year since then the industries are tied up months and months at a time" by "continuous strikes." He made no mention of the muddled state there of automobile assembly, the confusing variety of bodies on Model Ts, and the degree of vested interest within a disorganized Ford network.[83] Ford Canada's shipments to Australia would pick up in 1919–20 but would fall off again the following year.

Sidestepping the inconclusive nature of the Ottawa conference, McGregor carefully shifted his focus to living conditions in his summary of the conference at a dinner at the Essex Golf and Country Club following his return to the Border Cities, where, in the postwar slump, the cost of living was spiraling.[84] Industry's concern with the business profits tax, municipalities grappling with the proposed costs of joint utilities, labor dissatisfaction, provincial grants for housing, the uncoordinated building boom, the fruitless enthusiasms of the EBUC and the chamber of commerce for town planning and cantonments for the homeless, and the probe into the cost of living by the chamber and the Border Retail Merchants' Association all contributed to a degree of public malaise. In an address to the chamber, British planning expert Thomas Adams termed local development "haphazard" and called for regional coordination. Irritating to some were the outspoken critiques by Alderman Hooper. In moving once again to hold up the council's grant to the chamber of commerce, he bluntly claimed the Border Cities were overcrowded, the promotions of industrial commissioner Sclanders had overachieved, and the auto industry was content with revolving-door employment. In an oft-repeated summary, he said: "Everywhere you look in Ontario you see the words, 'Go to the Border Cities for a job.' They come here all right. They find their way from all over, and still they come, and there's nowhere to stay, and the rents are still soaring high."[85] Hooper's impression of the influx of labor was confirmed even by the *Star*. In contrast, McGregor smugly and naïvely observed in his account in early October that manufacturers "had contributed their share toward rendering living conditions better," and, correspondingly, "further advances in labor costs were not anticipated." In predictable partisan fashion, at a local Liberal nomination meeting, he passed the blame on to the provincial Conservative government, which he felt had "outlived its usefulness."[86]

An addendum to McGregor's manufacturing perspective came from his second in charge, Wallace Campbell, who, as a special "safety week" ended (with entertainment by a kilted band from Ford Canada), praised the work of Captain James H. (Jack) Robbins, secretary since July of the American-inspired Border Cities Safety Council. (Robbins would leave in April 1922 to become industrial commissioner of the Detroit Board of Trade.) Safety committees operated not just at Ford, where some deaths and accidents nonetheless continued to occur, but also at many Border plants. The movement was sweeping through businesses throughout the country, with modest effect. Interpretation of this effect varies. Naylor argues it was both a means of reducing workers' compensation assessment and an "innocuous" method of demonstrating corporate cooperativeness while shifting the blame for accidents to workers' carelessness. Hooker sees the movement, which he examines in detail at Ford Detroit, as a means of giving workers a stake in contributing to increased production. In December, at a chamber of commerce meeting in Windsor, J. H. Goldie of the Cadillac Motor Car Company of Detroit lectured on the foreman's place in accident prevention. At Ford Canada, L. W. Lee ran a "school of safety instruction," which may have engaged workers—the company showed safety films from Ford Detroit—and been influenced by the theories of Lee's sociological department.[87]

In the aftermath of the pay increase at Ford in May, worker resentment seems to have been subdued, despite the general labor dissatisfaction that carried into the fall and winter. In the form of the employees' welfare and housing fund set up in September, the company, as McGregor said in Ottawa, had made some effort to ameliorate the cost of living, but confirming detail on the fund is not available. In late October, the chamber of commerce and the Border Retail Merchants' Association announced their intent to launch a joint probe into the cost of living. The *Star*, however, did not make any investigative examination. It was the thrilling story that continued to catch the public's attention, with old prejudices remaining in play. In late November, for example, the Ford company easily distanced itself from employee William Stark when charges of his carrying a weapon and "violating" a young girl produced righteous indignation and sensational headlines. Another instance was the case that came to Windsor's Police Court after May Brooks attacked Percy Ulch, who, readers of the *Star* were led to conclude, was a European. May's husband, Donald, and Ulch both lived on Langlois Avenue and both worked at Ford. No doubt with some provocation, Ulch told his managers that the Brookses had two boarders—still a cardinal sin with Ford Canada, even in a housing crisis. Donald and Percy subsequently came to blows, and May jumped in and thumped Percy with a chunk of wood. After two hours of rancorous testimony in court, a "weary" magistrate deferred judgment.[88]

The National Industrial Conference in September and the debates on housing and cost of living did not visibly occupy McGregor. At the end of July, buoyed by the pay raise and just before closing his plant for a short time for inventory, he announced his projections for Ford's "biggest year" of production: 60,000 automobiles, an extremely ambitious target after the disappointing output of 39,126 cars in fiscal 1919. The actual result—an amazing 55,616—would come close, though this 42 percent increase would pale beside the 89 percent increase achieved at Ford Detroit. McGregor had been primed for this announcement by his attendance, along with his staff and eight branch managers, at the massive convention in Detroit on July 18–25 of Ford's American branch managers and salesmen. In typical gestures, on the 27th he took a contingent of staff through his plant and then entertained them at his Kingsville cottage on the shores of Lake Erie.[89]

It was the enthusiasm and optimism from this launch, which was heightened by the quiet on the labor front, that McGregor brought to the CNE show and the start of the new season of production. On display at the show, the Model T for 1919 was little changed, but the company believed that its new electric starter (to replace the hand-operated crank) would attract interest. By contrast, the Chevrolet already had self-starters and had been restyled with rounded front fenders instead of straight ones, while Studebaker Canada was into its second year with a new line: a Big Six and a new Light Six in addition to its four-cylinder motor.[90] Still, by the time of the Ford shareholders' meeting on 27 October, McGregor could claim the company was "in a very flourishing condition," due mainly to the price increase in February. At the start of the fiscal year in 1918, accounts receivable were high, the result in part of the extraordinary sale of 2,790 cars to the British government for wartime shipment to India and Mesopotamia, orders for 4,000 cars for Ford Manchester (which could not take American Ford cars because of a British embargo) and 1,000 for Ford Detroit for the Buenos Aires market, and the downplayed work for Ford Detroit's tank contract from the American government. Branch receipts were up too because of the heavy call for service and parts "due to increased number of cars in operation."[91] Still, meeting the target of 60,000 automobiles would be a challenge without expanded plant facilities. The business profits tax remained a financial and political distraction, though less of a burden than McGregor professed.

Local competition from GM Canada would start to become a reality. By October 1919 the Walkerville plant of Canadian Products had began work under the thirty-three-year-old Major Howard Earl Blood, who had assumed its general managership in May and moved to Walkerville to rush completion. A university-trained mechanical engineer and the son of Maurice E. Blood, a veteran bicycle, automobile, and parts manufacturer of Kalamazoo, Michigan, he had wide experience as a machinist, production manager (Detroit Gear and Machine), aviator and flight engineer, and company manager. After delays caused by coal and steel shortages in the United States, the first railway-car load of Chevrolet FB motors was sent to Oshawa in December, eventually to be followed by motors, axles, and transmissions for GM's McLaughlin-Buicks, Oaklands, and other Chevrolet models.[92] For Ford, however, the greatest obstacles occurred in the Australian market, where shipping difficulties, chassis-only exports, and declining market share continued to burden Ford Canada. Model Ts nonetheless remained the leading automotive import into Australia.

Ford Canada had not acted on its plan in October 1918 to "discontinue" its Australian branch. This precipitate proposition had likely been made as a result of the company's problems there and Henry Ford's pruning of his overseas operations. In June 1919 McGregor sent his manager of sales, Neil Lawrence, abroad for a year "to explore new trade possibilities in the British Empire," Wilkins and Hill conclude.[93] Exploration may have been one goal. In reality, he tried to bring standardization to the variety of bodies being built in Australia for Model T chassis in what had become a flourishing subindustry spurred by wartime embargos on whole cars, and to correct market dysfunctions of supply, price, and dissatisfaction caused by poorly made bodies. As a result of Lawrence's trip, a "Body Building Committee" was formed, but nothing came of it and production remained chaotic by Walkerville/Detroit standards. The Australian tariff of 1920, which would double the duty on imported bodies, would continue to assure a market for local body builders. In addition, both McGregor and Lawrence were perplexed by a problematic state of labor in Australia, which was clearly beyond their control.[94] On the other hand, McGregor would have taken some satisfaction from the confirmation in October by visiting trade commissioners from Australia, New Zealand, and South Africa that Ford was the only American auto firm in Canada that did not sell directly to imperial markets and did not channel correspondence or finances through its American parent.[95]

Closely integrated with the export trade conducted by agencies of Ford Detroit, Ford Canada's international business no longer followed strict imperial lines. There were practical and territorial trade-offs, such as the shipments to Britain and Argentina—head office's "special orders." By 1919, as well, McGregor's company had pulled out of the small-market possessions in the Caribbean and Central and South America, where it had once had interests. In 1919 the manager of Ford Detroit's foreign department entered into a contract with a firm in the British colony of Trinidad. At the same time, in the Asian-Pacific market, where Ford Canada was very active, it had been supplying such nonimperial possessions as Java, Sumatra, and Thailand for a number of years.

The boosting of production and delivery was a carefully calculated process. In the fall and winter of 1919 reserve stocks of steel and coal allowed the company to ride out shortages (caused by strikes in the United States), though supplies of inferior steel from Canadian sources led to weak castings and problems with the metal in Ford's cylinder blocks. Such problems were a concern because Ford had shifted in 1918 to Canadian foundries, among them the Holmes plant in Sarnia, for engine blocks. There may have been

Dominion Forge and Stamping Company, Walkerville, pressing room with machines for making automobile fenders. *Canadian Machinery*, 7 June 1917. Photograph by Mark Coatsworth.

start-up problems in their manufacture, including inconsistent quality of metal. By mid-December 1919, however, McGregor's dire predictions of foreign closure—he was a strategic doomsayer and commentator—had given way to ebullience and typical dramatic announcement. "The business was never more healthy than at the present time," he told the *Star* on the 13th. The delay in order fulfillment was normal because of low demand, and the recovery of supply was well timed to meet the company's normal shift around February from production for export to escalation in manufacture for domestic trade. But even there, in a tightening of control, dealers (including Don McGregor's Universal Car agency in Windsor) were being required to produce evidence of actual orders from customers in order to receive their allotments.[96]

Buffered by its reserves of steel and coal, Ford Canada was quick to capitalize on the suffering of firms in the local supply chain and to score points in the still-troubled utilities debate. The shortage of steel had intensified problems at Dominion Forge and Stamping, an important supplier of fenders, gas tanks, mufflers, hoods, other sheet-metal pieces, forged axles and connecting rods, and frames for Ford. Workers there, frustrated by the lack of housing, walked out and in October Dominion imposed a lockout. By the end of the month Ford had snapped up the ailing firm and made plans for expansion.[97]

Ford's constant need to grow and rebuild in turn propelled steady negotiations with Ford City's municipal council for street and railway line alterations and reviews of assessments, a process that regularly ended in Ford's favor. The coal shortage affected many industries. In the ongoing negotiations over the joint water system, the coal shortage created a real though minor flare-up as winter approached. Statements of Ford's supply of coal to the depleted pumping station of the Windsor waterworks were vehemently denied by its chief engineer and the secretary of the water board, who wanted no truck with Ford and McGregor and, by extension, with the EBUC. Wallace Campbell calmly retorted that two carloads of coal had indeed been dumped at the pumping station on 11 December. Supported by this wider fuel crisis, the EBUC sought legislative permission to process and distribute natural gas. Whatever the public's reaction to these municipal games—polls on related bylaws routinely attracted few voters—Ford's image remained bright in the *Star*. It continued to boost the Border Cities as Canada's "Motoropolis," as an article by Verne Dewitt Rowell divinely described it on 31 December. This apt label stuck. Ford, Studebaker, Maxwell, and Canadian Products were all thriving. With over half of the Border's automobile workforce—McGregor now employed 3,323 plant workers and an office staff of 247, most of them women—Ford represented, in primary fashion, the "romance" and "boundless optimism" of the industry.[98]

No local politician or other industrialist wielded as much influence as Gordon McGregor. From his offices at Ford he entered into an amalgam of new business negotiations, municipal debates, and endless social functions. At the end of 1919 whatever gains had been made with labor by the wage increase were amplified by a change in the company's profit-sharing plan, which previously meant high wages. On 31 December 1919 Ford Detroit, soon followed by Ford Canada, allowed employees to deposit up to a quarter of their wages with the company and receive interest based on its rate of profits. They were assured an annual return of 6 percent, though during the first six years of the plan's operation in Canada the rate exceeded 14 percent. In addition to Ford Canada, McGregor's business interests included directorships in his brother Walter's firm in Walkerville, McGregor Banwell Fence, which made automotive springs as well as fencing, and the Border Cities Hotel Company Limited. The latter, whose board of directors first met in November 1919 and included Walter McGregor, E. N. Bartlet, and Sir Percival Perry of England, who was no longer with Ford, aimed to build a grand hotel (the Prince Edward) at the corner of Ouellette and Park streets in Windsor. The site was bought from Gordon McGregor and Perry for $100,000, with McGregor taking half this sum in shares. The selling of stock would begin in earnest in February, under the presidency of Hiram Walker. The hotel, designed by Eisenwein and Johnson of Toronto and Albert H. McPhail of Windsor, would be operated from its completion in 1922 under contract to the United Hotels Company of America, which managed the King Edward in Toronto, the Royal Connaught in Hamilton, the Clifton in Niagara Falls, the Mount Royal in Montreal, and a chain of hotels in the United States.[99]

Socially McGregor appeared everywhere—gala dances at the IODE and the golf club remained favorites. On 23 December, Gordon and Hattie happily hosted a gathering of eighty of the "younger social set" at the golf club to mark the return home for the holidays of their son, Bill, then a student at the University of Michigan in Ann Arbor, and their eldest daughter, Harriet, who was in her first year at the Ladies' College in Whitby, Ontario. A good-natured patron of many organizations, several of them at Ford, McGregor helped form the Border Cities Pipe Band in August from his brother's old regimental band and outfit it in McGregor tartan. A member of the Detroit Golf Club and the Detroit Athletic Club, in addition to the Essex golf club, in December he participated in the creation of the Border Cities Hockey League, which aimed to ice a team in the Detroit league as well. Photographed in dapper seasonal attire, McGregor skated but he did not play hockey. His own sportiness, however, nicely complemented his company's many teams and exceptional athletes.[100]

The call for McGregor to head the third and final Victory Loan campaign, which lasted from 27 October to 15 November 1919, was totally predictable. He begged off, however, citing the "pressure of business." He was busy, but he was undoubtedly conscious too that the campaign lacked the patriotic drive that had existed in actual wartime. In the Border Cities the mood was somber and cost-of-living concerns had taken hold. The chair went instead to Dr. Thaddeus Walker, though McGregor did join the manufacturers' section of the campaign's executive committee. Ford employees, 40 percent of whom were stated to be returned veterans, subscribed heavily, to the sum of $1,056,000. The company would quietly buy up the bonds from employees who could not pay for them in the months that followed. As usual, the *Star* opted not for close financial scrutiny but for the touching story. In one, a Ford worker, mumbling "Me pay up bonds, me pay up bonds," produced $1,500 in cash from an "old bandana handkerchief."[101] The image of the dutiful Ford worker, a foreigner perhaps, would not have been lost on readers. There were others, however, who did not buy into the hagiography of the *Star*'s treatment of Ford.

McGregor nonetheless remained the Border Cities' civic organizer par excellence: socially, politically, and as chair of the EBUC. He encouraged similar involvement for his senior staff. His private secretary and longtime office head, Grace Falconer, was active in Windsor's Girl Guides and Young Women's Christian Association. In early September 1919 Frank Nancekevill was appointed to the CMA's transportation committee. He also chaired the Great Waterways conference at Windsor on 18–19 November that led to the formation of the Canadian Deep Waterways and Power Association, with industrial commissioner Maclure Sclanders as secretary-treasurer. That same month, advertising manager E. G. Hogarth was appointed to the board of the Association of Canadian Advertisers. In December, the dour Wallace Campbell was named president of a local Christmas charity, the Border Cities' Goodfellows' Club, thus becoming the cities' "Santa-Claus-in-chief."[102] The humor in this match would not have been lost on McGregor, whose own civic involvement had elements of fun, amusement, and genuine charity, similar to the flavor of Jim Couzens's later philanthropic endeavors in Detroit.

McGregor was a natural selection in August to head the banquet committee for the much-anticipated visit of the charismatic

Prince of Wales to the Border Cities. He was to chair the grand dinner at the golf club on 23 October. McGregor was not too busy to accept this honor, even as he was planning the takeover of Dominion Forge and launching the Prince Edward Hotel project. Insisting on a "strictly informal" affair, with business suits rather than tuxedos, McGregor was charged with negotiating the guest list of 125 for this intensely popular event, a task that meant difficult exclusions. Initially invited because he was Detroit's mayor, James Couzens was dropped in a flash after he welcomed to his city Ireland's escaped republican president, Eamon De Valera, who was anathema to British authorities. Some unnamed Windsor councillors were also excluded, a move that intensified the council's running feud with McGregor. With McGregor as toastmaster and master of ceremonies, and his ubiquitous film crews covering the event, the dinner was still a resounding success. Henry Ford, always capable of social faux pas, attended, and he was watched by the press; his brief exchanges with the prince were dutifully reported. Invited to tour the auto chief's Detroit factory, Edward asked him, "Will you sell me a tractor?" Quite familiar with the prince's newly purchased western ranch, Ford replied sharply, "I'll show you how to make that Alberta farm of yours a paying proposition." At some point, according to family lore, the prince visited Gordon McGregor's Victoria Avenue home. The dining room chair in which he sat was afterward marked with a brass plaque by the head of Ford Canada, who was delighted by this brush with royalty.[103]

McGregor moved ceaselessly from social function to corporate office to meeting rooms to back rooms. His only real public mandate was the EBUC, to which he would be reelected and reappointed chair in January 1920. Progress on the joint water system remained blocked, mainly by the repeated obstructions of Windsor, with the other municipalities all sharing some doubts. Unproductive debate over apportionment and amalgamation, rivaling engineering reports, inconclusive public votes, and referrals to the Ontario Railway and Municipal Board ground on through late 1919 and into 1920 with an inglorious display of petty jealousies and infighting. To increase Windsor's influence, councillor Archibald Hooper called for representation by population on the commission. Some councillors took exception to its move to new and larger offices in September in the Heintzman Building at Ouellette and London. Slowly, however, under McGregor's direction and broad view, the EBUC gained more and more authority, its new board of health being a good example. McGregor wanted to use health as grounds for taking over the individual water systems, and repeated attempts were made by the EBUC to take control of town planning, the production and distribution of natural gas, and parks as well as water. Petty, lingering resentments over exclusion from the prince's dinner, Windsor's withholding of support for the chamber of commerce, and Ford's supply of coal to Windsor's water board all figured in this mix of contending interests, with McGregor a pivotal player.[104]

Back-to-back elections, provincial in October 1919 and municipal in January 1920, took him into a more political role, aggressively prominent but never a candidate save for the EBUC. Nominated in October by McGregor for the Liberal candidacy in Windsor, Major J. C. Tolmie (McGregor's pastor before his enlistment in 1915) was one of the few to survive the sweep of the United Farmers Party in Ontario. Backed by McGregor's formidable coterie and with no labor candidate on the ticket (only Windsor and Guelph were uncontested by International Labour), Tolmie's campaign paid lip service to the interests of labor, including the minimum wage and the eight-hour day.[105] No sooner had the provincial contest ended than campaigning began for January's municipal vote. Approached in November to run for mayor of Windsor, McGregor declined, again citing the proverbial pressures of business. Within days, however, he was selected as president of the newly formed Municipal Electors' Association of Windsor, a heavily publicized promotional lobby that briefly introduced a new dynamic to the Border Cities' political life: the progressive urge of businessmen to reform municipal politics from outside the confines of elected councils and with links to experiments in the United States and elsewhere in Canada (notably St. John's and Montreal) with citizens' committees and commission and city manager forms of local government.

The Municipal Electors' Association, which identified Dayton, Ohio, as its model and business as a stimulus to progressivism, brought McGregor's interests squarely to bear on the councillors and issues in the town that had challenged his civic place. Ostensibly the association was formed to spur public interest, promote "better government," and outline the issues facing voters. By no coincidence, the chamber of commerce launched a major membership drive, with a flood of self-serving publicity. Claiming no brief against Windsor's council (but meaning to undermine it), McGregor told the *Star* on 28 November that he was untroubled with his characterization (along with the rest of the EBUC) by a "certain member" of council (Hooper) as the "biggest crowd of tricksters ever got together." Sounding very much like a candidate, he proceeded to comment at length on a range of concerns, including ferry links with Detroit and other public services that Windsor had to address "to justify hopes for her future progress." Initially no slate of favored candidates was forthcoming—the association just wanted to see more public interest. Windsor needed councillors, McGregor believed, who would "forget class distinctions." Not surprisingly, labor councillors Hooper and George Wood took strong exception to this undemocratic and autocratic association, which looked too much like the chamber of commerce or Ford on the hustings. This hostility was shared by the mayor and aldermen of London, Ontario, who saw a threat to the conventional electoral process. By 10 December the association had moved beyond the selective backing of candidates and begun an aggressive membership drive, with a special team devoted to factories.[106]

Though the association proposed a newcomer for mayor, realtor Leo Page, the decision by incumbent E. B. Winter to run again led to his acclamation. As the association's president, McGregor was in the forefront of nominators for aldermanic candidates. His slate, which included auto distributor Arthur O'Neil and safety council head J. H. Robbins, was decidedly business oriented. McGregor took a particular interest in the position for the water board, on which he wanted members sympathetic to the EBUC. The contest was between Malcolm G. Campbell (chamber of commerce president, manager of Kelsey Wheel Canada, and a McGregor ally), former mayor C. R. Tuson (a florist, undertaker, and McGregor adversary), and board chairman James F. Smythe. Nominated by A. D. Bowlby (McGregor's early Ford associate) and Archibald Hooper and with the backing of labor, Smythe had opposed a joint water system but within days, without explanation, he withdrew.[107]

Under the auspices of the East End Citizens' Association (of which little is known), Campbell and Tuson met, with McGregor in the chair, to debate the water issue on the evening of 30 December in the "new Jewish school." The matter was fully "threshed out," the *Star* reported, with McGregor, as expected, urging a broad metropolitan view. Suddenly, in the midst of the debate, Samuel K. Baum of Baum and Brady, home furnishings dealer (and proud user of Ford trucks), jumped up and charged to the front of the assembly, waving copies of deeds for properties on Victoria Avenue, the fashionable street where McGregor and several associates lived. The documents, Baum blasted, contained evidence that Tuson had registered restrictions prohibiting sales to Jews of land he was privately advertising for sale. This exclusionary device, known as a restrictive covenant, was legal and not uncommon in Ontario, but that evening, in a Jewish school and in the hands of a respected Jewish businessman, the confrontation created explosive tension. So blindsided, his candidacy and position on the water issue seriously sidetracked on the eve of the election, Tuson erupted and the meeting was immediately closed. In the end, Campbell was elected. If McGregor had any foreknowledge of Baum's action, he said nothing. His own mild anti-Semitism would later be drawn out by Henry Ford's anti-Semitic diatribes.[108]

With Windsor's opposition on the utilities issues reduced, McGregor quickly moved the interests of the EBUC forward, though not without some continuing opposition. The Municipal Electors' Association faded away. Within days of the election, McGregor had been reappointed chair of the EBUC, and its parks scheme had received the backing of the chamber of commerce and the councils of both Windsor and Walkerville. In March Windsor's water committee withdrew its latest appeal to the Ontario Railway and Municipal Board on apportionment in favor of a joint report. In June the EBUC received additional statutory allowance from the province to allow for the control of drainage works, the issue of related debentures, the authorization of town planning, the formation of a metropolitan parks board, and the power to submit questions to electors, whose turnout on such issues would continue to be low. Not surprisingly, Sandwich found problems in the planning of the commission's parks committee, and both Ford City and Walkerville balked at the prospect of municipal amalgamation, still a contentious topic. Windsor councillor Archie Hooper remained a thorn: he fully supported the council's refusal of funding to the chamber of commerce. It continued to ignore workers, he explained, and its "argument about having a housing scheme is nothing more than camouflage."[109]

Through most of 1920, however, there was a fragile harmony on the utilities question, despite the inflammatory arguments of Windsor councillor and former mayor Arthur Jackson in December that the EBUC was usurping the powers of the council, arguments that carried no weight at Queen's Park. At the same time, Windsor's medical officer of health, G. R. Cruickshank, continued to find serious problems with the town's water supply. Its chlorination system was improperly operated; "the caretaker should be arrested for manslaughter," he bluntly reported. Even if amalgamation was a problem for some, Ford City's new mayor, Edmund C. Poisson, recognized the salutary links between the EBUC, McGregor, Ford Canada, and his town. Ford Canada knew its way around and through the town's weak administrative structures—since 1913 the town, according to its auditor, had maintained no ledgers. The company's property needs regularly went before Poisson's council, of which Ford manager and chamber executive Frank Nancekevill was a member. Between 1919 and 1921 Ford and the town were engaged in a steady sequence of complicated negotiations dealing with property expansions and exchanges, street widenings, taxation, spur lines, and smoke nuisance. On 6 January 1920 Poisson went on record in support of Ford as his town's backbone; it should not be "knocked," he maintained, as some former councillors had done.[110]

McGregor's response to this upturn for Windsor and the EBUC, starting with the election, is unclear, but he surely must have been satisfied. The press coverage of one incident suggests he harbored a complacency bordering on contempt. On 12 March the *Star* reported that McGregor "threw something in the nature of a bombshell into the meeting of the Essex Border Utilities Commission today when he calmly announced that he was taking Major [William James] Baxter, the secretary, away from the commission, to make him advertising manager" of Ford Canada to replace the recently resigned E. G. Hogarth. Baxter no doubt had a say, but not too subtly the *Star*'s emphasis is on McGregor's arbitrariness, which few challenged. Ford was that much intertwined with the Border Cities. In April 1920 Ford's W. J. Wells would represent the company, along with other members of the Border Cities Safety Council, at the convention in Toronto of the Canadian National Safety League and the Ontario Safety League.[111]

With production moving steadily that winter and spring, McGregor was quite content to fulfill his social and philanthropic roles: a patron of the grand ball put on in January by his wife's chapter of the IODE in aid of the Boy Scouts, a reelected director of the Essex golf club, a main sponsor of Hattie's spearheading of the Essex County Health Association's drive to rebuild its sanatorium (burned on 29 April) at a new site on Prince Road in Sandwich, and, as head of Ford, the munificent benefactor of numerous other events and causes, including in November the Salvation Army's renewed drive for its Grace Hospital. For this drive Wallace Campbell's wife, as a promotional gag, rode in a cement hoist up to a roof to canvass workers there. The 241st Border Battalion's social association, formed in May and headed by Walter McGregor, found Ford's film of war training wonderfully entertaining and amusingly out of touch with European experience. The motor tour through the Border belt by the Michigan Pike's Association was musically accompanied, with McGregor's permission, by his plant's "Ford Quartette" in a Ford car taken straight off the line and which, to produce a nice piece of publicity, went 1,600 miles without adjustment or tire change.[112]

McGregor had more time as well to spend publicly on business interests apart from automobiles, which were being spewed out endlessly. High on his agenda was his continuing promotion, together with his brother Walter, of the Border Cities Hotel Company and its Prince Edward Hotel, where Gordon's experience with realty promotion and corporate finance paid off. In June 1920, at the annual meeting of the Merchants' Bank in Montreal, one of Ford Canada's main banks, he was made a director. The *Star*, in lauding the local boy made good, proudly if mistakenly ranked him as the first man to be elected from southwest Ontario to the board of a major bank, a boastful claim that was quite simplistic in the context of his company's strategic use of different banks, as would become clear the following year.[113] What did not become publicly clear, on the automotive front, were the competitive consequences for Ford Canada of its parent company's move to boost production to unprecedented levels at Ford Detroit's new superplant on the Rouge River.

CHAPTER 6

Motoropolis

Whatever hat Gordon McGregor wore, the world of automotive production and sales was his primary environment. The development of the parts business and the consolidation of automobile insurance were just two signs of the industry's maturation in Canada. Ford Canada's growth over sixteen years was another; McGregor's ride on Henry Ford's comet had been spectacular. With production climbing to 55,616 vehicles in 1920 and a network of 685 dealers and more than 2,500 service garages throughout the country, Ford dominated the national industry. Given Henry Ford's preeminence, however, McGregor would never enjoy personally the national recognition enjoyed, say, by the Eaton family of Toronto. Among Canadian automakers, T. A. Russell still claimed the limelight, if not the political weight. McGregor nonetheless had prominence as president of the Automotive Industries of Canada (which how had forty-nine members and from which he would retire later in 1920) and as an executive member of the Canadian Manufacturers' Association. Locally he remained the Border Cities' undisputed industrial leader, a position he would retain until illness undermined his capacity and abruptly terminated his career in 1922.

The Border Cities' first full auto show, an extravaganza of lights, music, and automobiles, with the distinct smells of oil, rubber, and paint, was organized in February 1920 by R. M. Jaffray in conjunction with the formation of the Border Cities' Automotive Dealers' Association, headed by William R. Woollatt. The opening ceremony for Champion Spark Plug's new branch factory that same month was also the type of venue relished by McGregor. At the last minute he had to cancel his appearance at the car show, probably to join in the EBUC's lobby at Queen's Park in Toronto. In Essex the public was well accustomed to seeing large groups of Ford employees on social and athletic outings; in July 1920, for instance, 125 toolmakers took the train to Kingsville for a picnic. The biggest showing of Ford's executive gang came on 30 August, automotive day at the CNE in Toronto, where Ford had major exhibitions and demonstrations of cars, trucks, and tractors. Viewers admired Ford Canada's introduction of a touring-car top that could now be folded up or down by just one person, not two. McGregor, Wallace Campbell, Harry S. Pritchard, J. D. Isaacs, Frank Nancekevill, and others proudly mingled and strutted along with Henry Ford and his new henchman and private secretary, the insidious Ernest Gustav Liebold. Approached by the press, Ford admitted to no difficulties at Ford Detroit while McGregor, in his element, brushed off questions in order to extol "Canada's only National Motor Show."[1]

Despite its surging production of cars and trucks, a condition aided by unusually high demands that winter, McGregor's firm was not immune to the economic slump of the early 1920s. The depression in the United States was particularly devastating, with employers in Detroit suffering acute shortages of labor and materials. At Ford Detroit, war-induced inflation undermined the financial incentive of the $5 day. Labor insurgency was equally disruptive; in 1919 the Automobile Workers' Union had mounted a strike against a major supplier of Ford automobile bodies. Ford Detroit faced a collapse in sales, severe overstocking, rail and steel strikes, and sharp rises in the costs of materials and consequent price increases on Model Ts in March 1920. Henry Ford, however, was himself an economic force. To stem the reversal, the American company slashed prices in September and shifted inventory and much of the financial burden onto its suppliers and dealers. Personally, the unpredictable Henry Ford began an ill-advised, almost vindictive purge of executives, including Frank Klingensmith (James Couzens's successor). In similar erratic fashion, he now disclaimed any corporate organization, lines of authority, and systems of records. More and more authority was assumed by the autocratic Liebold, who would front for Ford and with whom McGregor would have to deal directly, increasingly through formal letter writing.[2]

Wilkins and Hill conclude that McGregor at Ford Canada, in contrast to Ford at Ford Detroit, "cautiously" felt his way during the postwar slump. Seeing no need to emulate his president, he quietly recognized the need for carefully kept records and up-to-date office equipment. Shortages of raw materials, notably steel from the United States, and of railway cars caused a continued resort to inferior steel and a cutback in hours at the Ford City plant in April 1920, but it and Dominion Forge managed to remain open. The following month McGregor was obliged to deny rumors of plant closure. In the wake of depression, many automotive firms such as Kelsey Wheel laid off workers and closed for periods of time. Studebaker shut down, Canadian Products cut its staff by half, and Windsor Machine and Tool reduced its wages by 12 percent. Reductions occurred too at such nonautomotive plants as W. J. Peabody's clothing factory, which claimed that public agitation for lower prices for commodities had created "unbalanced markets."[3]

The labor scene became unsettled, with large numbers of autoworkers moving over from Detroit only to find shortages of jobs and housing—workers' housing could not be built fast enough and building inspectors could not keep up. The EBUC attempted to have new housing conform to planning principles, though it is uncertain if the major developers always complied. Between July and September, in an exercise of its newly legislated powers, the EBUC reviewed nearly two dozen plans and made adjustments in some. When faced with Windsor's latest obstruction on the water and parks scheme, the commission made vague threats about blocking the town's plans that did not "fit in" with its poorly explained schemes. Still, many developers built where and what they could. In such turmoil, the little-known autoworkers' union that emerged in Windsor in 1920, a local of the Automobile, Aircraft, and Vehicle Workers of America, dropped out of sight the next year, with no evidence that it had ever secured a foothold in the Ford plant. In November 1920, after months of accounts of "unsettled" conditions in the Border's auto sector, the federal *Labour Gazette* reported that although "all automobile factories at Windsor laid off a large number of workers . . . the Ford plant alone continued about normal."[4]

The slump nonetheless appears to have caused delays in McGregor's plans for his company. In the fall of 1919 he had told shareholders that plant extensions, despite his claim of flourishing conditions in other respects, had to be set aside. He blamed his favorite whipping boy, the federal business profits tax, which the chamber of commerce also continued to attack, going so far as to call it "class legislation." General Motors Canada felt only that, in general terms, the motor industry was "unduly taxed." Ford Canada had nonetheless managed to benefit from the slump by taking over Dominion Forge. In July 1920 Ford's directors authorized a major expansion program of $2.5 million, the culmination of months of detailed technical planning, complex site assemblies, and negotiations with Ford City over property exchanges and rights of way. In such negotiations, the town was often outweighed. At a meeting in the mayor's office in May, for instance, the town was urged to allow the Canadian Pacific Railway (CPR) to take over part of Caron Avenue for more freight facilities. Councillor and Ford traffic manager Frank Nancekevill assured the town it would be "amply repaid" if it did. The matter, however, was not decided at the municipal level—it was the federal board of railway commissioners that gave the CPR permission, without notifying the town's solicitor. At the annual meeting of shareholders on 25 October, McGregor concluded that the expansion once again had to be deferred because of a "slackening of business," despite Ford Canada's own reduction of prices. Other factors included slow sales, fluctuating supplies, and a hurtful increase in railway rates by the federal railway board, a measure vigorously opposed by traffic manager Nancekevill.[5]

More negative news was delivered by sales manager Neil Lawrence who, after sixteen months away assessing Ford's foreign market, returned in October, thoroughly dejected about Canada's weak presence in the export market. His surprisingly unexpected findings were presented in an address to the chamber of commerce entitled "Darkest Canada," which apparently attracted considerable attention. Lawrence's thoroughness of investigation and representativeness are open to question, but he had distinct impressions. Canadian products, he claimed, were "stamped as American rather than British," a reasonable confusion in the case of the American-designed Model Ts. In Australia, he observed (in the portion of his speech printed in *Industrial Canada*), labor had industry "by the throat." Moreover, the Australian tariff of 1920 would continue to guarantee the bulk of the market to local auto body builders. The speech found its way into trade debate in the House of Commons, where Essex North's W. C. Kennedy quoted Lawrence: "During my entire sixteen months abroad, I never met a single representative of any Canadian enterprise. On the other hand, the activity of American representatives in these same countries is so decidedly marked that one could safely say that to-day American industries are invading the whole of the British overseas possessions."[6]

Lawrence should not have been surprised at the American dominance. For years consuls and trade representatives had viewed Ford Canada as Canadian in name only. Lawrence's report probably contributed to McGregor's decision to delay expansion overseas, a situation that would change in a few years. Despite the imperial advantage, American exports dominated. During a four-month period at the end of 1919, for example, 4,015 American-made motorcars went into India compared to 616 British and 510 Canadian-made cars, but trade flows could shift with amazing speed. Though the market in India was glutted, Ford Canada sent in some 3,600 cars and chassis in 1919–20, while in the Malay States demand for Canadian-made cars remained strong in mid-1920. Overall, however, as Lawrence had reported, Ford Canada's exports dropped dramatically throughout 1920.[7]

McGregor's firm may have benefited from some collective arrangement on international shipments. In early 1922 the federal Department of Trade and Commerce alluded to a recently concluded agreement between Canadian and American car manufacturers that blocked, in some undetailed manner, the export of Canadian-made automobiles with the exception of Ford cars.[8] The benefit of this arrangement may not have been significant, however. Dodge and the General Motors Export Company had both been serving imperial markets from the United States since before the war and until after 1922. This fact suggests the imperial access of McGregor's company was becoming a diminishing need of the Canadian operation and even a factor in the formation of assembly operations abroad in the 1920s. A review of the export figures printed in this study (see tables 2 and 3 in chapter 3) suggests too that any collective arrangement on shipments is a complex piece of business to sort out.

On the home front there had been no strong resistance from industry in general to the business profits tax during the war. Chambers of commerce across Ontario predictably stood out as the exceptions. In the economic slump, the tax had become the bête noire of the Border Cities Chamber of Commerce, for no one more than Gordon McGregor. The less taxation on the auto industry the better, he reasoned—with much self-interest. He liked the possibility of a reduced import tax on automobiles, put forth in the federal budget of May 1920. "They can't expect the auto industry to bear the whole burden of taxation," he told the *Star* on 19 May in his guise as a spokesman; he was joined in this sentiment by Howard Blood.[9] For years McGregor had railed against the business profits tax, partly for political reasons and in part because of his company's enormous profitability.

At the shareholders' meeting in October he defensively explained in detail his company's fiscal position in relation to both the tax and current economic trends. During the previous year, in a deft stroke of accounting, the firm's cash balance of $3,903,273.40 had been reduced by $1,832,000 primarily to create a reserve for the payment of the business tax, which was to expire on 31 December. This reserve was more than enough to cover the $735,200 owing in tax for the ten months prior to 31 July as well as the additional five months since, but McGregor had other, peevish reasons for reducing the cash balance. If the government learned of Ford's healthy balance, he feared unreasonably, it might reenact the tax, as if Ford Canada was Ottawa's only corporate signpost. Furthermore, public knowledge of the larger balance could lead to an increase in Ford's local property assessment, incite shareholders to clamor for dividends, and somehow spark new labor demands. "On account of the labor situation at the close of our fiscal year," he stated without fuller explanation, "we felt it was inadvisable to show large cash balances."[10]

The summer of 1920 had begun well for McGregor. His son, Bill, returned from the University of Michigan in June for the summer break, and Gordon and Hattie soon moved to their cottage at Kingsville. The directors' meeting on 9 July was auspicious and there was progress in the promotion of the Prince Edward Hotel. Within weeks, however, family tragedy intruded. McGregor's beloved mother, who had been living with her daughter Margaret Bartlet in Walkerville and had been ailing for some time, died of colon cancer in her mid-seventies on 18 July; she was buried privately. Gone was McGregor's link to the family's early days on the river. On 3 August his sister Edith Ellen Malcolmson of Winnipeg passed away in a Toronto hospital. On 10 November, after a directors' meeting of the Merchants' Bank in Montreal, McGregor himself underwent surgery at the city's Royal Victoria Hospital, the

Star claimed, for appendicitis, which had reputedly troubled him "on other occasions." His trouble may, in fact, have been the cancer or other illness that was to claim his life in sixteen months. Hattie and brother Walter left on the afternoon of the 10th to join him; he was visited too, in early December, by Wallace Campbell and Henry Ford. A second operation took place that month. McGregor's stay in the hospital until 16 January and subsequent weakness suggest some serious ailment, although its exact nature is unknown.[11]

McGregor's sickness and long absence brought out the laudatory impulses of the *Star* toward the Border Cities' industrial champion, whom it portrayed with wonderfully grand exaggeration as a nationally known industrial giant. "Few men stand higher than Mr. Gordon McGregor in the Canadian industrial world, and few have devoted themselves so unstintingly to the advancement of their respective communities." There was homespun praise too, along with some fuzziness and a bit of Fordist mythmaking, in the recollections of Ford City pioneer H. R. Askin, published in the *Star* on 13 November: "He remembers too, a young man named McGregor, who started in business as a hog-killer. After a year or two, McGregor took to repairing wagons, and later to manufacturing them. He used to make a special kind of wagon, and, as the years went by, he stopped making wagons and started with automobiles. The automobile business prospered, and finally developed into the Ford Motor Company of Canada."[12] If McGregor had started out killing hogs, Ford Canada's publicists never saw fit to highlight the experience.

McGregor's operations and recuperation in Montreal prevented his testimony in person before the federal tariff commission at its local hearings in the chamber of commerce building on 30 November. This hearing was Ford Canada's first opportunity to address head-on the growing and increasingly political movement in Canada for reduced tariffs and lower prices on automobiles. The debate, which the company had heard before, had its origins in various farmers' organizations, journals, and provincial governments, including the Canadian Council of Agriculture, which since 1916 had been brooding over the need for low-priced machinery and lower car license fees as well as Canada's protective tariff. Many farmers wondered why Model Ts from Ford Detroit could not be imported directly in volume even with the duty, a notion reinforced by a proliferation of stories of Ontario and western farmers who ventured across the border and brought back new cars. But this was a debate with no clear winner. Some politicians believed that the proportion of farmers who needed or owned automobiles was overrated. One such critic cited a survey of Ottawa valley farmers by the *Ottawa Farm Journal:* of the 63 percent of 1,000 farmers who responded to the survey, only 24 percent owned cars; more had organs and pianos. For years Ford Canada, in the comfort zone of the Border Cities, had been ignoring its reputation as a subsidiary formed to take advantage of the price differential created by the tariff and the knowledge, based on advertisements and hearsay, that prices were higher in Canada than in the United States.[13]

The Border Chamber of Commerce had begun organizing in August of 1920 for the commission hearing planned for the fall. Locally it was felt that the automobile industry merited particular attention. The testimony presented by Ford on 30 November was, in McGregor's absence, given by secretary and assistant manager Wallace Campbell, but it had McGregor's imprimatur if not his authorship.[14] In the estimate of the *Star*, the testimony was a "categorical refutation" of charges that Ford Canada "had taken undue advantage of the tariff to maintain a high scale of prices for Ford cars."[15] Both McGregor and Campbell were quite adept at nuancing the formation of Ford Canada, and here the need for a company to access the imperial market advantageously was put on a par with one formed to provide domestic production. To dispel the notion spread by farmers' organizations, the company was portrayed in Ford's testimony as no mere assembly plant, but once again as a distinctly Canadian corporation responsible for an automobile that was 77 percent Canadian made and of higher quality and with more features than the American version. Not since the war had Ford spun its Canadian identity so strongly. No mention was made of the absence of original technological contribution from the Canadian company. Unlike Ford Detroit, where Henry Ford reigned, Ford Canada was committed to shareholders who expected profitability, Campbell explained. He contrived to take the tariff out of the debate. On any price differential, several arguments were put forward, the main one, economies of scale, being the substantial difference in overhead between a company that made 55,000 units with a seasonal market versus one (Ford Detroit) that made 1 million units, subject to capricious pricing by Henry Ford. Ford Canada contributed substantially to the Canadian economy in the form of industry-leading wages and its stimulation of the accessories and parts trades. Model Ts were owned by more farmers than by any other category of occupation, a fact methodically tracked by Ford Canada.

In a barrage of figures that defy easy comparative analysis, Campbell argued that his company's prices accurately reflected the costs of production. Though Canadian prices on Model Ts had risen from $590 in 1915 to $675 in 1920, he boldly concluded, based on a series of perplexing calculations, that a T bought in the United States, plus duty, would cost the Canadian buyer $117.44 *more* than the Canadian T. The difference could be even greater, he confidently explained, because his company had been competing against the American company under "abnormal conditions" in an "extremely hazardous period": for much of 1920 Ford Detroit, on Henry Ford's instructions, had been selling dramatically below cost.[16] What McGregor and Campbell likely knew, but did not state, was that under existing conditions, American Model Ts were not easily obtained by Canadian customers distant from the border. At the same time, prices and figures presented by a company executive at a single hearing in Ontario were unlikely to influence perceptions and a political debate that were gaining momentum across the country.

None of the counterarguments matched Campbell's calculations in terms of dollars and numbers; statements of price differentials were always vaguely given and they varied. But this was not a debate that Ford Canada was going to win—it was not about opposing reckonings by accountants. Strong testimony contrary to Campbell's was received by the tariff commission elsewhere in its tour, from Robert John Deachman (editor of the *Calgary Westerner*), John Livingstone Brown (president of the United Farmers of Manitoba), and Thomas Wakem Caldwell (an MP and president of the United Farmers of New Brunswick). They still saw lower prices in the United States and wondered why Ford's large profits were not going into the development of the industry in Canada, a concern that overlooked Ford Canada's solid achievements in marketing. Reinforcing these arguments were the almost irrefutable, even sentimental ones of need. United Farmers' organizations, such as the one in Alberta, no longer saw motorcars as the preserve of "wealthy town people" but as a "real necessity" for "up-to-date" farmers. As

Unloading Model T Ford chassis and cars from Canadian Pacific Railway boxcars, Medicine Hat, Alberta, late 1910s. The Esplanade: Archives, Medicine Hat, Alberta, image no. 0104.0004.

economic argument, the Ford testimony, though loaded with revealing data, was shaky in places: the commission's chair, federal finance minister Sir Henry Drayton, knew enough to question the accuracy of Campbell's figures and calculations, an intervention not reported by the *Star*.[17] As political argument, the testimony changed no minds in the low-tariff camp or among critics who saw no difference between branch plants created to assemble and those set up to manufacture.

The testimonies of other automobile executives in the Border Cities—V. A. Clemen (Fisher Body), W. P. Shillington (Studebaker), and M. G. Campbell (Kelsey Wheel)—did not substantiate Ford Canada's argument. Campbell and Shillington (whose plant would reopen in January 1921) and several other local industrialists with branch affiliations made no bones about the tariff as the primary factor in the creation of their Canadian branches. "We are merely a subsidiary of the Studebaker Corporation of South Bend, Indiana," Shillington testified, without equivocating or posing as a stand-alone Canadian company. Further, he explained: "We are in

Walkerville purely because of the tariff on the completed automobile and because we could assemble the parts in Walkerville, make some purchases in Canada and reduce the cost slightly. If it were not for the present tariff on the completed automobile it would simply be a case of there being no advantage in being over here. That is all there would be to it. We have our plant at South Bend and we would simply ship from there."[18]

At other times, McGregor and Campbell could and did enthuse about their proximity to the United States and the omnipresence of branch plants and their role in defining the industrial character of the Border Cities. Their presence at innumerable gatherings and meetings at Ford Detroit attest to this sentiment. The relationship was reciprocal: in 1920 more than a quarter of the workforce at Ford Detroit was Canadian born. The souvenir booklet prepared by the Border Cities Trades and Labor Council with financial support from McGregor and Campbell, among others, for the meeting of the Trades and Labor Congress of Canada in Windsor in September 1920 had stressed the cities' closeness to America. The foremost champions of this proximity remained the chamber of commerce and industrial commissioner Maclure Sclanders, who gave typically upbeat testimony to the tariff commission on 30 November. Praising the efficacy of the protective tariff, he proudly identified 206 industries in the Border Cities, of which more than half were American. "The general development of these Border Municipalities has been literally phenomenal. They have leaped from the small town category into the truly metropolitan. . . . Protection is the cause. The splendid effect is evidenced in all our American factories. . . . Without this cause there would be no effect. We should have no American industries."[19]

Sclanders broadcast this message effusively wherever he went. Pro-protective organizations such as the CMA were receptive listeners, but not everyone was impressed. "The wholly exceptional rapidity and nature of our growth had not yet been grasped by our friends in centres further east," a puzzled Sclanders would tell the *Monetary Times* (Toronto) in January. "Perhaps this is because most of it has its source in the United States."[20] Later, with American firms continuing to locate in the Border Cities in record numbers, he would muse in *Canadian Machinery and Manufacturing News* (Toronto) that "it would almost seem that we are here in a little kingdom of our own and to some extent apart and away from the outer world." To Sclanders, the outside world was "duller."[21]

By contrast, the *Toronto World* for one saw the Border Cities as a somewhat un-Canadian beehive of Yankee-style industry and municipal politics. In June 1920 the *World* wondered if the release of a suspect from a border jail, after a "persuasive argument" by "citizens," constituted "a phase of the Americanization of the Border Cities."[22] Such attitudes figured to a degree in the hostility felt, beyond the Border Cities, over the seemingly exploitative prices for Canadian-built automobiles, including Ford cars.

While McGregor was in the hospital in Montreal, the tariff issue died down—no change came as a result of the commission—though the issue would return to trouble him during the federal election of autumn 1921. He returned to Windsor on 16 January 1921 accompanied by his wife and under a physician's care. On the 26th he visited his office at Ford for the first time, "still weak" and only long enough to shake hands with his staff.[23] Earlier that month, across the river, Henry Ford's vice president and treasurer, his chief auditor, his advertising manager, and the head of his sociological department, among other important executives, had all left the company in a dramatic series of departures and firings, losses that would have repercussions for McGregor.[24]

Of immediate concern to the weakened McGregor was the local flare-up in the fractious utilities politics after the municipal elections at the beginning of the month. In a fast-paced campaign again led by Windsor alderman Archie Hooper, both Windsor and Ford City (which soon backed off) had applied to the provincial government to withdraw from the Essex Border Utilities Commission. Promptly dismissed from his job at the Grand Trunk Railway on the grounds that employees were forbidden to engage in politics, Hooper saw his disruptiveness, going back to the street railway dispute of 1919, as the reason. He mentioned too the decline in support he had received from the local Trades and Labor Council. He was nonetheless determined to stay his course, and he had three targets: the EBUC, Gordon McGregor, and perceived corruption within Windsor's board of education.[25]

By the time of McGregor's return, the commission was taking steps to block the municipal withdrawals. At the chamber of commerce meeting on 20 January, where Walter McGregor now presided as president, Gordon raised some routine matters, such as overcrowding on the Detroit River ferries, but it was the threatened withdrawals that claimed his reduced energy and his ire. He knew he needed Windsor's support. Attributing the secessionist drive to Hooper's "ancient grudge" against the EBUC, he was fully prepared, health permitting, to fight the withdrawal at Queen's Park, where the United Farmers were in power. At the same time, Walter was fending off other attacks against the chamber, notably from court registrar and former Windsor mayor Henry Clay, who, like Hooper, argued that the chamber had no business usurping the place of an elected mayor and council. At Queen's Park on 23 February, Windsor's application to withdraw from the EBUC was rejected by the private bills committee, which another labor alderman, Albert W. Strong, described in frustration as "the finest little band of autocrats I have ever had the misfortune to meet." As chairman of the EBUC, Gordon McGregor quickly moved to smooth the waters with conciliatory words. "We realize that without the co-operation of the city of Windsor we can accomplish very little," he told the *Star* on the 26th.[26]

Subsequent negotiations produced some mutual concessions, but by 8 March an exhausted and frustrated McGregor could no longer tolerate the Windsor councillors, who found his handling of the affair "autocratic and dictatorial." "If this is their attitude," he ranted in the *Star*, "it is quite evident they will be satisfied with nothing less than a commission composed of mollycoddles who will submit to their every whim and fancy." A chastised council, ignoring Hooper, resumed negotiations, only to see the issue of a joint system rise and fall until 1922, when new engineering proposals, backing from the ORMB, and a conclusive public vote for a joint system laid permanent groundwork for the construction of a new filtration plant, pumping station, and reservoir in Ford City in 1926.[27]

For McGregor, however, the matter and the pressures ended in 1921. On the advice of his doctors, he resigned the chair of the EBUC on 21 March and his seat for Ford City the next day. He refused to reconsider. For almost five years he had, with respectable vision, pushed and negotiated the legislated agenda of the EBUC, which was almost unique in Ontario, on the important if lackluster issues of metropolitan water and sewage systems, municipal amalgamation (which would come about in 1935), town planning, parks, and public health. After his departure, momentum slowed. So too did the personalized attacks. Without strong public interest, McGregor had faced the fractious reaction of local town councillors, who, with some legitimate concerns, resented the commission's encroachment on their turf and McGregor's heavy-handed corporate style.

The slump in the automotive industry could not be dealt with so easily. It continued into 1921 with greater severity. Canadian and American analysts wishfully looked for positive signs of turnaround from the major auto shows, notably New York's in January 1921 and the coincident annual meeting of the National Automobile Chamber of Commerce. McGregor's debilitation and slow recovery left him unable to deal with day-to-day business matters with his usual energy and authority, let alone the new challenges within the broader industry. With much glitz, the Border Cities auto show was opened on 21 February by Walter McGregor. Gradually, some responsibility at Ford shifted to Wallace Campbell, a move that may not have been universally welcomed within the Canadian company. On 2 April, McGregor, his wife, son, and teenaged daughter Harriet (now a student at the new Knox preparatory school for girls in Cooperstown, New York) left for one of his favorite resorts, White Sulphur Springs in West Virginia. He stayed there until mid-May, with a side trip to Washington, and then spent the summer at Kingsville. During McGregor's recuperation and time away in Montreal and Virginia, which did aid his recovery, Campbell was left to deal with numerous demands. He deflected the usual stream of wild rumors about wage reductions, the construction of a plant at Oshawa, and Henry Ford's disposal of Ford Canada stock. In addition, he put together a report for Henry Ford, who was now searching far afield for raw materials, on the production of lead in Canada. Walter McGregor pitched in too during his brother's absence, to host a luncheon and tour by the Canadian Manufacturers' Association members at the Ford plant in April. The same month, Ford Canada announced a return to full-time production after six months of closure on Fridays and Saturdays. Equally optimistic was Edward C. Mackie, general manager of Studebaker Canada, who boasted, "We cannot build enough cars to fill our orders." In January, George W. Parkes, the local president of Maxwell Motor, was also prematurely optimistic, in part because he felt the industry could count on the "willingness on the part of labor to conform to readjusting conditions."[28]

Beginning in the fall of 1920 and carrying into 1921, production and business at Ford had dropped to around 46,000 automobiles and trucks, a decline due in part to depression on the prairies and the reduced operations at the Ford plant between November 1920 and May 1921. Having dropped so many of his executives, Henry Ford was not content to leave Wallace Campbell in Ontario to deal with Canadian conditions. Ford had a strong sense of ownership in his Canadian operation, which he would use as he saw fit. "Ford thought a lot of Mr. Campbell," Canadian production head George Dickert recalled. "They were very close together. I think he had something to do with helping out cutting down on inventory." During Ford's purge of executives in January and February he brought Campbell over to run his mammoth plant at Highland Park as Frank Klingensmith's possible successor as vice president and general manager. But in Dickert's estimate, Campbell was "not a production man." With Ford Detroit "in more or less of a state of chaos" because of more executive resignations linked to Ford's anti-Semitism, according to *Automotive Industries* (New York), the fit did not work. Campbell returned to the Canadian company, no doubt to McGregor's relief.[29]

The Detroit link, for both McGregor and Campbell, remained Ernest Liebold, Henry Ford's impersonal secretary, who had quickly picked up on Ford's treatment of Ford Canada as a useful tool for implementing his pet plans and projects. When Liebold needed information in early February on the banking of Henry Ford's personal funds in Canada, McGregor promptly gave him an answer that included a summary of the Canadian company's arrangements. Apart from Ford Canada's use of the Canadian Bank of Commerce and the Merchants' Bank in Walkerville—he professed to avoid banks in Windsor for some reason—his choice of banks nationally was extremely fluid, depending on which head offices offered the best rates and sent the most favorable circulars to its branches "concerning the financing of Ford shipments at this season of the year." Even locally, McGregor and Ford Canada used the Commerce in addition to his main bank, the Merchants', in order to keep the former "in good humour to have them competitive" for foreign transactions.[30]

With production stabilizing more at Ford Canada than at

other local manufacturers, the company was able to force price cuts in June and September 1921 in response to cuts at Ford Detroit, the Canadian tariff debates, and new competitive developments in the Canadian market. Further, a 15 percent dividend was declared at a directors' meeting on 7 June, even though production was heading toward 46,832 at year's end in September, down from 55,616 the previous year. Early in June, Canadian Products had been compelled to cut half its workforce back to three days a week, but that fall, a decision by General Motors headquarters in the United States to concentrate the manufacture of its automobiles for export (except Cadillacs and GM trucks) at Oshawa was expected to produce a boom at Canadian Products, which made the motors and axles for Oshawa. Under Howard Blood, Canadian Products had started to pick up its work schedule, with attention focusing as well on McLaughlin Park, the subdivision developed next to the GM land in Walkerville by the Windsor-Detroit realty firm of Good, McGivern, Currie. In addition, GM Canada had set up a tractor division.

For buyers, the launch of new models by McLaughlin, Studebaker, and Overland, among others, at the Montreal auto show in January 1921 was starting to draw attention to Ford's outmoded styling and conventional marketing, though with the introduction of a one-person folding top, demountable wheel rims, and electrical starter in 1920, Ford Canada believed it was moving forward. Even in its trucks, a new optional gear made speeds of 20 to 25 mph possible. Like the Dodge Canada Company incorporated in July 1921, which could not afford to remodel annually (and made an economic virtue of this fact in its advertising), Ford rationally resisted the spiral of depreciation and obsolescence caused by annual change.[31] At the same time, in both Canada and the States, Ford Motor ignored such trends as installment financing, sliding gearshifts, and the use of colored paints and fabrics—critical features with many women. McGregor and his associates left no records of ever discussing these fundamental changes in automotive marketing, though their advertising suggests reaction. "Why pay more for an over-powered engine?" asked one series, with reference to six-cylinder vehicles. Even if most advertising media, including *Everywoman's World* (Toronto), with a focus on female drivers, continued to identify Ford as the leader in ownership and preference in the period 1919–21, there were also trails of dissatisfaction in 1921 among both dealers and McGregor's executive corps.[32]

The elimination of the excise tax on 20 December 1920 left Canadian dealers holding unsold but previously taxed automobiles. Forums for dealers to vent their concerns varied between Canada and the United States. American Ford dealers were vigorously discouraged from belonging to clubs and associations but in Canada local and regional associations abounded, and they included a number of Ford dealers and branch managers. Dealers in general were not a happy lot. "For many years manufacturers of automobiles have sold their product to dealers on a contract one-sided in every respect and without deviation or stability," one anonymous dealer told *Saturday Night* in January 1921. That same month, 400 dealers lobbied finance minister Drayton for refunds on the excise tax on unsold stock. Two major manufacturers, the GM group (McLaughlin, Chevrolet, and Oldsmobile) and T. A. Russell's Willys-Overland, agreed to split the charges faced by dealers. Ford Canada refused to go along, however: it telegraphed the Toronto Automobile Trade Association that it would defer a decision until after the convention of Ford dealers at the end of January. What happened then is uncertain—Ford's records are mute—but in the end, *Canadian Automotive Trade* (Toronto) reported in July, more than one maker reneged.[33]

The automobile dealers' sections in Ontario and Saskatchewan of the Retail Merchants' Association (RMA) of Canada were leaders in this lobby and debate. In Toronto, Ford branch manager Fred Fox was active within the Ontario group, whose president, Joseph James Duffus, was a reputable Ford/Gray-Dort/Dodge dealer in Peterborough. Additional pressure on dealers as a result of low prices would continue into the winter of 1921–22. At the end of the period, the London *Advertiser* hoped that the trend was over: "To say that most manufacturers and probably a majority of dealers have had enough of price reductions to last them until doomsday expresses a body of sentiment that in time will have its effect upon the situation, but which up to now has been powerless to stem the tide. 'They can't go lower without going broke,' as one observer tersely, if cruelly, put it."[34]

Another problem facing the dealers was the move by Canadian tire manufacturers in September 1921 to reduce the margin of retail profit, producing a new low-price scale that lasted through the winter. Dealers in convention in Saskatchewan concluded that the scale on tires (a necessary piece of equipment that seldom lasted for high mileage) "practically compels the dealer to operate without profit." The "tire situation" was still concerning the Ontario automotive section of the RMA at its annual convention in Toronto in early February. This price cutting on tires was linked primarily to price cuts at Ford, which were used aggressively to force suppliers to drop their prices. From its perspective, GM Canada would begin attacking, in its advertising, Ford's "bogey of low price for initial investment" as early as mid-1922, shortly after McGregor's death. Ford and other low pricers "produced and sold in volume something that would run, but there could be neither comfort nor convenience in operation, no economy in cost of using until various and sundry accessories were purchased and attached to complete the job."[35]

Whatever dissatisfaction was felt among Ford dealers, the exodus of a cluster of key executives in 1920–21, not to mention Wallace Campbell's brief stint in Detroit, disturbed McGregor, who moved to find suitable replacements. The departures began in April 1920 with assistant superintendent and education department head Lawrence W. Lee, who left to become vice president and general manager of a new auto-top making outfit in Toronto, General Top Company of Canada Limited. (Its president, R. C. Kilgour, was also president of the Packard-Ontario Motor Car Company, a used-car enterprise.) Lee's brother John of Ford Detroit's sociological department had already left the American company in 1919. The Canadian resignations in March 1921 of W. G. Wells from the superintendent's department and of B. Ross McKenzie, the longtime general purchasing agent, prompted McGregor to issue an announcement that no new policy had been adopted to cause such exits nor were they the start of a Henry Ford–style purge or "reorganization." The unfortunate loss of innovative sales manager Neil Lawrence in August might have been predicted. He was disillusioned with Ford's status as an exporter. Although he and his wife had been fêted in June, Wilkins and Hill cite his "clash of personalities" with others in the company. As well, he had quarreled with the *Border Cities Star* over his public opposition to full Prohibition, which he believed was unattainable in a liquor-manufacturing and emerging bootlegging center. He left Windsor in November for an unspecified job in London, England, and was replaced by Harry S. Pritchard, a Chatham-born lawyer who had come to Ford in 1912 or 1913 via the Detroit auto trade and was already making his mark in the sales department by early

1920, when he wrote an analysis of the company's steel supply. At a chamber of commerce conference in June 1921 on the area's high cost of living, he had resolutely defended Ford's high wages and high profits against arguments of inflationary contribution. The "welfare of a community depends on good wages," he argued before launching into other Fordist economics. "Prices for productive labor are not unreasonable but there is much unproductive labor here." The fast-paced Pritchard was backed up in the sales department by the sharp, analytic Hubert C. French, who became assistant sales manager on Pritchard's promotion in August. (A former manager of the Cadwell Sand and Gravel Company in Windsor, French had come to Ford in 1919 and had impressed both McGregor and Campbell; in 1924–25 he would start up Ford Australia.) Equally as distressing as Lawrence's departure was the resignation in October of traffic manager Frank Nancekevill, who gave up the difficult job of contending with Canada's fatigued railway system to become Ford's district distributor in Brantford, Ontario.[36] He was succeeded by W. R. Burgin, who became equally adept at giving addresses on shipping and transportation. The reasons for these turnovers are uncertain, but McGregor's weakening health, the departures at Ford Detroit, and the trade slump and resulting pressures may have been factors. Rounds of below-cost price slashing to keep pace with American levels probably created operating difficulties.

During the summer and early fall of 1921, McGregor, still recovering and at his cottage for much of the time, maintained a light schedule of business and public involvement. He sat on the committee to develop a public golf course at Devonshire Park, a project backed by the Essex club and to be operated by the Western Racing Association. The *Star* believed that golf was a "rich man's game" that needed to be opened up to others. As well, McGregor continued to chair the advisory committee of the Essex Health Association for the erection of the new sanatorium in Sandwich. He visited Detroit frequently, once for the marriage of a niece. In July he applauded his brother Don's major expansion of the Universal Car Agency in Windsor. His health allowed for some golf, though a photograph taken at White Sulphur Springs around this time reveals an overweight McGregor supporting himself with a cane, nattily attired in a tweed jacket and matching plus fours, checked cap, tartan stockings, and shining shoes. The onetime clothing salesman

Gordon McGregor on vacation at White Sulphur Springs, West Virginia, c. 1921. Courtesy of Gordon McGregor Rock.

never lost his sense of sartorial style or love of golf. Like McGregor, Howard Blood belonged to the Detroit Athletic Club and the Essex County Golf and Country Club, among others, and the two auto men met socially as well as through industry. In October McGregor accompanied Hattie to Montreal for an operation for an undisclosed ailment that had been troubling her for a year.[37]

Though reports of beer- and rum-running, neighborhood bootlegging, and related crimes were beginning to pervade the news in the Border Cities, with provincial authorities intervening wherever possible, the industrial milieu remained decidedly automotive. New ventures took off; many crashed. None held a candle to Ford Canada. Organized in 1921, Brock Motors Limited of Amherstburg made the Brock, a "thoroughly Canadian product." Financially strapped, the firm folded after putting together one car. That same year Reo Motor Car of St. Catharines bought a factory site in Walkerville and another company, the veteran Windsor Machine and Tool Works, expanded with much publicity into making automotive pistons. At a banquet on 31 October at the Hotel Statler in Detroit, a group of New York and Pennsylvania capitalists, organized as Colonial Motors Limited, announced its intention to begin building in January, in the former Detroit Lubricator Company plant on Walker Road in Walkerville, the six-cylinder "Canadian," with a novel independent front suspension.[38] It never went into production. This and other false starts, but most noticeably the streams of new vehicles from Ford and Studebaker and the tons of parts from other makers, set the character of the industry in the Border Cities.

At Ford, Campbell was increasingly the company's lead spokesman, but it was McGregor who issued the annual statement of 28 September 1921, including the stupendous annual revenue of $37,836,473.40. As well, he was in the chair for the annual meeting of 24 October, where the removal of the business profits tax was announced. No board meeting was ever held without an American director present. Present in October, or at least named, was Ford Canada's second vice president, Henry's twenty-seven-year-old son Edsel, who had taken over from the ousted Frank Klingensmith. McGregor liked Edsel and his friend, Ford lawyer Ernest C. Kanzler, whom McGregor knew from his involvement in the early production of Fordson tractors. McGregor was never shy about involving American executives in his company's affairs as familial courtesy;

in 1921 he encouraged both Edsel and Kanzler to join him for a round on the golf links and for lunch to talk over business.[39]

By contrast, Henry Ford and especially Ernest Liebold were more inclined to use McGregor's offices, with minimal comradeship, to serve their projects and flawed visions. McGregor catered to Ford as president, of course, and also partly out of friendship. A book provided by Windsor lawyer H. O. Fleming, a member of the committee on the St. Lawrence Seaway, was sent over by McGregor in October to Ford, "as he is so vitally interested in the development of water powers throughout this continent." (Ford was then pushing to acquire control of a complex of dams and generating plants in the Tennessee region.) Mindful of Ford's purchase of the Detroit, Toledo, and Ironton Railroad in 1920, McGregor also forwarded information on a high-speed reverse gear that brother Walter had found in use in a Model T adapted to run on a lumber railway in the Parry Sound district of Ontario. McGregor in turn asked if Ford (regardless of his antiurban streak) would invest in the Prince Edward Hotel project, but Liebold brushed him off: "It is entirely out of Mr. Ford's line of thought to make any investments such as mentioned."[40]

McGregor discreetly monitored and protected Henry Ford's local monetary assets, which Ford really did not know much about. (Asked once if he was president of Ford Canada, Ford said he did not know, but this story is apocryphal—he was not that ignorant.) Reporters interested in his stockholdings in Ford Canada, some of which were rumored to have been sold in March 1921, were stonewalled by McGregor's office. In 1919–20 Henry Ford had reduced his holdings to about 20 percent by selling 4,305 shares to finance construction at his Rouge River site, but this was not the sort of divestment that McGregor would discuss publicly. As president of Ford Canada, Ford drew dividends and a local salary on which Ford City attempted repeatedly to levy municipal assessments. "They have tried this for two or three years and we have always bluffed them off, and the assessment to Mr. Ford has been dropped," McGregor told Liebold on 1 November 1921, in the belief that the town had no right to tax his boss. When it moved to do so again, McGregor appealed on Ford's behalf and gruffly gave notice of his strong impatience: he had his company's lawyer, A. R. Bartlet, prepare a legal action that Bartlet was quite willing to take to the Supreme Court of Canada. McGregor would tolerate no municipal intrusion, and evidently he was successful. In 1922 the $2 million that Henry Ford had in a Windsor bank reportedly sat there free of local taxation.[41]

Ford's line of thinking included a common but nonetheless nasty streak of anti-Semitism, which historian Robert Lacey explains "went back to his farm-boy, populist suspicion of financiers and middlemen" and the paranoia he felt about sinister Jewish influence at the time of his peace ship escapades during the war.[42] Incensed by the ability of finance capital to manipulate industry, Ford loathed what he saw as the Jewish influence on Wall Street. In the spring of 1920 he had turned his personal newspaper, the *Dearborn Independent*, to chronicling the imagined international Jewish menace facing America, including a hedonistic worldview antithetical to Ford's vision of family values. Management of the Dearborn Publishing Company was entrusted to Ernest Liebold, a vicious anti-Semite himself, who took every opportunity to disseminate and fan Ford's paranoia. Many in the Ford company who openly disagreed with the campaign were purged. Treasurer and Ford Canada vice president Frank Klingensmith was ousted because of differences on corporate borrowing on the American side and maybe because he had tried too hard to help Edsel Ford master the business, but Liebold saw another reason when he dismissively labeled Klingensmith "half-Jewish." Windsor's Jewish community was conscious of Ford's anti-Semitism and Liebold's close scrutiny of what took place within that community. At Dearborn Publishing, Liebold gathered together the most aggressive anti-Semitic articles printed in the *Independent* between May 1920 and March 1921 and published them as two small volumes entitled *The International Jew: The World's Foremost Problem.*[43]

Freely available at all Ford dealers in the United States, this malicious little publication generated violent reaction. One historian described it as a "colossal misstep" by Ford, who was eventually forced to back off. There was less recorded response in Canada, where anti-Semitism and nativist strains, the latter remnants of the war years, permeated society. The newspaper of the respected Woman's Christian Temperance Union, for example, freely reprinted anti-Jewish material from the *Dearborn Independent.* Within the clubby automotive trade, Jewish stereotypes were played for laughs in countless jokes and published cartoons. *Canadian Automotive Trade* picked up, from the magazine of the Timken Detroit-Axle Company of Detroit, the Rosenheim cartoon character. In one strip, where he visits his banker, another character claims "a Jewish Christmas account would be like the Anti-Saloon League savin' up for a champagne banquet."[44]

McGregor's anti-Semitism, which seemed temperate, fed into Ford and Liebold's campaign in an obsequious way. In July 1921 a Kitchener friend of McGregor's assistant secretary, Philip Grandjean, asked him for copies of *The International Jew*. Grandjean and Liebold eagerly obliged. "This book is on sale in all the [American] branches at 25¢ each," Liebold told his Canadian colleague. "If you have sufficient inquiries for them from the public, we would be glad to send you a supply to be handled in this manner." It is uncertain if Ford Canada accepted the offer. Later that summer, Henry Ford wanted to send *The International Jew* to Lord Northcliffe, the British press magnate who was traveling across Canada and was rumored to be anti-Semitic. Liebold had McGregor's staff forward the books to Ford Canada's Vancouver office in the hope of their reaching Northcliffe before he sailed.[45]

Such cooperation, which included McGregor's demeaning hack reporting to Liebold on Jewish activity in the Border Cities, would continue into the winter, but the reignition of the tariff and price debate claimed McGregor's full attention. This issue had never fully gone away. Despite Ford's price slashing in September 1921 and the revival of demand, Canadian automobiles still cost more than their American counterparts, according to industry analysts, even allowing for duty, exchange, and production cost differences. "Motor wise Canadians know these things," *Automotive Industries* (New York) claimed in its report on the CNE show in September 1921, "and some of them have foregone automobiles on the out and out objection to the price differential, regardless of its justice." Ford cars were not the only culprits. *Automotive Industries* bunched them together with the other American-based products—the Walkerville-Oshawa Chevrolets, Windsor-made Maxwells, and Canadian Dodges, which in June 1921 began to be distributed from a building on Windsor's waterfront. In January 1922 the *Monetary Times*, after its own juggling of figures, sided with the low-volume/higher-prices argument but observed that "to produce a low price car in Canada many intricate factors are involved which stock salesmen do not understand or discuss when trying to peddle their offerings."[46]

The tariff debate was inflamed almost single-handedly by William Edgar Raney, the pugnacious attorney general in the United Farmers' government elected in Ontario in 1919. The Border Cities initially became his concern as a result of crime. Since the advent of Prohibition under the Ontario Temperance Act of 1916 and national Prohibition in the United States in 1920, the Detroit River was becoming a notoriously steady and sometimes violent channel for rum-runners and organized crime. No longer did the illicit traffic in automobiles and parts seem as newsworthy. With 352,534 vehicles from the United States passing through customs at Windsor in 1920, automotive and ferry traffic was congested but commonplace. Practically, the attorney general knew the Border Cities well; politically, it was not his favorite region. Determined, with the backing of the churches and the Social Service Council to take on the province's horse racing tracks, the moralistic Raney understood that the Windsor Jockey Club Limited and the Western Racing Association had the highest gate receipts and amounts wagered next to Toronto's clubs. Most of the bettors came from Detroit. In addition to the moral dimension, problems arose too, he had discovered as an investigating counsel in 1919, from altered financial accounts at the tracks, loose controls of receipts, and the surfeit of petty crime drawn to the tracks—pickpocketing and the like. Similarly, with the Hiram Walker and Sons distillery and the Walkerville Brewery, Raney and his federal customs associates knew what to watch for: inflated figures for wastage, fictitious consignees, the suspicious redirection of shipments, false landing certificates, improper vouchers for payments, and unpaid taxes and fraudulent returns. Though "neither vindictive nor fanatical," in the estimate of his premier, Raney focused his Prohibitionist crusade on the Essex border, an effort that netted the province much revenue in fines and publicity but gave the Border Cities nothing extra for policing. In the legislature, J. C. Tolmie (Windsor) and Robert Livingstone Brackin (Kent West), both Liberals, took the government to task for its weak measures of enforcement in Essex. Even so, support there for Prohibition was not a given. In Windsor, the *Plain Dealer* newspaper was launched to fight Prohibition as the official journal of the Border Cities branch of the Citizens' Liberty League for Moderation, in which both Ford's Neil Lawrence and Walter McGregor were active.[47] But there were also industrial and electoral factors along the border that drew the ire of the United Farmers and their crusading attorney general.

Campaigning for the federal election of 6 December 1921 began in September. The incumbent prime minister, Conservative Arthur Meighen, meant to preserve the protective tariff as the keystone of economic nationalism. Under William Lyon Mackenzie King, the Liberals avoided any clear position on trade policy, but the third party in the race, the Progressives, adopted a farmers' platform drafted by the Canadian Council of Agriculture. It condemned protection as wasteful and as grounds for fostering a "privileged class." When King had visited the Border Cities in August, he and a delegation of the region's top Liberals lunched at the Ford plant, but trade policy was on no one's agenda there. King, who knew of McGregor's strong Liberal background, privately had a low opinion of Canadian automakers—in 1923 he would castigate them as a hard-nosed lot and Ford executives in particular as "a genuinely brute force gang"—but in 1921 he played it safe and praised the local state of Canadian-American relations. At the start of the campaign, the Progressives received support from many of Ontario's United Farmers' MLAs, vehemently so from William E. Raney.[48]

Raney took to the hustings in support of the Progressives early in the fall of 1921. His big blow came on Friday, 18 November, in the rural eastern Ontario village of Winchester, well away from Essex. After commenting on the national debt, railway deficits, and unemployment, he attacked the 35 percent tariff on automobiles and the higher prices of Canadian-made vehicles over their American equivalents. When Detroit makers established branches in Canada, he calculated, "the tariff ceases to be for revenue and becomes a tariff for protection and the U.S. manufacturer, with a branch in Canada, is able to add to his profit on his Canadian sales a sum approaching or perhaps quite equaling the Canadian duty." To illustrate this contention, he used the respective costs of Ford cars, and only Fords, and concluded that Ford Canada was benefiting unduly. Warming to the topic, he vigorously launched into a detailed critique of Ford's profits, dividends, and assets, and denounced the government and the tariff for their support of big business. Ford Canada's profitable position, which rivaled the tale of Aladdin's fabled lamp, was a veritable diamond mine. In debates elsewhere, other large corporations, such as Riordan in Quebec, took similar hits, much as the jockey clubs were slammed as vested interests, but in the Border Cities, Raney's address struck a raw nerve, in part because of its spread through the Canadian press. The *Toronto Star* and the *Winnipeg Free Press* printed the Winchester address in full and backed Raney's thrust. "It will be said in reply to Mr. Raney that the Ford case is an exceptional one," the Toronto newspaper editorialized. "It may be. Yet it gives the plainest illustration of the way the tariff in full play works." In the opinion of the *Star*, a cleanup was needed.[49]

On Monday morning, 21 November, when reporters from the *Border Cities Star* approached McGregor's office for comment, executives there, caught off guard, were glumly reticent as they considered a response. Raney's "remarks were made at a political meeting for a purpose and until the elections are over," one said, "I do not wish to make any statement whatever nor be brought into any controversy over the matter. After the election, I will be pleased to give you any information you may wish, or statistics." By that evening, however, an aggravated Gordon McGregor had decided to throw himself aggressively into the campaign, partly to support Essex North's Liberal incumbent, his friend W. C. Kennedy, and in part to meet Raney's blunt challenge.[50] McGregor, Ford, and the tariff question would dominate the campaign in both Essex North and South, with the full support of the *Border Cities Star*. At a Liberal meeting at the Oddfellows' Hall in Walkerville on Monday night, chaired by Walter McGregor, Kennedy was joined onstage by Gordon McGregor, local MLA Major J. C. Tolmie, William M. Grant (manager of Parke Davis and Company), and Frank H. Joyce. Joyce, the former secretary-treasurer of American Auto Trimming in Windsor, was now cohead and secretary-treasurer of the Gotfredson-Joyce truck corporation in Walkerville. (By this time Harry Neal, the popular head of a Windsor baking company, had entered the fray as an independent Conservative, though he would never pose a serious challenge.) Kennedy told the partisan audience that the tariff was not an issue for the Liberals, but the recovering McGregor, with his typically humorous yet pretentious snubs, had more than that to say to a receptive audience. He artfully avoided any direct discussion of the tariff. Ford was his game. The Liberals had always supported Ford Canada, beginning in the Laurier era, and they would continue to do so, he predicted. Reining in his true sentiments with a laugh, he settled for dismissing Raney as a nobody: "He thinks he has thrown a monkey-wrench into the machinery but the Ford Motor Company was already a going concern before Mr. Raney was anywhere in particular and will continue to exist long after that gentleman has been forgotten. . . . Many of the things he said were gross misrepresentations." Recognizing that he was in no forum for boring statistical argument, he declined a rebuttal based on the myriad numbers his office could generate. Ford's production said it all. At the end of McGregor's remarks, his brother (whose support of the Ontario Temperance Act (OTA) and Prohibition was qualified) added, to much applause and laughter, "Raney knows no more about the Ford Motor Company, nor any other motor company than he did about the OTA." The only contrary statement of the evening came at the end from the plainspoken Frank Joyce, who claimed succinctly (in the *Star*'s summary) "that the Ford Motor company had done all that Raney had said and more." "'In fact,' he added, 'their story makes Aladdin's lamp appear like a tallow candle in comparison.'" Evidently no one asked Joyce, who had no axe to grind with Ford, to expand on his opinion.[51]

On the following day, Tuesday the 22nd, McGregor privately reviewed the Raney matter, including an explanation of the politics involved, with Henry Ford over the telephone. He promised to send Ford a copy of Raney's speech, which went out that afternoon, and subsequent newspaper commentary.[52] That same afternoon, at the official nomination meeting at the Sandwich courthouse, Kennedy and Neal staked out their respective positions. Gordon and Walter McGregor and Frank Joyce would not be supporting him, Kennedy reasoned, if they believed Liberal policy would ruin their businesses and close their factories. Neal, despite his independence, backed Meighen's position on the tariff, which was responsible for the American control of 50 percent of the industries on the Canadian border. The decided underdog, he faced a steady barrage of heckling at the nomination meeting—his "light weight bread" was a favorite dig—but he gave as good as he got. As a longtime member of the Windsor Gas Company, Kennedy shared responsibility for Essex's gas shortages, Neal claimed, not to mention the large blocks of Victory Bonds Kennedy and other capitalists had bought because they were tax free, regardless of McGregor's professed intolerance of speculation.

At subsequent meetings in Windsor and Sandwich and at the Ford and Canadian Products factories, Kennedy and Neal gave low-key performances. Neal took it easy on his "old friend" McGregor. At each event, proceedings were dominated by McGregor, a skilled stage speaker who also campaigned in Essex South; he spoke at gatherings in Essex and Amherstburg (where his family was still well known) in support of George Perry Graham, a veteran Liberal from Laurier times. At meetings in support of Neal, it was Windsor barrister Frederick C. Kerby who delivered penetrating, lengthy attacks, not against Kennedy but against McGregor, the "millionaire" head of Ford, the company's monopoly on the production of Model Ts in Canada, and its consequent disregard of tariff protection. McGregor could easily afford to back the Liberals whatever their position on the tariff, Kerby maintained. As he saw it, a lower tariff would tip the balance of trade against Canada and increase the exchange rate, thus making Detroit automobiles more expensive, not cheaper.

Deliberately ignoring Kerby's interpretation, which Kennedy found "absurd," McGregor repeatedly challenged Raney's assertions instead. He was normally reluctant to mix business with politics, but here he did just that, with numbing analyses of statistics and trade policy and a corporate branding of Liberal politics in a contest fought primarily by noncontestants. Raney, he argued, was no friend of the farmer regardless of his affiliation. It was Henry Ford, after all, who had given Canada 1,000 tractors to help overcome food shortages during the war. At Essex and Amherstburg, toward the end of the campaign, McGregor took Graham's backers through a detailed breakdown of the prices, profits, taxes, exchange rates, and freight and other charges on imported Fordson tractors and on Canadian and American Model Ts. His arguments and humor frequently came laden with such quantitative analysis and convoluted economics. On 2,495 tractors, on which the tariff had been abolished in 1917, Raney calculated a profit for Ford Canada of $300,000; McGregor's figures left it with only $17,000.

In the end, voters gave Kennedy and Graham overwhelming majorities and King a national government. McGregor had given his plant workers Tuesday the 6th off to vote, on the condition that they make up the time on the Friday, when the factory would normally have been closed. Harry Neal, who was forced to forfeit his electoral deposit, reentered public life in early January, when he was reappointed chair of Windsor's board of education, where McGregor's brother Don sat on the commercial and industrial advisory committees. Raney came to the Border Cities on 23 December, possibly on a Prohibition matter, but during a quick trip to Ford City he skipped a planned visit to the Ford plant—a perverse invitation on someone's part—in order to catch the 4:10 P.M. train.

After the election, the pricing controversy receded into front-porch grumbling. The company would reduce prices again on 17 January, to an extent that surpassed reductions by Ford Detroit. McGregor relaxed the vigorous personal pace he had kept during the contest. No longer was he involved in the maze of utility politics and municipal elections. By 16 December his daughter Harriet and his son were home for the Christmas holiday. In their honor, on the 23rd Gordon and Hattie hosted a gala dinner and dance for young people at the Essex County Golf and Country Club. This was followed on the 28th by the first ball in the new clubhouse of the Elmcourt Country Club, whose entertainment committee consisted of the fun-loving Hattie, her youngest daughter (Nancy), and Mrs. W. C. Kennedy. Together they would also organize programs of afternoon tea "dansants" beginning in January, to the sound of records—waltzes, foxtrots, and the popular recordings of Paul Whitman—played on the new Victrola donated by the McGregors. They celebrated New Year's Eve with more than 200 others at a grand dinner and dance at the Essex club that the *Star* billed as "the most brilliant social event of the year." Each table had a centerpiece consisting of miniature snow-covered trees trimmed with holly and sparkling crystal; favors included whistles, bells, noisemakers, and colored-tissue hats. The automobile crowd was strongly represented, by, among others, the Gordon McGregors, the Don McGregors, and the Border Cities' other large retail dealer, Frank M. Foster (Maxwell-Chalmers, Willys-Overland, Packard, Cleveland, Franklin, Chevrolet, and Paige) and his wife.[53]

Some entertainments emanated from the Ford offices. On 13 December, McGregor, advertising manager W. J. Baxter, and several participating actors had attended a private première of the new Christmas film produced by Ford for the charitable Goodfellows' Club, of which Wallace Campbell had been president and "Santa-Claus-in-chief" in 1919–20. The 1,000 foot drama, written locally and featuring local actors and settings, was directed by Major Andrew Cory of Baxter's department. It was meant to be shown at intermissions in cinemas along with feature presentations, such as (at the Walkerville Theatre) Wallace Reid in *Too Much Speed*, "a racing romance of youth, roaring with speed cars and running on laughs and love." In a scene of charitable giving in the Goodfellows' film, the character of Widow Muldoon, played by Mrs. Stanley Wallace, registers great joy when she receives a Christmas hamper from the Goodfellows. It is possible that the club's determination of need and its "investigating committees" also drew upon Ford expertise. The Goodfellows-Ford film, an interesting piece of corporate welfare, was important for two reasons. First, in a decidedly modern turn, Ford films had become an industry within an industry, something McGregor was proud of. By late August his company's film crews had returned from a cross-country tour with enough material for "26 complete subjects a year"—double the previous year's production—for its most popular educational series (industrial, scenic, historical, and scientific subjects), which drew enthusiastic response. This series paralleled the Canadian Industrial Series made earlier by Pathéscope of Toronto for the Canadian Reconstruction Association to promote Made in Canada. The Ford films had wide circulation, in theaters, clubs, church groups, and industrial cafeterias and auditoriums. Their impact was the same as that of the Model T: reducing distances and class distinctions.[54]

Ford was not the only automotive group to utilize film. In the United States, in addition to the work of Ford Detroit, both Maxwell and Essex were using it for promotional purposes by 1918. In 1920 Canadian-born silent-film star Nell Shipman made *Something New* for Maxwell. It featured rocky terrain, Mexican bandits, chase scenes, and a trusty Maxwell with "speed—the only salvation." (The three broken transmissions suffered during filming did not appear.) To achieve this aesthetic of the speeding automobile, young bloods in Ford cars throughout North America ceaselessly beefed up and streamlined Model Ts for racing. How many Canadian companies used film is unknown. Goodyear Tire and Rubber of New Toronto, for one, recognized the "industrial value of moving pictures." Films shown in its cafeteria, the *Labour Gazette* reported in 1920, were well received, "a blessing to the working men," though the films that promoted morale and the prevention of time loss on the shop floor clearly had ulterior motives.[55]

The Goodfellows' film also underlined the social realities of poverty and unemployment in the Border Cities, where the slump in the automotive industry on both sides of the river was having definite effects, with no concerted public response. In late December, Ford Canada took on 200 "old hands" in its four-day-week schedule (in place since September) in the hope that it could return to full-time in January. High unemployment over the past six months prompted the *Star* to advise on 11 January 1922, in a rare piece of criticism, "that the Ford plant and other companies would do well to look after the residents of Ford City in regard to employment of outsiders coming in." Ford took some responsibility that winter: while the municipality reportedly looked after thirty-six or more families, "numbers of others" received direct help from Ford Canada. As in previous slumps, civic authorities were angered by the uncontrollable stream of unemployed, many of them autoworkers, who poured into the Border Cities looking for work. The number of openings was small: the placement of fifty men at Ford and other industries in early February was considered good, but municipal care was erratic. In January Ford City's council had rejected the proposal of local women to set up a soup kitchen because a number of councillors were averse to "advertising" Ford City as a public welfare center.[56]

On 28 January, on the grounds that the "low point in industry has definitely passed," Wallace Campbell announced that Ford Canada would be returning to an eight-hour-day, five-day-week on 3 February. Unabashedly, he tied his company's round of price cuts effected 17 January into the social fabric of the industrial upswing, consumer demand for cheap transportation, and political debate: "We base our optimism on the fact that we endeavour to serve the public by constantly reducing our prices commensurate with our reductions in costs, and take our losses on shrinkage of inventories. We are confident in our belief that if all industrial concerns would lower their prices to a rock-bottom minimum, the answer to sales and unemployment would be very quickly found."[57]

Rarely did Campbell make such announcements unless he had one eye on company strategy; the connections would often be identified at the branch levels. On 4 February, on the eve of the National Automobile Show of Western Ontario in the London armories, London branch manager M. F. Smith proudly stated that "at this very moment the Ford Motor Company is launching the greatest sales campaign ever launched in the Dominion," a culmination of the "[en]closed car campaign" launched by head office in September to push its enclosed two-door coupes and center-door sedans, which happened to be the company's most expensive models, even after substantial price cutting.[58]

Ever watchful for signs of better times, the *Star* was quick to headline that "Motoropolis has a bright future" and run promotional features on its bright stars: McGregor, Campbell, and Major Howard Blood, general manager of GM's Canadian Products. The *Star* even stretched to cast Henry Ford's abrasive acquisition of the prestigious Lincoln Motor Company from the highly respected Henry Martyn Leland in early 1922 as a benefit for the Border Cities: the acquisition of the Lincoln plant ought to assure the "further prosperity and expansion of Detroit. In this progress the Border Cities are vitally interested, for the forward march of their sister city across the river is usually accompanied by expansion on this side of the narrow water." McGregor and Campbell likely agreed, but in this instance there is no hint, recalling their position on tractors four years earlier, that they thought Lincolns could be made in Canada. Like tractors, these luxury cars would be imported. If McGregor was failing in health, his brother Walter was fast becoming a cross-border cheerleader. In his annual address to the chamber of commerce in January he lauded the 236 industries operating in the Border Cities. On 9 and 10 March he spoke to Detroit's Rotary Club on the fine state of Canadian business relations with the United States.[59]

Amid such buoyant proceedings, contrary views were drowned out. On 21 January, the unrepentant former labor councillor Archie Hooper, still McGregor's nemesis, was charged and fined in police court for running a common betting house at his cigar stand in the waiting room of the hydroelectric railway company at Sandwich and Ferry streets. On 29 January and 5 March, George F. Ramsay, a Socialist member of the Detroit Educational Society, spoke at the Windsor Open Forum on Pitt Street East, where he characterized Ford workers as the exploited "slaves" of capitalist organizations, but his audiences were small and his views were dismissed by the *Star* as nonsensical "hot air." Elsewhere in Ontario, dealers were ruthlessly being pushed to the margins to promote low prices and the Fordist concept of "cheap transportation."[60]

From January to March Wallace Campbell, in addition to making a number of announcements for Ford, did much of the company's public legwork. Surprisingly, he did so in bolder fashion than associates had witnessed with the confident but cautious McGregor. In December, in the shadow of the federal election, Ford Detroit workers resident in Canada had once again been hit by American authorities with a confusing nonresident income tax on back pay. Ford asked Washington for clarification on the effective date and an exemption allowance; with 2,500 to 3,000 Border Cities residents working in Detroit, many besides autoworkers were concerned. In February Campbell, Howard Blood, M. G. Campbell of Kelsey Wheel, George Duck of Universal Car, Charles T. Miller of the chamber of commerce (and secretary-treasurer of the Canadian Bridge Company), and W. M. Grant went to Ottawa for a CMA conference but also to meet with the minister of finance to urge a better reciprocal taxation agreement between Canada and the United States.[61]

Whatever the state of his health, McGregor handled an appreciable workload, largely from his office. Municipal affairs no longer engaged him—though he was probably pleased with Archie Hooper's charge and the "overwhelming defeat" of Windsor's labor aldermen in January's election. Rumors in December of a takeover of the Merchants' Bank by the Bank of Montreal drew no comment from McGregor, but he did go to Montreal for directors' meetings. In January the merger was openly confirmed, and on 8 February he traveled to Montreal again for a ratification meeting. Much of his automotive work now was routine: forwarding assembly data to Ernest Liebold in Detroit; attending the New York motor show in January with Howard Blood, Studebaker sales manager W. G. Palmer, and Frank Foster of the Maxwell-Chalmers franchise; and in February wading through a pile of letters to address all kinds of rumors about Ford, including its acquisition of a site in Sudbury, Ontario, for producing nickel. "Somebody always had the Ford Company buying something—factories or land or office buildings—somewhere," he complained.[62]

Equally demanding were the capricious requests of Henry Ford and Ernest Liebold. Between early January and late February, McGregor spent an inordinate amount of time dealing with Ford's interest in obtaining a hydroelectric site in Ontario. Ford had "surplus cash" in Canadian banks, McGregor told Sir Adam Beck, the head of Ontario's public hydro commission, and he wanted to develop a site for use in the manufacture of cylinders, valves, and other parts. Sites at Smiths Falls, Merrickville, Sault Ste. Marie, and St. Mary's River, as well as Montreal in Quebec, were all discreetly considered. McGregor had learned to keep such matters quiet to avoid speculation and rash offers from municipalities. He made special investigative trips to Montreal and Ottawa in February. Beck thought Ford was capable of undertaking a major development on the St. Lawrence, but this idea fell on deaf ears. Nor could Ford be made to understand the scarcity of sites, the maze of existing municipal utility contracts, the political turmoil surrounding public power in Ontario, and the bitter tensions between Beck and Ernest Charles Drury, the premier of the United Farmers' government. McGregor summed up the situation in a letter to Liebold on 15 February, with a strong hint that the project be dropped:

> The real issue between Drury and Beck is that Beck wants to electrify all the radial railways in the Province of Ontario so as to get a market for his power and to do that he wants the government to guarantee the bonds of all these radial railways. Drury, on the other hand, objects to doing this. . . . [I]n the meantime I am just pointing out what the situation is, to show you how hopeless it is to try and get anything in this Province in the way of water power development.[63]

Further demands were made by Ford and Liebold. McGregor was quite obliging regarding both the *Dearborn Independent* and their Jewish phobia. Liebold wanted to see the *Independent* distributed widely in Canada, especially in Montreal. McGregor sent him circulation figures and sales prices for other publications in Canada and even offered the services of his advertising head, W. J. Baxter, to delve into the matter further. "If there is anything you can suggest we can do," McGregor told Liebold on 16 January, "that would overcome a national prejudice applying to practically all American publications, we will be very glad to co-operate to increase the circulation of the *Dearborn Independent* in this country if at all possible." Seeing nothing wrong with its predisposition, the *Border Cities Star* matter-of-factly and uncritically acknowledged Henry Ford's campaign against the "international Jew."[64]

The *Independent* mysteriously stopped spewing out its anti-Semitic articles in January, but Liebold's venomous hostilities continued unabated and McGregor fed them. He subserviently kept Liebold posted on developments in Windsor's Jewish community. Edwin G. Pipp, the editor of the *Independent* who had quit in disgust over the Jewish articles and started his own weekly, had earned Ford Detroit's particular enmity. He came over from Detroit on 12 February to address the Hebrew Literary Society at the Windsor Hebrew Institute at Aylmer and Tuscarora streets. His talk was an unveiled attack on Henry Ford for his grossly ambitious desire to be president of the United States, his appalling treatment of Henry Leland for "financial gain" in the takeover of Lincoln, and his anti-Semitism. The *Star*'s resulting report of Pipp's remarks, which contained references to Liebold, was sent to him by McGregor. "It seems [Pipp's] continued and persistent prevarications are more or less amusement to our Hebrew friends," McGregor observed.[65]

The image of a desk-bound McGregor as the errand boy of Ford and Liebold is sadly revealing, but the public likely saw nothing unusual; some held McGregor in esteem, some hated his wealth, others simply were keen on his cars. Many may have been more interested in the Ford-owned Lincoln automobile as it débuted on 27 February at R. M. Jaffray's third annual auto show in the Border Cities, "the greatest automobile manufacturing center in all of Canada." (The energetic Jaffray would also launch an electricity and food show, and since January he had been the manager of the new market building on Ouellette Street.) Regardless of Henry Ford's treatment of Leland, the *Star*, in its analysis of the acquisition, managed to find a way to portray Ford as a "public benefactor." With characteristic effusiveness, the *Star* liked the Universal Car Agency's exhibit and hustle at the show: "As usual the Ford cars were the means of drawing many spectators but more particularly now on account of their recent price cut."[66] Not everyone was so taken. McGregor was the butt of much grumbling, just as his company was grist for the rumor mill, and there was one telling encounter.

In January salesmen from Universal Car had conducted a door-to-door canvass in the Border Cities looking for prospective customers for used Ford cars. After they called on Mrs. George Brode at 255 Windermere Road in Walkerville, they recorded that she might be in the market but not until April—her husband, a plumber and steamfitter, did not have steady work that winter. Little did they realize that she had very strong feelings about Gordon McGregor and the cost of Canadian Ford cars, sentiments she would share with Henry Ford, for whom she still had some respect. Raised in a rural mining community in Maryland, Mary Martin Brode had had limited education. She came to Detroit during the Great War and then moved to Walkerville. After the visit of the salesmen, her anger on the boil, she set out her concerns in no uncertain terms in a letter to Henry Ford on 16 January 1922:

> Can you explain why your car costs *so* much more on this side of the river. I'll tell you. Gordon McGregor, Dr. [Charles Westlake] Hoare and some more share holders are becomeing millionars on the huge proffits they are deriving. Now listen. The factory that bears your name on this side, dont do you justus. The [hei]ght of my ambition is a car, so my husband an four small kiddies can enjoy life a little. But never in this wide world will I buy a car and such a terribl difference in prices, and I know hundreds of other people with the same oppinion, I'll make my meager deposits in the bank when I can spair it, and sit on the front porch in my rocking chair, before I ever give those proffiteers their price, and the factory that bears your name, would be working full time if those old misers were not such hogs. Don't think either one of the stock-holders mentioned are rideing in a Ford Car. No Sir, they don't leave there money with the Ford Co[.] [J]ust saw where Dr. Hoare had his big Cadallac up for sale. Then too, compare liveing expences with Detroit. What I mean is groceries meats clothing shoes and yard goods. Dont think I am writeing this to drum up custom for Ford. Not so. For if Fords went idle forever it would not stop my pay check for my husband dont work their. He is a plumber and steamfitter. But I admire your system an way of thinking and if you never cut the price of your car on the other side, I dont believe any one would. Now listen, every one I ever hear speaking in regards to cars say never in this side would will they pay Fords of Canada such a price. They will go over an buy a Dodge for a few dollars more, So please use your influence.
> [Signed] Mrs. Geo. Brode

This remarkable letter stopped at the desk of Ernest Liebold. He calmly told Mary Brode that he was passing a copy on to McGregor for reply, "asking that he inform you regarding the difference in the price between the Ford car as constructed in Canada and Detroit." Whether Henry Ford ever saw the letter is uncertain. "Naturally it is very annoying to get letters of this kind," an angry McGregor wrote to Liebold about Mrs. Brode, "and possibly if she had lived in the community for a little while she might feel differently and know something of what she is talking about."[67] McGregor's response to Mary Brode has not survived, but clearly there was a clash of perception: if she, like William Raney and others, possessed the facts—Fordist minds loved facts—they would understand his position on prices, McGregor believed. Mrs. Brode saw him as a greedy profiteer; he had proclaimed two big dividends of 15 percent in 1921 and another of the same size would follow in 1922. Nothing Ford Canada, the *Star*, or the chamber of commerce said or did would alter that view, which, like the sentiments of the autoworkers and the dealers, represented strong undercurrents. Her concerns about the cost of living were well grounded. In 1919 a federal committee had verified that some food costs were higher in Windsor than in Detroit. Between February 1921 and September 1922 the highest costs in Ontario were reportedly being experienced in the Border Cities.

Well into the 1920s, Gordon McGregor, Wallace Campbell, and other government-protected capitalists remained targets. In *A War on Poverty* agrarian radical Edward Alexander Partridge would lambaste them for continuing "to prey upon that part of the poor bedevilled Canadian public who can't escape to the United States." At the same time self-interested analysts in the auto industry were starting to predict an economic rebound after 1921. "The automobile is not a luxury," reasoned William M. Gray of Gray-Dort Motors in Chatham in January 1922, "it is an economic necessity in Canada's agricultural, industrial and social activities and as such will again predominate in sales."[68]

On Saturday, 4 March, McGregor, accompanied by his son, visited for the final time his Ford office, where he wrote his last letter to Liebold, about the Model T adapted to run on railways. Then, not feeling "up to the mark," he underwent an X-ray examination. Although the results are not known, they were obviously alarming. On Sunday he was promptly sent to Montreal along with his wife and brother Walter; Bill and Harriet followed on Wednesday and brothers Don and Malcolm cut short their vacations in the States.

After three operations at the Royal Victoria Hospital, the last one on Wednesday, Gordon McGregor died at 3:30 A.M. on Saturday, 11 March 1922, at the age of forty-nine. At 8:45 A.M. Walter telegraphed Henry Ford that "Gordon passed away very peacefully this morning." Wallace Campbell had stayed in touch by telephone.[69]

Later that day the *Star* announced "Gordon M'Gregor Dead" in banner headlines of a size that had rarely been seen, even during the war. "Intestinal trouble arising out of an internal injury suffered in a railroad accident some years ago was the direct cause of death," it explained in extraordinary obituary coverage that lasted a week and rivaled in solemnity the war's worst news. In its close coverage of McGregor's life over many decades, however, the *Evening Record* and the *Star*, which seemed to follow his every movement, had never reported any railway accident. Though no one talked about his illness at the time, family members have confirmed it was cancer, the unspoken disease that ran in the family. Family pathology also points to a rare blood vessel disorder (hereditary haemorrhagic telangiectasia, or Osler-Weber-Rendu disease), which has been traced to Gordon McGregor.[70]

McGregor's remains were brought from Montreal to Windsor in the private railway coach of Grant Hall, vice president and general manager of the Canadian Pacific. A short funeral service, conducted by the Reverend Hugh Mortimer Paulin of St. Andrew's Presbyterian Church (J. C. Tolmie's successor in 1915 and a nativist of the first order), was held on the afternoon of Tuesday, 14 March, at the family residence at 490 Victoria Avenue. Interment followed at Windsor Grove Cemetery; the pallbearers were George Dickert of Ford, branch managers Fred Fox from Toronto and C. S. Hoben from Montreal, Malcolm G. Campbell of Kelsey Wheel, Frank Joyce, and Major Edward C. Kenning, a golfing mate and lawyer on the original incorporation of Ford in 1904. The cortège, perhaps the largest ever seen in Windsor, reached the cemetery before the last car had taken on mourners at the house. Extensive coverage was provided by the *Star*, with less effusive notice given by the *Detroit Free Press*. In a step-by-step account of the service at the residence, the *Star* dutifully noted that Henry and Edsel Ford "were present and stationed themselves in proximity with many of [McGregor's] employees and associates of lower standing." The *Free Press* had the Fords simply standing out on the verandah, "but within sound of the minister's voice." Municipal offices, the Ford plants on both sides of the river, and Kelsey Wheel, Standard Paint and Varnish, and other Ford feeders, as well as Dowsley Spring and Axle in Chatham, all closed. "The thousands of wheels in the machinery of the organization now so perfect, due to Mr. McGregor's wisdom, foresight and personality, were silent," the *Star* intoned. The Ford offices went into mourning. Tributes poured in from Ford Canada's board of directors, Hiram Walker and Sons, the Border Cities' mayors and religious leaders, various chambers of commerce, the GWVA of Ontario, the board of the Border Cities' Boys' Work organization, notable politicians from all levels and parties, and McGregor's many clubs: the Detroit, Windsor, Walkerville Tennis, Rotary, Kiwanis, Beach Grove Country, Elmcourt Country, Essex Golf and Country, Detroit Golf, and Detroit Athletic.[71]

For decades the *Evening Record* and then the *Star* had been fine-tuning a sanitized characterization of Gordon McGregor. It now found full, utterly respectful flourish: gone was the "motor magnate" of manly—even princely—proportions, the simple, modest, accessible, democratic, unspoiled industrial champion, the factory workers' true companion. Not surprisingly, Ford Canada was identified as his "greatest work," far ahead of his public contributions. One more time the *Star* proudly recounted his heroic efforts in forming Ford Canada, which "is representative in substance of the speed of progress of modern industrial Canada." The *Financial Post* carried the same image: "In spite of numerous prophecies made that this new venture was but a flash in the pan—handicapped by the lack of capital and faced with almost universal skepticism—he found the task of interesting prospective purchasers of stock a seemingly impossible one." No one paused to wonder how far the organization and automobiles of Henry Ford had carried McGregor. Noticed by the automotive journals and *Industrial Canada*, news of his passing appeared only sporadically (via the Canadian press) in daily and weekly newspapers throughout Ontario, where far more attention was paid to department store heir Sir John Craig Eaton, who fell ill in March and died in April.[72]

CHAPTER 7

McGregor's Legacy

Gordon McGregor's legacy can be seen at three levels: family, region and country, and company. Of these the most difficult to discern are the family context, because of the absence of letters and memoirs, and the company setting, within the presence of the Henry Ford juggernaut.

In the aftermath of McGregor's death, the bulk of his personal estate went to his widow, Hattie. Much had already gone to charity during his lifetime, and he had not stinted on his lifestyle. Valued at $1,235,537.03, the estate included twelve parcels of land ($259,750.35), mortgages ($58,487.91), bonds ($282,146.79), and stock ($599,280, of which $515,005 was in shares in Ford Canada). His primary executor was his brother Walter. For the next eleven years this mild-mannered man would have to deal with Hattie's apparently casual disregard (despite her reputation as the family disciplinarian, a role Gordon had never assumed, according to a nephew) for the details of investment and estate management and her regular requests for funds from the estate. In a conversation with the author in 2004, a grandson raised conjecturally the vague possibility of costly "family needs." By the time of Hattie's own death on 7 April 1933, she owed the estate over $7,800.[1]

After Gordon's death, she had been named to take his place for the duration of his term as a Ford director—a merely honorary gesture. She withdrew from most of her social and public involvements for a time. When she resumed activity in the summer of 1922, it was to finish the renovation of St. Andrew's Church, a project she and Gordon had planned before his death.[2] The Kingsville cottage continued to enjoy family use. Whatever personal or corporate papers Gordon left at his home, cottage, or office were destroyed. Many years later, in McGregor's basement in the Victoria Avenue house, a young nephew stumbled across his phonograph and some wax-cylinder recordings, which hauntingly re-created his fine, entertaining voice in renderings of such prewar Irish tunes as "The Rose of Tralee" and "Mother Machree."

At Ford Canada, without missing a beat, Wallace Campbell aggressively assumed direction of the company. On 16 March, two days after McGregor's funeral, the board moved him into his late colleague's positions as vice president and treasurer. The *Star* approved this promotion of a "Windsor product," as it called Campbell. On the 18th, he announced that the plant, with 2,714 employees in addition to office staff, would be operating on a full-time schedule of five and a half days a week. The executive transition may have generated—or provided an opportunity for—some managerial turnover. In April service manager Joseph D. Isaacs, a sixteen-year veteran of the company, left to become president and general manager of Middlesex Motors Limited in London. In June advertising manager W. J. Baxter, whom McGregor had plucked from the EBUC, resigned to join McConnell and Fergusson Limited, the noted advertising agency in London and Toronto that did work for Ford. Baxter's shoes in particular were hard to fill. In his two years with Ford under McGregor, its advertising, the *Star* noted, had gained international recognition and favorable mentions in *Printers' Ink* and other leading trade journals.[3]

According to Campbell and company advertisements, McGregor had played a part in the property negotiations and assemblies and other early groundwork for the major factory expansion launched with much fanfare in the summer of 1922 in a bid to boost production. The company's tunnel vision was intense. In welcoming the reunion of the Border Cities' "Old Boys" in August, the company was quick to laud, with a nod to the Boys, "the shrine of transportation's modern miracle—the universal Canadian Ford Car." Through greater volumes and economies, the expansion was meant to bring prices closer to those of American Ford cars and, as Campbell told shareholders on 23 October 1922, counter embarrassing "competition from our parent Company" since 1920 and, finally, achieve the lower prices expected from tariff protection. For years Ford Detroit had been pressing its Canadian offspring to produce more and had held it closely to company policy, but with no thoughts of synchronizing prices. Because of the parent's development of its own raw materials and the Rouge River complex, Campbell explained, the American Ford company "is now in a position to produce and sell cars at prices which in effect are keener competition to us than any other make of car." He acknowledged the moral need to give Canadians savings on car purchases in a protected economy, but instinctively he did not hesitate to recognize price increases as Ford Canada's proper response to the production of 1,800 fewer cars and the need to maintain satisfactory profits.[4]

To effect the expansion, which involved about 175 acres to the south of its crowded riverside complex (never an ideal site for growth), Ford Canada worked "hand in hand" with Ford City Council and the Reaume Real Estate Organization Limited. Its primary agents in this development were A. A. Little, Leonard P. Reaume, and Ulysses G. Reaume, who was also mayor of Ford City. Ford Canada's relation with the Reaume firm, which controlled nearly a third of the entire available acreage in Ford City, had, it seems, been carefully cultivated by McGregor. Their interests were the same. Whatever town planning he had promoted within the EBUC, planning in Ford City followed corporate needs or, as the Reaume outfit put it honestly enough in promotional literature, business "just followed the lines of least resistance." Here, the course of least resistance was defined by the needs of Ford Canada. This growth in Ford City was also part of the eastward expansion and intensification of the Border Cities: to the east of Ford City a section of Sandwich East Township had been subdivided for development in 1913, and in 1921 the area was incorporated as the town of Riverside, with a population of 1,155.[5]

The expansion at Ford Canada did have an immediate and expected impact on production, McGregor's parting achievement: from 50,266 cars in 1922 to 79,115 in 1923 and 71,726 the next year. Exports also soared: for instance, from 7,212 chassis to Australia in 1922 to 13,708 the following year. Plans were also made for a large assembly plant for Toronto on Danforth Avenue in East York (1922–23), the reorganization (with financing from Ford Detroit) of operations in South Africa (1923) and Australia (1924–25)—the latter facilitated by a new trade treaty—and the institution of time-payment arrangements for buyers (1923).[6]

This creation of new Ford companies in Australia and South Africa was the fruit of Ford Canada's, and McGregor's, leadership in the export field within the larger Canadian automotive industry. By the 1920s this industry was the second largest in the world next to America, but, as Tom Traves points out, in export sales on a per capita basis it surpassed those of the United States. After 1919, in many imperial markets lower tariffs were being charged on Canadian cars than on American vehicles. Consequently, in 1921 General Motors transferred its export offices to Oshawa and handed over the imperial market to its Canadian company.[7] But McGregor and Ford had been in the field since 1904 and were clearly the dominant Canadian players before the early 1920s. The complex marketing challenges created by Ford Canada's formation of assembly plants abroad fell largely on Wallace Campbell.

For the *Border Cities Star*, McGregor's premature death removed a long-favored son, an industrial beacon, and an eminent champion of Canadian-American relations along the Detroit River. Perhaps any smart businessman could have been Henry Ford's surrogate in Canada—a simplistic reduction—but McGregor had deep roots and connections in the Border region. His corporate achievements rested heavily on that foundation. After printing a profusion of eulogies in March 1922, between 22 April and 24 June the *Star* ran a feature series of nine articles on the impact of Ford on Essex, the county with the heaviest concentration of Model Ts in Canada. Here, the *Star* believed, was McGregor's influence writ large. As the county's industrial "mainspring," Ford Canada gave employment to 40 percent of the Border Cities' population, an astounding proportion if true. At the main plant, 3,809 men were employed (whatever women there were, except for the 125–50 office staff, were not counted); 3,432 others worked for the twenty manufacturers that supplied Ford and only Ford. The *Star* series also gave a national count, a summary of McGregor's significance within the dominion if one equates him with his cars, in the manner of Henry Ford. The Model T had taken Canada by storm. Throughout the country the company had 700 dealers; they engaged 744 salesmen, 2,252 mechanics, and 588 clerks; 2,633 Ford service stations employed 5,266 men; and 24,000 railway cars were needed annually to transport Ford cars, with another 12,000 needed to take Model Ts to the seaboards for export.[8]

In the midst of this series, in a wonderful little piece of nostalgic corporate bluster, McGregor was elevated to the iconic level of

Henry Ford: in the search for a means to open up the country with some speedy form of road transportation, "Henry Ford solved the problem for the world. The late Gordon McGregor solved it for Canada."[9] Scant attention was paid to either the minimal technological contribution of Ford Canada (never its strength or need) or the substantial contributions of McGregor's department heads, among them Dickert, Lawrence, Lee, Ranson, Nancekevill, Hogarth, and Baxter.

McGregor would remain at this rarefied height throughout the company's thirtieth, fiftieth, and hundredth anniversaries, in 1934, 1954, and 2004. In *Thirty Years of Progress*, Ford Canada saw no contradiction between its organization by "a handful of practical visionaries" and its full "accord with the clear principles laid down by Mr. Ford for the development of his great industrial concept."[10] As recently as the centennial of the company, its "Communications Network" proudly recognized that "with faith in his company, his country and the future, McGregor steadily built his dream."[11] None of these portrayals provides much insight into McGregor's personality, skills, and flaws or traces his development as an enormously engaging, rich, and prideful businessman capable of marshaling influential, often paternalistic actions at the civic and corporate levels. At no point, beginning with the eulogies of the *Border Cities Star*, has any examination probed the contradictions between McGregor's progressive engagements, as in the Essex Border Utilities Commission, and the paternalistic attitudes fostered by his upbringing in the Ford environment.

In the Border Cities, McGregor was further honored when an elementary school built on Alexis Road in Windsor was named for him in 1924, at which time his civic-minded brother Don was chair of the board. The previous year, when a Ford company accountant (William Egbert Disher) and a Ford City banker (Edward J. Colquhoun) were charged with siphoning off employee payments for Victory Bonds into their own accounts beginning in 1921 to pay for a stock deal, no one questioned the accounting procedures in place during McGregor's watch.[12] Even less attention was paid to the sniping of Partridge or to the likes of the feisty Mrs. Brode or to the mild critiques from other automobile executives. In death, McGregor proved as valuable a legendary figurehead as he had been between 1904 and 1922.

Wallace Campbell nonetheless opened up some distance from McGregor's more cautious management to propel the major expansion they had planned and in some instances to impart novelty and freshness to tested initiatives. In 1926, for example, claiming that no systematic program for "sales stimulation" had existed prior to that summer—and thus ignoring the many efforts before 1922—the company launched a flurry of new promotional folders, a new monthly salesmen's magazine, and "clinics" for dealer organization. Based on these and other factors, including the prolonged popularity of the Model T in Canada—longer perhaps than in the United States—Ford Canada experienced its best year ever in 1926. After General Motors' decision to send parts to Oshawa from the States and close its Canadian Products plant in January 1925, Ford Canada remained the Border Cities primary company in an industry that, under McGregor, had come to define and drive Canada's Motoropolis.[13]

Without question, the population of the Border Cities had exploded during McGregor's eighteen years at the helm of Ford Canada. Between 1911 and 1921, census figures reveal almost a twofold increase, from 24,888 in Windsor and Walkerville to 47,763 in Windsor, Walkerville, and Ford City. The surges in Ford's growth kept pace, and to a large extent the company's local leadership of the automotive industry in Motoropolis gave identity to that explosive growth. McGregor's direction of the company was exercised with a complex kind of authority: a dependence on Ford Detroit that could never disappear, a streak of independence granted by a separate corporate existence (and substantial Canadian ownership of shares), an initiative spurred by an unfettered use of proven technology, and, in his last years, a caution imposed by strong economic slumps. Sometimes within this caution lurked personal incertitude and an element of corporate subordination. McGregor's authority was also defined in part by subtle shifts in the nature of his "branch plant" operation, from one clearly linked to the tariff in the early years to a major regional gear in Henry Ford's larger North American machine, where national borders became blurred, especially as overseas business intensified and Ford Canada became a key center for foreign distribution. Wallace Campbell was well advised to create foreign subsidiaries in Australia and elsewhere.

The characterization of McGregor's successor by Wilkins and

Hill as a deeply thoughtful but unequivocal and "more venturesome" corporate head is furthered by the strong revival of business experienced by Ford Canada after 1922.[14] At the same time, Campbell's capabilities, his business personality and cadre of associates, his status and civic engagement in Motoropolis, and his reaction to strong competition from General Motors and Chrysler (something McGregor never really had to face head-on) have yet to be methodically scrutinized using the kinds of sources that have informed this study. The heights and reputation gained by Ford Canada under Campbell, who would remain at the helm until 1946, had their roots in McGregor's tenure as company head and one of the industry's more potent lobbyists and strategists. Many facets—the Ford negotiators portrayed as brutish by W. L. Mackenzie King in 1923, the company's tough lobbying over tariff changes in 1926, the bullish behavior of the parent company in Ford Canada's banking in 1927–28,[15] and Campbell's closeness to operations across the river—demonstrated behavior and models that had parallels or origins in McGregor's time. If, as probed throughout this study, McGregor's personal, public, and business personas fall short of being fully revealed, he nevertheless emerges as a dynamic figure in Canada's Motoropolis, in the overarching shadow of Detroit.

NOTES

INTRODUCTION

1. Examples of the company chronicles are Jaroslav Petryshyn, *"Made Up to a Standard": Thomas Alexander Russell and the Russell Motor Car Company* (Burnstown, Ont., [2000]); Heather Robertson, *Driving Force: The McLaughlin Family and the Age of the Car* (Toronto, 1995). Hugh Durnford and Glenn Baechler's important work is *Cars of Canada* (Toronto, 1973). Among the economic studies, I draw particular attention to Tom Traves, *The State and Enterprise: Canadian Manufacturers and the Federal Government, 1917–1931* (Toronto, 1979); I. M. Drummond, *Progress without Planning: The Economic History of Ontario from Confederation to the Second World War* (Toronto, 1987).

2. D. R. Smith, "'Profit and Not Patriotism': The Rise of Branch Plants and the Extension of Economic Boundaries in the Great Lakes Region" (paper presented at the annual meeting of the Organization of American Historians, Toronto, 22 Apr. 1999); I thank Dimitry Anastakis for bringing this paper to my attention.

3. Ibid., 8.

4. Tom Naylor, *The History of Canadian Business, 1867–1914* (Toronto, 1975), 2: chap. 11.

5. Smith, "Profit and Not Patriotism," 23.

6. Cleona Lewis, *America's Stake in International Investments* (Washington, D.C., 1938).

7. Smith, "Profit and Not Patriotism," 38.

8. Naylor, *History of Canadian Business*, 274.

9. N. F. Morrison, *Garden Gateway to Canada: One Hundred Years of Windsor and Essex County, 1854–1954* (Toronto, 1954).

10. These reports are quoted in ibid., 181–82.

11. Ibid., 231.

CHAPTER 1

1. Before confederation, Upper Canada was the name of the province that now comprises Ontario.

2. *Evening Record* (Windsor, Ont.), 4, 27 Apr., 19 May 1896; *Border Cities Star* (Windsor; formerly the *Evening Record*), 18 July 1920; private coll., Mary (McGregor) Mingay, Collingwood, Ont., Walter L. McGregor to Mrs. William McGregor, 5 Oct. 1917; G. B. Carruthers, unpub. family tree: "Descendants of John McGregor"; memoir of Margaret Hackett, 10 Jan. 1936, copy kindly supplied by J. McGregor Dodds, Grosse Pointe Farms, Mich.; *Commemorative Biographical Record of the County of Essex, Ontario* (Toronto, 1905), 28–29; *Lovell's Province of Ontario Directory for 1871* (Montreal, 1871); *Canadian Parliamentary Companion*

(Ottawa, 1878); J. S. Moir, *Enduring Witness: A History of the Presbyterian Church in Canada* ([Hamilton, Ont., 1974?]), 107.

3. National Archives of Canada, Ottawa (hereafter NA), RG 31, C1, 1871, Windsor, 1.

4. *Amherstburg Echo* (Amherstburg, Ont.), 29 Aug. 1930; photographs and memorabilia shared by J. McGregor Dodds.

5. Mingay coll., Walter L. McGregor to Mrs. William McGregor, 5 Oct., 24 Dec. 1917; *Border Cities Star*, 22 Apr. 1933.

6. Archives of Ontario (hereafter AO), RG 55-17-12-9, nos. 6 and 10; *Illustrated Historical Atlas of the Counties of Essex and Kent, 1880–1881* (reprint ed., n.p., 1973); *Amherstburg Echo*, 29 Aug. 1930; Frederick Neal, *The Township of Sandwich (Past and Present)* (Sandwich, Ont., 1909); Mary Mingay and Don Mingay, *Mingay: Memoirs of Mary and Don Mingay* ([Collingwood, Ont., 1994]), 6–7.

7. For example, see the notices and advertisements in *Windsor Eclipse*, 16 Feb. 1878; and *Essex Record* (Windsor), 9 Jan. 1884.

8. *Evening Record*, 14 Apr., 15 Aug. 1896, 14 May 1903; *Winnipeg Free Press* (Winnipeg, Man.), 15 May 1903; NA, MG 31, C1, 1881, Windsor, div. 2:40–41; *Henderson's Winnipeg Directory*, 1884, 1886–87; F. H. Schofield, *The Story of Manitoba* (Winnipeg, Man., 1913), 3:310.

9. *Border Cities Star*, 11 Mar. 1922.

10. Mingay coll., Walter L. McGregor to Mrs. William McGregor, 4 Mar. 1918.

11. *Amherstburg Echo*, 10 Aug. 1888, 19 Dec. 1890; *Border Cities Star*, 11 Mar. 1922; NA, MG 31, C1, 1891, Windsor, div. 2:49; *Detroit Directory*, 1888–92; *Windsor Directory*, 1888.

12. *Evening Record*, 10, 11 Dec. 1895, 8 Feb., 7 Mar., 15 June, 5 Sept. 1896, 20 Jan., 1 Feb. 1897; *Windsor Directory*, 1895; *Lovell's Business and Professional Directory of Cities and Towns of . . . Canada for 1896–97* (Montreal, 1896).

13. Canada, Royal Commission on Relations of Capital and Labor, *Report* 5 (1889): Ontario evidence, 369–435.

14. G. S. Kealey and B. D. Palmer, *Dreaming of What May Be: The Knights of Labor in Ontario, 1880–1900* (Toronto, 1987), 80–81; *Evening Record*, 23 Dec. 1895.

15. Royal Commission on Relations of Capital and Labor, 420, 434; Canada, *Census of 1911*, vol. 3 (manufactures), 242–43; *Lovell's Directory, 1896–97;* R. G. Hoskins, "Hiram Walker and the Origins and Development of Walkerville, Ontario," *Ontario History* 64 (1972), 129; N. F. Morrison, *Garden Gateway to Canada: One Hundred Years of Windsor and Essex County, 1854–1954* (Toronto, 1954), 119.

16. *Evening Record*, 18, 25 June, 29 Dec. 1897, 15, 28 Sept., 10 Oct. 1898.

17. Ibid., 15 Feb. 1896.

18. Ibid., 22, 28–29 Feb., 14 Apr., 1 May 1896.

19. Ibid., 23, 27 June, 9 July, 29 Aug. 1896. The quotation from the *Winnipeg Tribune* appears in the *Evening Record*, 15 Aug. 1896.

20. Ibid., 29 Aug., 1 Dec. 1896, 6, 20, 27 Feb. 1897, 3 Apr. 1898.

21. Ibid., 13 May, 5 June 1896.

22. Ibid., 2 Mar., 24–25 Apr., 5 May, 7, 18, 22 Dec. 1896, 18, 22, 26 Jan., 2

Mar., 20 Nov. 1897.

23. Ibid., 18 Jan. 1902; NA, MG 26, G: 9684–88.

24. *Evening Record,* 10 Dec. 1896, 1 Nov. 1902; *Border Cities Star,* 22 Apr. 1933; *Commemorative Biographical Record of the County of Essex,* 29.

25. *Evening Record,* 17, 26 Nov. 1897, 4 Feb. 1898.

26. Ibid., 20 Oct., 3 Nov., 24 Dec. 1898; NA, RG 31, C1, 1901, Windsor, div. 7:8; *Ford Graphic* (Windsor), 17 Aug. 1954, 4 (recollection of W. Donald McGregor).

27. Recollection of W. D. McGregor, as remembered by his son, Donald E. McGregor of Toronto: interview with author, 8 Jan. 1998.

28. *Evening Record,* 4 Mar. 1899, 23 Oct., 8, 29 Nov. 1902.

29. Ibid., 11 Dec. 1897, 9 Feb., 9, 21 July 1898; AO (microfilm), Sandwich Township, abstract index to deeds, conc. 1, lot 98 east, 22 Oct. 1897, 27 Dec. 1900, 2 Feb. 1901. In addition, McGregor and Curry experimented with the cultivation of hops; their attempt to grow cranberries near Harrow failed.

30. *Evening Record,* 9 Nov. 1901; *Ontario Gazette,* 22 Dec. 1900, 1455 (letters patent 14 Dec. 1900). These letters patent used the "waggon" spelling. To avoid confusion, I will hereafter use "wagon."

31. *Evening Record,* 6 Sept., 29 Nov. 1902.

32. D. R. Smith, "'Profit and Not Patriotism': The Rise of Branch Plants and the Extension of Economic Boundaries in the Great Lakes Region" (paper presented at the annual meeting of the Organization of American Historians, Toronto, 22 Apr. 1999).

33. *Evening Record,* 3 Aug., 3 Sept. 1901, 9 Apr., 29 Nov., 5 Dec. 1902, 27 Jan., 12 Feb. 1903.

34. Ibid., 4 Aug. 1898.

35. Hugh Durnford and Glenn Baechler, *Cars of Canada* (Toronto, 1973), 230.

36. *Evening Record,* 25 Jan., 28 Feb., 14, 16 Apr., 6 Aug. 1896, 16, 20 Feb., 20 July, 21 Sept., 19 Nov. 1897, 11, 18, 30 Jan., 6–7, 11 Feb., 31 Mar., 2 Apr., 4 Aug. 1898, 18–19 Dec. 1899, 27 Aug., 4 Dec. 1903; *Lovell's Directory, 1896–97; Ontario Gazette,* 16 Nov. 1899, 1334–35; *Canadian Annual Review* (Toronto, 1902): 311; T. A. McPherson, *The Dodge Story* (Osceola, Wisc., 1992), 4.

37. *Evening Record,* 16, 27, 29 Apr., 4 May, 2 July, 9 Nov. 1896, 2, 10, 15, 20, 23 Mar., 6, 22 Apr., 19, 21 May, 3 Aug., 8, 25, 27 Sept., 30 Oct., 3 Nov., 24 Dec. 1897, 1, 4 June, 2 July, 29 Aug. 1898, 3 Mar., 6 Apr. 1899, 22 May 1901. Quote is from ibid., 9 Nov. 1896.

38. Ibid., 31 Jan. 1896, 8, 20 Mar., 1 Apr., 13 May 1897, 12 Jan., 1 Mar. 1898, 2 May 1901; R. E. Ankli, "The Early Canadian Automobile and Machine Tool Industries" (paper presented at meeting of the Canadian Historical Association, Winnipeg, Man., May 1986); *Canadian Machinery and Manufacturing News* (Toronto), 27 June 1918, 679. The best overview of the bicycle industry in Canada is S. [A.] Babaian, *The Most Benevolent Machine: A Historical Assessment of Cycles in Canada* (Ottawa, Ont., 1998).

39. *Evening Record,* 19 Nov. 1896, 31 Mar., 31 July 1897, 3 Sept. 1902, 11 Mar., 26 May, 17 Aug., 10 Sept., 25 Nov. 1903, 13 Jan. 1904.

40. Ibid., 12, 14–15, 18 May 1903; *Winnipeg Free Press*, 15 May 1903.

41. *Evening Record*, 18 Jan. 1904, 30 May 1913. The records of the Essex County Surrogate Court (on microfilm at the AO) note that McGregor's estate file has been "misplaced." For Milner and the West Lorne Waggon Works (officially chartered 11 Mar. 1904), see *Elgin Sun* (West Lorne, Ont.), 16 Feb., 9 Mar., 14 Sept. 1905, 12 Apr. 1906, and esp. 28 Nov. 1912. Private coll., Donald E. McGregor, Toronto, "The Wm. McGregor Estate, Financial Statement as at December 31, 1914"; Mira Wilkins and F. E. Hill, *American Business Abroad: Ford on Six Continents* (Detroit, 1964), 14.

42. *Evening Record*, 25 Jan., 17 Feb., 31 Mar. 1904.

43. *Ford Graphic*, 17 Aug. 1954, 4.

44. Ford Motor Company of Canada, *A Fitting Tribute to Our Rich Heritage of Ninety-three Years in Canada: 1904–1997* ([Oakville, Ont., 1997]), copy at Ford Motor Company of Canada (hereafter FMCC), Historical Department, Oakville, Ont.

CHAPTER 2

1. D. F. Davis, *Conspicuous Production: Automobiles and Elites in Detroit, 1899–1933* (Philadelphia, 1988); J. B. Rae, ed., *Henry Ford* (Englewood Cliffs, N.J., 1969); Wayne Lewchuk, *American Technology and the British Vehicle Industry* (Cambridge, 1987), 235n. 42; G. S. May, *A Most Unique Machine: The Michigan Origins of the American Automobile Industry* (Grand Rapids, Mich., 1975), 329–30; Jan Jennings, ed., *Roadside America: The Automobile in Design and Culture* (Ames, Iowa, 1990), chap. 3; R. S. Tedlow, *New and Improved: The Story of Mass Marketing in America* (New York, 1990), chap. 3.

2. *Evening Record*, 30 May 1913; Donald E. McGregor, Toronto, interview with author, 8 Jan. 1998; *Ford Graphic*, 17 Aug. 1954, 2; Mira Wilkins and F. E. Hill, *American Business Abroad: Ford on Six Continents* (Detroit, 1964), chap. 2.

3. May, *A Most Unique Machine*, 272.

4. Vincent Massey, *What's Past Is Prologue: The Memoirs of the Right Honorable Vincent Massey, C.H.* (Toronto, 1963), 168.

5. The literature on Henry Ford is substantial and varies enormously in quality and insight. The composite given here is taken from: Rae, *Henry Ford;* May, *A Most Unique Machine*, 90, 267–68, 303; D. A. Hounsell, *From the American System to Mass Production, 1800–1932: The Development of Manufacturing Technology in the United States* (Baltimore and London, 1984), 220–23; D. L. Lewis, *The Public Image of Henry Ford: An American Folk Hero and His Company* (Detroit, 1976); Tedlow, *New and Improved*, 222; J. J. Flink, *The Automobile Age* (Cambridge, Mass., 1988), 52; Davis, *Conspicuous Production;* Allan Nevins, *Ford: The Times, the Man, the Company* (New York, 1954).

6. Wilkins and Hill, *American Business Abroad*, 15.

7. *Toronto Daily Star*, 14 Jan., 26 Apr. 1904.

8. *Evening Record*, 14 Mar. 1904.

9. Wilkins and Hill, *American Business Abroad*, 15, 463n. 4.

10. Waterloo Historical Society, *Reports* 59 (1971): 13; 65 (1977): 23.

11. Wilkins and Hill, *American Business Abroad;* Peter McCormack, "The Ford

Motor Company of Canada, 1903–1929: 'Canadian Content' in a Multinational Setting" (master's thesis, University of Windsor, 1991).

12. Canada, *House of Commons Debates* (7 June 1904), 4351.

13. *Evening Record*, 1 Feb. 1905.

14. Ibid., 22 Nov. 1921. On CMA pressure for high tariffs, see G. A. Niemeyer, *The Automotive Career of Ransom E. Olds* (East Lansing, Mich., 1963), 101; S. D. Clark, *The Canadian Manufacturers' Association: A Study in Collective Bargaining and Political Pressure* (Toronto, 1939), 14–15.

15. *Evening Record*, 2 July 1904; *Ford Graphic*, 17 Aug. 1954, 2 (recollection of W. Donald McGregor); AO, RG 8-1-1, file 4352, 1904.

16. *Evening Record*, 29 Aug. 1914.

17. Virginia Scharff, *Taking the Wheel: Women and the Coming of the Motor Age* (New York, 1991), 52, 112–14.

18. On McLaughlin: Tom Traves, "The Development of the Ontario Automobile Industry to 1939," in I. M. Drummond, *Progress without Planning: The Economic History of Ontario from Confederation to the Second World War* (Toronto, 1987), 211.

19. *Evening Record*, 30 May 1912, 12 Sept., 28 Oct. 1913; *Border Cities Star*, 11 Mar. 1922; Wilkins and Hill, *American Business Abroad*, 17.

20. AO, F 149 (William M. Gray papers).

21. *Ford Graphic*, 17 Aug. 1954, 4; AO, RG 8-1-1, file 2856, 1905; RG 8-1-1, file 1937, 1906.

22. Wilkins and Hill, *American Business Abroad*, 19; Mira Wilkins, *The Emergence of Multinational Enterprise: American Business Abroad from the Colonial Era to 1914* (Cambridge, Mass., 1970), 143.

23. Ford Motor Company of Canada (Oakville, Ont.), Legal Department, minute book, vol. 1 (1904–11), facing p. 1, agreement 10 Aug. 1904, charter 17 Aug. 1904 (unless designated "shareholders," all minutes are of directors' meetings); Wilkins and Hill, *American Business Abroad*, 19; Herb Colling and Carl Morgan, *Pioneering the Auto Age* (Tecumseh, Ont., 1993). The meaning of branch plant is well handled by Tom Traves in his chapter on the automotive industry in Ontario: "'Branch plant' is a slippery term that can mean various things. In this chapter it is applied to Canadian firms that, regardless of ownership, had close connections with American firms. Thus some 'branch plants' in the auto industry began with Canadian initiative, operated for some time with substantial Canadian ownership interest and under effective Canadian management, and passed only later into American ownership; others were, from the start, wholly owned subsidiaries of American parent firms. On a narrower application of the 'branch plant' label, only the latter would qualify." "The Development of the Ontario Automobile Industry to 1939," 465n. 5.

24. FMCC, MB, 1:1, 6–16, 27; AO, RG 8-1-1, file 4352, 1904; *Evening Record*, 20, 30 Aug. 1904; *Ford Graphic*, 17 Aug. 1954, 2–3.

25. *Evening Record*, 3 May 1922 (recollections of L. C. Wilkinson); *Industrial Canada* 5, no. 11 (June 1905): 780 (contains a good elevated photograph of the Ford Company buildings); *Ford Graphic*, 17 Aug. 1954, 4, 8. For assembly operations see Hounsell, *From the American System to Mass Production*, 220; and Lewchuk,

American Technology, 40–46, 52.

26. *Evening Record*, 10 Sept. 1906; *Monetary Times*, 26 Aug. 1904, 279.

27. *Evening Record*, 15 Sept., 2 Nov. 1904.

28. FMCC, MB, 1:53; University of Windsor Archives (hereafter UWA), Windsor, Ont., FMCC coll., box 5, file 59, 64–65.

29. *Ford Graphic*, 17 Aug. 1954, 4, 8.

30. *Industrial Canada* 5, no. 3 (Oct. 1904): 205.

31. UWA, FMCC coll., box 3, file 55, general ledger.

32. FMCC, MB, 1:33–34; *Evening Record*, 27 Feb. 1913; *Toronto Daily Star*, 27 Feb., 1 Mar. 1905.

33. *Ford Graphic*, 17 Aug. 1954, 4; undated article by Herman L. Smith from a Ford catalogue, copy in possession of Donald E. McGregor, Toronto.

34. Canadian National Exhibition (hereafter CNE) Archives, Toronto, Toronto Industrial Exhibition *Program* (1904), 1; Hugh Durnford and Glenn Baechler, *Cars of Canada* (Toronto, 1973).

35. U.S. Department of Commerce and Labor, *Monthly Consular Reports*, no. 291 (Dec. 1904): 293.

36. *Evening Record*, 11 Mar. 1922; *Canadian Gazette*, Canadian automobile number, 28 July 1927.

37. Wilkins and Hill, *American Business Abroad*, 20.

38. *Windsor Directory*, 1905–6, 1906–7.

39. *Evening Record*, 17 Dec. 1904.

40. Ibid., 21 Jan. 1905; *New York Times*, 15, 17–18, 21–23 Jan. 1905; May, *A Most Unique Machine*, 337.

41. *Evening Record*, 17 Dec. 1904, 27 Mar. 1905; *Industrial Canada* 5, no. 6 (Jan. 1905): 395; 5, no. 10 (May 1905): 656; 5, no. 11 (June 1905): 815; P. W. Laird, "'The Car without a Single Weakness': Early Automobile Advertising," in *Technology and Culture* (Chicago) 37, no. 4 (Oct. 1996): 796–812. For descriptions of the various early Ford models, see J. M. Flammang et al., *Ford Chronicle: A Pictorial History from 1893* (Lincolnwood, Ill., 1997); and *Ford Times* (U.S.) 4, no. 10 (June 1911): 262–63. (Some of Gordon McGregor's bound volumes of this edition of *Ford Times* are in the possession of his nephew Walter L. McGregor of Windsor.)

42. An undated, four-page leaflet for the Model C, in the author's possession, shows right-hand drive vehicles; the production of right- or left-hand drive vehicles depended on the province or country of destination. The operating manual for the Model C was kindly shared by Kevin Mowle of Kincardine, Ont. Distinctively Canadian features become most apparent in the Model T Ford cars made in Walkerville and (after 1912) Ford City, Ont.

43. *Evening Record*, 17 Dec. 1904; Heather Robertson, *Driving Force: The McLaughlin Family and the Age of the Car* (Toronto, 1995), 376.

44. *Ford Graphic*, 17 Aug. 1954, 4; Scharff, *Taking the Wheel*, chap. 8.

45. UWA, FMCC coll., box 3, file 56.

46. Robertson, *Driving Force*, 112–13.

47. *Evening Record*, 11 May 1905; FMCC, MB, 1:40.

48. Wilkins and Hill, *American Business Abroad*, 21–22.

49. *Evening Record*, 1, 14, 27 Mar. 1905; *Ford Graphic*, 17 Aug. 1954, 21.

50. FMCC, MB, 1:36.

51. Ibid., 37.

52. Wilkins and Hill, *American Business Abroad*, 20.

53. Ibid., 22.

54. UWA, FMCC coll., box 3, file 55, general ledger (lists, under liabilities, accounts with suppliers from October 1905); AO, F 149, McGregor to Gray, 18 Oct. 1905.

55. Davis, *Conspicuous Production*, 120–21; Hounsell, *From the American System to Mass Production*, 220; May, *A Most Unique Machine*, 279.

56. *Evening Record*, 30 May, 14, 26 July 1906. K price: UWA, FMCC coll., box 3, file 56, 1907—$2,040.81 (wholesale?); *Industrial Canada* 6, no. 8 (Mar. 1906); 6, no. 10 (May 1906): 625—$3,200. *Canadian Graphic* (Toronto) 5, no. 12 (7 Apr. 1906): 15–16; K difficulties: Ralph Stein, *The American Automobile* (New York, 1971); [G.] N. Georgano, *The American Automobile: A Centenary, 1893–1993* (New York, 1992). Eric Edwards of Baxter, Ont., kindly provided expert opinion and allowed the author to examine his Model K, one of the two dozen in existence.

57. Rae, *Henry Ford*, 17–19.

58. UWA, FMCC coll., box 4, file 58.

59. Durnford and Baechler, *Cars of Canada*, 89; "The Automobile Industry in Canada: Made-in-Canada Cars to the Front," *Industrial Canada* 7, no. 10 (May 1907): 781–83; Maw letter, quoted in Wilkins and Hill, *American Business Abroad*, 17; Ketchum: *Ottawa Journal*, 23 Nov. 1927; Leith Knight, *All the Moose . . . All the Jaw* (Moose Jaw, Sask., 1982), 56.

60. Hounsell, *From the American System to Mass Production*, 220–25; Lewchuk, *American Technology*, 44–52; Lindy Biggs, "Building for Mass Production: Factory Design and Work Process at the Ford Motor Company," in *Autowork*, ed. Robert Asher and Ronald Edsforth (Albany, 1995), 41 (this article pertains to Ford Detroit).

61. Henry Ford Museum Research Center Archives and Library (hereafter Ford Archives), Dearborn, Mich., accession 65-130.

62. Ibid.

63. Ibid.

64. *Evening Record*, 3 Nov. 1906, 11 Mar. 1922; *Ford Graphic*, 17 Aug. 1954, 8.

65. *Ford Graphic*, 17 Aug. 1954, 2; *Evening Record*, 28 Apr. 1922.

66. Ford Archives, Dearborn, Mich., accession 65-130.

67. *Ford Graphic*, 17 Aug. 1954, 8; A. D. Chandler, ed., *Giant Enterprise: Ford, General Motors, and the Automobile Industry, Sources and Readings* (New York, 1964), 11; *Evening Record*, 20 May 1922 (for Conklin's account).

68. AO, F 149; Durnford and Baechler, *Cars of Canada*, 353.

69. Durnford and Baechler, *Cars of Canada*, 353.

70. AO, F 149.

71. *Evening Record*, 29 July 1907; J. J. Flink, *The Car Culture* (Cambridge, Mass., 1975), 22–23; CNE Archives, C3-0-2-0-0-9 [official catalogue and program, 1907], 7.

72. *Evening Record*, 17 Mar. 1906; UWA, FMCC coll., box 4, file 58; Wilkins and Hill, *American Business Abroad*, 21–22, 27; Nevins, *Ford*, 361–62; T. T. N.

Coleridge, *Our Motoring Heritage* (Wellington, N.Z., 1973); Pam MacLean and Brian Joyce, *The Veteran Years of New Zealand Motoring* (Wellington, N.Z., 1971); Norm Darwin, *The History of Ford in Australia* (Newstead, Aus., [1986]); Geoff Easdown, *Ford: A History of the Ford Motor Company in Australia* (Sydney and Auckland, 1987); John Goode, *Smoke, Smell, and Clatter: The Revolutionary Story of Motoring in Australia* (Melbourne, 1969); Peter Stubbs, *The Australian Motor Industry: A Study in Protection and Growth* (Melbourne, 1971); R. H. Johnston, *Early Motoring in South Africa* (Cape Town, 1975).

73. B. H. Morgan, *The Trade and Industry of Australasia* (London, [1908]), 186.

74. Canada, Parliament, *Sessional Papers*, 1911, no. 10, pt. 1:181; pt. 3:14, 153.

75. FMCC, MB, 1:48; *Evening Record*, 5 May 1906, 25 Jan., 29 May 1908; *Border Cities Star*, 11 Mar. 1922; *Ford Graphic*, 17 Aug. 1954, 4.

76. *Ontario Gazette*, 16 Feb. 1907, 170; *Motoring* (Toronto and Montreal), Sept. 1906 (AO, Pamphlets 1906, no. 74); *Canadian Motor* (Toronto), Feb. 1906.

77. Canada, *House of Commons Debates* (31 Jan. 1907), 2398–400.

78. J. M. Cameron, *Pictou County's History* ([New Glasgow, N.S.], 1972), 57; *Industrial Canada* 8, no. 8 (Mar. 1908): 636–37; *Saturday Night*, 31 Mar. 1906.

79. Flammang, *Ford Chronicle*, 24–27.

80. *Ford Times* (Canada), Nov. 1914, 115. (McGregor's bound set of this journal is in the Historical Department of the Ford Motor Company in Oakville.) Fox's obituary appears in the *Globe and Mail* (Toronto), 11 Mar. 1946.

81. *Border Cities Star*, 11 Mar. 1922.

82. Ibid., 16 Jan. 1908. On the McMullens and the Chatham Motor Car Company, see Durnford and Baechler, *Cars of Canada*, 98–99. William Gray and Sons built bodies for Chatham cars as well as Ford cars.

83. *Industrial Canada* 7, no. 7 (Feb. 1907): 553; 8, no. 8 (Mar. 1908): 604–5; 8, no. 11 (June 1908): 1068.

84. Ibid., 8, no. 7 (Feb. 1908): 531; 8, no. 10 (May 1908): 749.

85. Ibid., 8, no. 8 (Mar. 1908): 636–37; *Toronto Daily Star*, 21–28 Mar. 1908; Bill Sherk, *The Way We Drove: Toronto's Love Affair with the Automobile in Stories and Photographs* (Toronto, 1993), 15.

86. *Evening Record*, 27 July, 25 Aug. 1908.

87. CNE Archives, Toronto Industrial Exhibition, *Annual Report* (1907), 16; (1908), 13.

88. Durnford and Baechler, *Cars of Canada*, 101–2.

89. *Evening Record*, 14 Mar. 1906; *Ford Graphic*, 17 Aug. 1954, 8.

90. *Monetary Times*, 20 Apr. 1906, 1414; *Eastern Chronicle* (Halifax), 7 Apr. 1908; *Canadian Annual Review* (Toronto, 1908): 292–93; H. C. Klassen, "Bicycles and Automobiles in Early Calgary," *Alberta History* 24, no. 2 (Spring 1976): 6; Deborah Stewart, "The Island Meets the Auto," *Island Magazine*, no. 5 (Fall–Winter 1978): 9–14; Kathleen Dewar, "John A. Dewar: The Principled Maverick," *Island Magazine*, no. 43 (Spring–Summer 1998): 4–5; Edward MacDonald, *If You're Stronghearted: Prince Edward Island in the Twentieth Century* ([Charlottetown, P.E.I.], 2000), 55–59.

91. *Evening Record*, 31 Mar., 8 Apr. 1908; *Toronto Daily Star*, 31 Mar. 1908; C. W. Humphries, *"Honest Enough to Be Bold": The Life and Times of Sir James Pliny Whitney* (Toronto, 1985), 170.

92. Humphries, *"Honest Enough to Be Bold."*

93. *Evening Record*, 28 June, 1 Sept. 1905, 14 Feb. 1906, 28 Aug., 3, 12, 28 Sept. 1908, 23 Feb., 4, 23 Mar. 1909; Paul-André Linteau et al., *Quebec: A History, 1867–1929* (Toronto, 1983), 346; W. A. Squires, *History of Fredericton: The Last Two Hundred Years*, ed. J. K. Chapman (Fredericton, N.B., 1980), 77–79; Mike Parker, *Historic Dartmouth: Reflections of Early Life* (Halifax, N.S., 1998), 45.

94. *Evening Record*, 12, 28 Sept., 24 Dec. 1908; David Gartman, *Auto Slavery: The Labor Process in the American Automobile Industry, 1897–1950* (New Brunswick, N.J., and London, 1986), 204. Assessing labor sentiment at the Ford plants in Walkerville and Detroit in 1908 is difficult, but there had been stirrings in Detroit as early as 1905, when the workers at the Reliance Automobile Company staged a full walkout, which Windsorites read about in the *Evening Record*, 16 May 1905. The following year, Gartman notes (182) unspecified elements of control were being instituted among the Ford workers in Detroit. The early open-shop, anti-union movement within the industry there is also discussed in Lewchuk, *American Technology*, 36–39; May, *A Most Unique Machine* 341–42; and J. S. Peterson, *American Automobile Workers, 1900–1933* (Albany, 1987), 7, 40. In Walkerville, where McGregor likely still knew many of his workers from wagon works days and where the number of employees was far fewer than at Ford Detroit, relations remained shrouded in bonhomie and craft brotherhood, though open-shop attitudes prevailed at management levels.

95. *Toronto Star Weekly*, 30 Dec. 1933, 5 (R. E. Knowles's interview with Henry Ford).

CHAPTER 3

1. Jan Jennings, ed., *Roadside America: The Automobile in Design and Culture* (Ames, Iowa, 1990), 38; R. S. Tedlow, *New and Improved: The Story of Mass Marketing in America* (New York, 1990), 151; D. A. Hounsell, *From the American System to Mass Production, 1800–1932: The Development of Manufacturing Technology in the United States* (Baltimore and London, 1984), 9; J. Couzens, "What I Learned about Business from Ford," *System* 40 (1921): 261–64; J. B. Rae, ed., *Henry Ford* (Englewood Cliffs, N.J., 1969), 154, 173.

2. D. F. Davis, *Conspicuous Production: Automobiles and Elites in Detroit, 1899–1933* (Philadelphia, 1988), 12; Terry Smith, *Making the Modern: Industry, Art, and Design in America* (Chicago and London, 1993), 94–98; David Gartman, *Auto Opium: A Social History of American Automobile Design* (London and New York, 1994), 39–49.

3. FMCC, Office of Public Relations, Toronto, press release, 27 Sept. 1958, "Golden Jubilee of the Model 'T' Ford": "Model T was the herald and the symbol of a new way of life." This Canadian release marked the anniversary of the T's purported appearance in the United States on 1 Oct. 1908.

4. Hounsell, *From the American System to Mass Production*, 218–22; Allan

Nevins, *Ford: The Times, the Man, the Company* (New York, 1954), chap. 16.

5. *Evening Record,* 28 Sept. 1908; Ford Archives, Dearborn, Mich., accession 575, box 16, and accession 65-130; *Industrial Canada* 9, no. 8 (Mar. 1909): 683; FMCC, MB, 1:55; G. T. Bloomfield, "Coils of the Commercial Serpent: A Geography of the Ford Branch Distribution System, 1904–33," chap. 4 in Jennings, *Roadside America* (this article treats the American system); B. W. McCalley, *Model T Ford: The Car That Changed the World* (Iola, Wisc., 1994), 478–79 (factory shipping invoices). Canadian production figures vary: McCalley gives 1,280 for "1909–10" (539), while Hugh Durnford and Glenn Baechler give 458 to August 1909 and another 1,280 in the year to August 1910 (*Cars of Canada* [Toronto, 1973], 353).

6. London *Times* (London, Eng.), 13–22 Nov. 1908.

7. *Toronto Daily Star,* 18, 20, 22, 24, 26 Feb. 1909.

8. Norm Darwin, *The History of Ford in Australia* (Newstead, Aus., [1986]), 11.

9. *Evening Record,* 6 Feb. 1909; *Toronto Daily Star,* 25 Feb. 1909.

10. *Toronto Globe,* 17 July 1909; *Evening Record,* 1, 19 May 1909.

11. Canadian dealerships: *Ford Sales Bulletin* (Walkerville), 3 July 1915, 335 (482, company's exact count); *Industrial Canada* 18, no. 12 (Apr. 1918): 1793 (more than 700); 20, no. 1 (May 1919): 25 (more than 750); *Border Cities Star,* 22 Apr. 1922 (700).

12. *Evening Record,* 27 Aug. 1909; Mira Wilkins and F. E. Hill, *American Business Abroad: Ford on Six Continents* (Detroit, 1964), 40–42.

13. Darwin, *History of Ford in Australia,* 5; Bill Tuckey, *True Blue: Seventy-five Years of Ford in Australia* (Edgecliff, Aus., 2000), 3–5.

14. *Evening Record,* 29 Jan. 1910; *Ford Times* (U.S.) 4, no. 1 (Sept. 1910): 31; Robert Conlon and John Perkins, *Wheels and Deals: The Automotive Industry in Twentieth-century Australia* (Aldershot, Eng., 2001), 4, 17–18, 22, 83; Darwin, *History of Ford in Australia,* 7–12, 89; Geoff Easdown, *Ford: A History of the Ford Motor Company in Australia* (Sydney and Auckland, 1987), chap. 1; Pam MacLean and Brian Joyce, *The Veteran Years of New Zealand Motoring* (Wellington, N.Z., 1971), 173; R. H. Johnston, *Early Motoring in South Africa* (Cape Town, 1975), 85–88; Shakila Yacob, "Beyond Borders: Ford in Malaya, 1926–1957" (paper presented at Business History Conference, 2003 [examined on Internet, 5 July 2004]); Virginia Scharff, *Taking the Wheel: Women and the Coming of the Motor Age* (New York, 1991), 191n. 26 (Queen of Fiji).

15. FMCC, MB, 1:60; Wilkins and Hill, *American Business Abroad,* 37, 39; F. R. Bryan, *Henry's Lieutenants* (Detroit, 1993), 227–29.

16. Wilkins and Hill, *American Business Abroad,* 39.

17. FMCC, MB, 2 [1911–25], 29.

18. *Evening Record,* 8 Oct. 1909–15 Dec. 1910; *Canadian Machinery and Manufacturing News* (Toronto) 6, no. 7 (July 1910): 64; *Ontario Gazette,* 3 Dec. 1910, 1878, 1882–83; Wayne Lewchuk, *American Technology and the British Vehicle Industry* (Cambridge, 1987), 47–48.

19. *Evening Record,* 11 Sept. 1909–29 July 1911; *Kingsville Reporter* (Kingsville, Ont.), 2 June 1910; Clarence Hooker, *Life in the Shadows of the Crystal Palace, 1910–1927: Ford Workers in the Model T Era* (Bowling Green, Ohio, 1997), chap. 2.

20. Lindy Biggs, "Building for Mass Production: Factory Design and Work Process at the Ford Motor Company," in *Autowork*, ed. Robert Asher and Ronald Edsforth (Albany, 1995), 43–44.

21. *Toronto Daily Star*, 24 Feb. 1910.

22. *Evening Record*, 7 Sept. 1910–1 Mar. 1911. Tudhope's advertisement is quoted in Durnford and Baechler, *Cars of Canada*, 109.

23. *Canadian Machinery and Manufacturing News* 6, no. 6 (June 1910): 33.

24. *Evening Record*, 7 Sept., 5 Oct. 1909, 11 Mar. 1910. Recollection of office in 1910 by L. C. Wilkinson: *Border Cities Star*, 3 May 1922.

25. Albert Kahn Associates Inc. (Detroit), Library Services and Archives, job no. 475 [blueprints 13 July–18 Sept. 1910]; *Statutes of Canada*, 1911, 1–2 Geo. 5, c. 146; *Canada Gazette*, 18 Feb. 1911, 2739; Canadian Cement and Concrete Association, *Annual Report* (1910), 8, 21–25, 96–101; (1911), 71–77; *Canadian Machinery and Manufacturing News* 6, no. 10 (Oct. 1910): 64; *Industrial Canada* 14, no. 1 (Aug. 1913): 91; *Construction* (Toronto) 4, no. 5 (Apr. 1911): 91; G. T. Bloomfield, "Albert Kahn and Canadian Industrial Architecture, 1908–1938," Society for the Study of Architecture in Canada, *Bulletin* 10, no. 4 (Dec. 1985): 4–10; Frederico Bucci, *Albert Kahn: Architect of Ford* (New York, c. 1993); W. H. Ferry, with an essay by W. B. Sanders, *The Legacy of Albert Kahn* (Detroit, 1987); Grant Hildebrand, *Designing for Industry: The Architecture of Albert Kahn* (Cambridge, Mass., and London, 1974); A. E. Slaton, *Reinforced Concrete and the Modernization of American Building, 1900–1930* (Baltimore, 2001).

26. *Canadian Machinery and Manufacturing News*, 2 Jan. 1913, 59; Walkerville machine inventory: UWA, FMCC coll., box 6, file 73; Lewchuk, *American Technology*, 49; Hounsell, *From the American System to Mass Production*, 224–28, 231–33; R. S. Woodbury, *Studies in the History of Machine Tools* (Cambridge, Mass., and London, 1972): "History of the Gear-Cutting Machine," 123, "History of the Grinding Machine," 10–11.

27. *Canadian Machinery and Manufacturing News* 5, no. 4 (Apr. 1909): 61; 6, no. 6 (June 1910): 31–33.

28. *Canadian Foundryman and Metal Industry News* (Toronto), 1, no. 6 (Nov. 1910): 7–8; 1, no. 7 (Dec. 1910): 8; n.s., 2, no. 8 (Aug. 1911): 14–15.

29. Ford Archives, Dearborn, Mich., accession 65-130 (Dickert reminiscences), 11.

30. *Ford Times* (U.S.) 4, no. 4 (Dec. 1910): 115.

31. Yacob, "Beyond Borders"; *Ford Times* (U.S.) 4, no. 13 (Sept. 1911).

32. *Toronto Daily Star*, 25 Feb.–4 Mar. 1911; *Ford Times* (U.S.) 4, no. 7 (Mar. 1911): 191.

33. Essex County Registry Office (Windsor, microfilm at AO), Sandwich Township (east) abstract index to deeds, conc. 1, lot 98 (McNiff's), east part, water frontage; FMCC, MB, 2:12, 26; *Evening Record*, 4 July, 10, 12 Aug. 1911, 11 May, 19 June, 20 Sept. 1912; *Toronto Daily Star*, 20, 27, 30 Apr., 29 May, 16 June 1909; *Canadian Machinery and Manufacturing News*, 2 Jan. 1913, 59. For the recollection on Walter Bartlet, I am grateful to Christopher Moore of Toronto.

34. Ford Archives, Dearborn, Mich., Dickert reminiscences, 13; Lewchuk, *American Technology*, 44–52.

35. Ford Archives, Dearborn, Mich., Dickert reminiscences, 12–13.

36. FMCC, MB, 1:74.

37. J. J. Flink, *The Automobile Age* (Cambridge, Mass., 1988), 54–55.

38. *Evening Record*, 20, 27 Jan. 1912; *Canada Gazette*, 23 Dec. 1911, 2419; Library of Congress (Washington, D.C.), James Couzens papers, box 139, McGregor to Couzens, 6 Feb. 1912; Windsor Public Library, Municipal Archives, John Stodgell coll., MS 24 II/5, McGregor to Stodgell, 6 Feb., 23 Mar. 1912.

39. Canada, *Census of 1911*, vol. 3 (manufactures), 242–43.

40. Hooker, *Life in the Shadows*, 50–52, 129.

41. *Evening Record*, 23 Nov., 14 Dec. 1910; FMCC, MB, 1:74.

42. *Evening Record*, 16 Sept. 1910.

43. Ibid., 15 Dec. 1911, 8 Apr., 11 May, 18 June, 20 Sept. 1912.

44. *Ontario Gazette*, 3 Dec. 1910, 1878; *Iron Age* (New York), 28 Nov. 1912.

45. *Evening Record*, 28 Apr. 1922; [L. R. Chandler], *A History of Essex Golf and Country Club, 1902–1983* ([1983]). This history was kindly drawn to the author's attention by Richard H. Carr of Grosse Pointe Farms, Mich., who also searched the club's records for information on McGregor.

46. *Evening Record*, 31 Aug., 7, 9 Sept., 17 Oct., 3, 7, 17, 19 Dec. 1910; Grace Julia Drummond, ed., *Women of Canada* (Montreal, 1930), 45.

47. *Evening Record*, 21, 22 Oct. 1910; *Canadian Foundryman and Metal Industry News*, n.s., 2, no. 11 (Nov. 1911): 17. The commission's report confirms but does not print McGregor's testimony.

48. *Globe* (Toronto), 27 Jan. 1911; *Iron Age*, 2 Feb. 1911, 313.

49. *Evening Record*, 27, 28 Jan., 24 Feb., 10, 12 Aug., 8, 12, 15 Sept. 1911; *Industrial Canada* 11, no. 3 (Oct. 1910): 281; 11, no. 6 (Jan. 1911): 637–42 (T. A. Russell's "The Grain Growers and the Manufacturers"); Franklin Hiram Walker: *Daily Mail and Empire* (Toronto), 1 Sept. 1911; Menard: ibid.; McLaughlin: ibid. and *Canadian Annual Review* (Toronto, 1911): 110–11; T. A. Russell, "What an Industry Employing 1000 Hands Means to a Community" (undated but noted as a reprint from the national edition of the *Toronto News*, 21 June 1911).

50. Library of Congress, Couzens papers, box 139, Couzens to McGregor, 23 June 1911; Wilkins and Hill, *American Business Abroad*, 37. In this context there is some relevance to the statement in Herbert Marshall, F. A. Southard, and K. W. Taylor, *Canadian-American Industry: A Study in International Investment* (New Haven, 1936), 69, that the Canadian Ford and McLaughlin-Buick "factories were evidently established with relatively little regard for tariffs."

51. *Evening Record*, 14 Aug. 1911.

52. Ibid., 8, 15 Sept. 1911.

53. Ibid., 15 Dec. 1911; D. L. Lewis, *The Public Image of Henry Ford: An American Folk Hero and His Company* (Detroit, 1976), chap. 3.

54. *Evening Record*, 12 Jan., 6 Sept. 1912.

55. Library of Congress, Couzens papers, box 139, McGregor to Couzens, 9 Apr. 1912 (marked "*Personal*"); *Evening Record*, 18 Feb., 9, 24 Apr. 1912; Tedlow, *New and Improved*, 141–43; H. L. Dominguez, *The Ford Agency: A Pictorial History* (Osceola, Wisc., 1981), 18–24.

56. *Ford Times* (U.S.) had been launched as a house journal by Couzens in

1908 as part of his overall supervision of sales and marketing, according to Robert Lacey, *Ford: The Men and the Machine* (London, 1986), 166. *Ford Times* marked a sharp transition in the printed promotion of automobiles. Magazine illustrations and posters of such expensive cars as the Pierce-Arrow, the Oldsmobile, and the Packard represented cutting-edge artistic advertising that never stooped to the common level. *Ford Times* did, with easy humor; the primary graphic for the Universal Car was the localized photograph.

57. *Ford Times* (U.S.) 4, no. 11 (July 1911): 298 and back cover.

58. Ibid., 4, no. 12 (Aug. 1911): 309–11, 322–23, 328.

59. *Evening Record*, 9 Apr. 1912; Lewchuk, *American Technology*, 37; Hooker, *Life in the Shadows*, 42.

60. *Evening Record*, 18 June 1912.

61. Canada, *House of Commons Debates* (19 Mar. 1912), 5492–98, 5508–19; *Toronto Daily Star*, 24 Feb. 1912; *Evening Record*, 5 Apr. 1912.

62. One of the Ford cars was delivered in May 1912 to the West Point Barracks in Victoria, "the first motor vehicle to serve with the Canadian forces on the Pacific coast," according to W. G. Taylor, *The Automobile Saga of British Columbia, 1864–1914* (Victoria, B.C., 1984), 101.

63. *Monetary Times* (Toronto), 6 July 1912, 117–18 ("Canadian Cult of the Automobile"); FMCC, MB, 2:13; *Evening Record*, 31 July, 9 Aug. (editorial, "The Cult of the Auto"), 7–9 Oct., 3, 5 Sept. 1912.

64. *Evening Record*, 1, 5 Nov. 1912, 6, 20, 28 Feb. 1913.

65. Ibid., 7, 28 Dec. 1912; private coll., Mary (McGregor) Mingay, Collingwood, Ont., Gordon McGregor to Esther Wigle, 30 Oct. 1912, Walter McGregor to Esther Wigle, 30 Oct. 1912; Mary Mingay and Don Mingay, *Mingay: Memoirs of Mary and Don Mingay* ([Collingwood, Ont., 1994]), 4–5.

66. Essex County bylaw, no. 306 (3 Dec. 1912); *Evening Record*, 11 Nov., 4 Dec. 1912, 8 Mar. 1913; Art Gallery of Windsor, *Ford City/Windsor*, exhibition catalogue, 30 July–2 Oct. 1994, curator Rosemary Donigan (copy Ontario College of Art and Design Library, VF-5911).

67. FMCC, MB, 2:29; Ford Archives, Dearborn, Mich., Dickert reminiscences, 14–15, 17; *Canadian Machinery and Manufacturing News*, 2 Jan. 1913, 59; *Industrial Canada* 13, no. 11 (June 1913): 1458; "Evolution of a Ford," *Ford Times* (Canada) 1, no. 8 (Mar. 1914): 354–59; Darwin, *History of Ford in Australia*, 11; Hooker, *Life in the Shadows*, 20 (but see Hounsell, *From the American System to Mass Production*, 10, 243); McCalley, *Model T Ford*, 159, 539; Kevin Mowle, "The Canadian 'T'—Made in Canada," *Old Autos* (Bothwell, Ont.), 2 Dec. 1996 (1913 Model Ts). That only the machining of engines (rather than full casting) began in 1913 is suggested by the company's acquisition that year of a 15-spindle, fixed-center drilling machine and vertical drilling machines. See UWA, FMCC coll., box 6, file 73.

68. FMCC, MB, 2:29. The 11,584 Ford cars made in 1912–13 far surpassed McLaughlin's production that season of 881 cars. As a result, the dozen or so other Canadian-built cars were left "jostling for scraps of a market dominated by the Model T." Heather Robertson, *Driving Force: The McLaughlin Family and the Age of the Car* (Toronto, 1995), 147–48. Couzens on dealer deposits: L. H. Seltzer, *A*

Financial History of the American Automobile Industry (Boston and New York, 1928), 20–21.

69. *Gas Power Age* (Winnipeg, Man.) 3, no. 1 (Jan. 1911): 30f–30h; 3, no. 3 (Mar. 1911): 30–42; *Evening Record,* 9 Aug. 1912; *Toronto Daily Star,* 26 Feb. 1913; *Monetary Times,* 6 July 1912, 117–18; 21 June 1913, 1043; United Church of Canada Archives, Toronto, Ernest Davidge, "Reminiscences" (microfilm), 31; U.S. Department of Commerce and Labor, *Monthly Consular and Trade Reports,* no. 354 (Mar. 1910): 222; no. 356 (May 1910): 48; no. 357 (June 1910): 2:221–22; M. L. Berger, *The Devil Wagon in God's Country: The Automobile and Social Changes in Rural America, 1893–1929* (Hamden, Conn., 1979); Gartman, *Auto Opium,* 37; *Technology and Culture* 37, no. 4 (Oct. 1996): introduction, 772; G. T. Bloomfield, "Motorisation on the New Frontier: The Case of Saskatchewan, Canada, 1906–34," in *The Economic and Social Effects of the Spread of Motor Vehicles,* ed. Theo Barker (Basingstoke and London, 1987), 165–93 (an earlier version of this article appeared as "'I Can See a Car in That Crop': Motorization in Saskatchewan, 1906–1934," *Saskatchewan History* 37, no. 1 [Winter 1984]: 3–24); Paul Voisey, *Vulcan: The Making of a Prairie Community* (Toronto, 1988); Don Kerr and Stan Hanson, *Saskatoon: The First Half-Century* (Edmonton, Alberta, 1982), 258–59; J. H. Thompson, *The Harvests of War: The Prairie West, 1914–1918* (Toronto, 1978), 65–66; Tony Casham, *The Alberta Motor Association* ([c. 1967]), 3–14; Marjorie Balfour, *Motoring with the Saskatchewan Motor Club, 1901–1980* ([c. 1980]), 6–13; Rod Bantjes, *Improved Earth: Prairie Space as Modern Artefact, 1869–1944* (forthcoming from University of Toronto Press); D. F. Davis, "Dependent Motorization: Canada and the Automobile to the 1930s," *Journal of Canadian Studies* 21, no. 3 (Fall 1986): 118–19; Davis, *Conspicuous Production,* 121–22; Jeremy Adelman, "Prairie Farm Debt and the Financial Crisis of 1914," *Canadian Historical Review* 71 (1990): 499; Jean-Pierre Kesteman et al., *Histoire des cantons de l'est* (Quebec, 1998), 686; Sasha Mullally, "The Machine in the Garden: A Glimpse at Early Automobile Ownership on Prince Edward Island, 1917," *Island Magazine,* no. 54 (Fall–Winter 2003): 23.

70. *Toronto Daily Star,* 20 Feb.–1 Mar. 1913.

71. Kesteman et al., *Histoire des cantons de l'est;* Mullally, "The Machine in the Garden"; *Ford Times* (Canada) 2, no. 7 (Feb. 1915): 253–56. For his review of Quebec regional and local histories, the author is grateful to Jean-François Drapeau.

72. *Border Cities Star,* 7 Mar. 1921.

73. Tuckey, *True Blue,* 20.

74. *Ford Sales Bulletin,* 13 Sept. 1913, 41; *Canadian Motorist* (Toronto) 1, no. 1 (Jan. 1914): 16. Lawrence's hustle reflected Henry Ford's dictum "A dealer or salesman ought to have the name of every possible automobile buyer in his territory, including all those who have never given the matter a thought," from Ford's *My Life and Work,* quoted in Seltzer, *Financial History,* 98. P. W. Laird, "'The Car without a Single Weakness': Early Automobile Advertising," *Technology and Culture* 37, no. 4 (Oct. 1996): 796–812, esp. 803–5; Smith, *Making the Modern,* 96–97; J. A. Barron, *The Law of Automobiles and Motor Vehicles in Canada* (Toronto, 1926), 38, 56, 361–66; Lewis, *The Public Image of Henry Ford,* 43. The corporate memory of Ford Canada had expiry dates. Despite the success of the marketing strategy of 1912–13, in the waning days of the Model T, around 1926, the company claimed that it had

had no systematic program for "sales stimulation" prior to the summer of 1926, probably because it was trying to clean the slate for the new national time-payment plan being instituted in 1926 or 1927. Admittedly, in 1912–13, dealers were unable to offer sales on a payment plan or at anything under company-set prices. See Toronto Public Library (Toronto Reference Library), Baldwin Room, Broadside coll., 192, Ford, "Sales Promotion" [1926]. *Six Talks by the Jolly Fat Chauffeur* has been reproduced on microfiche: Canadian Institute for Historical Microreproductions (Ottawa), no. 79912.

75. Some volumes of McGregor's personal, bound set of *Ford Times* (U.S.) are in the possession of a nephew, Walter L. McGregor of Windsor. Gordon McGregor's set of *Ford Times* (Canada) is held by the Historical Department of the FMCC in Oakville, Ont.

76. Campbell, quoted in Wilkins and Hill, *American Business Abroad*, 44; U.S. Department of Commerce and Labor, Consular report of James J. McBride of Winnipeg, Man., *Monthly Consular and Trade Reports*, no. 356 (May 1910): 48.

77. *Ford Times* (Canada) 1, no. 2 (Sept. 1913): 246; Berger, *Devil Wagon*, 39–45; Stephen Davies, "'Reckless Walking Must Be Discouraged': The Automobile Revolution and the Shaping of Modern Urban Canada to 1930," *Urban History Review* 18, no. 2 (Oct. 1989): 123–38. According to testimonials, many Canadian doctors swore by their Model Ts; in the United States as late as 1912, physicians organized symposia on automobiles.

78. *Ford Sales Bulletin*, 2 Aug. 1913, 17.

79. U.S. Department of Commerce and Labor, *Monthly Consular and Trade Reports*, no. 340 (Jan. 1909): 35 ("Canadian makes are built on the same lines as those made in the United States"); no. 343 (Apr. 1909): 94; no. 350 (Nov. 1909): 85; no. 354 (Mar. 1910): 222–23; U.S. Bureau of Foreign and Domestic Commerce, Special consular reports, no. 72: Henry D. Baker et al., *British India with Notes on Ceylon, Afghanistan, and Tibet* (Washington, D.C., 1915), 191, 195, 198, 574–88; Ontario, Legislature, *Sessional Papers*, 1914, no. 84:101; Darwin, *History of Ford in Australia*, 14; Wilkins and Hill, *American Business Abroad*, 46; MacLean and Joyce, *Veteran Years of New Zealand Motoring*, 178; Peter Stubbs, *The Australian Motor Industry: A Study in Protection and Growth* (Melbourne, 1971), 4–5; O. M. Hill, *Canada's Salesman to the World: The Department of Trade and Commerce, 1892–1939* (Montreal and London, 1977), 158–59.

80. Wilkins and Hill, *American Business Abroad*, 43. Wilkins maintained this estimate in *The Free-Standing Company in the World Economy, 1830–1996*, ed. Mira Wilkins and Harm Schröter (Oxford, 1998), 62n. 172: the Canadian affiliate in its early decades had an "immense" amount of managerial autonomy.

81. *Evening Record*, 20, 26 Apr., 4, 13, 16 May 1912, 12, 28 Apr., 12 Sept. 1913; *Canadian Foundryman and Metal Industry News* 4, no. 6 (June 1913): 98; *Canadian Machinery and Manufacturing News*, 14 Aug. 1913, 187–88 (Barker); 20 Aug. 1914, 164–65; Seltzer, *Financial History*, 113; Wilkins and Hill, *American Business Abroad*, 116; M. C. Sajatovich, "Taking the Wheel: Selected Aspects of Windsor's Automotive Working Experience" (master's thesis, University of Windsor, 1992), 26.

82. *Iron Age*, 13 June 1912, 1457–58. A colorful vocabulary of speed came to permeate factory operations. At the end of the assembly line in Walkerville, for

instance, the steady drop of assembled automobiles down a steep ramp was called "shooting the shutes" by the testers behind the wheels (*Evening Record*, 28 Mar. 1914). The psychological and physical effects on the workmen of speeding up the line could not be articulated as easily, though it was being noticed.

83. O. J. Abell, "Making the Ford Car," [Detroit], *Iron Age*, 6 June 1912, 1384–91; 13 June 1912, 1454–69; François Baby House Museum, Windsor, scrapbook 3d, 26: Arthur R. Graham, "I Remember When"; *Evening Record*, 28 Mar. 1914 (this article describes the assembly-line system of Ford Canada); Hounsell, *From the American System to Mass Production*, 229–30; Biggs, "Building for Mass Production," 39–63.

84. Ward: Sam Gindin, *The Canadian Autoworkers: The Birth and Transformation of a Union* (Toronto, 1995), 22. Accounts by other workers of their experiences at Ford Canada are so rare that one looks for clues in the few accounts from Ford Detroit. One of the best (and published) records from before World War I is machinist Charles Madison's "My Seven Years of Automotive Servitude," in *The Automobile and American Culture*, ed. D. L. Lewis and Laurence Goldstein (Ann Arbor, Mich., 1983), 10–23. See also *American Machinist* (New York), 24 June 1915, 1101–2, "Eliminating Labor from Manufacturing Costs": at Ford, "[w]ork has been so subdivided that special machines are built to perform but one operation and these as automatically as possible. This eliminates much that has been considered essential in modern management. By simplifying operations the foreman becomes the only instruction sheet necessary." *Evening Record*, 4 Oct. 1912, 26 Apr., 9 May 1913.

85. *Evening Record*, 21, 23 May, 18 June, 25 July, 5, 16 Dec. 1913; *Kingsville Reporter*, 26 June 1913; *Iron Age*, 5 June 1913, 1399. Water pollution: Ontario, Legislature, *Sessional Papers*, 1914, no. 21; Lewchuk, *American Technology*, 36–39; Steven Tolliday and Jonathan Zeitlin, eds., *The Automobile Industry and Its Workers: Between Fordism and Flexibility* (Cambridge, 1986), 30–31; C. H. Johnson, *Maurice Sugar: Law, Labor, and the Left in Detroit, 1912–1950* (Detroit, 1988), 48–63; David Gartman, *Auto Slavery: The Labor Process in the American Automobile Industry, 1897–1950* (New Brunswick, N.J., and London, 1986); V. C. Reuther, *The Brothers Reuther and the Story of the UAW: A Memoir* (Boston, 1976), 49–50; Stephen Meyer, *The Five-Dollar Day: Labor Management and Social Control in the Ford Motor Company, 1908–1921* (Albany, 1981), 9–36; James Naylor, *The New Democracy: Challenging the Social Order in Industrial Ontario, 1914–1925* (Toronto, 1991), 25; Larry Kulisek and Trevor Price, "Ontario Municipal Policy Affecting Local Autonomy: A Case Study Involving Windsor and Toronto," *Urban History Review* 16, no. 3 (Feb. 1988): 258.

86. *Evening Record*, 22, 23–26 Apr. 1913; Hooker, *Life in the Shadows*, 33; Rae, *Henry Ford*, 58; Steven Babson, *Working Detroit: The Making of a Union Town* (New York, 1984), 37. Much later, in a Ford "employees'" publication, the suspect Dew Drop Inn was recalled with different bias as a "favorite eating place for Ford employees at lunch time," where home-cooked meals could be bought cheaply. *Ford Graphic*, 17 Aug. 1954, 8.

87. *Evening Record*, 29–30 Apr., 1, 3, 7 May 1913.

88. Ibid., 9 May, 17–19 Dec. 1913, 19 Jan., 23 Feb. 1914.

89. Ibid., 29–30 May 1913; *Canada Tax Cases* (1917–27), 123, 283.

90. *Evening Record*, 30 May 1913.

91. Ibid., 12 July, 16, 29 Aug., 8 Oct., 12, 14 Nov. 1913; *Canadian Foundryman and Metal Industry News* 4, no. 6 (June 1913): 98; Davis, "Dependent Motorization," 109–11; Tom Traves, "The Development of the Ontario Automobile Industry to 1939," chap. 12 in I. M. Drummond, *Progress without Planning: The Economic History of Ontario from Confederation to the Second World War* (Toronto, 1987), 212. Patent transfers: UWA, FMCC coll., box 7, file 66; box 12, files 91 and 94 (patents in imperial territories outside Canada remained under the control of Ford Detroit).

92. *Evening Record*, 26 Aug., 13, 16 Sept., 8, 25 Oct., 24, 26, 29 Nov., 2, 6, 8 Dec. 1913; *Ontario Law Reports* 31 (1914): 261–74; *Canadian Machinery and Manufacturing News*, 25 Sept. 1913, 290–91; *Kingsville Reporter*, 21 Aug. 1913.

93. FMCC, MB, 2:33; *Evening Record*, 2, 28 Oct. 1913.

94. FMCC, MB, 2:33.

95. *Evening Record*, 28 Nov. 1912; John Manley, "Communists and Autoworkers: The Struggle for Industrial Unionism in the Canadian Automobile Industry, 1925–36," *Labour* 17 (Spring 1986): 106.

96. *Evening Record*, 7–8 Jan. 1914; *Canadian Machinery and Manufacturing News*, 25 Dec. 1913, 663–68; *Gas Power Age* 9, no. 3 (Mar. 1914); Wilkins and Hill, *American Business Abroad*, 43; Bloomfield, "Motorisation on the New Frontier."

97. *Evening Record*, 8–9 Jan., 12, 20–21 Oct. 1914; London *Advertiser* (London, Ont.), 6–7 Jan. 1914; *Globe*, 6 Jan. 1914; *Toronto Daily Star*, 7 Jan. 1914; London *Times* (London, Eng.), 8 Jan. 1914; *Canadian Machinery and Manufacturing News*, 28 May 1914, 519–22; *Canadian Foundryman and Metal Industry News*, n.s., 3, no. 9 (Sept. 1912): 20; n.s., 5, no. 2 (Feb. 1914): 29; n.s., 5, no. 4 (Apr. 1914): 64; *Industrial Canada* 9, no. 8 (Mar. 1909): 664, "Profit-Sharing as a Preventative of Labor Troubles" (a discussion of ideas raised at the recent meeting of the National Civic Federation in New York); National Civic Federation, Profit Sharing Department, *Profit Sharing by American Employers* (New York, 1921); *Industrial Union News* (Detroit) 3, no. 3 (Mar. 1914) re: profit sharing; S. D. Brandes, *American Welfare Capitalism, 1880–1940* (Chicago and London, 1976); Rae, *Henry Ford*, 38–39, 81, 174; Davies, "Reckless Walking Must Be Discouraged," 133–34, 142–43; Lewchuk, *American Technology*, 59, 63–64; Hounsell, *From the American System to Mass Production*, 11, 256–59; Hooker, *Life in the Shadows*, 110–13; Huw Beynon, *Working for Ford* (London, 1973), 21–25; Harry Barnard, *Independent Man: The Life of Senator James Couzens* (New York, 1958), 94, 337n. 45; S. W. Sears, *The Automobile in America* (New York, 1977), 111. The $5 day program is examined most thoroughly in Meyer, *The Five Dollar Day*, which nonetheless maintains there was an actual distribution of profits.

98. *Evening Record*, 15 Jan., 9 Mar., 20 Apr., 1 Aug. 1914; "Profit Sharing in the British Ford Plant," *American Machinist*, 11 June 1914, 1023.

99. *Evening Record*, 26 Feb. 1914; Dark: François Baby House Museum, scrapbook 3d, p. 12; McGregor-Klingensmith, quoted in Wilkins and Hill, *American Business Abroad*, 58.

100. FMCC, MB, 2:33; *Evening Record*, 17 Feb., 26 June 1914; *London Adver-*

tiser, 6 May 1914; *Ford Times* (Canada) 2, no. 5 (Dec. 1914): 163–64; *Contract Record* (Toronto), 17 Sept. 1913, 70; 25 Feb. 1914, 251; 1 Apr. 1914, 407; 6 May 1914, 545; Taylor, *Automobile Saga of British Columbia*, 94.

101. Library of Congress, Couzens papers, McGregor to Couzens, 26 Feb. 1914.

102. NA, RG 25, A-2, vol. 308, files T 5/81–T 6/25.

103. AO, RG 80-8-0-523, no. 12665.

104. *Evening Record*, 2 Feb., 17 Mar., 4, 6, Apr., 6 May 1914; *Ontario Law Reports* 31 (1914): 261–74.

105. *Evening Record*, 4, 27 Mar., 2, 7, 16 Apr., 8, 16, 22 June, 16 July 1914.

106. Ibid., 4 Apr., 12 May, 10, 16 Sept. 1914; Ford's openness: Hounsell, *From the American System to Mass Production*, 260; J. M. Linton and C. W. Moore, *The Story of Wild Goose Jack: The Life and Work of Jack Miner* (Toronto, 1984), 78–79, 113, 128.

107. P. G. Gott, *Changing Gears: The Development of the Automotive Transmission* (Warrendale, Pa., 1991), 13–15; *Ford Sales Bulletin*, 14 Feb. 1914, 131.

108. *Evening Record*, 18, 20 May, 5 June, 1 Aug., 3 Oct. 1914. The price decrease was widely advertised throughout Canada, e.g., *Elgin Sun* (West Lorne, Ont.), 10 Sept. 1914, advertisement of J. A. Campbell (Dutton) and H. A. Carmichael (West Lorne). This is the type of simple and cheap ad that Neil Lawrence was referring to in March 1914 when he stated that newspapers were the company's preferred form of advertising ("It localizes the message" [*Evening Record*, 20 Mar. 1914]). *Industrial Canada* 15, no. 2 (Sept. 1914): 113. The actual figure of 18,774 comes from an apologetic announcement on the rebate in *Ford Sales Bulletin*, 31 July 1915, 341.

CHAPTER 4

1. *Evening Record*, 15 Sept., 1, 15 Oct. 1914; Russell Hann, introduction to *The Great War and Canadian Society: An Oral History*, ed. Daphne Read (Toronto, 1978), 221 (note on autoworker Craig Pritchard).

2. *Ford Sales Bulletin*, 17 Oct. 1914, 262; *Canadian Machinery and Manufacturing News*, 20 Aug. 1914, 164–65; Hugh Durnford and Glenn Baechler, *Cars of Canada* (Toronto, 1973), 305, 314; Mira Wilkins and F. E. Hill, *American Business Abroad: Ford on Six Continents* (Detroit, 1964), 80; J. J. Flink, *The Automobile Age* (Cambridge, Mass., 1988), 75; Martin Adeney, *The Motor Makers: The Turbulent History of Britain's Car Industry* (London, 1988), 85; *Evening Record*, 20 Nov. 1914.

3. *Evening Record*, 10, 16 Sept. 1914; *Ford Sales Bulletin*, 26 Sept. 1914, 253–54; 3 Oct. 1914, 258; J. C. Keith, *The Windsor Utilities Commission and Its Antecedent Commissions* (Windsor, Ont., 1957), 28.

4. FMCC, MB, 2:41; *Ford Times* (Canada) 2, no. 5 (Dec. 1914): 163–64; *Canadian Machinery and Manufacturing News*, 31 Dec. 1914, 643–44; Durnford and Baechler, *Cars of Canada*, 352–53. For the impact of a crane-way on the handling of automotive materials, see Lindy Biggs, "Building for Mass Production: Factory Design and Work Process at the Ford Motor Company," in *Autowork*, ed. Robert Asher and Ronald Edsforth (Albany, 1995), 54–55.

5. *Evening Record*, 29 Aug., 16, 31 Dec. 1914; *Ford Sales Bulletin*, 9 Jan. 1915, 286.

6. *Industrial Canada* 16, no. 2 (June 1915): 136–38 (response to critique of Made in Canada policy in *University Magazine*); (July 1915): 360–72; Jaroslav Petryshyn, *"Made Up to a Standard": Thomas Alexander Russell and the Russell Motor Car Company* (Burnstown, Ont., [2000]), 86–93. For a late Made in Canada advertisement by McLaughlin Motor, see *Toronto Daily Star*, 23 Feb. 1915.

7. *Evening Record*, 16 Oct.–20 Nov., 1 Dec. 1914; *Ford Sales Bulletin*, 15 Aug. 1914, opposite p. 234; 31 Oct. 1914, 268; 12 Dec. 1914, 278; 7 Nov. 1915, 269; *Industrial Canada* 15, no. 3 (Oct. 1914): cover.

8. *Ford Times* (Canada) 2, no. 6 (Jan. 1915): 196; homily: 2, no. 7 (Feb. 1915): inside front cover.

9. *Evening Record*, 12 Nov. 1914.

10. *Industrial Canada* 15, no. 6 (Jan. 1915): 603.

11. *Ford Sales Bulletin*, 3 Oct. 1914, 259; *Canadian Motorist* 2 (May 1915): 148.

12. *Evening Record*, 23 Feb. 1915.

13. FMCC, MB, 2:51; *Evening Record*, 19 Jan. 1915; *Ford Sales Bulletin*, 6 Feb. 1915, 294; 20 Feb. 1915, 299; *Canadian Motorist* 2 (Jan. 1915): 20.

14. *Evening Record*, 23 Jan. 1915; U.S. Congress, Commission on Industrial Relations, *Final Report and Testimony*, 11 vols. (Washington, D.C., 1916), 7626–38; P. S. Foner, *History of the Labor Movement in the United States* (New York, 1965), 4:385, 389, 442; Craig Heron and Robert Storey, eds., *On the Job: Confronting the Labour Process in Canada* (Kingston, Ont., and Montreal, 1986), 349n. 9.

15. *Ford Sales Bulletin*, 20 Feb. 1915, 297; 6 Mar. 1915, 301.

16. *Evening Record*, 20 Feb. 1915; Jeffrey Limerick, Nancy Ferguson, and Richard Oliver, *America's Grand Resort Hotels* (New York, 1979), 75, 78.

17. *Evening Record*, 23 Feb., 13, 23 Mar. 1915; *Labour Gazette* (Ottawa), May 1915, 1283; *Maclean's Magazine* (Toronto), Dec. 1914, 111. On unskilled labor, analyst Harold Lucien Arnold noted in 1915 that Ford Detroit "desires and prefers machine operators who have nothing to unlearn, who have no theories of correct surface speeds for metal finishing, and who will do what they are told, over and over again," as quoted in Steven Babson, *Working Detroit: The Making of a Union Town* (New York, 1984), 31.

18. *Evening Record*, 21 Jan., 3–4 Mar. 1915; *Toronto Daily Star*, 23 Feb. 1915; *Saturday Night* (Toronto), 20 Feb. 1915; *Ford Sales Bulletin*, 6 Feb. 1915, 294; 20 Mar. 1915, 306–7; *Ford Times* (Canada) 2, no. 7 (Feb. 1915): 253–56.

19. *Canadian Motorist* 2 (July 1915), 232.

20. *Evening Record*, 21–22 Apr. 1915; *Canadian Motorist* 2 (May 1915): 142.

21. FMCC, MB, 2:44; *Ford Sales Bulletin*, 1 May 1915, 317–18, 320; *Ford Times* (Canada) 2, no. 10 (May 1915): 387–95; Charles Madison, "My Seven Years of Automotive Servitude," in *The Automobile and American Culture*, ed. D. L. Lewis and Laurence Goldstein (Ann Arbor, Mich., 1983), 18; John Manley, "Communists and Autoworkers: The Struggle for Industrial Unionism in the Canadian Automobile Industry, 1925–36," *Labour* 17 (Spring 1986): 106; V. G. Reuther, *The Brothers Reuther and the Story of the UAW: A Memoir* (Boston, 1976), 49–50; Terry Smith,

Making the Modern: Industry, Art, and Design in America (Chicago and London, 1993), 53; Stephen Meyer, *The Five-Dollar Day: Labor Management and Social Control in the Ford Motor Company, 1908–1921* (Albany, 1981), 119.

22. *London Advertiser,* 21 Apr. 1915; *Globe,* 22 Apr. 1915; J. R. Godfrey, "Keeping Men on the Job," *American Machinist,* 19 Nov. 1914, 901–2.

23. *Evening Record,* 21 Apr. 1915, 22, 29 July 1916.

24. *Ford Times* (Canada) 3, no. 9 (Apr. 1916): 421; *Evening Record,* 1 June 1917, 1 Nov. 1918.

25. *Evening Record,* 16 Oct. 1916 (on population); Clarence Hooker, *Life in the Shadows of the Crystal Palace, 1910–1927: Ford Workers in the Model T Era* (Bowling Green, Ohio, 1997), 85, 129; J. S. Peterson, *American Automobile Workers, 1900–1933* (Albany, 1987), 57.

26. C. H. Johnson, *Maurice Sugar: Law, Labor, and the Left in Detroit, 1912–1950* (Detroit, 1988), 60, 62–63, 91; James Naylor, *The New Democracy: Challenging the Social Order in Industrial Ontario, 1914–1925* (Toronto, 1991), 27, 131–32; J. A. Pendergast, "The Attempt at Unionization in the Automobile Industry in Canada, 1928," *Ontario History* 70 (1978): 245; J. D. Thwaites, "The International Association of Machinists in Canada: To 1919" (master's thesis, Carleton University, Ottawa, 1966), 104.

27. *Evening Record,* 21 Apr. 1915; *Ford Times* (Canada) 2, no. 10 (May 1915): 393–94.

28. *Evening Record,* 23 June, 24 July, 28 Sept. 1915, 10 Aug. 1916.

29. Ibid., 1 June 1917; *Ford Times* (Canada) 3, no. 9 (Apr. 1916): 421.

30. Ford Archives, Dearborn, Mich., Dickert reminiscences, 17; David Gartman, *Auto Slavery: The Labor Process in the American Automobile Industry, 1897–1950* (New Brunswick, N.J., and London, 1986), 190–92; Peterson, *American Automobile Workers,* 56–59, 63–67, 72, 96.

31. Samuel Haber, *Efficiency and Uplift: Scientific Management in the Progressive Era, 1890–1920* (Chicago and London, 1964), 55, 70n. 33, 74, 119; D. T. Rodgers, *The Work Ethic in Industrial America, 1850–1920* (Chicago and London, 1978), 25.

32. *Evening Record,* 23 Feb. 1915 ("Faster Is Cry at Ford Plant to Beat Record"), 23 Sept. 1916; *Ford Sales Bulletin,* 9 Aug. 1913, 22; 6 Dec. 1913, 91; 28 Nov. 1914, 275; 23 Jan. 1915, 290; 3 July 1915, 334–45; 17 July 1915, 338–39; Flink, *Automobile Age,* 118–19; Madison, "My Seven Years," 17–19; Peterson, *American Automobile Workers,* 58; *Canadian Motorist* 2 (May 1915): 142.

33. *Evening Record,* 24 Apr. 1915; *Canadian Motorist* 2 (July 1915): 232; 2 (Sept. 1915): 331; *Financial Post* (Toronto), 29 May 1915.

34. *Evening Record,* 29 Sept. 1915; *Ford Sales Bulletin,* 31 July 1915, 341, 344; Norm Darwin, *The History of Ford in Australia* (Newstead, Aus., [1986]), 14–15.

35. *Evening Record,* 8 May, 21 June, 9 Sept. 1915.

36. Ibid., 6, 9 July 1915.

37. Ibid., 31 July, 14, 23, 27, 30–31 Aug., 14, 29 Sept. 1915; G. T. Bloomfield, "Motorisation on the New Frontier: The Case of Saskatchewan, Canada, 1906–34," in *The Economic and Social Effects of the Spread of Motor Vehicles,* ed. Theo Barker (Basingstoke and London, 1987), 169.

38. *Evening Record,* 21 June–16 Sept. 1915; D. R. Williams, *Call in Pinkerton's:*

American Detectives at Work for Canada (Toronto, 1998), 176–83.

39. *Evening Record,* 21 July 1915. Industrial sabotage, in the form of worker slowdown or damage to materials and products, was not unknown: see C. A. Zabala, "Sabotage in an Automobile Assembly Plant: Worker Voice on the Shopfloor," in *Autowork,* ed. Robert Asher and Ronald Edsforth (Albany, 1995), 209–25. When examined by the author on 1 May 1997, McGregor's bank accounts for the Pinkerton's investigations were found at Ford Canada's Historical Department in Oakville, Ont., in an unmarked cardboard box containing unorganized early company records.

40. *Evening Record,* 8 Sept. 1915; F. R. Bryan, *Beyond the Model T: The Other Ventures of Henry Ford* (Detroit, 1997), 17; Michael Williams, *Ford and Fordson Tractors* (Ipswich, Eng., 1985), 22, 28–29, 35–43; R. C. Williams, *Fordson, Farmall, and Poppin' Johnny: A History of the Farm Tractor and Its Impact on America* (Urbana and Chicago, 1987), 48.

41. *Ford Sales Bulletin,* 29 May 1915, 325; 19 June 1915, 330; Anne Jardim, *The First Henry Ford: A Study in Personality and Business Leadership* (Cambridge, Mass., 1970), 133; Walter Millis, *Road to War: America, 1914–1917* (Boston and New York, 1935), 234; *Monetary Times,* 8 Oct. 1915.

42. *Canadian Annual Review* (Toronto, 1915): 352, 414, 434–35, 443–46; Jack Miner, *Jack Miner: His Life and Religion* (Kingsville, Ont., 1969), 237.

43. Millis, *Road to War,* 219–20.

44. AO, F1075-MU1293: M. O. Hammond diaries, 23 Nov. 1915; *Evening Record,* 30 Sept., 1–2, 18 Oct., 22 Nov. 1915; *Financial Post,* 6 Nov. 1915.

45. *Evening Record,* 5–6, 12–14, 21 Oct., 8, 17, 20 Nov. 1915, 18 Mar. 1916; *Toronto World,* 15 Oct. 1915; *Globe,* 8 Nov. 1915; William Greenleaf, *From These Beginnings: The Early Philanthropies of Henry and Clara Ford, 1911–1936* (Detroit, 1964), 1, 5, 21, 26, 176.

46. NA, MG 29, C103, 34:30, 389–91; *Evening Record,* 28 Oct., 3–4, 20, 22, 24, 30 Nov., 1, 4, 6 Dec. 1915; *Monetary Times,* 8 Oct. 1915, 10; 15 Oct. 1915, 20, 22; 22 Oct. 1915, 12; 29 Oct. 1915, 9. The question of whether workers made voluntary contributions in order to keep their jobs is raised in Naylor, *New Democracy,* 21. As the Victory Loan of 1918 would reveal, not every Ford worker was able to pay for his subscription.

47. FMCC, MB, 2:46–47; Library of Congress, Couzens papers, Couzens to Henry Ford, 13, 25 Oct. 1915, McGregor to Couzens, 18, 20, Oct. 1915; *Evening Record,* 12–13, 16 Oct. 1915; *Globe,* 13–15 Oct. 1915; *Toronto World,* 14 Oct. 1915; A. J. Kuhn, *GM Passes Ford, 1918–1938: Designing the General Motors Performance-Control System* (University Park, Pa., and London, 1986), 259; *Dictionary of American Biography* (s.v. Couzens); Carol Gelderman, *Henry Ford: The Wayward Capitalist* (New York, 1981), 74–76.

48. *Evening Record,* 23, 26–27 Oct. 1915; *Globe,* 17 Nov. 1915; *Monetary Times,* 22 Oct. 1915, 30; *Toronto Daily Star,* 15–16 Oct. 1915. Henry Ford eventually followed through on his $10,000 donation: see his tax records in Ford Archives, Dearborn, Mich., accession 384, L. J. Thompson research papers, box 1, Henry Ford philanthropies.

49. FMCC, MB, 2:55; Windsor Public Library, Municipal Archives, John

Stodgell coll., MS 24, II/9; *Evening Record,* 22 Nov., 15–16 Dec. 1915; *Canada Gazette,* 29 Jan. 1916, 2450; *Dominion Law Reports,* 25 (1915): 771–72. The dividends of 1915 received and recorded by one shareholder (and early Ford supplier), Robert Gray of Chatham, vary in size from those noted here: see AO, F149, FMCC file.

50. *Canadian Machinery and Manufacturing News,* 23 Dec. 1915, 44; *Ford Times* (Canada) 3, no. 5 (Dec. 1915): 247–52; 3, no. 6 (Jan. 1916): 3; no. 7 (Feb. 1916): 317–20; 3, no. 12 (July 1916): 565–66. The company's program of acquisition and replacement of machinery in 1915–16, and the increasing sophistication and size of that machinery, is documented in its inventory: UWA, FMCC coll., box 6, file 73.

51. *Evening Record,* 18, 20, 23 Dec. 1915, 31 Jan., 1 Feb. 1916; Essex Golf and Country Club (Windsor, Ont.), board minute books, 22 Jan. 1916 (courtesy of Richard H. Carr); [L. R. Chandler], *A History of Essex Golf and Country Club, 1902–1983* ([1983]), 42. During the Prohibition years (from 1916), the club condoned the operation of "entertainment cubicles" (with space for storing liquor) in the men's locker-room area (46); Jeff Mingay and R. H. Carr, *One Hundred Years: A History of Essex Golf and Country Club, 1902–2002* ([Windsor], 2002), 23–25.

52. Library of Congress, Couzens papers, McGregor to Couzens, 17, 21 Dec. 1915.

53. Ibid., Couzens to McGregor, 18, 23 Dec. 1915; *Evening Record,* 17 Dec. 1915, 28 Oct. 1916; Canadian Association for the Prevention of Tuberculosis, *Annual Report* (1918), 167–72; Harry Barnard, *Independent Man: The Life of Senator James Couzens* (New York, 1958), 186; F. R. Bryan, *Henry's Lieutenants* (Detroit, 1993), 70.

54. Library of Congress, Couzens papers, McGregor to Couzens, 27 Dec. 1915, Couzens to McGregor, 29 Dec. 1915.

55. Ibid., McGregor to Couzens, 5 Jan. 1916; *Evening Record,* 4 Jan. 1916.

56. *Evening Record,* 20 Jan., 3, 17, 23, 25 Feb., 3 Mar. 1916; Walker: 28 Oct. 1916, 22 Feb. 1917; R. C. Brown and Ramsay Cook, *Canada, 1896–1921: A Nation Transformed* (Toronto, 1974), 230–31.

57. *Evening Record,* 7, 21 Feb., 1 May 1916. On the auto men in Detroit's associational life, see G. S. May, *A Most Unique Machine: The Michigan Origins of the American Automobile Industry* (Grand Rapids, Mich., 1975); and D. F. Davis, *Conspicuous Production: Automobiles and Elites in Detroit, 1899–1933* (Philadelphia, 1988), esp. 103–6.

58. *Evening Record,* 5 Aug., 30 Sept. 1916, 5 Apr. 1917; *Ford News* 2, no. 7 (Apr. 1918): 6–7. Cottingham's recollection appears in *Ford Graphic,* 17 Aug. 1954, 17.

59. E. P. Neufeld, *The Financial System of Canada: Its Growth and Development* (Toronto, 1972), 328; *Globe,* 24 Feb. 1915: consideration of auto insurance at annual convention of the Mutual Fire Underwriters' Association of Ontario.

60. FMCC, MB, 2:62–63.

61. Ibid.; *Financial Post,* 15 July 1916. Nancekeville: *Border Cities Star,* 12 Oct. 1921; *Globe,* 12 Dec. 1916; *Ford News* 1, no. 5 (Dec. 1916): "extra issue" of Jan. 1917 (reprints *Globe,* 3 Jan. 1917 on scarcity of railway cars). Australian trains: S. S. Cheney, *From Horse to Horsepower* (Adelaide, Aus., 1965), 143–45.

62. *Evening Record,* 10 June, 24 Oct., 6 Dec. 1916. McGregor's letter of 5 Dec.

1916 and the branch responses were found on 1 May 1997 in an unmarked box of early company records at the Historical Department of Ford Canada in Oakville.

63. *Evening Record,* 25 Feb. 1916.

64. Ibid., 4, 11, 25 Mar., 23 Sept., 28 Nov. 1916; *Toronto Daily Star,* 19 Feb. 1916; *Industrial Canada* 16, no. 11 (Mar. 1916): 1199; 17, no. 1 (May 1916): 13; 17, no. 2 (June 1916): 125; *Canadian Motorist* 3 (Mar. 1916): 80.

65. *Canadian Machinery and Manufacturing News,* 27 Jan. 1916, 78; Peter Morris, *Embattled Shadows: A History of Canadian Cinema, 1895–1939* (Montreal, 1978), 51, 57–58, 247–48.

66. Kevin Brownlow, *Behind the Mask of Innocence* (New York, 1990), 380.

67. *Ford Sales Bulletin,* 7 Feb. 1914, 126; 17 Oct. 1914, 263; 3 Apr. 1915, 310–11; Smith, *Making the Modern,* 100.

68. *Evening Record,* 18 Mar., 23 Sept. 1916; *Ford Times* (Canada) 3, no. 5 (Dec. 1915); 3, no. 11 (June 1916): 507–15.

69. *Evening Record,* 18 Mar., 28 Nov. 1916; NA, National Film, Television, and Sound Archives, Australia National Film and Sound Archives coll., accession 1994-0215, video no. V1 9902-0002.

70. *Evening Record,* 5 May 1916.

71. Ibid., 12, 19–20 May 1916; *Canadian Motorist* 3 (June 1916): 210.

72. Windsor Public Library, Windsor scrapbook, 27:18.

73. *Evening Record,* 1 Dec. 1916, 28 Apr. 1917.

74. Ibid., 20 Mar., 30 June, 5–6, 22 July, 28 Oct., 20 Nov., 2 Dec. 1916, 24 Feb. 1917; private coll., Mary (McGregor) Mingay, Collingwood, Ont., Walter McGregor to Mrs. William McGregor, 26 Jan. 1917.

75. *Evening Record,* 17 Oct., 5 Dec. 1916, 4 Jan. 1917; *Amherstburg Echo,* 23 June 1916.

76. *Evening Record,* 10 June, 18–19 July, 1 Nov. 1916; *Amherstburg Echo,* 9, 30 June, 21 July 1916; N. F. Morrison, *Garden Gateway to Canada: One Hundred Years of Windsor and Essex County, 1854–1954* (Toronto, 1954), 251–52.

77. Mingay coll., Walter McGregor to Mrs. William McGregor, 26 Jan. 1917. On American enlistment in the Canadian forces before and after April 1917, see *Canadian Annual Review* (Toronto, 1917): 354–57.

78. NA, MG 26, G: 192436a, 192446 (microfilm at AO); R. MacG. Dawson, *William Lyon Mackenzie King: A Political Biography, 1874–1923* (Toronto, 1958), 226, 231.

79. *Evening Record,* 26 Jan. 1917; Thomas Adams, "Town Planning, Housing, and Public Health," in Canada, Commission of Conservation, *Report* (1916): 126–27.

80. Ontario, Legislature, *Journals* (1916): 16, 91, 238; *Statutes of Canada,* 1916, 6 Geo. 5, c. 98; 1917, 7 Geo. 5, c. 69; Keith, *Windsor Utilities Commission,* 14–16; Larry Kulisek and Trevor Price, "Ontario Municipal Policy Affecting Local Autonomy: A Case Study Involving Windsor and Toronto," *Urban History Review* 16, no. 3 (Feb. 1988): 255–70; Naylor, *New Democracy,* 411–12 (on Wickett).

81. UWA, J. C. Keith papers, subseries C, box 4, files 47 and 48; subseries G, oversize box 1, scrapbook; Ontario, Legislature, *Sessional Papers,* 1918, no. 50:123, 127; *Evening Record,* 5 Jan., 5, 20, 22–24 Mar., 6, 27 Apr., 18 May, 12–13 July, 4

Sept., 9 Nov. 1917.

82. *Industrial Canada* 17, no. 6 (October 1916): 693 (advertisement for 1917 Ford tourer); Kevin Mowle, "1917 T—The Steel Ts," *Old Autos*, 7 Apr. 1997, 29; FMCC, MB, 2:76–77.

83. United Church of Canada Archives, Toronto, Ernest Davidge, "Reminiscences" (microfilm), 123–27; *Monetary Times*, 27 Oct. 1916, 24; *Ford News* 2, no. 3 (October 1917): 3; Canada, Dominion Bureau of Statistics, *Canada Year Book, 1918* (Ottawa, 1919), 422–25; Bloomfield, "Motorisation on the New Frontier"; J. H. Thompson, *The Harvests of War: The Prairie West, 1914–1918* (Toronto, 1978), 65–66; Paul Voisey, *Vulcan: The Making of a Prairie Community* (Toronto, 1988), 23–24, 63, 68–70. The other local histories consulted are too numerous to list.

84. *Ford Sales Bulletin*, 29 Nov. 1913, 88; 3 Oct. 1914, 259; 17 Oct. 1914, 262; 23 Jan. 1915, 289–91; 29 May 1915, 238, 330; *Ford News* 2, no. 1 (Aug. 1917): 3; Russell Johnston, *Selling Themselves: The Emergence of Canadian Advertising* (Toronto, 2001), 67; Heron and Storey, *On the Job*, 202.

85. *Ford Sales Bulletin*, 7 Mar. 1914, 142 ("Women Prospects"); *Ford News* 2, no. 3 (October 1917): 6–7; *Toronto Daily Star*, 23 June 1917; Kuhn, *GM Passes Ford*, 246; H. L. Dominguez, *The Ford Agency: A Pictorial History* (Osceola, Wisc., 1981), 24, 29; G. T. Bloomfield, "No Parking Here to Corner: London [Ontario] Reshaped by the Automobile, 1911–61," *Urban History Review* 18 (October 1989): 145 and n. 43.

86. Smith, *Making the Modern*, 96, 100.

87. FMCC, MB, 2:76–77; Darwin, *History of Ford in Australia*, 15–17; Peter Stubbs, *The Australian Motor Industry: A Study in Protection and Growth* (Melbourne, 1971), 6; Cheney, *From Horse to Horsepower*, 148–49; Shakila Yacob, "Beyond Borders: Ford in Malaya, 1926–1957" (paper presented at Business History Conference, 2003 [examined on Internet, 5 July 2004]).

88. Ford Archives, Dearborn, Mich., accession 384, L. J. Thompson research papers, box 1, Henry Ford properties, Sandwich, Ont.; ibid., Dickert reminiscences, 21; Reginald Pound and Geoffrey Harmsworth, *Northcliffe* (London, 1959), 565–66; C. E. Sorenson and S. T. Williamson, *My Forty Years with Ford* (New York, 1956), 237; Williams, *Ford and Fordson Tractors*, 35–43.

89. Library of Congress, Couzens papers, A. W. Anglin to A. R. Bartlet, 29 May 1917, McGregor to Couzens, 11 June 1917, Couzens to McGregor, 12 June 1917; *Canada Gazette*, 17 Feb. 1917, 2193–94; *Evening Record*, 20 Feb., 26 May, 2 June, 23 Oct. 1917, 13 Feb. 1918.

90. *Evening Record*, 12, 17, 21 May, 3 Aug. 1917; *Amherstburg Echo*, 7 Dec. 1917.

91. Library of Congress, Couzens papers, McGregor to H. S. Morgan, 21 Apr., 4 May 1917; Morgan to McGregor, 21 Apr., 4 May 1917, W. K. George to McGregor, 28 Apr. 1917.

92. *Evening Record*, 24 Mar., 18, 20 Apr., 25, 27 Oct. 1917.

93. Ibid., 27 Aug., 12 Sept., 29, 31 Oct. 1917.

94. *Detroit News*, 24 Apr. 1917 (the author is grateful to J. McGregor Dodds for sharing his copy of this issue); Mingay coll., Walter McGregor to Mrs. William McGregor, 5 Oct., 16, 24 Dec. 1917; Esther McGregor to Mrs. William Mc-

Gregor, n.d. (the undated poem by T. D. Niven, apparently from a newspaper, is in this collection); *Evening Record,* 17, 26 July 1917.

95. Mingay coll., Walter McGregor to Mrs. William McGregor, 25, 29 Apr., 31 July, 29 Oct., 6 Nov. 1917; *Evening Record,* 9–10 Aug., 18 Sept. 1917; *Amherstburg Echo,* 10 Aug. 1917.

96. *Evening Record,* 22 Aug., 18 Oct., 21 Nov., 17, 31 Dec. 1917; *Canadian Machinery and Manufacturing News,* 12 July 1917, 67 (which mistakenly names the new commissioner "James M." Sclanders); Border Chamber of Commerce, *Border Brieflets* (Windsor, 1917), on microfiche as CIHM, no. 73624; I. M. Drummond, *Progress without Planning: The Economic History of Ontario from Confederation to the Second World War* (Toronto, 1987), 98–99.

97. *Evening Record,* 23 May 1917.

98. Ibid., 7 Feb. 1916, 23, 26, 29–30 May 1917.

99. Ibid., 16 Dec. 1916, 10 Apr., 26 May, 2 June, 22 Sept., 6, 10 Oct. 1917.

100. FMCC, MB, 2:76–77; Library of Congress, Couzens papers, FMCC financial statement, fiscal year-end 31 July 1918; *Evening Record,* 27–28 July, 3–4, 8 Aug. 1917.

101. Sir [William] Thomas White, *The Story of Canada's War Finance* (Montreal, 1921), 62; *CAR* (1917): 300–302; Christopher Armstrong, *Blue Skies and Boiler Rooms: Buying and Selling Securities in Canada, 1870–1940* (Toronto, 1997), 7, 85–86.

102. *Evening Record,* 16–17, 23 Oct. 1917.

103. The *Evening Record*'s daily coverage of the Victory Bond campaign began on 10 Nov. 1917. F. S. Snell, ed., *Leamington's Heritage, 1874–1974* (Toronto, 1974), 96.

104. Larned is quoted in the *Evening Record,* 13 Nov. 1913.

105. Ibid., 14 Nov. 1917. On 5 Nov. the *Evening Record* reported Campbell's wounding.

106. Ibid., 16 Nov. 1917.

107. For the Miss Canada character, see *Canadian Encyclopedia,* 2nd ed. (Edmonton, Alberta, 1988), 1366.

108. *Amherstburg Echo,* 23 Nov. 1917.

109. Dodges: *Evening Record,* 12 Mar. 1917; Durnford and Baechler, *Cars of Canada,* 269. *Evening Record,* 9 Mar. 1918: by this date the Dodge Brothers' "Commercial Car" (apparently a truck) was being sold by Copeland Motor Sales in Windsor. *Evening Record,* 23 Oct., 27 Nov. 1917; *Amherstburg Echo,* 30 Nov. 1917. Cleona Lewis, *America's Stake in International Investments* (Washington, D.C., 1938), 300: Ford Canada did not offer its stock publicly until 1929, but stock (from private sales) was listed earlier on the Toronto and Detroit exchanges and the New York curb.

110. *Evening Record,* 26 Nov. 1917.

111. Ibid., 7 Dec. 1917, 5 Feb. 1918.

112. Ibid., 11, 13, 15, 18, 20 Dec. 1917, 31 Jan., 4, 6, 13, 21 Feb., 5, 12, 16, 23, 25, 30 Mar., 9, 18 Apr. 1918.

113. Ibid., 11, 13–14, 21, 31 Dec. 1917, 4, 10–11, 15, 18–19, 26, 30 Jan., 7–8, 12–13, 16 Feb. 1918; Ontario, Legislature, *Sessional Papers,* 1919, no. 50:33–34,

62–79; Drummond, *Progress without Planning*, 99.

114. *Evening Record*, 18, 29–20 Jan., 14, 26 Feb., 1 Mar. 1918.

115. Ibid., 2 Feb. 1918.

116. Ibid., 18 Jan., 12, 18 Feb. 1918.

117. Ibid., 15, 19 Feb. 1918.

118. Ibid., 20 Feb. 1918; *CAR* (1918): 178; B. M. Baruch, *American Industry in the War: A Report of the War Industries Board [Mar. 1921]* (New York, 1941), 289–92; R. D. Cuff, *The War Industries Board: Business-Government Relations during World War I* (Baltimore and London, [1973]), 204–19; G. B. Clarkson, *Industrial America in the World War: The Strategy Behind the Line, 1917–1918*, rev. ed. (Boston and New York, 1924), 332–34, 339–43; O. M. Hill, *Canada's Salesman to the World: The Department of Trade and Commerce, 1892–1939* (Montreal and London, 1977), 178; Flink, *Automobile Age*, 80. The exact nature and volume of materials imported by Ford Canada, on which it could claim drawbacks (duties refunded on exported product), is difficult to determine. An indirect indicator is the amount of the drawbacks themselves. In May 1917, in response to a question from Lambton West MP Frederick F. Pardee, customs minister John Dowsley Reid reported the payment of drawbacks to Ford of $127,066.10 in 1916 (fiscal year-end 31 Mar.) and $371,481.29 in 1917: Canada, *House of Commons Debates* (30 May 1917), 1818.

119. *Evening Record*, 27, 29–30 Apr., 2 May 1918; *Saturday Night*, 27 Apr. 1918; *Toronto Daily Star*, 13 June 1916.

CHAPTER 5

1. Ford Canada's surviving records of the period make no mention of this extracorporate activity by McGregor.

2. Documentation on the Automotive Industries of Canada is scarce. A two-page statistical report by the AIC, dated 21 Feb. 1919, is in the William M. Gray fonds, AO, MU 1150, F149, ser. A, articles file. Other mentions are in *Canadian Motorist* 5 (Aug. 1918): 495–500; 5 (Sept. 1918): 589–90.

3. *Evening Record*, 3, 15 June 1918; *CAR* (1918): 430–31; Margaret Prang, *N. W. Rowell: Ontario Nationalist* (Toronto, 1975), 237.

4. *Toronto Daily Star*, 5 June 1918.

5. *Evening Record*, 20 Feb. 1918. Accurate quantitative analysis was not the strong suit of the *Evening Record*, which often reported only as much as local companies, including Ford, disclosed.

6. Ibid., 13, 19 Feb., 26 Mar., 17 May 1918; *Toronto Daily Star*, 25 Feb. 1918; *CAR* (1918): 503; J. B. Rae, ed., *Henry Ford* (Englewood Cliffs, N.J., 1969), 90–92: "Price Policy and Prices of Model T Cars."

7. *Toronto Daily Star*, 15 Feb., 18 Mar. 1918.

8. *Evening Record*, 8, 18, 22 Mar., 4 Apr. 1918.

9. *Detroit Labor News*, 18 July, 2 Aug. 1918; *Industrial Banner* (Toronto), 6 Sept. 1918; IAM, *Machinists' Monthly Journal* (Washington, D.C.) 30, no. 5 (May 1918): 455; David Gartman, *Auto Slavery: The Labor Process in the American Auto-*

mobile Industry, 1897–1950 (New Brunswick, N.J., and London, 1986), 161–69; C. H. Johnson, *Maurice Sugar: Law, Labor, and the Left in Detroit, 1912–1950* (Detroit, 1988), 69–75, 91, 111; Mark Perlman, *The Machinists: A New Study in American Trade Unionism* (Cambridge, Mass., 1961), 51. In trade journals of this period, the notion of speeding up production had gained the ethical dimension of efficiency. At Ford Detroit, with orders exceeding production, the "spirit of catching up is omnipresent," *Iron Age* had noted in 1912 in an article on cross-calculations of materials, time, and production (13 June 1912, 1457–58).

10. *Industrial Banner,* 21, 28 June 1918; James Naylor, *The New Democracy: Challenging the Social Order in Industrial Ontario, 1914–1925* (Toronto, 1991), 131–33.

11. *Amherstburg Echo,* 28 June 1918; *Evening Record,* 28 June 1918.

12. D. H. Avery, "Ethnic and Class Tensions in Canada, 1918–20: Anglo-Canadians and the Alien Worker," in *Loyalties in Canada: Ukranians in Canada during the Great War,* ed. Frances Swyripa and J. H. Thompson (Edmonton, Alberta, 1983), 79–98; Elliot Samuels, "The Red Scare in Ontario: The Reaction of the Ontario Press to the Internal External Threat of Bolshevism, 1917–1918" (master's thesis, Queen's University, Kingston, Ont., 1972), 341: there were twenty-one charges in Windsor, second to Toronto with twenty-seven. *Evening Record,* 11–13, 17–18, 20–22 June 1918.

13. *Labour Gazette,* May 1918, 314; July 1918, 476; *Iron Age,* 18 July 1918, 151.

14. *Evening Record,* 12–13, 25 Mar., 4–5, 13 Apr., 4, 6, 8, 25 May, 10, 28 June 1918.

15. Ibid., 24 Apr. 1918.

16. Humfrey Michell, *Profit-Sharing and Producers' Co-operation in Canada* (Kingston, Ont., 1918); National Civic Federation, Profit Sharing Department, *Profit Sharing by American Employers* (New York, 1921).

17. *Evening Record,* 11 June, 29 July 1918; *Ford Graphic,* 17 Aug. 1954, 6.

18. *Evening Record,* 6–8 June 1918.

19. *Iron Age,* 8 July 1918, 151.

20. *Evening Record* coverage of labor action daily from 29 June to 7 Sept. 1918, and 1 Dec. 1920. As a result of a change in ownership, the *Evening Record* became the *Border Cities Star* on 3 Sept. 1918.

21. *Industrial Banner,* 12, 19 July, 27 Sept. 1918; *Amherstburg Echo,* 5, 11–12 July, 16 Aug., 20 Sept. 1918; FMCC, MB, 2:82; *CAR* (1918): 313, 492–93; Judy Fudge and Eric Tucker, *Labour before the Law: The Regulation of Workers' Collective Action in Canada, 1900–1948* (Toronto, 2001), 98–99.

22. *Evening Record,* 29 June 1918.

23. Ibid., 6 July 1918; "State of Mind of the Foreigner in This Land," *Canadian Machinery and Manufacturing News,* 23 Oct. 1919, 419, 56 [*sic*]; "The Problem of the Foreigner" (editorial), ibid., 16 Oct. 1919.

24. R. A. Frager, *Sweatshop Strife: Class, Ethnicity, and Gender in the Jewish Labour Movement of Toronto, 1900–1939* (Toronto, 1992), 241n. 27.

25. *Toronto Daily Star,* 8–10, 12, 15, 20, 22 July 1918.

26. *Industrial Banner,* 27 Sept. 1918.

27. *Chatham Daily Planet* (Chatham, Ont.), 9, 12 July 1918.

28. London *Times* (London, Eng.), 23 July 1918.

29. *Labour Gazette*, Aug. 1918, 557, 565, 573–74, 611–12; Sept. 1918, 700; *Evening Record*, 3 Sept. 1918. For the production of submarine chasers at Ford Detroit, see *American Machinist*, 23 May 1918, 894; 7 Nov. 1918, 841–44; Ford Archives, Dearborn, Mich., Dickert memoirs, 18; D. A. Hounsell, "Ford Eagle Boats and Mass Production during World War I," in *Military Enterprises and Technological Change: Perspectives on the American Experience*, ed. Merritt Roe Smith (Cambridge, Mass., 1985), 175–202.

30. *Labour Gazette*, Apr. 1916, 1059 (order in council of 23 Mar. 1916); *CAR* (1918): 270–71; Paul Craven, *"An Impartial Umpire": Industrial Relations and the Canadian State, 1900–1911* (Toronto, 1980), 288–98.

31. *Evening Record*, 22 Aug. 1918; *Border Cities Star*, 12 Sept., 4 Oct. 1918; *Amherstburg Echo*, 30 Aug. 1918.

32. *Evening Record*, 23, 25 July 1918; *Industrial Banner*, 27 Sept. 1918.

33. *Detroit Labor News*, 19 July 1918.

34. *Border Cities Star*, 7 Sept. 1918.

35. *Industrial Banner*, 27 Sept. 1918.

36. *Evening Record*, 21, 29 June, 19 July 1918; *Border Cities Star*, 31 Dec. 1921, 27 Nov. 1922.

37. *Border Cities Star*, 12 Sept. 1918; *Chatham Daily Planet*, 31 July 1918.

38. *Border Cities Star*, 4 Oct. 1918.

39. Ibid., 5 Oct. 1918; FMCC, MB, 2:89, 103.

40. *Evening Record*, 24, 27 Aug. 1918; *Border Cities Star*, 17, 20–21, 23–25, 28 Sept., 25 Oct., 1, 25, 28 Nov. 1918; *Amherstburg Echo*, 25 Oct. 1918; *Canada Gazette*, 23 Nov. 1918, 1754–55; *Canadian Motorist* 5, no. 11 (Nov. 1918): 725.

41. *Canadian Motorist* 5, no. 8 (Aug. 1918): 495.

42. *Toronto Daily Star*, 8 Aug. 1918.

43. *Border Cities Star*, 19, 23, 26–27 Sept. 1918.

44. *Toronto Daily Star*, 19 Feb. 1918.

45. Ontario, Legislature, *Sessional Papers*, 1919, no. 15:16; NA, National Film, Television, and Sound Archives, accession 1994-0215, video no. V1 9901-0038. The call to conserve gasoline led some communities, among them London and Kitchener, Ont., to restrict the use of automobiles on Sundays (see *Kitchener News Record*, 7–15 Sept. 1918; *London Advertiser*, 13, 16 Sept. 1918).

46. NA, National Film, Television, and Sound Archives, accession 1994-0215, video no. V1 9902-0015; O. M. Hill, *Canada's Salesman to the World: The Department of Trade and Commerce, 1892–1939* (Montreal and London, 1977), 389.

47. The *Border Cities Star*'s coverage of the campaign extends from 3 Oct. to 28 Nov. 1918.

48. FMCC, MB, 2:87; Library of Congress, Couzens papers, McGregor to Couzens, 15 Nov. 1918; *CAR* (1918): 486–87; Christopher Armstrong, *Blue Skies and Boiler Rooms: Buying and Selling Securities in Canada, 1870–1940* (Toronto, 1997), 88–89.

49. *Border Cities Star*, 4 Oct. 1918.

50. Ibid., 9, 27 Nov. 1918; *Amherstburg Echo*, 8 Nov. 1918. On the embezzle-

ment, see chapter 5.

51. *Border Cities Star*, 10, 12, 18–19, 21, 25, 28–31 Oct., 2, 13, 19, 22, 26, 30 Nov., 2–5, 10–12, 18–21, 23 Dec. 1918, 4, 22 Feb., 1 May 1919.

52. Ibid., 26 Nov., 3–4, 6, 9, 16 Dec. 1918, 13, 24 Jan. 1919.

53. Ibid., 20 Nov. 1918, 1 Aug. 1919.

54. Ibid., 4, 13, 16–17, 27 Dec. 1918, 3, 6, 14 Jan., 4, 8 Feb., 4, 25 Apr., 17, 21 May, 7, 20 June 1919; *Industrial Canada* 19, no. 8 (Dec. 1918): 51–52; Clarence Hooker, *Life in the Shadows of the Crystal Palace, 1910–1927: Ford Workers in the Model T Era* (Bowling Green, Ohio, 1997), 109–17.

55. *Border Cities Star*, 6, 12–14 Dec. 1918, 4 Feb., 15–17 Apr. 1919.

56. Ibid., 3, 16 Jan., 4 Feb., 4 Apr. 1919; *Amherstburg Echo*, 9 Aug. 1918.

57. *Border Cities Star*, 22 Nov., 18, 23 Dec. 1918, 4, 29, 22 Feb., 5–6 Mar., 1 May 1919.

58. Ibid., 1 Jan., 16 Dec. 1918, 25 June, 23 July 1919; Ontario, Legislature, *Sessional Papers*, 1921, no. 50:76, 159; Michael Simpson, "Thomas Adams, 1871–1940," in *Pioneers in British Planning*, ed. G. E. Cherry (London, 1981), chap. 2; J. F. Vance, *Death So Noble: Memory, Meaning, and the First World War* (Vancouver, B.C., 1997), 208.

59. Ample coverage of the water and sewer issue during the period September 1918–July 1919 was provided by the *Border Cities Star*, which remained biased toward McGregor and the EBUC. Ontario, Legislature, *Sessional Papers*, 1920, no. 21:4, 260–61.

60. *Border Cities Star*, 23 Jan., 1, 3–4, 17–20, 21–22, 27 Mar. 1919.

61. Ibid., 11 Feb., 1, 17, 20, 27 Mar., 9 June, 2, 26, 28 Aug., 6 Nov. 1919; *Amherstburg Echo*, 8 Nov. 1918.

62. *Border Cities Star*, 6 Dec. 1918, 11 Feb., 12 Mar., 22, 30 Apr., 20 June, 19 July 1919.

63. Jeff Mingay and R. H. Carr, *One Hundred Years: A History of Essex Golf and Country Club: 1902–2002* ([Windsor], 2002), 26–27.

64. FMCC, MB, 2:95. When McGregor moved up from driving Ford cars is uncertain. There is a photograph of his 1919 Packard car in the "G. M. McGregor" file in the FMCC Archives. When his chauffeur, John Saunders, a onetime foreman at the Ford plant, married the McGregors' maid, Jeanie Gordon, McGregor gave them a tall oak clock, which is now in the possession of Ronald Onuch of Windsor.

65. *Border Cities Star*, 9, 16 May 1919.

66. Ibid., 6 Mar. 1919.

67. Ibid., 29 Mar., 11, 14, 29 July 1919.

68. *Industrial Canada* 19, no. 9 (Jan. 1919): 195–96.

69. *Border Cities Star*, 8 Mar., 11–12 Apr., 7, 11, 23 June, 12, 14–15, 30 Aug., 18 Sept. 1919; *Industrial Canada* 20, no. 6 (October 1919): 144; *Canadian Motorist* 6, no. 8 (Aug. 1919): 546.

70. *Border Cities Star*, 21, 25 Feb., 11–12 Apr., 1, 13, 20 May, 6 June, 4 July, 9 Aug., 13 Sept. 1919; *Monetary Times*, 7 Jan. 1921; *Canadian Machinery and Manufacturing News*, 10 Apr. 1919, 366; 8 Jan. 1920, 25; 30 Dec. 1920, 576.

71. *Ford Graphic*, 17 Aug. 1954, 14.

72. *Border Cities Star*, 13 Sept. 1919; Naylor, *New Democracy*, 67; advertisement from a Ford dealer in Carleton Place, Ont., reproduced in Claudia Smith, *Gypsies, Preachers, and Big White Bears: One Hundred Years on Country Roads* (Burnstown, Ont., 1998), 120.

73. *Border Cities Star*, 7–8, 12–13, 28 Feb., 1 Apr. 1919.

74. Ibid., 21 Mar., 5 June 1919.

75. Ibid., 21 Mar., 12–14, 22, 30 May, 3–5, 12, 23, 25 June, 7 July, 30 Aug. 1919; IAM, *Machinists' Monthly Journal* 31, no. 4 (Apr. 1919): 363.

76. *Border Cities Star*, 21 May–8 Aug., 19 Dec. 1919.

77. Ibid., 2 Jan., 10 May, 30 July, 23, 29 Aug., 1 Dec. 1919; FMCC, MB, 2:95, 101. Bonus and benefit plans or other forms of profit sharing were often discredited by labor, which, as at Ford Canada, favored unrestricted pay raises. An opposite employer's perspective is contained in an editorial in the *Border Cities Star*, 21 Aug. 1920: "Far-seeing employers of labor also look upon this plan as insurance against labor disturbances and other forms of industrial unrest, as it undoubtedly is."

78. Craig Heron and Myer Siemiatycki, "The Great War, the State, and Working-Class Canada," in *The Workers' Revolt in Canada, 1917–1925*, ed. Craig Heron (Toronto, 1998), 36.

79. NA, RG 33/95-95.

80. *Canadian Motorist* 6, no. 3 (Mar. 1919): 138.

81. Donald E. McGregor of Toronto: interview with author, 8 Jan. 1998; *Industrial Canada* 20, no. 3 (July 1919): 233; 20, no. 4 (Aug. 1919): 53.

82. Harry Bruce, *Frank Sobey: The Man and the Empire* (Toronto, 1985), 63–65; Robert Lampard and Calvino Cheng, "Snow Problem? No Problem! Three Medical Men and Their Snowmachines," *Saskatchewan History* (Fall 2001): 36–40; "Correspondence, Notes, and Comments," ibid. (Spring 2003): 4.

83. National Industrial Conference, *Official Report of Proceedings and Discussions* ([Ottawa, 1919]), 2, 39, 71–73; *Industrial Canada* 20, no. 5 (Sept. 1919); Heron and Siemiatycki, "Great War," 36; Richard Allen, *The Social Passion: Religion and Social Reform in Canada, 1914–28* (Toronto, 1971), 134–37; Norm Darwin, *The History of Ford in Australia* (Newstead, Aus., [1986]); 16–20, 23.

84. *Border Cities Star*, 30 Sept., 3 Oct. 1919.

85. Ibid., 19, 27 Sept. 1919.

86. Ibid., 3–4 Oct. 1919.

87. Ibid., 25 Apr., 20 June, 11, 13, 20, 30 Sept., 20–21, 5, 19 Dec. 1919, 25 Apr. 1922; *Iron Age*, 1 May 1919, 1160; Naylor, *New Democracy*, 167; Hooker, *Life in the Shadows*, 109.

88. *Border Cities Star*, 30 Oct., 4, 27 Nov. 1919.

89. Ibid., 31 July 1919.

90. Kevin Mowle, "The Canadian 'T'—1919," *Old Autos;* Hugh Durnford and Glenn Baechler, *Cars of Canada* (Toronto, 1973), 249, 262.

91. FMCC, MB, 2:103.

92. *Border Cities Star*, 9 Aug., 12, 31 Dec. 1919; *Canadian Automotive Trade* (Toronto), October 1919, 35; *Industrial Canada* 20, no. 7 (Nov. 1919): 68; *Who's Who and Why, 1921*, ed. B. M. Greene (Toronto, n.d.), 233.

93. Mira Wilkins and F. E. Hill, *American Business Abroad: Ford on Six Conti-*

nents (Detroit, 1964), 115.

94. Darwin, *History of Ford in Australia*, 20; Peter Stubbs, *The Australian Motor Industry: A Study in Protection and Growth* (Melbourne, 1971), 10; Bill Tuckey, *True Blue: Seventy-five Years of Ford in Australia* (Edgecliff, Aus., 2000), 7–8.

95. *Border Cities Star*, 17 Oct. 1919.

96. Ibid., 12–13 Dec. 1919, 21 Jan. 1920.

97. Ibid., 9, 14, 29 Oct., 12–13 Dec. 1919; FMCC, MB, 2:106; *Canadian Foundryman and Metal Industry News* 8, no. 8 (Aug. 1917): 114–17; *Canadian Machinery and Manufacturing News*, 26 Dec. 1918, 295 (illustrated advertisement for Dominion Forge and Stamping); 20 Nov. 1919, 516, 518, 520 ("High Premiums Being Offered for Auto Sheets"); 10 June 1920, 559; *Industrial Canada* 20, no. 7 (Nov. 1919): 130.

98. *Border Cities Star*, 6, 8, 11–13, 15, 17, 31 Dec. 1919.

99. Ibid., 12 Nov. 1919, 12–13, 18 Feb., 30 June, 10, 22–23 July, 17, 24 Sept. 1920, 3 June 1922; *Who's Who and Why, 1919–20*, ed. B. M. Greene (Toronto, n.d.), 400; National Civic Federation, *Profit Sharing*, 291–92; M. E. McCallum, "Corporate Welfarism in Canada, 1919–39," *Canadian Historical Review* 61 (1990): 54–55.

100. *Border Cities Star*, 16 Aug., 25 Sept., 16, 24 Dec. 1919.

101. Ibid., 3, 9, 31 Oct. 1919.

102. Ibid., 24 Nov., 2 Dec. 1919, 16 Feb., 21 Apr. 1920; 27 May, 10 July 1922; *Industrial Canada* 20, no. 6 (October 1919): 58; *CAR* (1919): 120.

103. *Border Cities Star*, 10, 16, 22–24, 27 Oct., 3 Dec. 1919. For this information on the chair I am indebted to Ann Bartlet Brush of R.R. #5, Harrow, Ont., whose mother and aunts knew the McGregor family.

104. *Border Cities Star*, 7, 20, 24 June, 5, 12, 25, 30 July, 9, 21, 23, 27, 30 Aug., 30 Sept., 15, 18, 28–29 Oct., 3–6, 18, 20, 25–26 Nov., 6, 17, 23, 29, 31 Dec. 1919.

105. Ibid., 4, 11, 21 Oct. 1919; Naylor, *New Democracy*, 127.

106. *Border Cities Star*, 22, 25, 28–29 Nov., 5, 10, 15–16, 18, 20, 23–26 Dec. 1919, 8 Jan. 1920; Naylor, *New Democracy*, 83; Judith Sealander, *Grand Plans: Business Progressivism and Social Change in Ohio's Miami Valley, 1890–1929* (Lexington, Ky., 1988); J. C. Weaver, *Shaping the Canadian City: Essays on Urban Politics and Policy, 1890–1920* (Toronto, 1977), 64–71.

107. For assistance in examining records pertaining to the municipal election, I am grateful to Linda Chakmak of Windsor.

108. *Border Cities Star*, 30–31 Dec. 1919; Stephen Speisman, "Antisemitism in Ontario: The Twentieth Century," in *Antisemitism in Canada: A History and Interpretation*, ed. Alan Davies (Waterloo, Ont., 1992), 121.

109. *Border Cities Star*, 9 Jan., 3, 16, 24–25, 28 Feb., 2 Mar. 1920.

110. Ibid., 6 Jan., 4, 6, 8, 16 Mar., 6–7, 13 Apr., 31 May 1920, 1 Nov. 1922; Windsor Public Library, Municipal archives, Ford City Council minutes, bylaws; Ontario, Legislature, *Sessional Papers*, 1921, no. 17:367–68.

111. *Border Cities Star*, 6 Jan., 12 Mar. 1920.

112. Ibid., 3, 6, 8, 16–17 Jan., 11 Feb., 30 Apr., 1, 4, 11, 14–15, 18, 27–29 May, 1–2 June, 28 Aug., 9–10 Nov. 1920; Canadian Association for the Prevention of

Tuberculosis, *Annual Report* (1921), 106.

113. *Border Cities Star*, 12 Feb., 4 June 1920, 4 Jan. 1922; *CAR* (1921): 39.

CHAPTER 6

1. *Border Cities Star*, 21, 29, 31 Jan., 19, 23–24, 27 Feb., 1–2 Mar., 26 June, 31 Aug., 3 Sept. 1920; *Kingsville Reporter*, 29 July 1920; *Toronto World*, 17 Apr. 1920; *Monetary Times*, 14 Mar. 1919, 16; 6 Dec. 1919, 36; 5 Mar. 1920, 10; *Canadian Motorist* 7, no. 2 (Feb. 1920): 107; 7, no. 9 (Sept. 1920): 768–69, 771; *Industrial Canada* 20, no. 11 (Mar. 1920): 136; Kevin Mowle, "The Canadian 'T' . . . The Decade of Change—1920," *Old Autos*, 7 July 1997 (other new features are noted in Ford advertising, e.g., *Liberal* [Richmond Hill, Ont.], 6 May 1920). On Liebold, see F. R. Bryan, *Henry's Lieutenants* (Detroit, 1993), 169–72.

2. *Border Cities Star*, 20 Apr., 21, 23 Sept., 23, 30 Oct. 1920; D. L. Lewis, *The Public Image of Henry Ford: An American Folk Hero and His Company* (Detroit, 1976), 109; A. J. Kuhn, *GM Passes Ford, 1918–1938: Designing the General Motors Performance-Control System* (University Park, Pa., and London, 1986), 246, 260, 285, 298; Carol Gelderman, *Henry Ford: The Wayward Capitalist* (New York, 1981), 201; Thomas Klug, "Employers' Strategies in the Detroit Labor Market," in *On the Line: Essays in the History of Auto Work*, ed. Nelson Lichtenstein and Stephen Meyer (Urbana and Chicago, 1989), 61–62; Stewart Macaulay, *Law and the Balance of Power: The Automobile Manufacturers and Their Dealers* (New York, 1966), 13; L. H. Seltzer, *A Financial History of the American Automobile Industry* (Boston and New York, 1928), 114–18, 197–202; Stephen Meyer, *The Five-Dollar Day: Labor Management and Social Control in the Ford Motor Company, 1908–1921* (Albany, 1981), 185–87.

3. Mira Wilkins and F. E. Hill, *American Business Abroad: Ford on Six Continents* (Detroit, 1964), 116. *Border Cities Star*, 20, 26 Apr., 28 May, 21, 23 Sept., 6, 8 Oct. 1920.

4. *Border Cities Star*, 20 Aug., 4, 7 Sept. 1920; *Labour Gazette*, Apr. 1920, 380; June 1920, 638; July 1920, 751; Sept. 1920, 1117; October 1920, 1270; Dec. 1920, 1588; Canada, Department of Labour, *Labour Organization in Canada* (Ottawa, 1921), 221, 294 (for 1920); Canada, Department of Labour, *Labour Organization in Canada* (Ottawa, 1922), 123, 213, 250 (for 1921); *Canadian Motorist* 7, no. 3 (Mar. 1920): 180; H. A. Logan, *Trade Unions in Canada: Their Development and Functioning* (Toronto, 1948), 232; Craig Heron and Robert Storey, eds., *On the Job: Confronting the Labour Process in Canada* (Kingston, Ont., and Montreal, 1986), 202.

5. *Border Cities Star*, 31 Dec. 1919, 20 Feb., 21 Apr., 31 May, 4, 24, 30 Aug., 1 Sept. 1920.

6. Ibid., 17 Apr., 16, 19 Nov. 1920; *Industrial Canada* 21, no. 11 (Mar. 1921): 60–63; Canada, *House of Commons Debates* (14 May 1921), 3409.

7. Canada, Department of Trade and Commerce, *Weekly Bulletin*, 28 June 1920, 1421; 22 Nov. 1920; 11 Apr. 1921, 590; 18 Aug. 1923.

8. Ibid., 29 Apr. 1922, 668.

9. *Border Cities Star*, 19 May 1920; "Motor Industry Taxed to the Limit, Finds Going Hard," *Canadian Machinery and Manufacturing News*, 14 Oct. 1920; ibid., 10

Mar. 1921, 60.

10. FMCC, MB, 2:114.

11. *Border Cities Star*, 16 June, 19 July, 3, 5 Aug., 11, 24 Nov., 8, 11, 20–21, 24 Dec. 1920.

12. Ibid., 13 Nov., 21 Dec. 1920.

13. United Farmers of Alberta, *Annual Report* (1918), 211; *CAR* (1919): 326, 364–68; K. A. Badgley, *Ringing in the Common Love of Good: The United Farmers of Ontario, 1914–1926* (Montreal and Kingston, Ont., 2000), 60–63, 72, 86, 105, 225–26; L. A. Wood, *A History of Farmers' Movements in Canada* (Toronto, 1924; repr. Toronto, 1975, intro. F. J. K. Griezic), 225–70; B. J. Rennie, *The Rise of Agrarian Democracy: The United Farmers and Farm Women of Alberta, 1909–21* (Toronto, 2000), 194; Tom Traves, *The State and Enterprise: Canadian Manufacturers and the Federal Government, 1917–1931* (Toronto, 1979), 22–23.

14. *Border Cities Star*, 24, 30 Aug., 17 Sept., 2 Oct., 29 Nov., 1 Dec. 1920.

15. Ibid., 1 Dec. 1920.

16. Campbell's testimony, which was covered in the *Border Cities Star*, 1 Dec. 1920, appears in its entirety in NA, RG 36, ser. 8, 23:4312–34.

17. NA, RG 36, ser. 8, 5:786–819, 9:1304–1450, 15:2221–32, 23:4312–34.

18. Ibid., 23:4287–89, 4355–80; *Canadian Machinery and Manufacturing News*, 17 Feb. 1921, 67; 26 May 1921, 117.

19. *Border Cities Trades and Labor Council, Eighteenth Anniversary Complimentary Souvenir, 1902–1920: To the Delegates, Trades and Labor Congress of Canada, Windsor, Ontario, September 13th to 20th, 1920* (Toronto, 1920); Sclanders's testimony appears in Canadian Manufacturers' Association, *The Tariff: Why Canada Needs It* (1921), 81–82; Clarence Hooker, *Life in the Shadows of the Crystal Palace, 1910–1927: Ford Workers in the Model T Era* (Bowling Green, Ohio, 1997), 52, 129.

20. *Monetary Times*, 7 Jan. 1921.

21. *Canadian Machinery and Manufacturing News*, 26 May 1921, 69–70.

22. *Toronto World*, quoted in *Border Cities Star*, 4 June 1920.

23. *Border Cities Star*, 17, 27 Jan. 1921.

24. Ibid., 7, 26–27, 31 Jan. 1921.

25. Ibid., 5–6, 20 Jan., 15 Feb. 1921; Ontario, Legislature, *Sessional Papers*, 1923, no. 50:151–54; J. C. Keith, *The Windsor Utilities Commission and Its Antecedent Commissions* (Windsor, Ont., 1957), 99, 108.

26. *Border Cities Star*, 21, 24–25 Jan., 1, 12, 1–22, 24–26 Feb. 1921.

27. Ibid., 1–2, 4–5, 8–12, 14–17, 21–22, 26 Mar., 26, 28 July, 5, 18 Aug. 1921.

28. Ibid., 13, 18 Jan., 3, 7, Feb., 1, 10 Mar., 2, 27, 29 Apr., 9, 14 May 1921; *Industrial Canada* 21, no. 9 (Jan. 1921): 159–60; 21, no. 12 (Apr. 1921): 81.

29. *Border Cities Star*, 28 Jan. 1921; Ford Archives, Dearborn, Mich., Dickert reminiscences, 20; *Automotive Industries*, 3 Feb. 1921, 243; 5 May 1921, 983; 23 Mar. 1922, 685.

30. Ford Archives, Dearborn, Mich., accession 285, box 9, file 14, McGregor to Liebold, 23 Feb., 3 Mar., 4 Apr. 1921.

31. *Border Cities Star*, 8–9 Jan., 3, 19 Sept., 29 Oct. 1921, 11 Mar. 1922; FMCC, MB, 2:130; *Canadian Automotive Trade* (July 1921): 28; (Nov. 1921): 16; *Industrial*

Canada 22, no. 2 (June 1921): 91.

32. *Selling Cars in Canada, 1919–20* (Toronto, 1919) was put out by Continental Publishing, publisher of *Everywoman's World. Border Cities Star*, 6 Apr. 1921.

33. *Saturday Night*, 29 Jan. 1921, 13; *Canadian Automotive Trade* (July 1921): 3–5; *Border Cities Star*, 10 Jan., 10, 16 Sept., 29 Oct. 1921, 2–3 Feb. 1922; *Automotive Industries*, 6 Jan. 1921, 41; 27 Jan. 1921, 189; H. L. Dominguez, *The Ford Agency: A Pictorial History* (Osceola, Wisc., 1981), 41.

34. *Canadian Automotive Trade* (Apr. 1921): 14; (Aug. 1921): 1; (Feb. 1922): 9, 23; *London Advertiser*, 18 Mar. 1922. On J. J. Duffus's earlier years with Ford, see *Ford Sales Bulletin*, 9 May 1914, 178.

35. *Border Cities Star*, 10, 16 Sept., 29 Oct. 1921, 2 Feb., 17 June 1922; *Canadian Automotive Trade* (Apr. 1921): 4; (July 1921): 6; (Feb. 1922): 9, 23.

36. *Border Cities Star*, 7, 22 Mar., 2 Apr., 10, 13 June, 11, 15, 24 Aug., 11–13, 29 Oct., 1, 10 Nov. 1921; 5 Jan. 1922; *Industrial Canada* 20, no. 10 (Feb. 1920): 118, 120; 20, no. 12 (Apr. 1920): 111; Wilkins and Hill, *American Business Abroad*, 117.

37. *Border Cities Star*, 2, 15 June, 30 July, 8 Sept., 6, 21, 29 Oct., 5 Nov. 1921, 15 Apr. 1922.

38. Ibid., 3, 7 Sept., 1, 23–24 Nov. 1921; Hugh Durnford and Glenn Baechler, *Cars of Canada* (Toronto, 1973), 164–65, 248. The two partners in Windsor Machine and Tool (founded in 1910) had both trained in the machine-craft era that had helped spawn the local automotive industry: Adolph Morrell with Canadian Typograph and Lorne Wilkie with Evans and Dodge Bicycle (*Canadian Machinery and Manufacturing News*, 27 June 1918, 679).

39. Wilkins and Hill, *American Business Abroad*, 115.

40. Ford Archives, Dearborn, Mich., accession 285, box 28, file 9, McGregor to Liebold, 15 Oct., 9 Nov. 1921 (includes circular from Border Cities Hotel Company Limited), Liebold to McGregor, 15 Nov. 1921; box 57, file 10, Liebold to McGregor, 8 Nov. 1921, McGregor to Liebold, 15 Oct., 12 Nov. 1921, Liebold to Joseph Galumb, 18 Oct. 1921.

41. *Border Cities Star*, 29 Sept. 1922; Ford Archives, Dearborn, Mich., accession 285, box 28, file 9, McGregor to Liebold, 1 Nov. 1921 (includes opinion of A. R. Bartlet, 29 Oct. 1921); Wilkins and Hill, *American Business Abroad*, 114.

42. Robert Lacey, *Ford: The Men and the Machine* (London, 1986), 205–6.

43. *The International Jew: The World's Foremost Problem* (Dearborn, Mich., 1920). Vol. 2, though generally included under the title *The International Jew*, had a separate title: *Jewish Activities in the United States* (Dearborn, Mich., 1921). Albert Lee, *Henry Ford and the Jews* (New York, 1980); Neil Baldwin, *Henry Ford and the Jews: The Mass Production of Hate* (New York, 2001); Steve Fraser, *Every Man a Speculator: A History of Wall Street in American Life* (New York, 2005), 367–71.

44. R. A. Frager, *Sweatshop Strife: Class, Ethnicity, and Gender in the Jewish Labour Movement of Toronto, 1900–1939* (Toronto, 1992); *Canadian Automotive Trade* (Mar. 1921): 8–9.

45. Ford Archives, Dearborn, Mich., accession 285, box 28, file 9, Liebold to Northcliffe, 5 Aug. 1921, Liebold to "Miss Faulkner" (Grace Falconer), 5 Aug. 1921, Liebold to Ford Canada (attention W. R. Campbell), 18 Aug. 1921, Liebold to P. Grandjean, 30 July 1921, Campbell to Liebold, 15 Aug. 1921, Grandjean

to Liebold, 27 July 1921; Reginald Pound and Geoffrey Harmsworth, *Northcliffe* (London, 1959), 805–6, 845–46.

46. *Automotive Industries*, 8 Sept. 1921, 459–60; *Monetary Times*, 6 Jan. 1922, 230.

47. *Ottawa Citizen*, 16 Aug. 1921; *Toronto Daily Star*, 31 Aug. 1920; *CAR* (1921): 442, 549, 559; Canada, Royal Commission in Racing Inquiry, *Report of J. G. Rutherford* (Ottawa, 1920), 20–21, 50–59; Canada, Royal Commission on Customs and Excise, *Interim Reports (nos. 1 to 10)* (Ottawa, 1928), 103–4, 114–15; E. C. Drury, *Farmer Premier: Memoirs of the Honourable E. C. Drury* (Toronto and Montreal, 1966), 126; G. A. Hallowell, *Prohibition in Ontario, 1919–1923* (Ottawa, 1972), 86; N. F. Morrison, *Garden Gateway to Canada: One Hundred Years of Windsor and Essex County, 1854–1954* (Toronto, 1954), 287–90.

48. *Border Cities Star*, 24–26 Aug. 1921; Traves, *The State and Enterprise*, 108; J. H. Thomson and Allen Seager, *Canada, 1922–1939: Decades of Discord* (Toronto, 1985), 14–17.

49. *Border Cities Star*, 21 Nov. 1921; *Winnipeg Free Press*, 19, 24, 26 Nov. 1921; *CAR* (1921): 497–99. The *Toronto Star* was quoted in the *Free Press*.

50. *Border Cities Star*, 22 Nov.–10 Dec. 1921.

51. For Joyce's loaded remark, see ibid., 22 Nov. 1921.

52. Ford Archives, Dearborn, Mich., accession 285, box 28, file 9, McGregor to Henry Ford, 22 Nov. 1921.

53. *Border Cities Star*, 24 Nov.–12 Dec. 1921, 3, 6, 17 Jan. 1922.

54. Ibid., 14–17 Dec. 1921; *Industrial Canada* 20, no. 7 (Nov. 1919): 74. Films advertising Canada were also made under Raymond S. Peck, editor in the Department of Trade and Commerce, ibid. 20, no. 8 (Dec. 1919): 60–61. Much like Ford's films, these movies included reels on fishing, lumbering, and water power: see Ford Archives, Dearborn, Mich., accession 285, box 9, file 14. The reduction of distance and class is fundamental in Ford advertising for all model versions and trucks. The theme is also developed in the literature of the period, including Virginia Woolf's *Mrs. Dalloway*, originally published in 1925.

55. The aesthetic of speeding automobiles is nicely treated in Lynne Kirby, *Parallel Tracks: The Railroad and Silent Cinema* (Durham, N.C., 1997) and Kay Armatage, *The Girl from God's Country: Nell Shipman and the Silent Cinema* (Toronto, 2003). (Copies of the Maxwell films were kindly lent to me by Professor Armatage.) Nell Shipman, *The Silent Screen and My Talking Heart: An Autobiography* (Boise, Idaho, 1987), 87–88; Roland Marchand, *Advertising the American Dream: Making Way for Modernity, 1920–1940* (Berkeley and Los Angeles, 1985), 62–63; *Labour Gazette* 20, no. 10 (Oct. 1920): 1263–64; *Industrial Canada* 21, no. 5 (Sept. 1920): 89.

56. *Border Cities Star*, 27 Dec. 1921, 11, 25, 28 Jan., 6, 8 Feb. 1922.

57. Ibid., 28 Jan. 1922.

58. Ibid., 27 Dec. 1921, 17, 25 Jan. 1922; *London Advertiser*, 4 Feb. 1922.

59. *Border Cities Star*, 31 Dec. 1921, 14, 19–20, 30 Jan., 28 Feb., 3 Mar. 1922.

60. Ibid., 21, 23, 30–31 Jan. 1921, 6 Mar. 1922.

61. Ibid., 7 Dec. 1921, 16–17 Feb. 1922.

62. Ibid., 17 Dec. 1921, 4, 10, 21 Jan., 24 Feb., 5 Sept. 1922.

63. Ford Archives, Dearborn, Mich., accession 285, box 57, file 10, Liebold to McGregor, 27 Dec. 1921, 21 Jan., 3, 20 Feb. 1922, McGregor to Liebold, 19, 29 Dec. 1921, 18, 25, 27 Jan., 6, 15 Feb. 1922, McGregor to Beck, 4, 7 Jan. 1922, Beck to McGregor, 6 Jan. 1922.

64. *Border Cities Star*, 16 Jan. 1922; Ford Archives, Dearborn, Mich., accession 285, box 57, file 10, McGregor to Liebold, 16 Jan. 1922, Liebold to McGregor, 19 Jan. 1922.

65. *Border Cities Star*, 13 Feb. 1922; Ford Archives, Dearborn, Mich., accession 285, box 57, file 10, McGregor to Liebold, 15 Feb. 1922, Liebold to McGregor, 18 Feb. 1922.

66. *Border Cities Star*, 29 Dec. 1921, 14 Jan., 24–25, 27 Feb., 1, 6 Mar. 1922.

67. Ibid., 25 Nov. 1922; *CAR* (1922): 513; Ford Archives, Dearborn, Mich., accession 285, box 57, file 10, Mrs. G. Brode to Henry Ford, 16 Jan. 1922, Liebold to Mrs. Brode, 23 Jan. 1922, McGregor to Liebold, 27 Jan. 1922. I am grateful to Patrick Brode of Windsor for family background on his wonderfully outspoken grandmother, who apparently did acquire a Ford later in the 1920s.

68. E. A. Partridge, *A War on Poverty* (Winnipeg, Man., [1925]), 63; *Industrial Canada* 22, no. 9 (Jan. 1922): 138.

69. *Border Cities Star*, 9–11 Mar. 1922; *Amherstburg Echo*, 10, 16–17 Mar. 1922; Ford Archives, Dearborn, Mich., accession 285, box 57, file 10, McGregor to Liebold, 4 Mar. 1922, Walter McGregor to Henry Ford (telegram), 11 Mar. 1922.

70. The blood vessel disorder is being investigated by Gordon McGregor's grandniece Mary McGregor-Clewes of Toronto.

71. *Border Cities Star*, 13–18, 28 Mar. 1922; *Detroit Free Press*, 10–12, 14–15 Mar. 1922; *Montreal Gazette*, 13 Mar. 1922; *Automobile Topics* (New York), 18 Mar. 1922, 374; FMCC, MB, 2:134, 138, 141, 145.

72. *Border Cities Star*, 11 Mar. 1922; *Financial Post*, 17 Mar. 1922; *Automotive Industries*, 16 Mar. 1922, 636; *Canadian Motorist* 9, no. 4 (Apr. 1922): 208; *Industrial Canada* 22, no. 12 (Apr. 1922): 100, 102.

CHAPTER 7

1. AO, RG 22-311 (1922), no. 99 (1933), no. 147; Colonel Walter Leishman McGregor (Gordon's nephew and Walter's son), Windsor, interview with author, 27 Oct. 1997; Gordon McGregor Rock (grandson), Toronto, interview with author, 16 Aug. 2004.

2. *Border Cities Star*, 4 Apr., 11 Sept. 1922; *New York Times*, 5 Apr. 1922.

3. *Border Cities Star*, 16 Mar., 28 Apr., 3 June 1922.

4. Ibid., 27 June, 7–8, 10, 20, 22, 26–27, 29 July, 5, 7, 11, 22 Aug., 24 Oct., 27–29 Nov. 1922; FMCC, MB, 2:145, 153, 157, 162.

5. "lines of least resistance": *Border Cities Star*, 11 Aug. 1922; *Iron Age*, 9 Nov. 1922, 1257.

6. *Contract Record and Engineering Record*, 26 Dec. 1923, 1271–72; *CAR* (1924–25): 65–67; Johnston, *Early Motoring in South Africa*, 185; Mira Wilkins and F. E. Hill, *American Business Abroad: Ford on Six Continents* (Detroit, 1964), 118–19.

7. Tom Traves, "The Development of the Ontario Automobile Industry to

1939," in I. M. Drummond, *Progress without Planning: The Economic History of Ontario from Confederation to the Second World War* (Toronto, 1987), 214, 216.

8. The Essex series appeared in the *Border Cities Star* on 22, 29 Apr., 6, 13, 20, 27 May, 3, 10, 24 June 1922.

9. Ibid., 20 May 1922.

10. FMCC, *Thirty Years of Progress, 1904–1934* ([1934]), 1, 3.

11. "The Birth of Ford of Canada," http://media.ford.com/newsroom/feature_display.cfm?release=18467.

12. I am grateful to Mrs. Milka Brown, principal of Gordon McGregor School, Windsor, for information on her school. *Border Cities Star*, 9, 13–14 Apr., 9 May, 13 June 1923; FMCC, Historical Department, box marked "42" and "Archives COB 5" (documents on the Disher/Colquhoun case of 1923).

13. Toronto Reference Library, Special Collections Centre, Baldwin Room Manuscript Coll., Broadside coll., 1920s, Ford; *Industrial Canada* 25, no. 10 (Feb. 1925): 55; 25, no. 11 (Mar. 1925): 53.

14. Wilkins and Hill, *American Business Abroad*, 118.

15. On this point I am grateful to Dr. John Turley-Ewart of Toronto, who provided pertinent information from the minutes of the Executive Council of the Canadian Banking Association.

INDEX

Adams, Fred A., 193
Adams, Thomas, 191, 202
Adler automobile, 99
Advertiser (London, Ontario), 233
Agawan Club, 16
Alberta, province of, 51
Allan, Norman McL., 8, 171
Allied war loan, 131, 133, 134, 164
All-Red Feature Company, 146
All Saints' Church (Windsor, Ontario), 175
American Auto Trimming (Canada), 166, 243
American Auto Trimming Company, 62
American Federation of Labor, 125, 175
American Machinist (New York), 123
American Motor Car Manufacturers Association, 34
Amherstburg (Ontario): impact of auto, 5; and G. M. McGregor, 11, 12, 167, 245; and M. P. McGregor, 128
Anglin, Arthur White, 158
Anglo-French Loan, 131
Angove, H., 58
Ann Arbor Country Club (Michigan), 112
Arkell and Douglas, 60
Arnold, Harold Lucien, 283n. 17
A. R. Williams Machinery Company, 87
Asheville (North Carolina), 120
Askin, H. R., 223
Association of Border Americans, 187
Association of Canadian Advertisers, 210
Association of Licensed Automobile Manufacturers, 24, 34
Australian Motorist (Melbourne), 60
Autocar automobile manufacturer, 33
Automobile (Philadelphia), 41
Automobile, Aircraft, and Vehicle Workers (AAVW), 197, 198, 219
Automobile and Sportsmen Exhibition Limited (Montreal), 47
"Automobile Corner" (Toronto), 26, 33
automobile shows, 26, 93; Border Cities, 217, 230, 252; Boston, 50; Canadian National Exhibition (CNE) (Toronto), 47, 79, 86, 92, 121, 184, 201, 204, 218, 240; CCM (Toronto), 33, 34, 37; Chicago, 50; Detroit, 119; Granite Rink (Toronto), 39, 47; Industrial Exhibition (Toronto), 17, 32, 33, 50, 52, 173; Leduc (Alberta), 89; Minnesota, 89; Montreal, 121, 232; National Automobile Show (Western Ontario), 248; National Motor Show (Toronto), 184, 201; New York, 34, 50, 92, 230, 250; Olympia (London, Ontario), 57; St. Lawrence (Toronto), 51, 57, 58, 63; Toronto, 48, 50, 73, 89, 92; Winnipeg, 89, 107
Automobile Workers Union, 182; Local No. 27, 178; strike activity, 218
Automotive Industries (New York), 231, 240
Automotive Industries of Canada (AIC), 173, 184, 290n. 2; and G. M. McGregor, 200, 217
Auto Specialties Manufacturing, 100
Auto Workers' News (Detroit), 197
Avery, William H., 33

Bain, John, 152
Baird, Annia R., 138
Bank of Montreal, 250
Banwell, Henry, 16
Barker, Charles L., 100, 116
Bartlet, Alexander Robert, 158, 177, 238

Bartlet, Edgar Nelson, 132, 159, 161, 209
Bartlet, Margaret Anne. *See* McGregor, Margaret Annie
Bartlett, Walter, 74
Baum, Samuel K., 214
Baum and Brady, 214
Baxter, William James, 215, 251, 258; and Ford Canada, 261; and Ford film, 246
Bay of Fundy: in Ford film, 186
Beach Grove Country Club (Walkerville, Ontario), 256
Beck, Sir Adam, 105, 116, 251
Belle Isle (Michigan), 18, 50
Bennett, Charles H., 29
Benz, 23, 39, 41
bicycle model types: Brantford Red Bird, 19; Detroit, 19; King of Scorchers, 19. *See also* Evans and Dodge Bicycle
Bixler, Elizabeth. *See* McGregor, Elizabeth
Blake, Lash, Anglin, and Cassels, 158
Blood, Howard Earl, 237, 250; and Canadian Industries, 8; and Canadian Products, 205, 232; and taxation, 222, 249
Blood, Maurice E., 205
"Body Building Committee," 206
Bognie Brae (Amherstburg, Ontario), 12
Boharm (Saskatchewan), 42
Boland, John Francis, 157
Borden, Sir Robert Laird, 152, 166, 168, 169, 172
Border Brieflets, 162
Border Cities, 63, 107, 208; and American industry, 227; and automobile shows, 217; and automotive industry, 62, 99, 116, 123, 138, 163, 197, 237, 248; and branch plants, 171, 227; community, 61, 167; competition within, 7; crime, 241; and Detroit, 190; employment, 5, 106, 122, 260; and Ford automobile, 252; and Ford Canada, 6, 224; and Ford production, 144; growth, 1, 4, 62, 128, 259; housing, 254; and IAM, 180; identity, 77, 83; industrial sabotage, 129; labor flow, 248; labor tension, 103, 182; and G. M. McGregor, 147, 148, 152, 217, 223, 240, 256, 261; politics, 212; population, 202, 262; and profit sharing, 108; and F. Maclure Sclanders, 162; and taxation, 141, 193, 243; union activity, 182, 198; Victory Bond campaign, 165, 210; and World War I, 115, 118, 132, 151, 165, 189. *See also under* Ford City, Ojibway, Sandwich, Sarnia, Walkerville, Windsor
Border Cities' Automotive Dealers' Association, 217
Border Cities' Boys' Work organization, 256
Border Cities Chamber of Commerce, 100, 152, 153, 163, 171, 176, 183; and Border region, 192, 193; challenges to, 8, 191; and EBUC, 214; and Ford employment, 198; and foreign market, 172; and Archibald Hooper, 199; and G. M. McGregor, 170, 184, 190, 192, 228, 254; publicity, 212; and taxation, 219, 221, 224; and town planning, 202; Victory Bond campaign, 165, 168, 187; and Windsor, 227; and World War I, 161
Border Cities' Goodfellows' Club, 210
Border Cities Hockey League, 209
Border Cities Hotel Company Limited, 209, 216
Border Cities' "Old Boys," 258
Border Cities Pipe Band, 209
Border Cities Safety Council, 190, 203, 213
Border Cities Social Service Council, 241
Border Cities Star, viii, 291n. 20; and benefit plans, 294n. 77; and Border Cities, 190, 203, 249; and W. R. Campbell, 258; and Detroit, 249; and EBUC, 189; and Ford

Canada, 188, 208, 224; and Ford employment, 248; and Henry Ford, 251, 252; and golf, 235; and Archibald Hooper, 183; and A. N. Lawrence, 234; and E. G. Liebold, 252; and G. M. McGregor, 188, 215, 216, 223, 246, 254, 255, 260, 261; and Motoropolis, 249; and G. F. Ramsay, 249; and Victory Bond campaign, 186, 187, 210, 292n. 47. See also *Evening Record*
Border Cities Trades and Labor Council (TLC), 175, 182, 227; and Ford lockout, 181; and Archibald Hooper, 228; labor tension, 178; and war production, 181
Border Manufacturers' Farmers Association, 176;and Ford film, 185
Border real estate board, 191
Border region, 191, 192, 260. *See also* Border Cities
Border Retail Merchants' Association, 183, 190, 202, 203
Bowlby, Andrew Douglas, 213; and bicycle industry, 19; and Ford Canada, 132; Ford sales agent, 20, 38, 62
Boyde, John R., 64
Boy Scouts of Canada, 216
Brackin, Robert Livingstone, 241
branch plant, 1, 6, 30, 61, 79, 116, 269n. 23; American manufacturers, 17, 18, 104; employment, 6; formation of, 3–5, 46; and G. M. McGregor, 262; relationship, 30; and taxation, 141, 171; war production, 183
branch plants (American-owned): American Lamp and Stamping, 100; Baker Electric, 100; Chalmers Canada, 79, 141; Dominion Stamping, 100; Fisher Body, 100, 196; Hupp, 100; J. T. Wing Company, 17; Kelsey Wheel, 100, 104; Maxwell-Chalmers, 196; Maxwell Motor Company, 104, 141; National Auto Body, 100; Overland, 100; Peters Cartridge, 17; Saginaw Salt and Lumber, 17; Saxon Motor Car, 141; Tate Electric, 100; Tudhope, 100; W. E. Seagrave Company, 17
Brandon (Manitoba), 15
Brandywine Falls (British Columbia): in Ford film, 147
Brazil, Jules, 121
Brett, W. G., 187
British American Film Company, 146
British Columbia, province of, 33, 51
British Red Cross, 150
Brock Motors Limited, 237
Brode, George, 252
Brode, Mary Martin, 252–54, 261
Brooks, Donald, 204
Brooks, May, 204
Brooks, Mel S., 94
Brown, John Livingstone, 225
Bryan, William Jennings, 131
Bullis, G. S., 117
Burgin, W. R., 235

Cadillac automobile, 232
Cadillac Automobile Company, 24, 34, 41, 57; strike, 101
Cadillac Motor Car Company, 203
Cadwell Sand and Gravel Company, 235
Caldwell, Thomas Wakem, 225
California, state of, 149, 153
Cameron, Robert H., 136
Campbell, Gladyes Emily. *See* Leishman, Gladyes Emily
Campbell, Malcolm G., 213, 226, 250; and G. M. McGregor, 255
Campbell, Wallace Ronald, 8, 38, 43, 61, 78, 117, 128, 148, 246, 289n. 105; and Detroit, 234; and Ford Canada, 224, 230, 237, 248, 250, 258, 262, 263; and Ford City fund, 134; and Ford expansion, 86; and Ford foreign market, 260, 262; and Henry Ford, 218; as Ford officer, 134; and Ford prices, 225; and Ford profits, 106; and Ford sales, 95;

Campbell, Wallace Ronald (*continued*) and labor tension, 178, 182; and Lincoln Motor Company, 249; and G. M. McGregor, 150, 194, 223, 255, 258; as political figure, 210, 214, 254; and safety, 203; and Victory Bond campaign, 166; and Windsor, 208
Camp McGregor, 151
Canada Cycle and Motor Company (CCM), 18, 26, 29, 47; automobile promotion, 32; and Ford Canada, 48; and Ford Motor Company, 26; Ford sales contract, 33; and Russell automobile, 42
Canada Food Board: and Ford film, 185
Canadian Annual Review (Toronto), 196
Canadian Army Medical Corps, 193
Canadian Automotive Museum (Oshawa, Ontario), 57
Canadian Automotive Trade (Toronto), 233, 240
Canadian Auto Top Company, 62
Canadian Bank of Commerce, 231
Canadian Bridge Company, 27, 100; employment, 198
Canadian Commercial Motor Car Company Limited, 62, 142
Canadian Cement and Concrete Association, 65
Canadian Council of Agriculture, 223, 242
Canadian Credit Men's Trust Association, 194
Canadian Deep Waterways and Power Association, 210
Canadian Expeditionary Force (CEF), 115, 181
Canadian Foundryman (Toronto), 84, 104, 108
Canadian Graphic (Toronto), 39
Canadian Gray Motors Limited, 62
Canadian Industrial Series, 247
Canadian Industries, 7, 8
Canadian Machinery and Manufacturing News (Toronto), 67, 84, 107, 118, 227
Canadian Manufacturers' Association (CMA), 27, 32, 63, 80, 104, 105, 118, 200, 227, 230, 250; and foreign market, 172; and G. M. McGregor, 195, 200, 217; and R. S. McLaughlin, 200; transportation committee, 210
Canadian Motor (Toronto), 47
Canadian Motorist (Toronto), 121, 122, 127; and G. M. McGregor, 145, 184
Canadian National Exhibition (CNE). *See* automobile shows
Canadian National Safety League, 216
Canadian Pacific Railway (CPR), 143, 145, 198, 220, 255
Canadian Patriotic Fund, 133
Canadian Products, 208, 220; closure, 262; and depression, 219, 232; profits plan, 196, 199, 200; and Walkerville, 196, 205
Canadian Reconstruction Association, 193, 247
Canadian Red Cross Fund, 133
Canadian Safety Council, 190
Canadian Salt Company, 105, 171, 200; and profit sharing, 108
Canadian Shredded Wheat Company, 118
Canadian Sirocco Company, 183
Canadian Top and Body, 77
Canadian Typographical Company Limited, 18, 27, 31, 100, 298n. 38
Canadian war loan, 134
Carlisle, Arthur, 175
Carrick, "Comrade," 198
Carriage, Wagon, and Automobile Workers, 125
Cascaden, Gordon, 197
Casgrain, Henri-Raymond, 51, 111
C. F. F. Wearne and Company, 67
Chalmers Canada, 7, 172; and automotive industry, 141; Ford City plant, 149; foreign market, 172
Chalmers, Hugh, 79, 172
Chamber of Commerce and Convention

League of Detroit, 17
Chamberlain, Joseph, 29
Champion Spark Plug Company of Canada, 163, 196, 217
Chaplin, Charlie: in Ford film, 186
Chaplin Wheel Company, 33
Chatham (Ontario), 4, 27, 29; and G. M. McGregor, 29; as supplier, 43
Chatham/Anhut automobile, 61
Chatham Daily Planet (Chatham, Ontario), 181
Chatham Motor Car Company, 48
Cheakamus Canyon (British Columbia): in Ford film, 147
Cherniak, Isadore, 125
Chevrolet, 163; and automobile dealers, 139, 233; FB motors, 205; and GM Canada, 196
Chevrolet automobile, 205; Chevrolet 490, 139; and CNE, 204
Chicago (Illinois), 163
Chrysler Motor Company, 263
Citizens' Liberty League for Moderation, 241
Clan Campbell, 151
Clarke, Alfred Henry, 79
Clarke, Frederic Colburn, 146
Clay, Henry, 229
Clemen, V. A., 226
Cleveland, Grover, 15
Clifton Hotel (Niagara Falls), 209
C. M. Mayes and Company, 78
Coderre, Louis, 121
Cody, Henry John, 195
Colonial Motors automobile: Canadian, 237
Colonial Motors Limited, 237
Colonial Office (imperial), 110
Colorado, state of, 133
Colquhoun, Edward J., 261
Comfort, William Levington, 128
Commercial Motor Vehicle Company, 18
Commission of Conservation, 152
Conklin, Robert, 44
Connaught, Duke of, 111
Conservative Party, 152
Consumers Glass, 170
Copeland Motor Sales, 163, 289n. 109
Cory, Andrew, 246, 247
Corliss, John Blaisdell, 15
Cottingham, H. R. (Pat), 142
Couzens, James Joseph, 24, 25, 29, 55; and Border region, 192; and Chevrolet, 139; and Detroit, 189, 210; and employee relations, 138; and Henry Ford, 168; and Ford Motor Company, 25, 89, 158; and *Ford Times*, 276–77n. 56; and foreign market, 45, 61; image of, 46; income, 32; and G. M. McGregor, 60, 76, 80, 83, 99; as political figure, 137, 211; post-Ford, 135; and profit sharing, 106, 107; resignation, 134
Cowan, Mahlon K., 140
Cozak, Stephen, 130
Crawford House (Windsor, Ontario), 15, 30
Crothers, Thomas Wilson, 178, 179, 181, 182
Crouchman, Harry, 160
Cruickshank, George Robert, 193, 215
Currie, George, 178, 182
Curry, John, 17, 21, 25, 29; and Ford Canada, 30; and G. M. McGregor, 27, 28, 37, 103–5; and Walkerville Waggon Company, 23
Curry, William George, 17
Curry Hall (Windsor, Ontario), 86, 111

Daisy Air Rifles, 29
Dark, James, 109
Dartmouth (Nova Scotia), 52
Davidge, Ernest, 154
Davidson, Harley, 18
Davis and Fehon, 59
Dayton (Ohio), 212
Deachman, Robert John, 212
Dearborn Independent (Dearborn, Michigan), 239, 251
Dearborn Publishing Company, 239
Delany, Michael Augustine, 77, 78

Department of Trade and Commerce (Canadian), 46, 99, 110, 186, 221, 299n. 54
Detroit, 11, 253; and automobile registration, 149; automotive industry, 20, 21, 23, 26, 28, 58, 116, 147, 249; and automotive shows, 34; Border Cities interests, 62; and Border region, 192; and James Couzens, 135, 138; and daylight savings time, 172; and depression, 218; employment, 4, 126; and Ford Canada, 30, 37, 38, 62, 64; and Ford dealers, 87; and Ford production, 175; and IAM, 180; industry, 6, 8; labor flow, 32, 76, 83, 219; labor tension, 108, 125, 169; and G. M. McGregor, 26, 29, 142, 235, 263; and M. P. McGregor, 14; and Model T, 55; and profit sharing, 177; recession, 101; relationship with, 99; as supplier, 136; and taxation, 79; and Victory Bond campaign, 187; and Windsor, 147; Windsor-Walkerville interests, 17, 61, 86; and World War I, 115, 151
Detroit, Toledo, and Irontown Railroad, 238
Detroit Athletic Club, 209, 237, 256
Detroit Board of Commerce, 46, 149
Detroit Board of Trade, 79, 80, 203
Detroit City Council, 102
Detroit Educational Society, 249
Detroit Employers' Association, 149
Detroit Free Press, 144, 255
Detroit Gear and Machine, 205
Detroit Golf Club, 137, 209, 256
Detroit Hockey League, 209
Detroit Lubricator Company, 237
Detroit News, 160
Detroit River, 11, 35, 60, 74, 104, 188, 229; and Border region, 192, 260; crime, 241; and Ford Canada, 128, 136, 170; labor flow, 123
Detroit Rotary Club, 256
Detroit Shipbuilding, 193
Detroit Street Railway Commission, 134
Detroit Truck Company, 163; Tonford truck, 163
De Valera, Eamon, 211
Devonshire, Duke of, 177
Devonshire Park golf course (Windsor, Ontario), 235
Dewar, Peter A., 80, 81
Dew Drop Inn (Ford City, Ontario), 102, 280n. 86
DeWitt (Michigan), 29
Dickert, George, 42–44, 57, 67; and W. R. Campbell, 231; and Ford Canada, 88, 126, 261; and Fordson tractors, 157; and G. M. McGregor, 255; and war production, 181
Dickinson, Nancy. *See* McGregor, Nancy
Disher, William Egbert, 261
Dixon, George, 43
Dixon, James R.: Ford sales agent, 38
D. M. Ferry and Company, 14
Dodds, Bruce, 86
Dodds, Harriet (Hattie) (McGregor), 15, 16, 78, 82, 86, 111, 112, 140, 209, 223; death, 257; and Elmcourt, 246; health, 237; and Union, 159
Dodds, John J., 15
Dodge, Henry T., 67
Dodge, Horace Elgin, 18, 168
Dodge, John Francis, 18, 106, 134, 135; and Henry Ford, 168
Dodge, V. A., 67
Dodge and Seymour, 67, 73
Dodge automobile, 253
Dodge brothers: and automotive industry, 19; and Border Cities, 168; "Commercial Car," 289n. 109; and Ford Canada, 31, 33, 37, 88, 132, 168; and Henry Ford, 24, 131; and Ford Motor Company, 42; as supplier, 43
Dodge Canada Company, 232
Dodge works, 64; foreign market, 221
Dominion Automobile Company Limited, 47
Dominion Forge and Stamping, 100,

199; and depression, 219; and Ford Canada, 220; lockout, 208; and G. M. McGregor, 211; safety, 190
Dominion Grange, 51
Dominion Motors Limited, 62, 63, 77, 81
Dominion Police, 129
Dowsley Spring and Axle, 256
Drayton, Sir Henry, 226
Drouillard, Arsas, 101, 102
Drouillard, Theodore, 192
Drury, Ernest Charles, 251
Duck, George, 250
Duck, Jean Mabel. *See* McGregor, Jean Mabel
Duck, John Morton, 86, 106, 117
Duffus, Joseph James, 121, 233
Duncanson, Mary Reford (Gooderham), 159
Dunlop Tire, 59
Durance, Robert J., 59, 60, 94

East End Citizens' Association, 213
Eastern Chronicle (New Glasgow, Nova Scotia), 47
Eaton, Sir John Craig, 83, 256
Edison, Thomas Alva, 120, 131
Edison Company, 43
Eisenwein and Johnson, 209
Elgin County (Ontario), 20
Elmcourt Country Club, 246, 256
E-M-F automobile company, 7, 62, 63, 74, 81, 86, 104
E-M-F Canada, 62
Employees' Welfare and Housing Fund, 200
Essex auto-dealers' association, 163
Essex Border Utilities Commission (EBUC), 9, 153, 193, 228; and Archibald Hooper, 228; and housing, 219; and G. M. McGregor, 170, 176, 191, 211, 217; and politics, 208; "South Detroit," 153; and town planning, 202, 212, 259; and Victory Bond campaign, 187; "Vimy Ridge," 153
Essex Country Club (Sandwich, Ontario), 112
Essex County (Ontario), 5, 87; and film, 247; Ford agents, 38; and Ford Canada, 218, 260; labor tension, 189; and G. M. McGregor, 245; prohibition, 241; Victory Bond campaign, 165, 186–88
Essex County automobile club, 86, 111
Essex County Golf and Country Club Limited (Sandwich, Ontario), 78, 117, 128, 235, 286n. 51; and G. M. McGregor, 137, 194, 202, 209, 216, 246, 256
Essex County Health Association (EHA), 138, 216; and G. M. McGregor, 150, 164, 235
Essex North (riding), 76, 85, 112; fall fair, 185; and Liberal party, 152; and G. M. McGregor, 16; and W. D. McGregor, 14; and taxation, 243; Victory Bond campaign, 165; and E. S. Wigle, 169
Essex South (riding): and Ford Canada, 62, 112; and Liberal Party, 152; and G. M. McGregor, 245; and taxation, 243; Victory Bond campaign, 165
Evans, Frederick Samuel, 17, 18, 20; industrial ambitions, 18, 19
Evans, Lillian (McGregor), 21
Evans and Dodge Bicycle (E&D), 18, 298n. 38; and Ford Canada, 31; manufacturing, 19
Evening Record (Windsor, Ontario), 6, 80, 291n. 20; and automobile center, 86; and automotive industry, viii, 19, 27, 83, 99, 141; and Detroit, 62, 273n. 94; and Ford Canada, 31–33, 52, 57, 85, 104, 105, 132, 135, 290n. 5; and Ford City, 129; and Ford film, 151; and Henry Ford, 131, 132, 134; and Ford production, 43, 121, 142; and industrial sabotage, 129; and labor tension, 103, 175, 177–79, 273n. 94; and G. M. McGregor, 7, 16, 38, 50, 53, 61, 77, 86, 103, 113, 117, 148,

Evening Record (*continued*)
169, 255, 256; and politics, 171; and profit sharing, 108; and taxation, 79, 141, 164; and Walkerville, 81; and Walkerville Waggon Works, 20; and Windsor, 18; and World War I, 118, 125, 145, 151. See also *Border Cities Star*
Everywoman's World (Toronto), 232

Fairbanks, Douglas, 186
Falconer, Grace E., 32, 34, 154, 155, 210
Farm Journal (Ottawa), 224
Fauré, Gabriel, 15
Ferry City, 192
Fielding, William Stevens, 27, 47
Financial Post (Toronto): and G. M. McGregor, 127, 256; and World War I, 143
First Presbyterian Church (Walkerville, Ontario), 46, 78
Fisher Body, 8, 160, 226; bonus plan, 200, 294n. 77; labor tension, 178; union activity, 182
Flanders, Walter E., 104
Flavelle, Sir Joseph W., 83
Fleming, H. O., 238
Flett, John A., 201
Ford, Clara, 158
Ford, Edsel, 237, 239, 255
Ford, Henry, vii, viii, 1, 61, 120, 148; and advertising, 82, 95, 156; and automotive industry, 21, 42, 92; and W. R. Campbell, 231; and H. Chalmers, 172; and employee relations, 122, 198; and Ford boycott, 133; and Ford Canada, 3, 29, 30, 34, 53, 112, 117, 143, 168, 195, 230, 238; and Ford Detroit, 195; and Ford prices, 218, 225; and Ford sales dividends, 143; and Fordson tractors, 157, 245; and *Ford Times*, 84; and foreign market, 44, 205; ideology, 49, 94; image of, 24, 35, 84, 110, 116, 118–20, 125, 130, 133, 136, 140, 145, 157, 166, 168, 201, 211, 231, 239, 240, 252, 261; and industrial training, 79; and labor flow, 76; and labor tension, 108; lawsuit against, 76; and liquor dispute, 101; and J. A. Macdonald, 131; and G. M. McGregor, 9, 16, 20, 25–27, 37, 61, 99, 158, 195, 223, 255, 256; and Percival Perry, 157; personal finances, 32, 46, 238, 239; and profit sharing, 106–8; and public opinion, 254; and racing, 19, 26; and Red Cross, 134, 135, 285n. 48; relations with, 43; as "Skipper," 134; and taxation, 194, 239; and Union, 159; and Victory Bond campaign, 167, 187; and Windsor, 239; and World War I, 115, 131, 132
Ford and Malcolmson Company, 19
Ford Australia, 235, 262
Ford automobile, 23, 26, 33, 35, 49, 58, 60, 67, 74, 89, 111, 185; advertising, 74, 95, 156; and automobile shows, 116, 252; dealerships, 86; distribution, 260; and foreign market, 221; and politics, 85; prices, 99, 224, 228, 240, 242, 258; production, 88, 277n. 68; and publicity, 216; and public opinion, 253; and racing, 163; registration, 117; sales, 92, 94, 121; suppliers, 177; used market, 143; war production, 116; and World War I, 197
Ford automobile models, 35, 237; "999," 19, 26; Ford tourer, 154; Model A, 41, 45; Model B, 35, 37, 39, 44, 45; Model C, 34, 35, 37, 38, 43, 44, 270n. 42; Model K, 39, 43, 44, 56, 271n. 56; Model N, 39, 41–46, 49, 56, 57; Model R, 44, 56; Model S, 44, 49, 56, 57; Model T, vii, 39, 41, 53, 55, 56, 57–60, 63, 64, 67, 74, 77, 80, 81, 83, 86, 89, 92, 94, 96, 154, 174, 260, 270n. 42, 274n. 5, 277n. 67; and advertising, 95, 119, 121, 156, 194, 197; and Canadian market,

107, 201, 225, 262; and CNE, 204; and Ford film, 146, 147, 247; and foreign market, 98, 202, 205, 260; and politics, 245; prices, 145, 174, 218, 225; production, 142, 245; used market, 100, 154; war production, 116
"Ford boycott," 132
Ford branches and plants, 75, 84, 88, 93, 122, 123, 143, 144, 183; Adelaide (Australia), 59; Australia, 59, 174, 183, 205; Britain, 108; Buffalo (New York), 101; Calgary, 75; Detroit, 106, 109, 273n. 94; East York (Toronto), 259; England, 60, 61; Ford City, 87, 102, 108, 219; Hamilton, 67, 154; Highland Park (Detroit), 63, 64, 66, 101, 117, 122, 231; London (Ontario), 75, 109, 119; Manitoba, 89; Montreal, 67, 93, 121, 143; Oshawa, 230; Piquette Avenue (Detroit), 43; Rouge River, 216, 238, 259; Saint John, 109, 119, 183; Saskatoon, 75; Toronto, 42, 48, 67, 86, 92, 109, 121, 127, 146; Vancouver, 75, 154; Walkerville, 39, 42, 47–49, 57, 58, 66, 67, 83, 109, 115, 119, 273n. 94; Windsor, 79, 117, 193; Winnipeg, 67, 78, 119
Ford Canada bowling teams: Chassis, 170; Coupes, 170; Millwrights, 170; Sedans, 170; Toolmakers, 170; Torpedoes, 170; Touring, 170; Trucks, 170
Ford Canadian market: Alberta, 89, 107; British Columbia, 33, 107; Buffalo Hills, 154; Calgary, 44, 89; Edmonton, 89; Fort William (Thunder Bay), 41; Fredericton, 41; Gleichen, 154; Goderich, 41; London, 112; Manitoba, 33, 89, 107; Maritimes, 52; Montreal, 38; Moose Jaw, 41; Newfoundland, 93; North Battleford, 89; Northwest Territories, 33; Ontario, 98; Prince Edward Island, 93; Quebec, 47, 93, 95; Ridgetown, 41; Saskatchewan, 47, 89, 107; Toronto, 33, 38, 74; Vancouver, 38, 41; Victoria, 98, 277n. 62; Walkerville, 53; Winnipeg, 38, 41, 95, 98; Yarmouth, 98; Yukon, 95
Ford catalogue, 117
Ford City (Ontario), 1, 87, 100, 107; and automotive industry, 129, 162; and daylight savings time, 172; and EBUC, 153, 214, 228, 229; and Ford automobile, 270n. 42; and Ford Canada, 6, 220; and Ford employment, 248; and Ford expansion, 136, 158; and Fordson tractors, 130; housing commission, 191; industrial sabotage, 129, 130; and labor tension, 99, 103, 123; and liquor dispute, 102, 103; and G. M. McGregor, 105, 112, 117, 229; population, 123, 262; relationship with, 99; town planning, 152, 259; Victory Bond campaign, 167, 186; and Walkerville, 6; and World War I, 151
Ford City Board of Trade, 141
Ford City Council, 259
Ford City fund, 134
"Ford City hustlers," 168
Ford Educational Weekly (Detroit), 146
Ford England, 116, 205
Ford film, 107, 145, 146, 150, 158, 170, 176, 185, 216, 299n. 54; as industry, 247; and G. M. McGregor, 184; and publicity, 167, 185; and Victory Bond campaign, 165, 186, 188
Ford foreign market, 59, 61, 109, 110, 127, 143, 220; Aden, 67; Argentina, 206; Asia, 197; Asian-Pacific, 206; Australia, 45, 46, 48, 59, 67, 94, 95, 98, 111, 127, 144, 156, 205, 220, 259; Belize, 110; Bombay, 59; Borneo, 67; Britain, 127, 157, 206; British empire, 30, 73, 206; British Honduras, 110; Buenos Aires, 205; Burma, 60, 67; Calcutta, 45, 59;

Ford foreign market (*continued*)
Caribbean, 206; Central America, 206; Ceylon, 59, 60, 67, 81, 99; China, 73; Colombo, 99; Delhi, 81; Denmark, 45; Durban, 45; Dutch East Indies, 67; Egypt, 45, 197; Fiji, 59; France, 127, 197; India, 45, 48, 59, 60, 67, 156, 205, 221; Italy, 60, 197; Jamaica, 48; Java, 206; London (England), 45, 60, 110; Malaya, 60, 67, 73, 156, 221; Malaysia, 67; Mesopotamia, 197, 205; Natal, 45; New South Wales, 94; New York City, 110; New Zealand, 30, 45, 46, 48, 59, 60, 67, 98, 111, 144, 206; Paris, 60; Penang, 73; Perak, 73; Port Elizabeth, 60; Pretoria, 48; Singapore, 60, 73; South Africa, 30, 60, 67, 82, 206, 259; South America, 206; Straits Settlements, 156; Sumatra, 206; Thailand, 67, 206; Trinidad, 48, 206

Ford Glee Club, 179

Fordism, 84, 112

Fordist economics, 235

Ford Manufacturing Company, 39, 42

Ford Monthly: and Ford film, 147

Ford Motor Company (Ford Detroit), 19, 20; advertising, 35, 156, 299n. 54; and automobile shows, 34; and automotive industry, 142; Eagle submarine chasers, 181, 188; employment, 76, 113, 122, 125, 126, 177, 179, 199, 227, 283n. 17; factory, 42; and film, 247; and Ford Canada, 33, 106; and Henry Ford, 39, 168, 231; Ford market, 83; foreign market, 44, 61; growth, 67, 250; labor tension, 101, 218, 280n. 84; and Lincoln Motor Company, 252; and G. M. McGregor, vii, viii, 1, 26, 29, 63, 138; and Model T, 55, 57–59, 223; as parent company, 2, 7, 33, 48, 55, 80, 258, 262; prices, 143, 174, 225, 232, 246, 258; production, 100, 142, 144, 204, 216, 224, 232, 280n. 84, 291n. 9; profits, 225; profit sharing, 107, 177, 208; publicity, 249; public opinion, 253; safety, 191, 203; sales, 48; as supplier, 42; and taxation, 205; technology, 41; Victory Bond campaign, 167; war production, 181, 183, 205; and World War I, 132

Ford Motor Company of Canada Limited (Ford Canada), vii, viii, 1, 7, 21, 141, 177; advertising, 35, 97, 131, 132, 194, 278–79n. 74; and agriculture, 158, 159; and AIC, 173; and automobile dealers, 233; automobile registration, 48; automobile regulations, 51; and automobile shows, 44, 92, 184, 218; and Border Cities, 215; branch company, 80, 84; branch plants, 48, 99; and W. R. Campbell, 263; and Canadian market, 89, 93, 146; and J. Couzens, 138; and daylight savings time, 172, 176; and depression, 220; early stages, 32, 33; employee clubs and teams, 170, 176, 179, 194; employee relations, 106, 125, 148, 170, 204; employment, 76, 85, 122, 123, 126, 162, 179, 198, 200, 294n. 77; and film, 186; and Ford City, 136, 215; and Ford Detroit, 88; and Henry Ford, 39, 238; and Fordson tractors, 158; Ford Walkerville, 87; foreign market, 44–46, 60, 67, 73, 99, 156, 168, 172, 202, 205, 206, 221, 259, 260, 262; growth, 48, 50, 59, 66, 67, 75, 104, 123, 135, 140, 217, 262; historical conscience, 2; housing, 191; image of, 208, 221, 261; import market, 37; inauguration of, 30; as industry leader, 8, 111, 119, 121, 162, 207, 225, 232, 237, 262; labor tension, 101, 125, 176, 177, 179, 180, 182, 280n. 84; and E. G. Liebold, 231; lockout, 181; "Made-in-Canada" promotion, 88, 117, 118, 129,

145, 147, 162, 165, 168, 181, 247; and E. Marand, 136; and G. M. McGregor, viii, 2, 6, 9, 33, 223, 254, 256; officers of, 30, 31; and Ontario Hydro, 105; and politics, 81, 86; prices, 57, 113, 143, 149, 174, 196, 220, 231, 234, 240, 259; and H. S. Pritchard, 235; production, 99, 100, 142, 144, 145, 153, 174, 204, 216, 224, 230, 232, 248, 259; profits, 52, 86, 237, 242, 245; profit sharing, 107, 108, 113, 122, 127, 177, 208; safety, 190, 203; sales, 38, 93, 96, 99, 262; sales dividends, 38, 112, 143, 161, 168, 232; and Salvation Army, 190; stock, 168, 195, 289n. 109; suppliers, 87, 100, 102, 120, 179, 196, 208; and taxation, 38, 164, 194, 222–34, 276n. 50, 290n. 118; and truck production, 163, 174; union activity, 182, 198, 199; Victory Bond campaign, 166, 167, 187; war production, 133, 181, 197; and World War I, 115, 116, 118, 133, 145

Ford Motor Company Victory Bond account, 189

Ford News (Canadian), 144, 154

"Ford Quartette," 216

Ford Sales Bulletin (Canadian), 94, 95, 117, 282n. 108; and Dodge brothers, 131; and Ford employment, 123, 127; and World War I, 118

Fordson tractor, 131, 157, 176, 185, 237; and Britain, 158; Dearborn plant, 130, 157; Ford City plant, 130, 133, 148; and Ford film, 185; and G. M. McGregor, 158; and politics, 245; production, 130; sales, 174; Sandwich plant, 148, 157

Ford Times (American), 84, 95, 144, 276–77n. 56; and Border Cities, 84; and Detroit, 84

Ford Times (Canadian), 84, 94, 95, 144; advertising, 96, 156; and Ford automobile, 154; and Ford employee relations, 123; and Ford film, 147; and Ford production, 136; and Model T, 110; and World War I, 116–18

Ford Tractor Company of Canada Limited, 158

Ford trucks, 185, 232; and advertising, 201; and automobile shows, 201; TT, 174

Forduplex Truck and Auto Company of Canada, 157, 163

Foster, Frank M., 246, 250

Fox, Frederick Isenbard, 48, 57, 58, 74, 92, 109; and Ford Canada, 175; and Ford sales, 97; and G. M. McGregor, 159, 255; and Model T, 92; and RMA, 233; and taxation, 174

Fox, Thomas, 175

Frederick Stearns and Company, 14, 144, 147

French, Hubert C., 235

French, John H., 102

Gadelius and Company, 60, 73

Gas Power Age (Winnipeg), 63, 89, 107

General Motors, 232; competition with, 263; foreign market, 260

General Motors Export Company, 221

General Motors of Canada Limited (GM Canada), viii, 8; competition with, 7, 205; and Ford Canada, 234; and Ford City, 184; GM trucks, 232; and McLaughlin Park, 232; and taxation, 220; tractor production, 232; and Walkerville, 196

General Top Company of Canada Limited, 234

George V, 81

George, William Kerr, 159

Girl Guides of Canada, 210

Globe (Toronto), 58, 108, 132, 133

Gotfredson-Joyce truck manufacturer, 7, 8, 243

Goldie, J. H., 203

Good, McGivern, Currie, 232

Gooderham, Albert Edward, 159
Gooderham, Mary Reford. *See* Duncanson, Mary Reford
Goodfellows' Club: and film, 246–48
Good Roads Association (Quebec), 52
Good Roads movement: in Ford film, 185
Goodyear No-Rim-Cut News (Toronto), 96
Goodyear Tire and Rubber Company, 96, 97; and film, 247
Gordon, Jeannie (Saunders), 293n. 64
Gordon McGregor School (Windsor, Ontario), 301n. 12
Gorrie (Ontario), 57
Gottlieb, F. W., 163
Gourley, W. J., 44
Grace Hospital (Windsor, Ontario), 216
Grady, J. E., 142
Graham, Arthur R., 100
Graham, George Perry, 80, 245
Gramm Motor Truck Company of Canada Limited, 62, 81; and automotive industry, 142; industrial sabotage, 129; war production, 116
Grandjean, Philip W., 165, 168, 176, 178, 190; and Victory Bond campaign, 186
Grand Rapids (Michigan): and F. Maclure Sclanders, 162
Grand Trunk Railway, 31, 183; and Archibald Hooper, 228; union activity, 198
Grant, William M., 243, 250
Gray, John Simon, 31, 39
Gray, Robert, 29, 286n. 49
Gray, William M., 254
Gray automobile, 62
Gray-Dort Motors, 254
Great Eastern Railway, 183
Greater Food Production movement: in Ford film, 185
Great Lakes region, 3, 4, 9
Great War Veterans' Association (GWVA), 167, 197, 198; and G. M. McGregor, 256
Great Waterways conference (Windsor, Ontario), 210
Green, Fred W., 41
Gregory, William T., 165, 169; and Victory Bond campaign, 186, 188
Grey, Earl, 50
Griffith, William Linny, 110
Grosse Pointe (Michigan), 19
Grove Park Inn (Asheville, N.C), 120
Guaranty Securities Corporation, 143
Gundy, J. H., 174

Hagen, Frank, 32
Halifax County (Nova Scotia), 105; regulatory laws, 52
Halifax explosion: in Ford film, 186
Hall, Grant, 255
Hamilton (Ontario), 41, 167
Hanna, William John, 102, 112, 159
Harrison, Robert H., 198
Harrow (Ontario), 267n. 29
Hawkins, Fred, 41
Hawkins, Norval A., 83, 89
Hayes, Arthur J., 196
Haynes automobile manufacturer, 126
Healy, A. F., 193
Hebrew Literary Society, 252
Heck, Charlotte, 148
Heintzman Building (Windsor, Ontario), 211
Henderson, Ernest George, 105, 171, 200
Henry Ford Company, 19
Herald Square Exhibition Hall (New York), 34
Herman, William F., 183
Hertzberg, C. S. L., 65
Hewer, J. R., 166
Hezzelwood, Oliver, 37
High Park (Toronto): in Ford film, 147
Hill, John H., 169
Hiram Walker and Sons, 14, 65, 241; and G. M. McGregor, 256; safety, 190; and taxation, 141
Hoare, Charles Westlake, 177, 253
Hobbart, Harriet. *See* McGregor, Harriet (Hobbart; Rock)

Hoben, C. S., 255
Hoffmeister, Art, 32
Hogarth, E. Gifford, 185, 210, 215; and Ford Canada, 261; and Victory Bond campaign, 186
Holmes engine plant (Sarnia, Ontario), 206
Holy Trinity Church (Ford City, Ontario), 159
Home Guard, 129
Hooper, Archibald E., 183, 191, 249; and Border Cities, 202; and Chamber of Commerce, 214; and EBUC, 229; and G. M. McGregor, 199; as political figure, 213; and politics, 211, 228; and union activity, 198
Hotel Statler (Detroit), 237
Hot Springs (Arkansas), 111
Hot Springs (Virginia), 149
House of Commons (Canada), 85, 220
Hudson auto plant (Detroit), 64
Hughes, Sir Samuel, 85, 86, 132
Hungry Hollow slum (Ford City, Ontario), 102
Hupmobile automobile, 41, 86
Hupp automobile manufacturer, 6, 7, 62, 141, 142

Ideal Fence and Spring Company, 177, 194
Imperial Oil Company, 102
Imperial Order Daughters of the Empire (IODE), 159, 216; and Ford film, 150; Mary Gooderham Chapter, 128; and G. M. McGregor, 150, 194, 209; and W. P. McGregor, 151
Importers Automobile Salon, 34
Industrial Banner (Toronto), 180, 182
Industrial Canada (Toronto), 32, 35, 47, 104; and A. N. Lawrence, 220; and G. M. McGregor, 145, 195, 197, 256
Industrial Disputes Investigation Act (IDIA), 178, 179, 181, 182
Industrial Workers of the World (IWW), 120, 176, 178, 197
Information Bureau (Liberal Party, Ottawa), 152
International Association of Machinists (IAM), 101, 125, 182; and Ford lockout, 181; labor tension, 175, 176, 178; Local Lodge 718, 175, 182, 198; strike activity, 199; Windsor Local, 198; and women, 199
International Business Machines, 155
International Jew: The World's Foremost Problem, 239, 240
International Labour Party, 212
International Time Recording Company, 121
International Waterways Commission, 101, 177, 192
Iron Age (New York), 100, 291n. 9
Isaacs, Joseph D., 43, 218, 258
Ivanhoe automobile, 33

Jackson, Arthur: and EBUC, 215
Jackson, E. S., 142
Jaffray, Robert Miller, 47, 50, 63, 116, 136, 141, 163, 171; and automobile shows, 184, 217, 252
Jeffries, Edward J., 175
Johnson, Emily Pauline, 84
Johnson, Fred, 74
Johnson, Sarah, 74
Joly, Sir Henri-Gustave, 16
Jones, John E., 89
Joyce, A. W., 160
Joyce, Frank H., 8, 243, 244; and G. M. McGregor, 255
J. P. Morgan and Company, 132
Judicial Committee of the Privy Council (Britain), 111

Kahn, Albert, 46, 64
Kahn, Gustave, 46, 65
Kahn architectural firm: and Ford expansion, 64–66
Kaltschmidt, Albert, 129
Kanzler, Ernest C., 237, 238
Kay, Mr., 20

Kelsey Wheel Company, 8, 116, 226; and depression, 219; labor tension, 179; and G. M. McGregor, 256
Kennedy, Michael A., 92
Kennedy, William Costello, 80, 166, 169; and American industry, 220; as political figure, 243–45; and taxation, 193, 243; wife of, 246
Kenning, Edward C., 255
Kent County (Ontario), 180
Kerby, Frederick C., 245
Kerr Engine, 27, 100
Ketchum and Company, 41
Kilgour, R. C., 234
King, William Lyon Mackenzie, 242, 245, 263
King Edward Hotel (Toronto), 209
Kingston Industrial Works (Jamaica), 73
Kingsville (Ontario): and Ford Canada, 62, 218; impact of auto, 5; and G. M. McGregor, 78, 82, 128, 149, 158, 161, 178, 204, 222, 230, 257
Kinnucan, A. J., 77
Kitchener, Lord, 131
Kitchener (Ontario), 292n. 45
Kiwanis Club, 256
Klingensmith, Frank L., 106, 109, 135, 218; and W. R. Campbell, 231; and Ford Canada, 237, 239
Knowles, Morris, 192
Knox preparatory school (New York), 230
Krit Motor Car: strike, 101
K. W. Magneto Company (Cleveland): Victory Bond campaign, 166

Labour Gazette (Ottawa), 121; and film, 247; and labor tension, 176; and lockout, 181; and Windsor, 219
Ladies' College (Whitby, Ontario), 209
Lake Erie, 78, 204
Lake St. Clair, 19, 26
Lambton County (Ontario): Ford agents, 38
Larned, Abner E., 166
Lauder, Harry, 148, 166
Laurier, Sir Wilfrid, 15, 79, 80; and G. M. McGregor, 152, 169
Lawrence, Augustin Neil (Gus), 88, 93, 107, 117, 190; and Canadian Patriotic Fund, 134; and employee relations, 121; and Ford advertising, 95, 282n. 108; and Ford Canada, 188, 234, 261; and Ford film, 146; and Ford production, 108, 113; and Ford sales, 95, 98, 112; and foreign market, 110, 205, 220, 221; and Victory Bond campaign, 186, 187; and World War I, 118
Lee, John R., 123, 234
Lee, Lawrence W., 123, 125, 126, 234; and Ford Canada, 261; and safety, 203
Leishman, David, 13
Leishman, Gladyes Emily (Campbell), 78
Leishman, Margaret (McGregor), 11
Leishman, Robert, 13
Leland, Henry Martyn, 23, 249, 252
Lennox, Haughton, 104
Lewis, Cleona, 4
Liberal Party, 8, 80, 81, 112, 241–45; and Ford Canada, 243, 244; and G. M. McGregor, 152, 203; and taxation, 243; and J. C. Tolmie, 212
Liberty Bond campaign (Detroit), 166, 187; and Ford film, 186
Liberty Loans (Detroit), 165, 186
Lickman, John, 102
Liebold, Ernest Gustav, 218, 239; and Ford Canada, 231, 238; and Ford Detroit, 218; image of, 254; and G. M. McGregor, 250; and Windsor, 239, 252
Light, Oliver A., 147
Lincoln Motor Company, 249, 252
Little, A. A., 259
Lockwood, Robert M., 45, 60, 61
Locomobile automobile, 39
Log Cabin Inn (Detroit), 84
Logie, Louis, 77, 104, 142
London (Ontario): and automotive

industry, 292n. 45; and G. M. McGregor, 123; Victory Bond campaign, 167
Lozier Motor Company, 77, 104
Lucking, Alfred, 158

Mabley and Company, 14
Macdonald, George, 148
Macdonald, James Alexander, 131, 133
Machinery Moulders Union, 85
Machinists' Monthly Journal (Washington), 199
Mackie, Edward C., 230
Maclean, William Findlay, 47
Maclean's Magazine, 121
Madison, Charles, 280n. 84
Magrath, C. A., 170
Mail and Empire (Toronto), 79
Maisonville, Barney, 74
Malcolmson, Alexander Y., 39
Malcolmson, Edith Ellen. *See* McGregor, Edith Ellen
Malcolmson, George Alexander, 78, 86, 140
Manitoba, province of, 51
Manley and Slater, 146
Manufacturers' Association of Great Britain, 45
Marand, Edward, 136
Maritime Motor Car Company Limited, 109
Maritime Six automobile, 92
Markt and Hammacher, 60
Martin, Peter Edmund, 56
Mary, Queen, 81
Massey, Charles Vincent, 24
Maw, Joseph, 41
Maxwell Canada, 77, 208
Maxwell Motor Company, 6, 7, 230; and automotive industry, 141; and film, 247
McClennan, James, 175
McConnell, Thomas J., 188
McConnell and Fergusson Limited, 258; and Ford advertising, 155
McDougald, John, 37
McGregor, David, 13, 20
McGregor, Edith Ellen (Malcolmson), 12, 78, 222
McGregor, Elizabeth (Bixler), 111, 128
McGregor, Esther Margaret. *See* Wigle, Esther Margaret
McGregor, Gordon M., 7, 11, 12, 20, 21, 78, 235; and advertising, 34, 35, 42, 58, 94, 95, 232; and AIC, 173, 184; and automobile dealers, 234; automobile ownership, 37, 46, 195, 293n. 64; and automobile shows, 44, 50, 58, 92; and automotive industry, 23, 63, 111, 128, 217, 262; and automotive regulations, 51, 52, 117; and Border Cities, 8, 9, 170, 203, 210; and Border region, 260; and W. R. Campbell, 231; and Canadian market, 47, 75, 93, 252; and Canadian Patriotic Fund, 134; childhood, 14; and J. Couzens, 25, 109, 139; and Curry estate, 104, 105, 111, 136; death, 189, 255–58, 261; and depression, 218, 219; and Detroit, 20, 84, 147; early career, vii, viii, 1, 2, 6, 8, 14, 17, 24, 29, 34; and EBUC, 153, 210, 213, 214, 229, 230, 261; and EHA, 138; and employee relations, 85, 88, 100, 106, 122, 123, 125, 148, 180, 200, 273n. 94; and F. S. Evans, 18; and Ford boycott, 133; and Ford Canada, 3, 30, 99, 104, 105, 119, 140, 154, 208, 250, 251, 254, 263; and Ford City, 195; and Ford City fund, 134; and Ford Detroit, 60, 87, 97, 112, 113, 218, 228; and Ford employment, 199; and Ford expansion, 67, 74, 86, 87, 120, 127, 220; and Ford film, 246; and Henry Ford, 9, 20, 25–27, 49, 120, 131, 194, 218, 238, 244, 250; and Fordist technology, 41, 63; and Ford prices, 195, 205; and Ford production, 144, 183, 195; and Ford sales, 44, 52, 95; and Ford sales dividends, 143, 168, 188;

McGregor, Gordon M. (*continued*)
and Fordson tractors, 130, 157; and Ford trucks, 157; and foreign market, 59, 61, 80, 110, 202, 206, 207, 221; and Archibald Hooper, 228; and hotels, 216; and housing, 191, 202, 204; image of, 2, 7, 15, 33, 50, 77, 83, 127, 136, 142, 158, 208, 213, 240, 260; and industrial sabotage, 129, 285n. 39; and industrial training, 79; and Kingsville, 149; and F. L. Klingensmith, 135; and labor tension, 101, 126, 176, 178, 179, 182; and E. G. Liebold, 240, 252; and Lincoln Motor Company, 249; and liquor dispute, 101–3; and lockout, 181; and Model K, 41; and Model T, 55, 57, 116; personal finances, 32, 46, 83, 135, 257; personal life, 16, 111, 128, 139, 140, 149, 169, 183, 194, 216, 228, 246; and Plymouth (Michigan), 28; as political figure, 9, 16, 79, 152, 169–72, 176, 192, 200, 212, 254; and politics, 15, 81, 85, 87, 103, 168, 191, 192, 197, 199, 212, 242–44; and profit sharing, 108, 201; and publicity, 107, 144, 147, 154, 159, 167; and public opinion, 253; and W. E. Raney, 244, 245; and safety, 190; and Salvation Army, 190; and taxation, 141, 164, 193, 194, 221, 222, 243; and Toronto press, 63; and town planning, 259; and Union, 159; and Victory Bond campaign, 165, 186, 187, 189, 209; and Walkerville, 56; and Walkerville Waggon Works, 17, 20; and war production, 181; and Windsor, 28, and World War I, 115, 116, 118, 131, 152, 161, 162, 190
McGregor, Gordon Jr., 111, 139
McGregor, Harriet (Hattie). *See* Dodds, Harriet
McGregor, Harriet (Hobbart; Rock), 111, 128, 209, 230, 246, 254
McGregor, James Duncan, 159
McGregor, Jean Mabel (Duck), 12, 149
McGregor, Jessie Lathrup. *See* Peden, Jessie Lathrup
McGregor, John, 11
McGregor, Lillian. *See* Evans, Lillian
McGregor, Malcolm Peden, 12, 14, 111, 128, 137, 149, 254
McGregor, Margaret. *See* Leishman, Margaret
McGregor, Margaret Anne (Bartlet), 12, 161, 222
McGregor, Nancy (Dickinson), 111, 246
McGregor, Walter Leishman, 12, 13, 21, 28, 78, 86, 105, 128, 140, 149, 161, 216; and automobile shows, 230; and Border Cities, 249; and Canadian Patriotic Fund, 134; and Ford Canada, 230; and Ford City, 141; and hotels, 216; and Ideal Fence and Spring Company, 194; and liquor dispute, 102; and McGregor-Banwell Fence Company Limited, 16, 209; and G. M. McGregor, 223, 254, 257; as political figure, 228, 229, 243; and politics, 169, 197, 244; and Victory Bond campaign, 188; Walkerville Waggon Works, 17; and World War I, 151, 160, 177
McGregor, William, 11, 13; and automotive industry, 17; death, 20; in House of Commons, 15; and Michigan, 13; as political figure, 15; as reeve of Windsor, 13; as warden of Essex County, 13
McGregor, William Donald, 12, 18, 21, 23, 27, 37, 86, 106, 128, 149; and automobile shows, 116; and Ford Canada, 111, 117; and G. M. McGregor, 246, 254; as political figure, 246, 261; and Universal Car Agency, 142, 207, 235
McGregor, William G., 111, 149, 209, 222, 254
McGregor-Banwell Fence Company Limited, 16, 128, 209

McKay, John A., 80, 183
McKee, William Johnson, 16, 30; and Walkerville Waggon Works, 17
McKenzie, B. Ross, 234
McKeough and Trotter, 38
McLaughlin, Robert Samuel, viii, 28, 200; and taxation, 80
McLaughlin automobile agency (London), 196
McLaughlin-Buick automobile manufacturer, 49, 57, 63; and GM Canada, 196, 200, 205; and taxation, 276n. 50
McLaughlin Carriage Company, 37
McLaughlin electric car, 92
McLaughlin Motor Car, 61, 118; and automobile dealers, 233; and automobile shows, 232; Chevrolet production, 139, 142; production, 277n. 68
McLaughlin Park (Walkerville, Ontario), 232
McLean, R. J., 147
McLeod, James B., 103
McMullen, Harold S., 48
McPhail, Albert H., 209
McRae, Milton A., 79, 80
Medbury Block (Windsor, Ontario), 34
Meighen, Arthur, 242, 244
Menard, Moise-L., 8, 51, 77; and taxation, 79, 80
Menard trucks, 7, 8, 51, 62, 163; and automotive industry, 142
Merchants' Bank of Canada, 129, 250; Montreal, 216, 222; Walkerville, 231
Merrickville (Ontario): and Ford Canada, 251
Mettawas Hotel/Inn (Kingsville, Ontario), 78, 112
Michell, Humfrey, 177
Michigan, state of, 29; automotive industry, 23, 28; and J. Couzens, 138; foreign market, 4, 30; State Fair, 130
Michigan Central Railroad: union activity, 198
Michigan Pike's Association, 216
Mickam, R. W., 155
Middlesex Motors Limited, 258
Military Hospitals Commission, 159
Miller, Charles T., 250
Miller, H. E., 34
Milner-Walker Wagon Works Company, 17
Milner, William, 17, 20
Miner, Jack, 112, 131, 158
Miss Canada: in Ford film, 167
Monetary Times (Toronto), 32, 132, 133; and American industry, 227; and Ford prices, 240
Montreal (Quebec): and AIC, 173; and Ford Canada, 251; and Ford film, 147; and G. M. McGregor, 223, 228, 230, 250, 254, 255; and Hattie McGregor, 237; politics, 212
Montreuil, Charles, 105, 153, 170, 198
Morgan, Ben A., 45
Morgan, H. S., 159
Morrell, Adolph, 19, 298n. 38
Morrison, Neil, 5
"Motor City," 190
Motoring (Toronto; Montreal), 41, 47, 136
"Motoropolis," 1, 8, 208, 249, 262; and G. M. McGregor, 263. *See also* Border Cities
Motor Times (Ontario), 63
Motor Trade in Canada (Toronto), 63
Mount Royal Hotel (Montreal), 209
Mulford, O. J., 33
Municipal Electors' Association (Windsor, Ontario), 212, 214
Muskoka (Ontario) 138
Mutual Fire Underwriters' Association of Ontario, 286n. 59

Nancekevill, Frank A., 143, 185, 190; and CMA, 210; and Ford Canada, 235, 261; and Ford City, 220; and Henry Ford, 218; and politics, 191; and Victory Bond campaign, 186
Nash, C. H., 58

National Automobile Chamber of Commerce (NACC), 172, 173, 230; and automotive industry, 184
National Automobile Club, 34
National Automobile Dealers' Association, 173
National Civic Federation (New York), 107, 177
National Cycle and Automobile Company Limited, 18
National Industrial Conference, 201, 204
National Spring and Wire Company, 177. *See also* Ideal Fence and Spring Company
Neal, Henry (Harry) James, 158, 190; and Ford film, 185; as political figure, 243–45
New Brunswick, province of, 51
New Dominion truck: and automotive industry, 142
New Glasgow (Nova Scotia), 47
New York City: and Henry Ford, 166; Ford Motor Company office, 61; and G. M. McGregor, 140
New York Times, 34, 131
Niagara Falls (Ontario): in Ford film, 147
99th Battalion, 150
Niven, T. D., 160, 289n. 94
North Carolina, state of, 120, 122
Northcliffe, Lord, 240
Northern automobile manufacturer, 34
North Essex Licence Commission, 101
North West Trading Company Limited, 13
Nova Scotia, province of, 38, 51

Oak Hall clothiers, 14
Oakland automobile, 205
Oak Ridge Golf Club (Sandwich, Ontario), 78
Oddfellows Hall (Windsor, Ontario), 15, 117, 243
Odette, Edmond-Georges, 77
O'Hara, Francis Charles Trench, 110, 111
Ojibway, 1; and EBUC, 153; and Ford film, 185; town planning, 152
Oldsmobile automobile manufacturer (Olds), 34, 41, 49, 57, 233; and advertising, 277n. 56; branch plant, 47
Olds Motor Works, 19, 24
O'Neil, Arthur, 213
Ontario, province of, 51, 77; automobile registration, 154; and automotive industry, 111; automotive proponents, 52; and Fordson tractors, 158; and Henry Ford, 131; and IAM, 180; and F. Maclure Sclanders, 162
Ontario Border Development Bureau, 105
Ontario County: and Victory Bond campaign, 188
Ontario Department of Highways, 185
Ontario Hydro, 87, 102
Ontario Motor Car dealership, 92
Ontario Motor League (OML), 50, 52, 58, 86, 92, 121
Ontario Motor Vehicles Act, 83
Ontario Municipal Association, 52
Ontario Railway and Municipal Board (ORMB), 170, 211, 214, 229
Ontario Safety League, 92, 191, 216
Ontario Temperance Act (OTA), 241, 244
Organization of Resources Committee, 158
Osler-Weber-Rendu disease, 255, 300n. 70
Ottawa (Ontario), 115, 171, 250; and Ford Canada, 181, 251; and Ford film, 147; Ford sales, 37; and G. M. McGregor, 140, 181; Victory Bond campaign, 167
Overland automobile manufacturer, 57, 163; and automobile shows, 232; and Border Cities, 196

Pacaud, Gaspard, 166
Packard automobile, 26, 33, 34, 46, 126, 195, 293n. 64; and advertising,

277n. 56
Packard Electric Company Limited, 47
Packard-Ontario Motor Car Company, 234
Paige-Detroit automobile manufacturer, 126
Page, Leo, 213
Palmer, W. G., 250
Pardee, Frederick F., 290n. 118
Parent, Eli, 62
Parke Davis and Company, 14, 243
Parkes, George W., 196, 230
Parry Sound (Ontario): and Model T, 238
Parsons, George K., 104
Parsons Motor Car Company of Canada Limited, 104
Partridge, Edward Alexander, 254, 261
Paterson, Simons Company, 73
Paterson Automobile Company, 62
Pathé Film (Montreal), 197
Pathéscope (Toronto), 247
Paulin, Hugh Mortimer, 255
Peck, Raymond S., 299n. 54
Peden, Jessie Lathrup (McGregor), 11, 149, 160, 222
Peden, Robert, 11
Peerless automobile manufacturer, 33
Perry, Sir Percival Lea Dewhurst, 45, 60, 209; and Ford England, 157; and G. M. McGregor, 158
Petrolia (Ontario), 16
Phillips, Franklin, 15
Photokrome Company, 16
Pickford, Mary, 186
Pierce-Arrow automobile manufacturer: and advertising, 92, 277n. 56
Pierce automobile, 39
Pinkerton National Detective Agency, 122, 129, 130, 136
Pipp, Edwin G., 252
Plain Dealer (Windsor, Ontario): and prohibition, 241
Plymouth (Michigan), 28, 29
Poisson, Edmund C., 215
Pope, Albert, 18
Prince Edward Hotel (Windsor, Ontario), 209, 211, 216, 222; and Henry Ford, 238
Prince Edward Island, province of, 51
Printers' Ink (New York), 258
Pritchard, Harry S., 93; and Ford Canada, 234; and Henry Ford, 218
Privy Council (England), 136
Progressive Party, 242
Pugsley, Jack A., 109

Quebec, province of, 51; and Ford film, 150; Ford sales, 47; public concern, 51
Quebec City: in Ford film, 186
Queen City Cycle and Motor Works, 27
Queen's Park (Ontario), 215, 217, 229
Queen's University, 177

Rambler automobile, 41
Ramsay, George F., 249
Raney, William Edgar, 242; and Border Cities, 241, 246; and G. M. McGregor, 254; and taxation, 241
Ranson, George E., 144, 147, 148; and Ford Canada, 261; and Victory Bond campaign, 186
Rapid Electrotype Company, 171
Rawlings, Frank, 197
Reaume, Leonard P., 259
Reaume, Ulysses G., 259
Reaume, W. G., 186
Reaume Real Estate Organization Limited, 259
Red Cross Society, 133–35; Victory Bond campaign, 165, 187
Redpath Motor Vehicle Company, 27
Regal Motor Car, 62
Reid, John Dowsley, 290n. 118
Reid, Wallace, 247
Reliance Automobile Company, 273n. 94
Reo Motor Car, 41, 61, 86; and Walkerville, 237
Retail Merchants' Association of Canada (RMA): and automobile dealers, 233
Reversing Falls (Saint John): in Ford film, 186

Riordan corporation, 243
Riverside, 259. *See also* Sandwich East
Robbins, James H., 203, 213
Robertson, James Wilson, 79
Rock, Harriet. *See* McGregor, Harriet (Hobbart; Rock)
Rocky Mountains: in Ford film, 150
Rolls-Royce automobile, 41
Rotary Club: and Ford Canada, 190; and G. M. McGregor, 256
Rouse and Hurrell Carriage Company, 60
Rowell, Verne Dewitt, 208
Royal Connaught Hotel (Hamilton), 209
Royal Victoria Hospital (Montreal): and G. M. McGregor, 222, 255
Russell, Thomas Alexander, 42, 52, 58, 118; and automotive industry, 104, 217; and Ford Canada, 48, 50; image of, 83, 196; and taxation, 80; and war production, 115, 181
Russell automobile, 42, 49, 57, 63; and automobile shows, 92
Russell Motor Car, 61; decline, 135; and IAM, 125, 178, 180; war production, 181

Saint John River: in Ford film, 186
Salvation Army, 190, 216
Sandwich, 1; and automotive industry, 104; and Border region, 192; and daylight saving time, 172; and EBUC, 153, 214; and EHA, 235; town planning, 152; and World War I, 151
Sandwich, Windsor, and Amherstburg Railway, 13, 199
Sandwich East, 6, 87, 259; and EBUC, 153. *See also* Riverside
Sandwich West, 6
Sarnia (Ontario), 4, 41
Saskatchewan, province of; and automobile dealers, 233; automobile registration, 154; Ford sales, 47, public concern, 51
Saskatchewan Motor Company, 117
Saskatoon (Saskatchewan): Ford sales, 154
Saskatoon Board of Trade, 162
Saturday Night (Toronto), 47, 172
Sault Ste. Marie (Ontario), 251
Saunders, Jeannie. *See* Gordon, Jeannie
Saunders, John, 293n. 64
Saxon Motor Car Company, 8, 126, 171; and automotive industry, 141
Schultz, John Christian, 13
Sclanders, F. Maclure, 162, 171; and advertising, 162; and American industry, 227; and automotive industry, 190; and branch plants, 162; and Chamber of Commerce, 171; and Ford film, 185; and housing, 191; as political figure, 210; and politics, 191; and taxation, 193, 227; and Victory Bond campaign, 168
Seagrave Fire Engines, 62, 81
Selden patent, 24, 34, 76
Serbian Relief Fund: and G. M. McGregor, 164
Sherwood, Sir Arthur Percy, 129, 134
Shillington, W. P., 226
Shipman, Nell, 247
Shortt, Adam, 118
Six Talks by the Jolly Fat Chauffeur with the Double Chin, 94
Smith, A. O., 43
Smith, David R., 2–4, 17
Smith, Frederick B., 17
Smith, George H., 139
Smith, Herman L., 2, 33
Smith, M. F., 248
Smith, W. A., 80
Smiths Falls (Ontario): and Ford Canada, 251
Smythe, James F., 213
Sobey, Frank H.: and Ford trucks, 201
Socialist Party of Canada, 197
Sorensen, Charles Emil, 157, 158
Sorenson, Daniel Mitchell, 42
Sosnowski, John B., 167
Sousa, John Philip, 166, 167

Sparks film company, 197
Spaulding, A. G., 18
Spence, Francis Stephen, 136
Spokane (Washington), 147
Standard Paint and Varnish, 256
St. Andrew's Presbyterian Church (Windsor, Ontario), 14, 15, 112, 255, 257
Staples and Brebner, 146
Stark, William, 204
St. Clair Auto and Boat Club, 194
Stephens box factory, 14
Stevens-Duryea Motor Company, 26, 33
St. John's (Newfoundland): politics, 212
St. Lawrence Seaway, 238; and Ford Canada, 251
St. Louis (Missouri): early automobile, 19
St. Louis, Lillian, 190
St. Mary's River (Ontario): and Ford Canada, 251
Stoddard-Dayton automobile, 92
Stodgell, Emma, 136
Stodgell, John, 76, 136
Straits Times (Singapore), 60, 73
Strong, Albert W., 229
St. Thomas (Ontario): and liquor dispute, 102
Studebaker automobile, 237; Big Six, 204; Light Six, 205
Studebaker Canada, 6, 7, 116, 163, 204, 208, 226; and automobile shows, 232; and automotive industry, 142; benefit plan, 200, 294n. 77; and depression, 219; and E-M-F, 62; foreign market, 172; production, 230; strike, 101
Studebaker Corporation, 226
Sudbury (Ontario): and Ford Canada, 250
Supreme Court of Canada, 239
Supreme Court of Ontario, 103
Sutherland, Kenning, and Cleary: and Ford incorporation, 34

Tabulating Machine Company, 155
Tarrant Motors Proprietary Limited (Melbourne, Australia), 60
Tate Electric automobile, 116, 129
taxation, 8, 260; American steel tax, 127; Australian tariff, 206, 220; and branch plants, 141, 226; Canadian tariff debate, 232; Canadian tax exemption, 193; cross-border taxation, 176; excise tax, 174, 233; federal excess business profits tax, 140–42, 164, 171, 194, 202, 205, 219, 221, 222, 237; federal tariff commission, 223, 225, 227, 228; and Ford Canada, 240, 262, 263; import tariff, 14, 25–27; income taxation, 194; Income War Tax Bill, 164; luxury tax, 172; and G. M. McGregor, 79, 193, 196; nonresident income tax, 250; protective tariff, 3, 61, 79, 223, 227, 242–44; reciprocal taxation agreement, 250; tariff advantages, 162; tariff debate, 38, 45, 175, 245; tariff percentages, 47; tariff protection, 80, 245, 258; tariff revisions, 47; tariff structure, 29; "tariff wall," 17
Tecumseh (Ontario): and liquor dispute, 102
Tennessee, state of: and Ford Motor Company, 238
Thomas automobile manufacturer, 33
Thompson, F. J., 15
Thompson, William B., 50
Tilbury Township (Ontario), 128
Times (London, England), 181
Timken Detroit-Axle Company, 240; strike, 101
"Tin Can Episode," 133
Tobin, F. M., 190
Tolmie, James Craig, 112, 152, 212, 241, 243, 255
Tonsmore Truck, 163
Toronto (Ontario): Ford boycott, 132; labor tension, 125, 291n. 12; and liquor dispute, 102; and G. M. McGregor, 123; public concern, 51;

Toronto (*continued*)
Victory Bond campaign, 167
Toronto Automobile Trade Association, 92, 121, 173; and automobile dealers, 233
Toronto Board of Trade, 3
Toronto Daily Star (Toronto), 26, 58; and automobile legislation, 63; and automobile shows, 74, 92; and automotive industry, 184; and Ford advertising, 156; and Ford Canada, 175; and Ford film, 185; and G. M. McGregor, 145; and Winchester address, 243
Toronto Industrial Exhibition. *See* automobile shows
Toronto Star Weekly (Toronto), 53
Trades and Labor Congress of Canada, 227
Trussed Concrete Steel Company of Canada Limited, 46, 65, 66, 100
Tudhope-McIntyre automobile, 57
Tudhope Motor Company, 63, 100; and Ford Motor Company, 109
Tuson, Charles Robert, 170, 188, 189, 192, 213; and politics, 214
241st Border Battalion (Canadian Scottish Borderers), 151, 160, 161; and Ford film, 167, 216

Ulch, Percy, 204
Union-on-the-Lake hospital (Union, Ontario), 138, 139, 159, 165
United Automobile, Aircraft, and Vehicle Workers of America, 182
United Counties of Leeds and Grenville (Ontario): and Victory Bond campaign, 188
United Farmers of Alberta, 225
United Farmers of Manitoba, 225
United Farmers of New Brunswick, 225
United Farmers of Ontario, 212, 241
United Farmers Party, 229, 242
United Hotels Company of America, 209
Universal Car Agency, 86, 95, 117, 207; and automobile shows, 129, 252; and Ford sales, 143; growth, 235; as industry leader, 163; and truck production, 163
Universal Fastener Company, 18
Universal Pictures, 149
University of Michigan, 209, 222

Vancouver (British Columbia), 127
Vancouver Young Men's Christian Association: in Ford film, 147
Victorian Order of Nurses, 150
Victor Manufacturing Company, 62
Victory Bond campaign, 161, 164–66, 185–87, 190, 285n. 46, 289n. 103; and Border Cities, 189; corruption of, 261; and Ford film, 167, 186; and G. M. McGregor, 168, 169, 188, 209; and taxation, 245
Vosburgh, Mr., 38

Walborn, Thomas S., 42
Wales, Prince of, 211
Walker, Chandler Merrill, 27, 29, 77
Walker, Edward Chandler, 65
Walker, Frank H., 17
Walker, Hiram H., 17, 27, 78, 209
Walker, Thaddeus, 153, 176; and taxation, 164; and Victory Bond campaign, 210
Walker Motor Car Company Limited, 62, 78
Walkerville (Ontario), 1, 4, 55; American involvement, 17; automotive industry, 28, 42, 51, 61–63, 84, 104; "Canadian Trade" advertising, 35; and Detroit, 61; and R. J. Durance, 60; and EBUC, 153, 214; Ford automobile models, 270n. 42; and Ford Canada, 30, 31, 65, 93, 126; and Ford Detroit, 32, 76; and Ford production, 109, 175, 279n. 82; and foreign market, 81; and GM Canada, 196; growth, 27, 37, 59; and IAM, 199; labor tension, 122, 182; and G. M. McGregor, 29; population, 81, 262; and profit

sharing, 177; and taxation, 79, 227; town planning, 152; workforce, 76; and World War I, 151
Walkerville and Detroit Ferry Company, 27
Walkerville and Ford City hospital, 106
Walkerville Board of Trade, 79
Walkerville Brewery, 241
Walkerville Carriage Goods Company, 62
Walkerville Electric Light and Power, 87, 105
Walkerville Malleable Iron, 27, 100
Walkerville Tennis Club, 256
Walkerville Theatre, 247
Walkerville Waggon Works Company Limited, 17, 25; decline, 20; and Ford Canada, 32; and G. M. McGregor, 20, 28, 52, 103
Wallace, Mrs. Stanley, 247
Walter, Robert, 110
Wanamaker, John, 131
Ward, Albert C., 101
War Industries Board, 172
War Labor Board (American), 175
War Production Committee, 159, 161
war revenue act, 174
War Trade Board, 174
Way, Ernest, 137
Wearne Brothers Limited: and Ford foreign market, 156
Weekly Herald (Calgary), 89
Wells, Pearson, 198; and politics, 199
Wells, W. G., 234
Wells, W. J., 215
Wells and Gray Limited (Toronto), 64, 161
Westerner (Calgary), 225
Western Racing Association, 235, 241
West Lorne Waggon Company Limited, 20, 31
Westminster Church (Detroit), 16
Westminster Church (Winnipeg), 15
West Virginia: and McGregor, 177
White, Sir William Thomas, 141; in Ford film, 167; and Victory Bond campaign, 165
White Sulphur Springs (West Virginia): and G. M. McGregor, 149, 194, 230, 235
Whitman, Paul, 246
Wickett, Samuel Morley, 153
Wigle, Ernest Solomon, 87, 166, 169
Wigle, Esther Margaret (McGregor), 87
Wilby, Ernest, 64
Wilcox, E. M., 92
Wilcox, Oliver James, 79, 85, 86
Wilkie, Lorne, 19, 298n. 38
Wilkinson, George, 128
William Gray and Sons Company, 29, 33, 272n. 82
William McGregor and Son, 14, 16
Williams, Mr., 166
Willys-Overland automobile manufacturer, 135; and automobile dealers, 233; labor tension, 176; publicity, 196
Wilmington (Delaware), 147
Wilson, Woodrow, 120
Wilson and Company, 33
Wilt Twist Drill Company of Canada Limited, 78
Winchester (Ontario), 242, 243
Windsor (Ontario), vii, 1, 4, 9, 18; and American industry, 241; American involvement, 17; automotive industry, 20, 28, 51, 61–63, 104, 147, 163; and Border region, 192; and branch plants, 104; and daylight saving time, 172; and Detroit, 147; and EBUC, 153, 214, 219, 228, 229; expansion, 5; fall fair, 185; and Ford expansion, 86; growth, 5, 6, 37; housing commission, 191; labor flow, 76; labor tension, 175, 176, 291n. 12; and Liberal Party, 152; and G. M. McGregor, 9, 11, 12, 14, 29, 83, 178, 228, 255; politics, 16; population, 81, 262; and profit sharing, 108; and taxation, 79; town planning, 152; union activity, 197; Victory Bond campaign, 167;

Windsor (*continued*)
waterworks, 208; workforce, 14, and World War I, 151, 188
Windsor Armouries, 129, 188
Windsor Auto Sales, 116, 163
Windsor Board of Education: and Archibald Hooper, 228; and H. J. Neal, 246
Windsor Board of Trade, 15, 116, 141, 152
Windsor Bureau of Industry, 128
Windsor Collegiate Institute, 163
Windsor Gas Company, 244
Windsor Grove Cemetery, 20, 255
Windsor Hebrew Institute, 252
Windsor Jockey Club Limited, 241
Windsor Machine and Tool Works, 19, 298n. 58; and depression, 219; growth, 237
Windsor Open Forum, 249
Windsor patriotic fund, 134, 159; and G. M. McGregor, 164
Windsor-Walkerville region: automobile industry, 51, 86
Winnipeg (Manitoba): and Ford Canada, 86; labor tension, 197, 199; and McGregor family, 13, 15, 127, 149
Winnipeg Free Press: and Winchester address, 243
Winnipeg General Strike, 199
Winnipeg Motor Trades Association, 89
Winnipeg Tribune, 15
Winter, Edward Blake, 192, 213; and labor tension, 199
Winton automobile, 39
W. J. Peabody garment factory: and depression, 219; industrial sabotage, 129, 130
Wollering, Max, 42
Wolseley automobile, 99
Woman's Christian Temperance Union, 239
Wood, George Herbert, 168, 199; as political figure, 213
Woodstock (Ontario), 57
Woolf, Virginia, 299n. 54
Woollatt, William R., 217
Woollatt Brothers, 163
World (Toronto): and Border Cities, 228
Wyndham, Arthur C., 92

Young Mens' Christian Association: and G. M. McGregor, 147, 150, 164
Young Womens' Christian Association, 210